The British Museum
Occasional Paper
Number 143

The Sarawak Museum

The Forest, Source of Life:
The Kelabit of Sarawak

Monica Janowski

**The British Museum
Occasional Paper 143
published with
The Sarawak Museum**

Publishers
The British Museum
Great Russell Street
London WC1B 3DG

The Sarawak Museum
Tun Abang Haji Openg 93566
Kuching
Sarawak

Production Editor
Dr Josephine Turquet

Occasional Paper No. 143, 2003
The Forest, Source of Life: The Kelabit of Sarawak
Monica Janowski

ISBN 0 86159 143 7
ISSN 0142 4815

Front cover: The longhouse community of Pa' Dalih, 1987. In the
distance can be seen part of the Apad Uat mountain range which
the Kelabit call the 'stone longhouse' (*ruma' batuh*). This is said to
have been petrified when some of its residents laughed at an
animal.

For a complete catalogue giving information on the full range
of available Occasional Papers please see the Occasional Papers
website: www/the britishmuseum.ac.uk/occasionalpapers
or write to:
Oxbow Books
Park End Place
Oxford OX1 1HN
UK
Tel: (+44) (0) 1865 241249
Fax (+44) (0) 1865 794449
e mail oxbow@oxbowbooks.com
website www.oxbowbooks.com
or
The David Brown Book Co
PO Box 511
Oakville
CT 06779
USA
Tel: (+1) 860 945 9329; Toll free 1 800 791 9354
Fax: (+1) 860 945 9468
e mail david.brown.bk.co@snet.net

Printed and bound in the UK by Henry Ling Limited

Frontispiece Balang Pelaba of Pa' Dalih replacing the rattan binding on the wooden handle of his *tongol* (bush knife) (BM5a, 9a, SM62; see **Pl. 65**), watched by little Balan, grandson of the headman of Pa' Dalih, Lawe Padan, 1987.

Preface

Like other parts of interior Borneo, the Kelabit Highlands were never as remote from the rest of the world as European writers once supposed. The links were, however, indirect, amounting to a vast but largely undocumented exchange of goods and ideas within and between ecological and cultural zones. Movement was in relays: few people travelled along much of the chain, let alone from one end to the other. Outside agents sought to regulate supply and demand, with and against the initiatives of local communities, leaders or entrepreneurs. Once European power became established on the coast and increasingly upriver, even those still out of its reach came inexorably under its influence but never entirely on its own terms.

Before the Second World War, Borneo was less known than imagined by most of the English speaking world, its reputation brokered by 'white rajas', traders and travellers. It was not until Tom Harrisson's monograph, *World Within: a Borneo Story* was published in 1959 that this part of central Borneo came to the attention of a significant readership. Harrisson's role in the development and popularisation of Bornean studies was outstanding if sometimes controversial, but the portrait of the Kelabit Highlands which he painted for his readers was characteristically engaging. Since then, anthropologists and other researchers have added their own interpretations while developing a database of factual information, and increasingly informants and collaborators, and scholars and specialists native to Borneo itself, have added their own voices, providing essential perspectives from the 'world within' to complement and often to correct those of outsiders.

The collections which the author of this Occasional Paper, Dr Monica Janowski, made among the Kelabit in the late 1980s for the Sarawak Museum and the British Museum, and which are catalogued here, have a special objectivity when set alongside her documentary notes and their interpretation, brought to life vividly by the accompanying photographs, mostly taken concurrently with the making of the collections. Here are things which local people have made or used in particular places and at particular times, and to which they attach significance. The objects in these collections are often of symbolic as well as practical use. Dr. Janowski points to this in her interpretation, linking it to the Kelabit relationship with the forest, the source of most of the materials of which the objects were made. She emphasises the continuing importance to the Kelabit of the forest and the broader natural environment of which it forms part, and relates this to Kelabit cosmology and religion, both pre-Christian and Christian.

The text and images provide a context for the two complementary collections held in Kuching and in London, one at each end of a 21st century chain of connection. Like the collections themselves, this publication results from collaboration between our two museums. It appears, appropriately, as both an Occasional Publication of the British Museum and a Special Publication of the Sarawak Museum Journal. We are pleased to acknowledge assistance from the University of Greenwich towards the cost of publication.

Brian Durrans, Deputy Keeper and Curator of Asian Collections, Department of Ethnography, the British Museum, London
Sanib Bin Said, Director, the Sarawak Museum, Kuching.

Acknowledgements

I would like to thank all those who have checked through and commented on drafts of this book, including Sinamo' Rinai Adun (Sinah Nakap Ayu) and Tamamo' Adeth Ulun of Pa' Dalih, now resident in Miri, Sarawak; Dr. Brian Durrans, Dr. Josephine Turquet and other staff of the British Museum; and my peer reviewers for the British Museum Occasional Paper series. Thanks also to Claire Thorne for the line drawings and to Sam Kirby for maps 1 and 2. Dr Bernard Sellato was very helpful in advising on the part of map 2 which is in Indonesia, and I thank him. I thank Jim Hamill of the British Museum, Tabitha Cadbury of the University of Cambridge Museum of Archaeology and Anthropology, Julia Nicholson of the Pitt Rivers Museum, Oxford, Susan Ramsay of the National Museums of Scotland and Lyne Heidi Stumpe of the Liverpool Museum for giving me information on their Kelabit holdings. I am grateful to Dr. Hanne Christensen for identifying many of the plants used in handicrafts.

I would like to thank my Ph.D. supervisor, Prof. Maurice Bloch, for his support and advice during and after fieldwork, primarily carried out in order to gather material for my thesis (Janowski 1991a). Thanks go to the Sarawak Museum for permission to reproduce their photographs, and to Lucas Chin, then Director of the Sarawak Museum, for arranging for transport of the two collections out of the Highlands by helicopter as far as Kuching courtesy of the Malaysian Air Force in 1988, and thanks also to the officers of the Air Force who organized this. Balang Ngelibun (Robert Lian-Saging) introduced me to his friend, Baye Ribuh, headmaster at the primary school in the community of Pa' Dalih. Over the years I have benefitted a great deal from the friendship of both, and from that of their wives Kit Pearce and Sinah Baye Ribuh, and I thank all of them. I am very grateful to my husband, Kaz Janowski, for all his help and support during fieldwork, including his photography, and to my daughter Molly, who provided me with a second occupation (motherhood) while doing fieldwork and whose presence helped me to understand the importance of the role of *lun merar* for the Kelabit. I would like to thank Sally Greenhill, who visited us in the Kelabit Highlands and some of whose photographs are included here.

Finally, and most importantly, I would like to thank all of the Kelabit who welcomed us, helped me in my fieldwork, made, sold and donated handicraft items for the British and Sarawak Museum collections, provided information about their functions and allowed themselves to be photographed making and using them. Special thanks go to all the people of Pa' Dalih, where most of the items were made, who provided hospitality for my family and me; particular thanks go to Sinah Ribuh Bala, Sinah Belan Paran, Sinah Baye Ribuh, Sinah Rang Bala, Balang Pelaba and Lawe Padan in Pa' Dalih and to Sinah Paran Belan and Rose in Remudu.

Editor's note

Measurements are given in feet (abbreviation ft or ') and inches (abbreviation in or ")

1 inch = 25.4mm
1 foot = .3048m
1 mile = 1.6093km

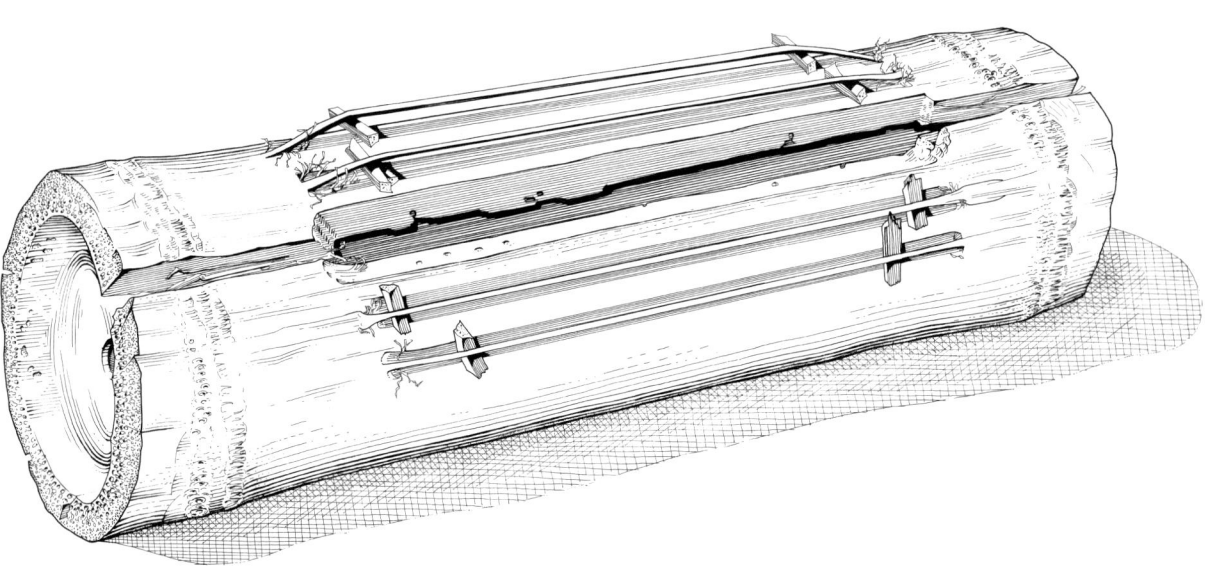

BM40 *Lotong,* musical instrument. Item in the British Museum collection, drawing by Claire Thorne.

Introduction

My aim in this book is to contextualize and provide an exegesis for the items in the two collections of artefacts which I made in 1986-88 in the Kelabit community of Pa' Dalih,[1] in the southern part of the Kelabit Highlands in the interior of Miri Division, Sarawak, Malaysia. In order to achieve this aim, it is my belief that it is necessary to provide more than a brief ethnographic description of the people of Pa' Dalih. This is because artefacts reflect the relationship which the makers have with the raw materials which they use as well as the use to which they are put. In the case of a community like Pa' Dalih, the vast majority of these raw materials still come from the natural environment which surrounds the settlement – the forest or *polong*. Therefore this book is as much an exploration of the relationship which the people of Pa' Dalih have with the forest as it is a description of the process of obtaining forest materials and making artefacts with them.

The Kelabit relate to their natural environment, on a practical level, in three ways: through the use of substances from the forest for craftwork; through hunting and gathering of food; and through agriculture. In order to understand one aspect of the relationship with the environment, it is important to see it in relation to other aspects of this relationship. Therefore I am devoting a substantial portion of this book to a discussion of hunting and agriculture.

Not only is the natural environment still the most important source of the physical substances necessary for biological life, but cosmology, traditional religious belief and social life are, for the people of Pa' Dalih, inextricably tied up with their relationship with the natural environment. This was not only true before the Kelabit became Christian; it remains true now, when they are devout Christians. This is expressed in a hymn often sung during our time in Pa' Dalih, in which the whole of the natural world was described as 'God's garden' (*late' Tuhan*). I will devote some space to exploring the spiritual role – in both a pre-Christian and a Christian context – of the forest for the Kelabit, and how this relates to their practical use of natural resources.

The making of the collections

The basis of this book is the two collections of Kelabit artefacts which I made in 1986-88, almost entirely in Pa' Dalih. These are now in the British and Sarawak Museums and are catalogued in Appendix 4.

My desire to make these collections was rooted in my interest in documenting the way in which the Kelabit relate to and use their natural environment, and why they relate to it in the way they do. This began with an interest in Kelabit rice agriculture, and the fact that both wet and dry forms of it are practised in the Highlands. Rice agriculture and the symbolic role of rice and the rice meal were the main focus of my Ph.D., for which I carried out fieldwork between 1986 and 1988. However, during my first period of fieldwork between 1986 and 1988 I became increasingly interested in the Kelabit relationship with the natural environment in a broader sense, since I found that their agricultural choices could not be understood without understanding this broader relationship. The Kelabit relationship with the wild natural environment surrounding them, including its expression through the song-stories which were told regularly sitting around the fire in the evenings until the 1960s, was the focus of my second period of fieldwork in 1992/93.

Before leaving the UK in 1986 for the Kelabit Highlands, I contacted Dr. Brian Durrans at the British Museum to discuss the possibility of making a collection of Kelabit artefacts for the British Museum. Dr. Durrans was supportive and agreed to cover the cost of purchasing the items. We decided that it would be ideal to make two parallel collections, one for the British Museum and one for the Sarawak Museum. When I arrived in Kuching and discussed the collection with Lucas Chin, then Director of the Sarawak Museum, he was supportive and happy to provide a home for a collection of Kelabit artefacts parallel to that made for the British Museum.

Most of the items in the British Museum and Sarawak Museum collections were collected towards the end of my first stay in Pa' Dalih, in late 1987 and early 1988. I waited until the end of my stay to make the collections because before embarking on this I needed to know a reasonable amount about Kelabit material culture and technology, and to develop a good relationship with the potential makers and sellers of the artefacts.

Many of the items in the two collections were commissioned. The procedure I used for commissioning items was to approach individuals who I knew to be skilled in making certain things and who I also knew would have the time and inclination to make these for me. Some of the items, whose making is considered to require particular skill, were ones which other Kelabit might also commission, and in these cases there was guidance as to how much to pay, and sometimes makers/sellers were quite clear how much they wanted. However, many items were things which would not normally be made for sale, and here I had to determine payment carefully. The maker would generally be reluctant to state a price, and I made a payment which I determined according to discussion with other Kelabit and my own assessment of what would be appropriate. My aim was to pay a little more than was strictly necessary but not an enormous sum which would be out of all proportion to what would be considered reasonable locally. In some cases the makers or owners of artefacts refused payment, and donated the artefact to the collection. The amounts paid, whether the item was donated, and whether the item was commissioned, is recorded for each item.

I felt that it was important to include photographs of the items in the collection being made and being used, and I set out to take photographs for this purpose from the start, using black and white film. Most of the photographs in this book were taken either by my husband, Kaz Janowski, or by me. Because I commissioned the making of the items in the collections, we were able in many cases to photograph the making of them. However, most of the photographs accompanying this volume of items being made were taken opportunistically, of people making items which I had not commissioned. The photographs of things being used were also taken opportunistically. None of the photographs was posed. Some of the photographs were taken by a friend who visited us in the Highlands, Sally Greenhill, who is a professional photographer. Some are photographs from the archives of the Sarawak Museum. I have indicated where photographs are from the Sarawak Museum or were taken by Sally Greenhill.

In late 1987 I commissioned a set of earthenware pots, of a kind made regularly until the 1970s and still occasionally in use in the 1980s, but no longer made normally at that time (Janowski 1991b). My husband Kaz and I photographed and filmed this process. Some of these pots are included in the collections, together with older examples of the pots, which were still in the possession of hearth-groups in Pa' Dalih.

Most of the items in the collections were collected in Pa' Dalih itself, although some were made (some on commission) and bought in Remudu, a neighbouring community in the southern part of the Kelabit Highlands. A few items are from Bario and others are from other Kelabit communities nearby or from communities in the Kerayan and Ba Rian areas just across the border with Indonesia from the Kelabit Highlands.[2] Items from Bario were bought there, and those from communities across the border were bought from visitors, or in some cases from Pa' Dalih people in possession of them. Communities across the border are closely related by kinship to Kelabit communities and there is a good deal of visiting to and fro.

Some of the items in the collection were made by nomadic Penan. The Penan are especially skilled in working metal and in basketry, particularly fine basketry, and this is reflected in the presence of knives and baskets made by Penan in the collection. No items were bought or commissioned from the Penan, however; all Penan-made items were in the possession of Kelabit and were bought from them.

The reason for buying items outside Pa' Dalih is, in most cases, because certain communities are specialised in making certain items, and Pa' Dalih people normally do buy these items from those communities. Thus in buying these I was reflecting what the people of Pa' Dalih themselves do, and recreating a portfolio of items which reflects what one would normally find in Pa' Dalih.

For some items, the reason for their being made in other communities is because certain raw materials are more available in one area than another – for example Remudu, a

southern Kelabit community three hours' walk from Pa' Dalih, is at a lower altitude, which favours a grass known by the Kelabit as *da'un berpah*, which is used in making a kind of mat. Because of this, Remudu has become specialised in making these mats. Other items are the specialisation of certain communities, such as one kind of sunhat from the Kerayan area across the border.

Eventually the two museum collections amounted to a total of 265 items. It would have been difficult, even impossible, to have arranged for enough porters to carry all of these items out through the forest to Bario, a difficult 12-hour walk. It would also have been very difficult to get the collections down by air from Bario to the coast, since the tiny plane which comes up to Bario is always oversubscribed. Fortunately, Lucas Chin at the Sarawak Museum was able to arrange with the Malaysian Air Force for transport by Sikorski helicopter from Pa' Dalih all the way to Kuching for the collections. From here the collection for the British Museum was shipped to the UK while that for the Sarawak Museum, after I had catalogued it, remained in Kuching.

Fieldwork in the Kelabit Highlands

I have carried out two periods of fieldwork in Pa' Dalih: 20 months of Ph.D. fieldwork in 1986-88, resulting in my Ph.D. thesis (Janowski 1991a), and a further four months in 1992-3. During both periods of fieldwork I was accompanied by my husband Kaz and my daughter Molly, who was born in 1985.

The Kelabit inhabit an area at the headwaters of the River Baram in the Fourth Division of Sarawak, in the highest inhabited part of Borneo, at the border with East Kalimantan. This area is unreachable by boat, and was in the past accessible only on foot; the Kelabit are great walkers. Nowadays, it is possible to fly in to Bario in the northern part of the Kelabit Highlands, currently the main Kelabit population centre, and within the last couple of years it has also become possible to get in by logging truck. It was by flying into Bario that I entered the Kelabit Highlands for the first time in June 1986, together with Kaz and 10-month old Molly. From Bario, we went on foot to Pa' Dalih, a distance of about 20 miles. We were eventually able to do this distance in eight or nine hours, but on this first occasion it took twelve hours, with Molly on Kaz's back.

After a month staying with Baye Ribuh, headmaster of the primary school in Pa' Dalih, we moved into the larger of the two longhouses, taking over the apartment which belonged to the school cook. She, like the school teachers, was provided with a separate house and was not currently occupying her longhouse apartment. One of the main implications of moving into the longhouse was that we set up our own hearth (*tetal*) and had to both obtain raw materials for cooking and to organise the cooking of rice meals for ourselves. Rice could be bought from other members of the community but other foods are not normally sold in Pa' Dalih; they are gathered, hunted or fished, with any left over being given to neighbours and kin. This meant that, since our skills were limited and people would not accept money for most foods, we relied, especially at the beginning, on being given meat, fish and vegetables to eat with our rice, brought in from the forest or from their fields by members of other hearth-groups. We were also often able to buy vegetables and sometimes meat at auctions held at the SIB Church (see below) in Pa' Dalih, to which inhabitants donated produce for auction to benefit the Church.

We gradually settled into life in the longhouse, getting used to the long dark building with shafts of sunlight coming in through windows during the day (**Pl. 1, Pl. 96**), the smoke from cooking fires and above all the constant company of other people. The living and cooking area (the *dalim*, literally the 'inside') of Pa' Dalih longhouse (**see Fig. 3**) is open-plan, without divisions between hearth-group apartments, and offers no privacy. It is common to see men or women sitting cooking or tending the fire at their hearth, apparently talking to themselves – but in fact holding a conversation with a neighbour at another hearth. It is possible to see what everyone, all down the longhouse, is doing. In this context, handicraft skills are easily observed in action. Displaying craftmanship is a matter of pride; being skilled and hard-working is an important basis of status among the Kelabit. Children can often be seen intently observing the making of a mat or a carrying basket, picking up the skills involved (**Frontispiece, Pl. 70, Pl. 92**), which they start to imitate at a young age.

Crafting forest materials

We very quickly became aware, living in Pa' Dalih, of the way in which the forest both facilitated and dominated human life there. It was a vital source of food and of craft materials; it was also conceived of as a place full of living beings, both animals and spirits. The forest was both threatening, an important source of meat and wild plants – and a source of spiritual potency.

The forest was, for the people of Pa' Dalih, a source of life in a number of connected ways. Physically, it provided food and materials for handicrafts. In 1986–88, when I made these collections, forest materials were basic to all handicrafts in Pa' Dalih, since communications with the outside world were difficult, time-consuming, and on foot – although town-bought materials and goods were becoming increasingly important. Socially, food and handicraft material from the forest enabled the people of Pa' Dalih to operate as a cohesive social group; involvement together in the process of taming and organizing wild resources, including hunting and gathering and rice agriculture, was the basis of social and kin bonds between individuals. Finally, the forest had, in the pre-Christian context, a spiritual role as source of a wild life force which the Kelabit call *lalud*, which, when brought together with rice at the rice meal, made *ulun*, or human life, possible (see Chapter 9).

With the coming of Christianity, the wild, the natural world not under human control, has continued to have a spiritual role. It is still associated with *lalud*, but this is accessed through Christ rather than through forest spirits, which Kelabit no longer *maya'* – a word generally translated by Kelabit into English as 'follow' – although they still believe that they exist. While these deities and spirits may be conceived of now, at least by some Kelabit, as associated with the devil, I never met a Kelabit who did not believe that they existed.

The Kelabit, like all *orang ulu* (Malay; literally 'people of

the interior'), as the interior tribal peoples are generally described within Sarawak (both by non-*orang ulu* and, in relations with outsiders, by interior peoples themselves), are very skilled in working materials collected from the forest. A man on a hunting trip in the forest will, where necessary, quickly make a cup or a cooking vessel using a node of bamboo, set up a simple hearth, erect a shelter for the night using wood and rattan with bark or palm leaves for flooring, or carry out emergency repairs to his basket with a length of rattan. Back at the longhouse, much more sophisticated handicraft work is done by both men and women, using materials from both primary and secondary forest to produce finished objects which are often (to my eyes, at least) of great beauty, and which are shown in the photographs here.

The items in the collection are not precious in the sense that the materials of which they are made are costly in themselves. For the Kelabit, the materials from the forest of which the objects are largely made have little monetary or trading value in their raw form. Even salt, used as currency in the area up to the Second World War, is only valuable once it has been gathered as brine from forest springs, boiled down, poured into bamboo nodes and then broken out of these and wrapped in leaves. It is craftsmanship, human skill in utilizing the natural environment, which is valued, and which makes the items beautiful to Kelabit eyes. This is expressed most strongly in the use of some items as house decorations nowadays by Kelabit resident in town, who see these objects as beautiful expressions of their traditional culture (Janowski 1997a).

The structure of the book

After giving some general background on the Kelabit in Chapter 1, Chapters 2-6 are primarily descriptive, while Chapters 7-9 make an attempt at analysis. I will work 'from the inside out' in the descriptive part of the book, as Tom Harrisson, a central figure in recent Kelabit history, did when he was parachuted into the Kelabit Highlands to organise resistance against the Japanese in 1945 (Harrisson 1959); and as is, I feel, appropriate, given what I will suggest is a Kelabit concern with the distinction, and complementary opposition, between inside and outside. I will start with the individual person in Chapter 2, going on in Chapters 3 and 4 to a description of the way in which the longhouse and hearth, the most domesticated and 'inner' (*dalim*) part of the material world, are constructed and used in Pa' Dalih. Chapter 5 looks at the technology and organization of rice agriculture, moving out from the centre which the longhouse represents towards that which is less 'inner' but which is still very much controlled; and in Chapter 6 we move even further outwards, to look at the utilization, for both craftwork and food, of wild resources from the forest, that most untamed area, the antithesis – but also the complement – of what is 'inside'.

This leads into the more analytic chapters of the book. In Chapter 7 I will take a closer look at the wild and at *lalud*, the life force which is associated with it. In Chapter 8 I will look at the way in which *irau* feasts, both in megalithic, pre-Christian times and after the Kelabit became Christian, have acted as means of underlining the importance of both status based on rice on the one hand and possession of *lalud* on the other. Building on this, chapter 9 is an analysis of the way in which, in pre-Christian Kelabit cosmology, a human way of life, *ulun*, is set up through the 'correct' relationship between inner and outer, tamed and wild, female and male, and of how the core notions of *ulun* and *lalud* have been affected by Christianity.

In addition, I have provided Appendices containing a Kelabit word list (Appendix 1), descriptions of the materials and techniques used in craftwork (Appendix 2), the botanical names of many of the materials used (Appendix 3) and the catalogues of the two collections at the British Museum and Sarawak Museum (Appendix 4).

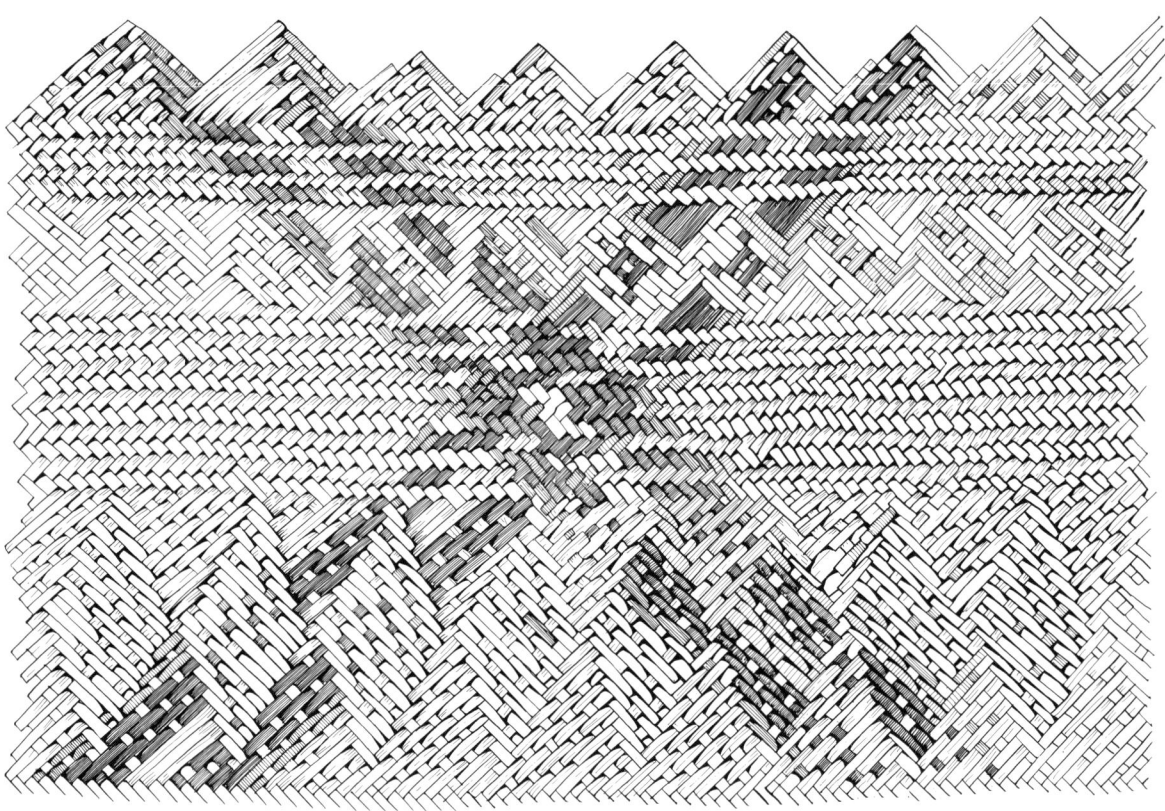

BM157 *Tarub siar barit,* mat made of *siar* grass. Item in the British Museum collection, drawing by Claire Thorne.

1. The Kelabit: Background

The Kelabit are one of many peoples living on the island of Borneo who have been described as tribal. The category of 'tribal' people includes groups such as the Iban, Kayan, Kenyah and Melanau as well as many smaller groups.[3] Most such groups lived, until the 1960s or 1970s, only in the interior of the island, and they are described as *orang ulu* (Malay), 'people of the interior'. Groups on the coast tended to become islamicized and to 'become Malay' (Malay; *masok melayu*). Many of those now described as Malay are probably descendants of converted tribal peoples.

The Kelabit are part of a larger linguistic grouping, the Apo Duat (Hudson 1977). Most people who speak languages belonging to this group live in an interior tableland area, the Kerayan-Kelabit highland, which includes the highest inhabited part of the island, the Kelabit Highlands itself (**Map 1**). The main part of this tableland lies in Kalimantan in the headwaters of the Kerayan River (Harrisson 1949: 134), with the rest divided between two Divisions of Sarawak, the Miri Division (the Kelabit Highlands, at the headwaters of the Baram River) and the Limbang Division (the Murut/Lun Dayeh Highlands, at the headwaters of the Trusan). It lies within a narrow rectangle about 50 miles north and south, 30 miles east and west and over 3,000 ft above sea level. Some Apo Duat-speaking people live outside the tableland, downriver in the Miri and Limbang Divisions of Sarawak; a number live in Brunei and a few in Sabah. Apo Duat-speaking peoples live in East Kalimantan, the Limbang and Miri Divisions of Sarawak, and in Brunei and include those who have also been described as Murut (except some of those known as Murut in Sabah, who belong to a different grouping altogether – see Appell 1969, Prentice 1970, Crain 1970: 17-35), the Lun Dayeh and Lun Bawang, the Kerayan and Ba Rian peoples in the part of the tableland in Kalimantan immediately across the border from the Kelabit Highlands, and the Treng, the Adang, the Sa'ban or Saban, the Libun or Nyibung, and the Potok, Milau and Berau (Janowski 1991: 17-21).

The term 'Kelabit' appears to derive from a place name, 'Pa' Labid',[4] as it was misheard by a government officer in the early part of this century (LeBar 1972: 159).[5] The division between the Kelabit and other Apo Duat peoples is not as great as the existence of a separate term for the Kelabit might suggest. However, there are some significant cultural differences between the Kelabit and their cousins across the border in the headwaters of the Kerayan River, and the cohesion of the group now called Kelabit has increased greatly since the 1960s due to the increasing importance of the political boundary between Malaysia and Indonesia, which separates the Kelabit Highlands from the Kerayan. Early in this century the Kerayan was effectively under the control of the Brooke administration in Sarawak. By the middle of this century the Kerayan Highlands were clearly situated in Dutch Borneo while the Kelabit Highlands were under Sarawak, but the administration on neither side ventured into the interior often and the fact that they were in different countries had little practical significance. Since the Second World War this has changed, and the implications of being Malaysian or Indonesian have come to mean a good deal. Services provided by the administration, as well as employment opportunities in town, have been better on the Sarawak side. This has meant that the Kelabit have had an advantage compared with their relatives on the other side of the border, and they have developed a heightened awareness of being a distinct cultural group, to the extent that they have now taken up the exonym 'Kelabit' as an endonym. In town, the Kelabit have been successful in education and employment, with a number gaining degrees and some obtaining senior positions in government service, and this has strengthened their Kelabit identity; the degree of cohesion and the emphasis on ethnic identity as Kelabit among the Kelabit in town in particular is high (Amster 1998).

Although it is difficult to get exact figures, more Kelabit probably now live in towns in Sarawak, particularly Miri at the mouth of the Baram, than live in the Highlands. It is unlikely that there are more than three or four thousand living in the Highlands.[6] However, the number fluctuates due to migration to and from town and due to temporary or permanent in-migration from the Kerayan area of closely related people, most of whom are almost certainly not registered as resident in Malaysia.

There are a small number of semi-nomadic Penan hunter gatherers living in the Kelabit Highlands as well as Kelabit, based in the settlements of Pa' Tik and Pa' Berang. Their numbers are difficult to estimate since they are semi-nomadic, but it is not likely to be more than 100 or so.

Until 1997, when logging roads reached Remudu in the southern part of the Kelabit Highlands, there was no way to get to the Kelabit Highlands except by air to Bario or by boat to points much lower on the river and then on foot; the upper reaches of the Baram are not navigable for long distances. A government airstrip was built at Bario in 1961, and this provided scheduled services to Marudi, and later Miri. In the decades after the Second World War Mission planes visited the Highlands, and a number of Kelabit communities, including Pa' Dalih (in 1975), built short airstrips for the Mission planes. However, Mission planes no longer visit the Highlands. Charter planes are sometimes hired by Kelabit and Chinese entrepreneurs to bring goods up to the Highlands, and normally go to Bario. The ex-Mission airstrip at Long Dano in the southern Highlands is able to take charter planes, although it is quite dangerous to land there, and some goods reach the southern Highlands by that route.

Although there are no proper roads in the Kelabit Highlands, there is a limited network of dirt tracks that can be used by vehicles in the immediate Bario area, and a few pickup trucks and motorbikes had, in the late 1980s, been brought in by the 'Skyvan', a large plane sometimes chartered by individual Kelabit to bring goods and vehicles into the Highlands.

The community of Pa' Dalih

Pa' Dalih is nestled in the midst of the forest, surrounded by an area of buffalo pasture and rice fields, both dry and wet. In 1986–88, when I lived there first, it consisted of two longhouses, together with a school building and teachers' houses, and a small clinic (**Fig. 1**). It is approached on foot. Coming from Bario, the point at which one first sees the settlement is at the top of a hill and one has a good view over the whole community. One can also be seen. By the time of arrival at the longhouse it is generally known that visitors have arrived and, particularly if it is evening and people have

returned from the fields, all the children, followed, one by one, by the adults, will come and shake hands as one enters the longhouse.

The population of Pa' Dalih at the time that I carried out a simple census in October 1986 was 122. This included 63 people living in a 15-hearth group longhouse (where one hearth group apartment was vacant and another was occupied by my family), 29 in a six-hearth group longhouse and 32 in separate houses (*ruma' sebulang*). Of these separate houses, all except one was occupied by people with a family member employed by the school, the clinic or the Sidang Injil Borneo (SIB) Church (see below), and whose houses had been provided for them by the authorities. All of the inhabitants of Pa' Dalih were Kelabit with the exception, in October 1986, of the pastor of the SIB parish, who was a Penan. By 1992, when I returned to Pa' Dalih, a third longhouse had been built and was inhabited by people from the Kerayan area across the border in Indonesia, who were related to existing inhabitants of the community of Pa' Dalih.

Together with the communities of Remudu, Long Dano and Batu Patong, Pa' Dalih is situated in the southern part of

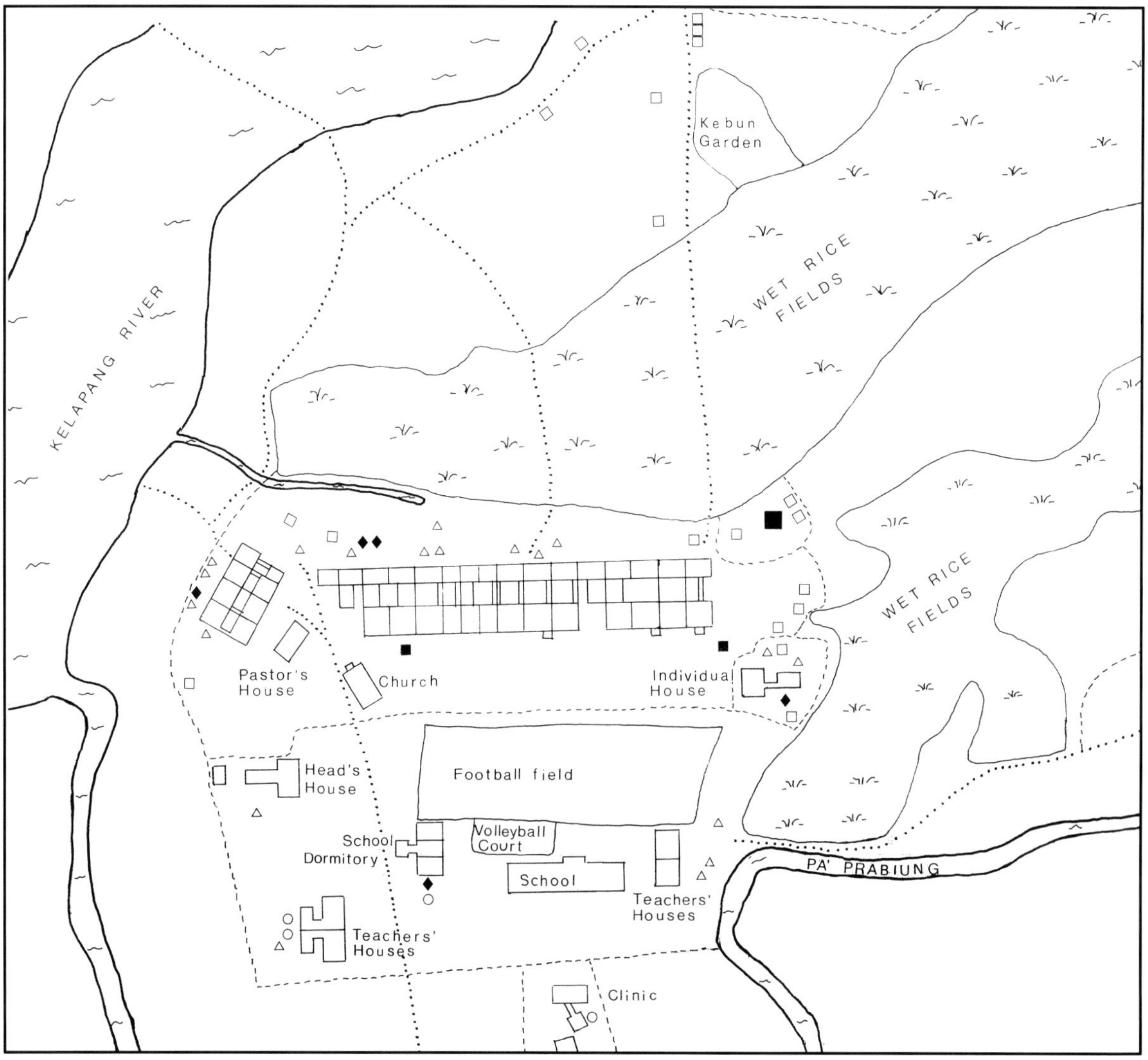

Figure 1 Plan of Pa' Dalih 1986-88

Key

■ Shops	◆ Pig huts	○ Separate toilets	⋯⋯ Footpath
△ Chicken huts	□ Padi storage huts	■ Rice-husking mill	----- Fence

the Kelabit Highlands. It is about 20 miles from Bario, and is actually just outside the tableland proper (see **Map 2**). The Kelabit of the Highlands are, politically and linguistically, divided into two groups: those of the northern part of the Highlands (*lun pedayeh*, or 'upriver people') and those of the southern part (*lun pela'ud* or 'downriver people') (Talla 1979: 106-7).

The paths between Remudu, Pa' Dalih and Long Dano form a triangle, with the distances between the communities taking between one and three hours to walk. These three settlements, together with Batu Patong (40 minutes walk from Pa' Dalih), are closely bound together, speaking the same form of Kelabit[7] and sharing a primary school, opened in 1964 (Talla 1979: 440-1) (which has a radio-call facility), and a small government clinic (visited by the Flying Doctor by helicopter once a month), both situated in Pa' Dalih. Remudu and Long Dano are *bawang* (distinct communities with their own territories, delimited by boundaries marked by natural phenomena) as well as *sidang* (parishes of the SIB Church to which the Kelabit belong); Pa' Dalih and Batu Patong together form one *sidang* although they are technically separate *bawang*. Batu Patong, during the period 1986–88, only contained one hearth-group, which was effectively part of Pa' Dalih. By 1992, however, when a number of Lun Bawang people from the Kerayan had come to live in Pa' Dalih and Batu Patong, some of these had started to make wet rice fields at Batu Patong.

There is, nowadays, a sharp contrast between settlements in the area now known as Bario and those outside Bario. Originally, there was just one longhouse in the Bario area, called Lam Baa; but there has been a flood of migration from other communities into Bario since the 1960s. Although it is now the administrative centre of the area and the residence of the Kelabit chief (*penghulu*), Bario continues to be made up of longhouse communities. However, these are very close together and are separated by wet rice fields rather than by the forest which separates communities outside the Bario area.

One of the most important reasons for the migration to Bario which started in the 1960s was that in Bario, unlike in the communities in the southern part of the Kelabit Highlands (Pa' Dalih, Batu Patong, Remudu and Long Dano), a) there is a lot of land suitable for growing wet rice and b) after the airstrip was built in Bario it became possible to send rice by air for sale in town, since there are certain varieties of rice grown in wet fields in the Highlands which are much liked in town and fetch good prices. In Bario, since the 1960s, there has been more money to buy goods and easier access to town-bought goods. In the southern communities, by contrast, there has been much less money and transport has been difficult. Therefore, in a community like Pa' Dalih there was, even in the late 1980s, much more reliance on the forest, both for food and for making everyday items, than there was in Bario.

Research on the Kelabit

Although this part of Sarawak came under the rule of the English Brooke family as Rajahs in the 19th century, few Europeans visited the Kelabit Highlands before the Second World War, and this means that there was little written on the Kelabit. An expedition in 1908 was led by Douglas, Resident of the Baram Division of Sarawak. This was followed by another in 1922 led by Mjoberg, Curator of the Sarawak Museum, and by two in 1930 and 1936 led by Banks, also a Curator of the Sarawak Museum (Douglas 1909b; Douglas 1912; Mjoberg 1925; Banks 1937b). In 1945, Schneeberger, a geologist working for the Batavian Oil Company, visited the Apo Duat highland area, including the Kelabit Highlands (Schneeberger 1945; 1979).

Tom Harrisson (**Pl. 2**) has produced the greatest volume of writings on the Kelabit (Heimann 1997). He took a great interest in the Kelabit after the war when he became Curator of the Sarawak Museum, and wrote about them during the 1950s and 1960s, with many of his articles appearing in the new series of the *Sarawak Museum Journal*. One of the features of the Kelabit Highlands and of Kelabit life which particularly interested him was the megaliths of the Highlands (**Pl. 80**). However, he concentrated his interest on the people of Lam Baa, the original longhouse in the Bario area, and did not pay as much attention to other Kelabit communities.

Since the 1970s, when the first Kelabit young people who attended school began to emerge from university, there have been a number of Kelabit who have studied and published on their own people. These include Robert Lian-Saging (Lian-Saging 1976/77; Lian-Saging and Bulan 1989), Yahya Talla (Talla 1979), David Labang (Bulan and Labang 1979), Lucy Bulan (Bulan and Labang 1979; Bulan n.d.) and Poline Bala (Bala 2001).

Robert Blust, a linguist, has carried out some research on Kelabit language, and has published a vocabulary of Kelabit (Blust 1993). Recently, Matthew Amster, an American anthropologist, has carried out fieldwork in Pa' Ukat in the Kelabit Highlands and in Miri (Amster 1998; Amster 1999; Amster 2000).

Kelabit settlement

Bario was, by the late 1960s, the main centre of Kelabit settlement. From the early 1960s the presence of an airstrip there, together with the gradual concentration of government services including a primary school, a secondary school and a clinic, led to the in-migration of large numbers of people from other parts of the highlands. Most of the people living in Bario in the late 1980s were originally from outside it, predominantly from the southern part of the Kelabit Highlands from Pa' Main southwards (**Map 2**). Lian-Saging (1976/77) describes the patterns of resettlement of longhouse communities from other parts of the Highlands in Bario.

Bario, although it contained, by the 1980s, hundreds of people, was not a town nor even a continuous village. It was made up of a number of separate longhouse communities less than an hour's walk from each other, all but one constructed in pairs, with two longhouses built extremely close together: Bario Asal and Arur Layun; Ulung Palang Deta' and Ulung Palang Banah; Pa' Ramapoh Deta' and Pa' Ramapah Banah; and Arur Dalan. Each of these communities consisted of a single longhouse plus a few separate houses (*ruma' sebulang*). There was also a settlement, inhabited mostly by traders, at the airstrip in

Bario. The inhabitants of this settlement, Padang Pasir, built a new longhouse at Kampung Baru in the early 1990s, half an hour's walk away on the path to the southern part of the Highlands, to which they were gradually moving when I was in the Highlands in 1992/93.

Outside Bario, there were, in 1986, eight Kelabit longhouse communities within the Kelabit Highlands outside Bario: Pa' Lungan, Pa' Umor, Pa' Ukat, Pa' Derong, Remudu, Pa' Dalih, Long Dano and Batu Patong. The first four were within a couple of hours' walk north-east and north-west of Bario, while the last four were a day's walk or more away to the south-east (see **Map 2**).

The Kelabit Highlands are separated from other parts of the interior tableland by a low range of mountains, the Apad Uat (literally, the 'Root Range'; it is from this range that the term for the linguistic group to which the Kelabit belong, Apo Duat, derives) but this is easily crossed. The barrier between the Kelabit Highlands and other parts of the Miri Division of Sarawak is much greater, since the mountains are much higher (Janowski 1991: 5). Despite this, there were, in the late 20th century, Kelabit communities on the other side of these mountains, established within the previous century or so: Long Lellang, Long Seridan, Long Napir and Long Peluan (**Map 1**). There had been others, but all their inhabitants resettled in Bario. Until it became possible to travel by air, the Kelabit used to walk to very distant communities for the purposes of trade or to visit kin. However, links between Kelabit communities in and outside the Highlands were, by 1986, via Marudi or Miri, and the Kelabit rarely walked long distances any longer. The only time when they still walked to faraway communities in 1986-88 was as *pelawat* (Malay ?), which can be glossed as 'religious travellers'. *Pelawat* were groups of people from one parish or a small number of parishes who visited a circuit of other parishes to pray with the people there (see below for discussion of Christianity among the Kelabit).

The Kelabit Highlands are fairly closely linked to other parts of the interior tableland inhabited by related Apo Duat peoples, situated in East Kalimantan, in Indonesia. The border runs roughly north-south, along the Apad Uat range, and is only a couple of hours' walk from any Kelabit community in the highlands to the first communities in Kalimantan. This means that both northern and southern communities are able to make contact with people across the border quite easily. Bario's links across the border are with a Lun Bawang area in the headwaters of the Kerayan River, which the Kelabit call Ba Rian or Berian (Schneeberger describes this as Pa Rian; Schneeberger 1979, **Map 1**). Pa' Dalih has its links across the border to the Lun Bawang communities of the area which they call the Kerayan, which also forms part of the headwaters of the Kerayan river. As in the past, there was in the 1980s and 1990s a good deal of intermarriage between Kelabit and Kerayan people, and a significant amount of immigration, both temporary and potentially permanent, into the Kelabit Highlands from the Kerayan and Ba Rian areas, because of Sarawak's relative economic prosperity and the opportunities for employment. There was very frequent contact across the border. As far as Pa' Dalih was concerned, many of the teenagers belonging to hearth-groups (households) with kin links across the border

spent part of their time there and part of their time in Pa' Dalih. Kerayan people often came to Pa' Dalih to get employment during my stays there, particularly in the making of new wet rice fields. People from the Ba Rian area went to Bario for employment in wet rice fields there, in much larger numbers than in Pa' Dalih because the wet rice areas are bigger, there is more work, and there was more money to pay them than there is in Pa' Dalih. Talla says that in Bario in the 1970s at least 60% of the labour force in the wet fields in Bario was provided by such immigrants from the Ba Rian area (Talla 1979: 308).

Kelabit communities, known as *bawang*, are nucleated around between one and three longhouses. Outside Bario, each settlement was, in the late 1980s, cut off quite clearly from other settlements by primary or very old secondary forest, which was described as *polong raya*, literally 'big forest' (see note 28). Each settlement had its own territory within the forest, both for making fields and for hunting and gathering, known as *tang* (Talla 1979: 91). Even Bario consisted of a number of distinct longhouse-based settlements with separate farming land, even though these were very close to each other.

The Kelabit and the SIB Church

The Kelabit were converted to Christianity in the 1950s by the Borneo Evangelical Mission, but it was not until what is called the Revival of 1972 that they believe themselves to have become whole-heartedly Christian (Lees 1979) and to have abandoned their pre-Christian practices. In the late 1980s and early 1990s, all Kelabit – except a small number of people married to Muslims and one eccentric individual living in Bario who had become Muslim for reasons which were somewhat unclear – were, as far as I know, members of the Sidang Injil Borneo Church, which grew out of the BEM.[8] The SIB Church is now (2002) based in Miri, on the coast, and has parishes throughout the Apo Duat areas of Sarawak as well as in major towns. The Apo Duat peoples in Kalimantan belong to a different, but similar, Indonesian Church called KINGMI. Both the SIB and KINGMI Churches are evangelical and charismatic.

The SIB Church uses the national language, Bahasa Malaysia, in describing activities and organisational roles within the Church. Printed matter is normally in that language, although it is sometimes in Kelabit or Lun Bawang (the closely related language used in Apo Duat areas in the province of East Kalimantan and among Apo Duat peoples in the Limbang Division of Sarawak, which includes Lawas area and the Trusan River). The Bible has been translated into Lun Bawang, and the Kelabit use this quite easily. However, in Miri services in the SIB Church are held in English as well as Malay, and printed material is sometimes in English. English was the language of instruction in schools until the late 1970s, and some degree of knowledge of English is quite widespread among Kelabit who attended school in the 1960s and 1970s.

In Pa' Dalih during the time I lived there, services were held, as they were in other Kelabit longhouse settlements, every day at daybreak and and three times a week at nightfall as well. On Sundays there was a main service and a special womens' service; women attended both. A bamboo gong, *tobong* (BM85, SM34; **Pl. 100**), was beaten to announce the beginning of each service. The church building was made of planks, roofed with zinc, and furnished with plank benches, although in the longhouse people sat on the floor (even though some families owned tables and benches, these were little used). The church in Pa' Dalih was rebuilt in 1987, while we were living there, using community labour; while it was being rebuilt services were held in the public *tawa'* area of the longhouse (see Chapter 3).

The parish of Pa' Dalih was run by a group of about 10 deacons, *pelayan*, who were male. However, the election of a male *pelayan* implied his married status and the election of his wife too; in fact, it was really *pelayan* couples who were elected. This underlines the central significance of the couple as a male+female unit (Janowski 1995). Separately, there was a *kaum ibu*, a 'mothers' circle', which was very influential within the community. Although there was technically also a *kaum bapa*, a 'fathers' circle', this was dormant, and men did not, collectively as a gender, have the power that women had in the community. Both the *pelayan* as representatives of the whole community, and the *kaum ibu* as representatives of adult women (i.e. mothers) were able to deploy money, which was collected during services or raised through events such as cake sales (Malay; *pesta kek*) and spent on community activities.

Christianity, and the SIB Church in particular, was, at the end of the 20th century, strongly associated with the ethnic identity 'Kelabit'. For the people of Pa' Dalih, Christianity was associated with success in the modern world of the town. There was a belief that Christianity brought special access to the power, *lalud*, of God, on whom such success was believed to depend. Informants said that they believed that access to the power of God was the reason why white people had been so successful in the world. The association of Kelabit ethnicity with Christianity was expressed, for example, by placing Christian messages on artefacts which were emphatically Kelabit or Lun Bawang. These items were sometimes made to be displayed in Kelabit and Lun Bawang houses in town as *bunga ruma'*, literally 'house flowers/decorations' (see Chapter 3). The most common object to carry such a message was the *uyut* basket. *Uyut* belonged to individuals rather than hearth-groups. They were made for specific people and often had that person's name and a Christian message on them, frequently in English. Examples of Christian messages on *uyut* baskets in the collections are 'Love in Christ', Sing for Joy', God Bless you All' and 'The Truth of God' (BM51–53). Small *uyut* were often used for collecting money in church (BM59–60; **Pl. 3**), and these also had Christian messages woven into them, generally in Malay (because this is a language often used in church). An example is *'Persembahan Kami'* (Our Offering), which is on the collection basket shown in use in the church at Remudu in the late 1980s in **Plate 3**. The collection basket shown in this photograph is one of the pair of collection baskets which make up BM60 in the catalogue; some time after this photograph was taken, I bought the pair (another pair was ordered from Penan makers for the parish of Remudu, to replace these). Sometimes, I was told, the name of the parish for which they have been made is woven into such collection baskets.

Farmers in the forest

It is not known how long this Kerayan-Kelabit highland area has been inhabited.[9] Kelabit myth tells that humans originate here, with tribes other than the Kelabit and related peoples being washed downstream in a Great Flood (Lian-Saging 1976/77: 50-52). While the mountain ranges were, in the late 1980s and early 1990s, covered with primary and secondary forest (see note 28), with parts utilised for dry cultivation of rice and other crops, the flatter, bottom lands of the valleys in the area were generally used for wet rice agriculture, making the area distinctive for central Borneo.

For the people of Pa' Dalih at the end of the 20th century, the forest (*polong*) was the default environment which would exist everywhere, if it were not for human intervention. It was a vast world of thousands of living species in which all life, including human beings, originally developed, as well as a zone of mystery and of fear, since it was believed to be full not only of animals and plants but also of spirits, *ada'*. Through farming, the people of the community had thrust the forest back a little, to make space for areas that were under human control – cultivated fields and longhouses. For the people of Pa' Dalih, farming differentiated them from hunter-gatherer groups like the Penan, for whom the forest was even more dominant in everyday life. Farming, for the people of Pa' Dalih, meant rice cultivation. They emphasised their identity as rice-growers. Success in rice-growing was until the Second World War, and remained to a large extent at the time I lived there, the basis of status. While wealth was important for a person of status, rice-growing was also vital. In 1987 I heard a relative of a person from Bario with a successful job in town, who clearly felt uneasy about the fact that he was not making a rice field, say, in a tone that made it clear that she was making an excuse for him, that *kerja late' iah*, 'his job is his rice field'.

The people of Pa' Dalih had a complex relationship with the forest. While they certainly recognized their profound dependance on it, they tended in most contexts to downplay this, preferring to emphasise their dependance on rice-growing as their most important livelihood activity. Because of this, it would have been difficult for a casual outside visitor to fully realize the extent to which the forest was vital to life. The reason for down-playing their reliance on wild resources (see page 35) was because for the Kelabit this does not confer status. The attitude of agricultural groups like the Kelabit to a purely hunter-gatherer lifestyle is reflected in the fact that the nomadic Penan come under a lot of pressure to settle down and farm rice, not only from the government but from other, agricultural, tribal groups, including the Kelabit (Janowski 1997b). Nevertheless, the forest was profoundly important to the Kelabit of the Highlands in the 1980s and 1990s, on both a practical and a symbolic level. In many respects, agriculturalist peoples living in the forest in the interior of Borneo, like the Kelabit, are, in fact, as dependant on that forest as are the nomadic Penan/Punan.

The rainforest was, for the people of Pa' Dalih, a very rich source of substances necessary to sustain physical life and enable social life, through food and through crafts. Until the 1960s they had extremely limited access to goods from town and relied entirely on the forest for materials for building and handicrafts. After the Second World War, and particularly after the government-run airstrip was opened in Bario in 1961, an increasing number of substances and items available in town were enthusiastically adopted by the Kelabit in the Highlands. This was either because they were more durable or more effective than equivalent items made of forest materials, because they fulfilled a role or accomplished a task which was new and which could not be fulfilled by local materials at all, and/or because they were of high status. However, even in the late 1980s, all meat consumed on an everyday basis in Pa' Dalih, and a high proportion of other foods, derived from the forest. The vast majority of the materials used in craftwork also came from the forest. The people of the community were well aware that it was possible to live entirely off the forest, should they need to do so.

The forest was not only, even at the end of the 20th century, an important base of physical livelihood for the people of Pa' Dalih; it was also significant symbolically. Without wild foods, or foods treated as though they were wild,[10] the rice meal (*kuman nuba'*), which is the basis of Kelabit kin relations (see Chapter 9), could not take place.

Although it seemed from e-mail and letter contact with Kelabit informants in Miri that at the turn of the century much of the forest close to Pa' Dalih still remained, the primary forest in the Kelabit Highlands is likely to be lost soon. In 1997 logging roads reached the Highlands, reaching a spot near Remudu in the southern part of the Highlands within half a day's walk from Pa' Dalih. The impact of the loss of forest on livelihoods in the Highlands in general is difficult to predict. It is possible that the Kelabit Highlands has, as a 1985 study suggested, the potential to become a horticultural centre, where temperate crops could be cultivated for sale in town (Highland Development Technical Committee 1985). However, this would require a radical shift of emphasis in terms of subsistence strategy, and the intermediate stages are likely to be difficult. Already it is apparent that the reduced access to the forest in the Bario area is problematic on both a practical and a cultural level (Janowski forthcoming a). Since many of the materials which the Kelabit take from the forest for handicrafts are from primary forest, which is the area mainly affected by logging, its impact will also mean reduced access to many materials basic to everyday material culture.

BM53 The Christian message on an *uyut,* soft multipurpose basket. Item in the British Museum collection, drawing by Claire Thorne.

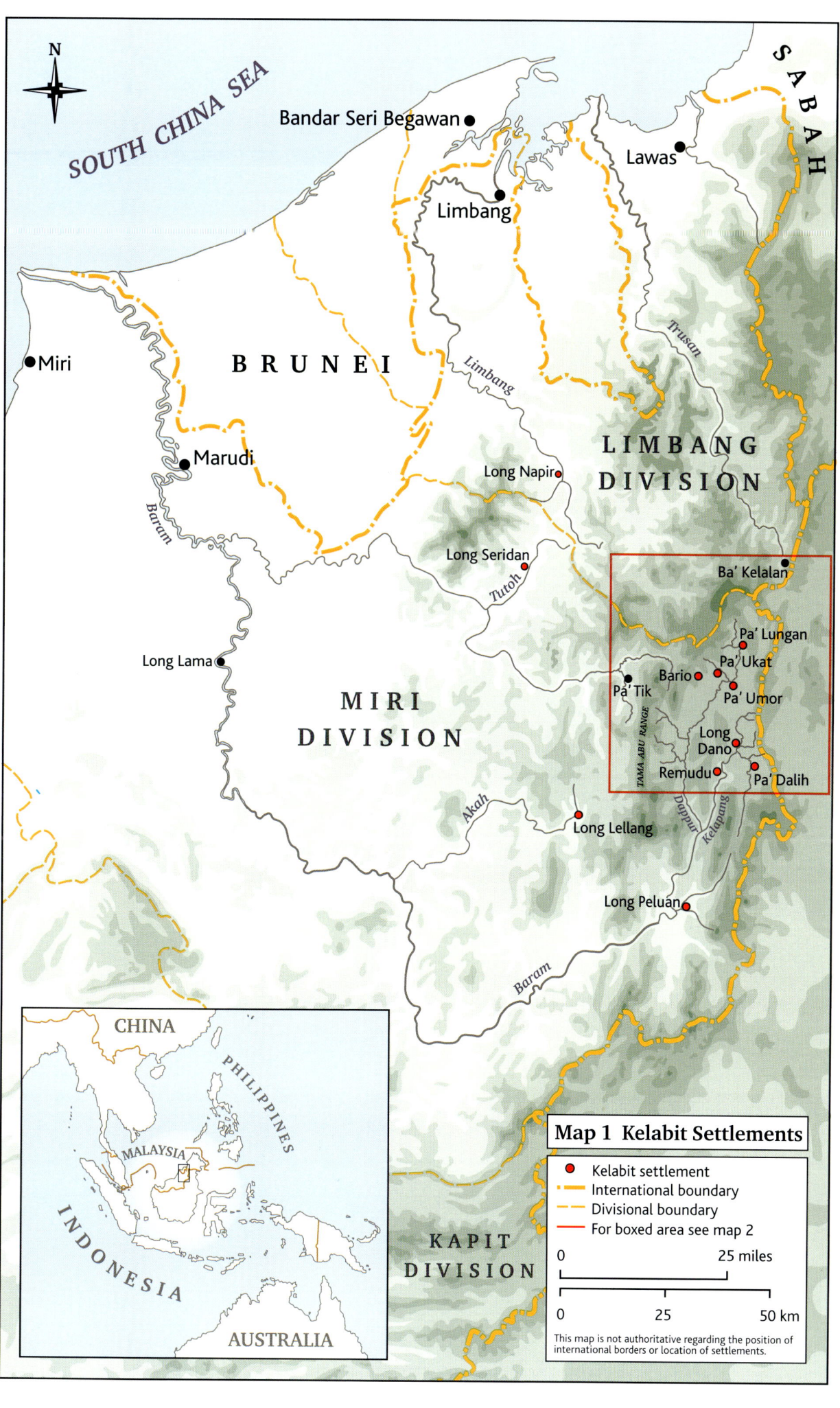

N

SOUTH CHINA SEA

Bandar Seri Begawan ●

Lawas ●

S A B A H

Limbang

● Miri

B R U N E I

Limbang

Trusan

● Marudi

L I M B A N G
D I V I S I O N

Long Napir ●

Baram

Ba' Kelalan ●

Long Seridan ●

Pa' Lungan ●
Pa' Ukat ●
Bario ● ●
Pa' Umor ●
Pa' Tik ●
Long Dano ●
Remudu ●
Pa' Dalih ●

Long Lama ●

M I R I
D I V I S I O N

Tutoh

TAMA ABU RANGE

Akah

Dapur

Kelapang

Long Lellang ●

Baram

Long Peluan ●

CHINA

PHILIPPINES

MALAYSIA

Map 1 Kelabit Settlements

● Kelabit settlement
▬ International boundary
▬ Divisional boundary
▬ For boxed area see map 2

0   25 miles

0   25   50 km

This map is not authoritative regarding the position of
international borders or location of settlements.

INDONESIA

AUSTRALIA

K A P I T
D I V I S I O N

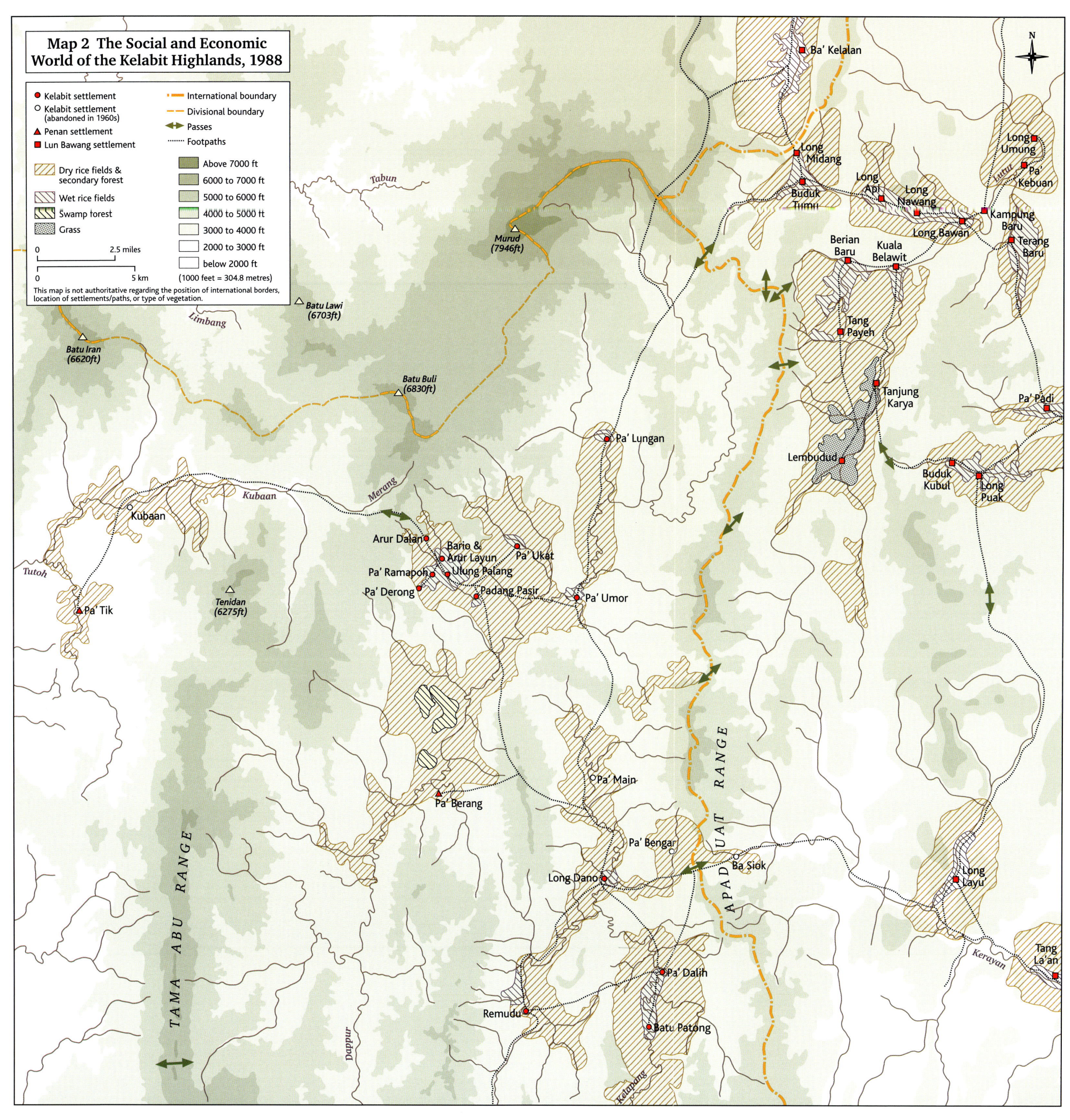

Map 2 The Social and Economic World of the Kelabit Highlands, 1988

Legend:

- ● Kelabit settlement
- ○ Kelabit settlement (abandoned in 1960s)
- ▲ Penan settlement
- ■ Lun Bawang settlement

- Dry rice fields & secondary forest
- Wet rice fields
- Swamp forest
- Grass

- ·—·— International boundary
- – – – Divisional boundary
- ◀▶ Passes
- ·········· Footpaths

Elevation:
- Above 7000 ft
- 6000 to 7000 ft
- 5000 to 6000 ft
- 4000 to 5000 ft
- 3000 to 4000 ft
- 2000 to 3000 ft
- below 2000 ft

(1000 feet = 304.8 metres)

0 — 2.5 miles
0 — 5 km

This map is not authoritative regarding the position of international borders, location of settlements/paths, or type of vegetation.

Labels on map:

Tabun

Murud (7946ft)

Batu Lawi (6703ft)

Batu Iran (6620ft)

Batu Buli (6830ft)

Limbang

Ba' Kelalan

Long Umung

Pa' Kebuan

Long Midang

Long Api

Long Nawang

Kampung Baru

Buduk Timu

Long Bawan

Terang Baru

Berian Baru

Kuala Belawit

Tang Payeh

Tanjung Karya

Pa' Padi

Lembudud

Buduk Kubul

Long Puak

Pa' Lungan

Kubaan

Kubaan

Merang

Arur Dalan

Bario & Arur Layun

Pa' Ukat

Pa' Ramapoh

Ulung Palang

Pa' Derong

Padang Pasir

Pa' Umor

Tutoh

Pa' Tik

Tenidan (6275ft)

Pa' Berang

Pa' Main

Pa' Bengar

Ba Siok

Long Layu

Long Dano

TAMA ABU RANGE

APAD UAT RANGE

Dappur

Pa' Dalih

Remudu

Batu Patong

Kalapang

Kerayan

Tang La'an

N

2 Clothes, Hair and Personal Adornment

Until the 1950s and 1960s the people of the Kelabit Highlands had little access to shop-bought clothing. Men wore loin cloths (*chawat*) made of bark cloth (*anit kayuh*) (**Pl. 99**), while women wore short skirts of bark cloth which met at the side but were not sewn together. Bark cloth jackets were sometimes worn by both men and women, which might be decorated with embroidery or cowry shells (*bee*) (Harrisson 1959: 10-15).

From the 1960s onwards, town-bought clothes became the norm. By the late 1980s, bark cloth was no longer worn, and there were no clothes of bark left in Pa' Dalih. Cotton *tekip* (the Malay *sarong*, a strip of cloth sewn up at the ends and wrapped around the bottom half of the body like a skirt) had become the usual clothing for adult women and men wore shorts or trousers. Both sexes usually wore a T shirt, sometimes a buttoned shirt, on their top half. On special occasions such as *irau* feasts, Kelabit women dressed in blouses and skirt made of *batik* or other high-quality fabric, similar to the formal *baju kebaya* (Malay) worn by Malay women (**Pl. 7**). In Bario all the women of the longhouse hosting an *irau* sometimes dressed in the same *baju kebaya*-like clothes to perform a dance and song (**Pl. 4**). Men attending *irau* wore a buttoned shirt, often made of *batik* cloth, and trousers (**Pl. 5**).

For neither men nor women was modesty a major issue when I lived in Pa' Dalih. It was, however, important for adult women to cover up their legs, something that does not appear to have been an issue before the Second World War. Kelabit women were, until the 1960s, tattooed on the arms and legs with a fine pattern of dots and lines (**Pl. 26**). The arm tattoos were abandoned first, so that when I lived there, there were a number of women in Pa' Dalih whose legs were tattooed but whose arms were not.

Clothing in the fields

Both men and women covered up as much as possible in the fields for protection from scratching from rice stalks, and, in dry fields, from stumps and branches. Naturally enough, everyone wore old clothes. Women usually wore a *tekip* and a long-sleeved shirt or blouse. Men, and sometimes women, wore trousers to protect their legs (although adult women rarely wore trousers when not in the fields), and both sexes tended to wear long-sleeved shirts in the fields, to protect their arms from the sun. Kelabit do not like to become browner than they naturally are; there is admiration for a fair body, and the heroes of their traditional sagas are described as having very white bodies (Rubenstein 1973: 868).

Both men and women wore head covering in the fields to protect them from the sun. Women, especially married ones, usually wore a wide hat called a *ra'ong* (**Pl. 34**). Men also quite often wore *ra'ong*, although they were considered to be more female than male attire. Those who did not wear *ra'ong* wore shop-bought caps and hats of various kinds, and sometimes a piece of cloth (**Pl. 43**). *Ra'ong* made in the Kelabit Highlands (BM46–47, SM54–55; **Pl. 29**) were made of the leaf of a fan palm, called *ilad* by the Kelabit (*Licuala valida*), while those made across the border in the Ba Rian area of the Kerayan headwaters (BM48, SM56) were made of *berpah* grass. *Ra'ong* are almost flat, with the edge, made of rattan, turned down. They are kept on the head with a woven cap (*oloh*) shaped to fit the top of the head, which is sewn on to the hat. They are often decorated, using all sorts of materials – tiny beads made into ornamental centres which may have messages woven into them (BM46; **Pl. 29**), wool sewn on into patterns (BM47), or shop-bought decorations. Ba Rian hats are often decorated with cloth (BM48). These were widely worn in Pa' Dalih when I lived there. Hats were often made for a particular individual whose name they might bear. This was particularly true of hats with beaded centres, which were the most highly valued.

In dry fields people often wore the rubber football boots that were also worn when walking in the forest in wet weather. They might also go barefoot. In wet fields people always went barefoot.

Clothing while hunting and in the forest

Men going hunting used before the Second World War to wear a bark loin cloth together with a bark jacket if they were going at night and a *tabir puet* (BM114) attached at the waist to sit on. In 1986-88, though, men going hunting, and young men in particular, tended to dress in clothing which had many elements of a soldier's uniform,[11] often wearing army or camouflage trousers, a T-shirt and jacket bought in town, and sometimes a cap. On their feet young men, and most older men, wore rubber football boots without socks, which were the usual forest footwear for both sexes. Some older men still went barefoot.

Women gathering wild vegetables wore similar clothing to that which they wore in the fields, although they did not make such an effort to protect themselves from scratches by wearing long sleeves. They would generally wear rubber flip-flops on their feet.

When travelling between settlements, men wore similar clothing, although interestingly it was often simpler, as though to underline the fact that when hunting they were engaging in an important male activity. Women travelling between settlements usually wore a *tekip* and T-shirt, as at home, but they might wear trousers instead of a *tekip*.

Hair

As they had before the Second World War, Kelabit adult women, in the late 1980s and early 1990s wore their hair long. Once a woman was married, and particularly once she had had a child, it was not considered appropriate for her to wear her hair short, although young unmarried women often did, particularly if they had spent some time in town. Long hair was worn at the back of the head, usually by simply tying it into a knot on itself.

Until the early 1960s, men had a more ornamental style of hairdo than women. The front part of their hair was cut in a bowl cut, with the sides of the head shaved (**Pl. 13**), while the back was left long and was worn in a bun, often with a hairpin through it (**Pls. 1, 109**). Many of these hairpins were apparently very beautiful and they were often carved. In 1986-88, although many older men still wore their hair cut in this way (**Pls 1, 28**), few used hairpins. Most younger men had a more Western style of haircut, although some continued to wear the traditional hairstyle, in what seemed to be a conscious display of 'Kelabit-ness'.

By the time I went to live in Pa' Dalih, hair was groomed using brushes and combs bought in town; until a couple of decades earlier bamboo combs were used. For removing lice, however, the combs called *kasib* made of bamboo (BM28, SM21) were used in the late 1980s, as they had been in the past.

Earrings and ear pendants

Practically all Kelabit men and women, until the 1970s, had their ear lobes pierced and extended with ear pendants, known as *abe*, as was common among 'tribal' peoples in Borneo until a few decades ago. In 1986-88, most adults in Pa' Dalih had had their ears extended in this way as children. However, from the 1970s onwards, the extension of ear lobes and the wearing of ear pendants fell out of fashion. People began to have their long ears surgically altered, removing the long flap of skin. By the late '80s, many younger women had had their ears re-pierced for small gold earrings, and most younger men no longer wore earrings. The last child to have her ear lobes extended and to wear heavy ear pendants in the Pa' Dalih area was a child called Esther living in Remudu, born around 1980 (**Pl. 8**). Young boys no longer had their ears pierced. Nevertheless, a number of older people still wore the *abe*, particularly at *irau* feasts (**Pls 5, 7**).

In the late 1980s, women who still wore heavy ear pendants had teardrop-shaped brass ones (**Pl. 7**). While these were bought on the coast, those made of lead had, until the 1960s, been made in the Highlands, as were the lead beads still being made and used in the late 1980s in bead caps, *petaa* (see below). Until the 1960s or 1970s, women often wore bunches of earrings called *abe ringgit* (BM146–147; **Pls 10, 21, 32, 38, 68**).

Men wore lighter pendants and consequently had shorter ear lobes than women, since it was the weight of the ear pendants that causes the ear to lengthen. When metal, men's ear pendants usually consisted of a single ring of brass (*abe tawak*) (BM148–149; **Pls 9, 13**) but they might be a bunch of rings (**Pl. 99**) or be made of carved hornbill ivory (**Pl. 6**). In addition to ear pendants, most men had the upper part of their ears pierced, through the cartilage, and wore clouded leopard (*Neofelis nebulosa*) fangs through these holes, with the points facing forwards and the ends attached together behind the head, often with tiny beads (**Pls. 13, 99**). These were almost never worn by the late 1980s, although I saw a few men wearing them in Bario (**Pl. 5**).

The ear pendants and earrings were heirlooms and were valuable; the metal many were made of, and some of the finished pendants, were bought outside the Kelabit Highlands at a time when the Kelabit had little cash. Both the long ears themselves and the ear pendants and earrings worn were, at least until the 1970s, considered to be beautiful. The emphasis appears to have been more on the beauty of the long ears in women, whereas in men the wearing of hornbill ivory and of clouded leopard fangs were a statement of maleness, as both substances derive from the wild, and these animals in particular are considered to be animals with a great deal of wild life force, *lalud* (see Chapter 7).

Beads

Old beads, *ba'o ma'on*, mainly made of glass and sometimes of stone, were still highly valued by the Kelabit at the end of the 20th century, as they had been before the Second World War. They were worn in necklaces (*bane ba'o*), as bead caps (*petaa*), and in belts (*brit*) (**Pls 4, 5, 7, 11**). Necklaces might be made up only of valuable, old beads; or of tiny, less valuable and newer beads strung to make bunches; or of a mixture of valuable old beads and newer, bunched beads (BM115; **Pl. 10**). It was usually men who wore the smaller, less valuable beads strung to make bunches, with or without valuable old beads, and it was clear that in the period immediately after the Second World War, and before that too, presumably, they wore far more of these than they did by the end of the 1980s (**Pls. 13, 99**).

Although it was those beads considered most 'ancient' (*ma'on*) which were the most valuable, there have clearly been fashions which have brought different ancient beads to the fore at different points in time. For example, at the beginning of this century the blue and green beads called *let* or *ba'o bata'* and the cornelian *ba'o burur* were in favour, but in the 1980s it was the small tubular *ba'o rawir* which were most sought after. Individual beads could be sold for as high as Malay $100 or more in 1986-88. This meant that a full bead cap, *petaa*, made of the most valuable beads, *alai*, was worth at that time the equivalent of about UK £20,000 (**Pl. 11**). A *petaa* made of *ba'o rawir* was worth the equivalent of about UK £5,000.

Bead-wearing, bead-stringing and bead-buying were significant concerns for women in Pa' Dalih when I was living there. Up to the Second World War, ceramics including plates and particularly old jars (*belanai*), metal gongs (*tawak*) and old beads (*ba'o ma'on*) were the main prestige possessions, passed on as heirlooms from generation to generation. Jars and gongs, which had been passed down the male line, were no longer of much interest to the people of Pa' Dalih in the late 1980s, but old beads, mainly passed down the female line, had retained their traditional role as a status symbol. With the increase in cash in the Highlands and the bids for status mobility that were going on, especially in Bario (Janowski 2003; see Chapter 8), the possession and purchase of beads had become almost an obsession. Although the best beads to own were said to be those inherited from ancestors, beads were being bought from people from the Kerayan and Ba Rian areas in Kalimantan, who had similar old beads to the Kelabit but less money, and so were willing to sell. This was much more significant in Bario, where there was more money, than in Pa' Dalih, but beads were sometimes bought from visitors from the Kerayan in Pa' Dalih too. The Kelabit themselves very rarely sold beads. Kelabit interest in beads contrasts with the situation among many other tribal groups in Sarawak, who have lost much of their interest in beads as prestige possessions.

Both men and women owned and wore beads in Pa' Dalih, but women wore them more often than men and they owned and wore the most valuable beads. Beads were considered to be a primarily female possession, just as Harrisson found to have been the case in Bario in the 1940s and 1950s (Harrisson 1959: 12-13). It was women who set bead fashions, and wore the beads considered most fashionable and most valuable, although men did wear beads which were considered very 'ancient' (**Pl. 12**). When men wore beads, it was as necklaces, *bane*. It was mostly young men who wore *bane*. Men did not wear *petaa* and *brit*.

Apart from the *bane*, the most common way of displaying old beads was in the *petaa*, or bead cap. Until the 1970s, when it became possible to sell rice to town by air, there were very few *petaa* and these were owned by women of very 'good' (*doo'*) origin. By the 1980s, however, far more women, especially in Bario, owned them, having purchased the necessary beads from people from the Kerayan.

Irau naming feasts (*irau pekaa ngadan*) were a particularly important occasion at which old beads were displayed in the late 1980s. Not only did individuals display their personal status through wearing *petaa* and *bane*, but the host longhouse as a unit also displayed its status and wealth through the beads which its women wore. One particularly clear display of this was at *irau* naming feasts (**Pl. 4**). During my stay in Pa' Dalih, I attended a number of these, both in Pa' Dalih and in Bario. It was quite obvious that women were careful to display their best beads at these.

Most beads were made of glass, although there were some made of stone and some made of shell. Although fashions dictating which beads are most highly valued change, it always seems to have been the case that those considered most ancient (*ma'on*) have been most highly valued. These were believed to carry life force, *lalud* (see Chapter 7).

Jewellery and ornaments other than beads

Until the 1960s or 1970s, both men and women wore bangles made of shell, *leko' olo' akap* (BM150) (**Pl. 99**), which were quite highly valued. These appear to have a marine origin and have clearly travelled some distance before reaching the Kelabit Highlands. By the late 1980s, however, bangles were not much valued or worn. Men also used to wear bands around their calves called *unus* (**Pls. 13, 99**) (Harrisson 1959: 12), said by informants in Pa' Dalih to strengthen the calf muscles and to protect the upper part of the body from danger which might enter the body through the ground.

In the late 1980s and early 1990s, women wore gold jewellery bought in town as well as or instead of beads (**Pl. 21**). Both were status symbols: beads within the Kelabit social world in the Highlands and to some extent the world of tribal peoples in town as well, and gold within both the Kelabit world and the outside world of the town. However, there did not seem any prospect in the foreseeable future of gold displacing beads entirely; gold was not seen as having the individual identity or accumulated life force or potency (*lalud*) from generations of being inherited that beads did, and this is likely to be a significant factor here. On the other hand, the value of gold was recognized by people of other ethnic groups in a way that beads were not. The different types of value ascribed to gold and beads were often brought together, particularly by those living in town, through having an old bead set in gold and wearing this as a pendant.

As well as valuable bead necklaces and sometimes bracelets, many individuals in Pa' Dalih wore plastic or base metal bangles and/or strings of plastic beads.

The *topi ulu*

Besides hats worn in the fields, there is another hat which was occasionally worn by the Kelabit while I was living in the Highlands. This was the *topi ulu* (BM97, **Pl. 5**), short for *topi orang ulu* (Malay), literally 'hat of the people of the interior'. This kind of hat was also worn by men of other tribal groups: the Berawan, Kenyah, Kajang, Kayan and Penan. The *topi ulu* was not worn on an everyday basis. Rather than being a practical item, it was a kind of badge of 'being tribal', something of which many of the interior peoples are proud in Sarawak. Such hats are worn on public occasions by some Kelabit men; I saw this in Bario on the occasion of the elections of 1987. I never saw the *topi ulu* worn in Pa' Dalih, probably because public occasions are much less common than in Bario.

BM9 Detail of carving and weaving on a *tongol* (bush knife). Item in the British Museum collection, drawing by Claire Thorne.

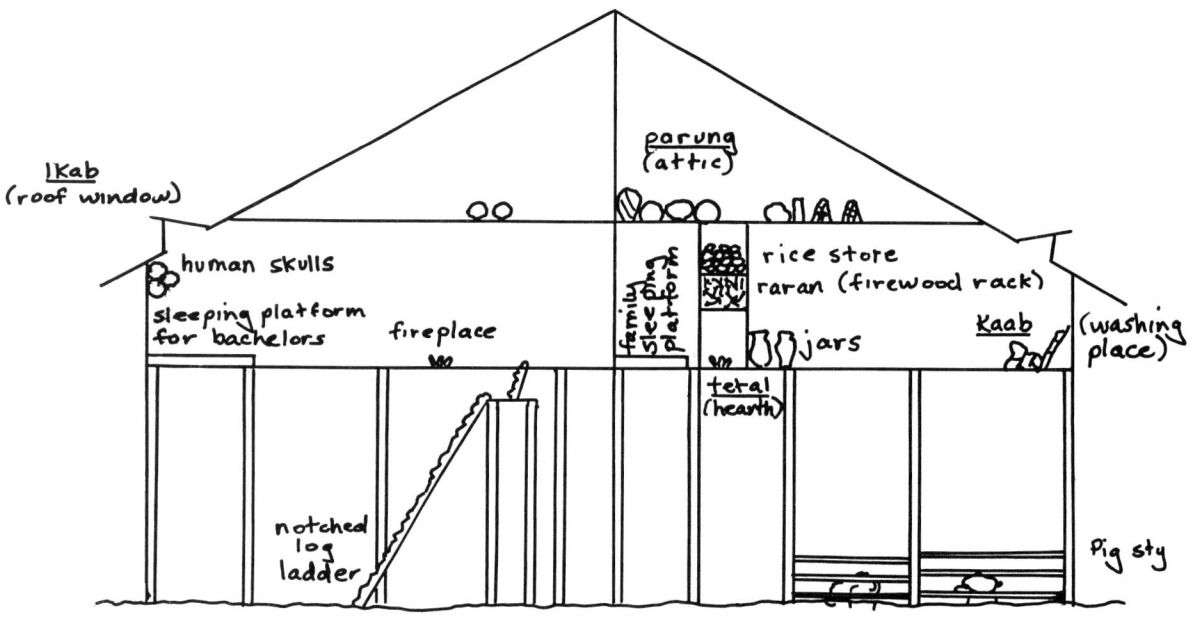

Figure 2 Cross-section of pre-1945 Kelabit longhouse (after Lian-Saging 1976/77: 126)

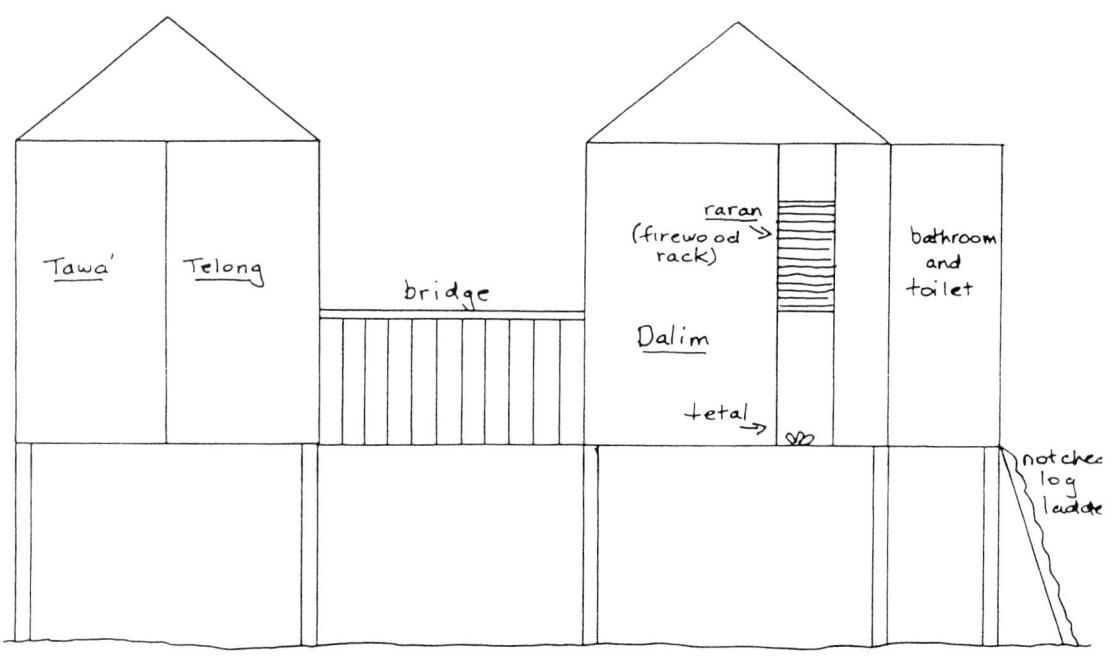

Figure 3 Cross-section of Pa' Dalih longhouse, 1986.

3 The Kelabit Longhouse

The Borneo longhouse

All of the 'tribal' peoples of Borneo appear to have lived in longhouses in the 19th century, and many still do. Depending upon the ethnic group, a whole community may live in one longhouse, or may be divided among several. Different groups have longhouses of different sizes and degrees of permanence. In some groups, they are only inhabited for part of the year, with the people spending part of the year in smaller, less permanent structures, sometimes themselves mini-longhouses, near their swidden fields.

The largest proportion of people still living in longhouses at the beginning of the 21st century is to be found in Sarawak, where the pre-Second World War Brooke government did not discourage this form of habitation, unlike the governments of Sabah and Kalimantan. Although there is a growing number of individual houses, in most Sarawak tribal communities the majority of people still live in longhouses.

The longhouse is a the focus of kinship and sociability and is the place where all activities outside it culminate. Here, the products of the forest and of the rice field – and nowadays, things brought in from town too – are brought together to create human society. The most important representation of this is the rice meal (in Kelabit described as *kuman nuba'*, literally 'eating rice') (**Pls 32, 35**).

The household/hearth group

Borneo longhouses are divided into areas built and inhabited by separate households – or hearth-groups, as I shall describe them. Among the Kelabit, the household is referred to as *uang ruma'* ('flesh of the house'), *lobang ruma'* ('house-cavity', probably meaning 'what is contained within the house'), or *tetal* (hearth). I use the term 'hearth-group' to refer to it because of the focal significance of the hearth and of the rice meal that is prepared at the hearth and eaten next to it (Janowski 1995; and see Chapter 9). A Pa' Dalih hearth-group is headed by one married couple, primarily responsible for rice cultivation and hence the provision of the rice meal for all hearth-group members. Once a couple has at least one child they enter the process of becoming adults (*lun merar* or 'big people'), and, once they are also primarily responsible for rice-growing within the hearth-group, they qualify to lead it. It is the fact of cultivating and consuming rice separately that defines a hearth-group as a distinct entity. My husband and myself, together with our one-year-old daughter, were urged to set up as a separate hearth-group within one of the two longhouses in Pa' Dalih, were lent a vacant apartment, and were given parental names (Batang Kelapang and Sinah Batang Kelapang, 'Kelapang River' and 'Mother Kelapang River') soon after we arrived (**Pl. 14**). These were used throughout our stay, since our English names were categorized as 'little' names (*ngadan i'it*), appropriate for those who do not yet have children, and their use would be improper in speaking to parents, such as we were (Janowski 2000). We were regularly urged to begin to grow rice, although we did not do this since it would have taken most of our time, inexperienced as we were. If a hearth-group is unable to produce enough rice to provide for regular rice meals it cannot continue to function as a separate hearth-group and its members must become dependant upon another hearth-group. If we had planned to stay permanently in Pa' Dalih there is no question that we would have had to begin to make rice fields.

Borneo longhouses are divided longitudinally into an inner and an outer area, and each hearth-group builds and owns a part of each. The inner area of each hearth-group is usually separated off by walls and is used almost entirely by its members. It contains the hearth where the rice meal is cooked, and is for this reason conceptually focal. It is sometimes, as among the Kelabit, literally described as 'inside' (*dalim* in Kelabit), and sometimes it is described using the term for the hearth-group itself, as among the Kayan, Kenyah and Maloh (King 1978; Rousseau 1978; Whittier 1978). Among some tribal groups the cooking area is separate from the main 'inner' area, to avoid contamination by smoke, but this appears to be a recent innovation – in most such cases the cooking hearth used to be in the main 'inner' area. The inner area may contain the area where rice is dried, and usually, at least until recently, it has contained the sleeping area for the married couple heading the hearth-group, their small children, and unmarried girls belonging to the hearth group. This inner area has been variously described by scholars working on Borneo 'tribal' groups as 'living room' (Geddes 1954; Freeman 1955), 'apartment' (Rousseau 1978; Whittier 1978) or 'compartment' (Appell 1978), and it has usually been considered by scholars to be the 'private' area, although the relevance of using the terms 'public' and 'private' is to be questioned, as Helliwell (Helliwell 1993) points out, since it implies an opposition between the community and the hearth-group/household which is inappropriate. The relationship between hearth-group and community might perhaps more usefully be seen as a nesting one, with the community being a higher-level version of the hearth-group (Janowski 1995).

The outer part of the longhouse is described among local people using terms that sometimes mean 'outer' (Helliwell 1993) although in many groups the term used has no literal meaning. In the literature on Borneo tribal groups it is called 'gallery' or 'verandah' (Freeman 1955; Appell 1978; Rousseau 1978; Whittier 1978); the use of these two terms emphasises the fact that it is not divided up by walls and that the parts of it built by different households form, as a whole, a long open area. It is used freely by everyone and is the area where people gather with members of other hearth-groups. It is usual for visitors to enter the longhouse through the outer area and they are usually entertained and fed here, and they often sleep here if they have no close relatives in the longhouse.

For all groups, physical divisions within the longhouse include a wall between the inner areas for all households, which are along one side of the longhouse longitudinally, and the outer areas, which are along the other side of the longhouse, as in Kelabit longhouses pre-1945 (**Fig. 2**). In addition, there are in most groups divisions between the inner areas of different households. However, this type of division is quite permeable, with openings and doors between households' inner areas (Helliwell 1993). Closely related households tend to have neighbouring apartments.

Longhouses are constructed on stilts, as is usual for houses throughout much of insular and mainland South East Asia. They are made of wood and/or bamboo, held together by rattan and/or nails (rattan is used to hold bamboo together, nails are used to hold wood together). Depending on the degree of permanence of the house, the proportion of wood and bamboo varies; the more permanent, the more wood. It is possible to build the whole house from bamboo and rattan. However among most tribes it appears always to have been considered desirable to use wooden planks at least for the floor, with the planks being re-used when the longhouse is rebuilt. Nowadays, with increasing permanence and the availability of chainsaws to make planks more easily, and of nails, wooden planks are used widely for both floors and walls, with nails holding them together. Roofs were until the Second World War made of wooden tiles, leaves (**Pls 52**, **107**) or grass; nowadays, corrugated metal is increasingly used.

Social hierarchy and the Borneo longhouse

Many Borneo tribal groups, such as the Kayan, Kenyah and Melanau, have status differentiation. Some of these have named hierarchical groups. These include what are described in the literature as 'aristocrats', a handful of related hearth-groups including one containing the male leader of the community, sometimes described as the chief in the literature. The second grouping, which includes the majority of households in the community, is the group often described in the literature as the commoners, while the third group is described as slaves. This last group consists of dependants of the aristocratic households and works for them.[12]

It is common, in hierarchically stratified groups, for the apartment inhabited by the hearth-group to which the chief belongs to be in the centre of the longhouse, with his close relatives or those of his wife on either side. Among the Iban, generally considered egalitarian (although it has been suggested that the Iban are not egalitarian when they are long-settled in an area [Rousseau 1980]) the apartment of the individual considered to be the direct descendant of the founder of the longhouse is also at the centre of the longhouse. The chief's apartment in stratified groups is often wider than other apartments, and the roof is

sometimes higher. Sometimes the 'gallery' area of the leader's apartment extends further out; it is usually here that visitors go initially if they do not have closer relatives in the longhouse. They may also be accommodated and fed here, sleeping in the gallery outside the chief's 'inner' area.

The households of those of lowest status, in both egalitarian groups and those with status differentiation, tend to be at the ends of the longhouse; their low status is usually associated with the fact that they or their ancestors were the last to arrive and were not associated with founding the longhouse. High status is associated in all groups with being directly descended from the founders of a longhouse (Leach 1950).

The centrality of the chief's or founder's descendants' apartment within the longhouse is arguably associated with the symbolic role of the longhouse as representation of kinship and cohesiveness. The chief's apartment is the site of feasts and rituals, drawing all members of the longhouse together and representing them as kin – 'people together' (*lun royong*), in Kelabit terminology. It is, I would suggest, the capacity of the chief to be this kind of centre of the longhouse that legitimates and underlines his role, and that of his hearth-group, as the centre of the community.

The Kelabit longhouse (See Figs 2 and 3 on page 14)

Kelabit call their longhouses *ruma' kadang* or *ruma' rawir'*, terms which both mean 'longhouse'. In the late 20th century, Kelabit longhouses consisted of between 5 and 25 hearth group areas or apartments arranged in a row (**Pls. 1**, **96**), consisting of a cooking and living area described as the *dalim* (literally 'inside') and a section of the part of the longhouse described as the *tawa'*. This was, in the early part of the 20th century, the outer and more public part of the longhouse; by the end of the 20th century, much of it had been divided up, as it had in Pa' Dalih, into private sleeping and storage rooms called *télong* (see **Fig. 3**). In Pa' Dalih, hearth-group areas within the longhouse were described as *ruma'* (house) or as *tetal*. The latter term is best glossed as 'hearth at which the rice meal is cooked' and this underlines the importance of the hearth and the rice meal. In the late 20th century, communities – *bawang* – usually consisted of two, sometimes one or three longhouses. By the mid-1990s, Pa' Dalih consisted of three longhouses but in 1986-88, when the collection was made, it consisted of only two.

As discussed above, Bario in 1986-88 consisted of eight longhouses as well as one settlement of individual houses at the airport. Bario was not one community (*bawang*) and one parish (*sidang*) as Pa' Dalih was, but was an agglomeration of *bawang/ sidang*, most consisting of two longhouses each.

I was told by the people of Pa' Dalih that at some unspecified point in the past there was a huge group of about 100 longhouses at Batu Patong nearby, 40 minutes walk from Pa' Dalih, where in 1986-88 only one hearth-group remained.[13] It is likely that this is an exaggeration, but it would imply that there are precedents for big groups of longhouses such as that which currently exists in Bario. The agglomeration in Bario has been the result of the concentration of government services, including an airstrip, in that area. Previous large groups of longhouses appear to have been due to strong leadership and were therefore probably relatively cohesive, at least when they were initially formed. The Bario group is, by contrast, less cohesive. In 1986-88 it was inhabited by people who had migrated to Bario since the 1960s from communities all over the highlands, and there was a certain degree of tension between representatives of the southern and northern Kelabit resident there. This is rooted in the strong sense of place which the Kelabit possess; as Crain and Pearson-Rounds point out, this is important, both for the Kelabit and the related Lun Dayeh, in creating identity, and an attachment to the place of origin persists when people move somewhere new (Crain and Pearson-Rounds 2000).

The 'proper' arrangement of a Kelabit longhouse is clearly that the apartment of the leading couple of a longhouse should be at the centre; when a new longhouse is built, the most prominent couple does have their apartment in the middle. The apartment of the leading couple – or leading couples, where there is competition for leadership (Janowski 2003) – is not normally different from the apartments of other households, except that it may contain some furniture bought in town or constructed locally on the basis of town models (e.g. tables and chairs may be built). However, the *tawa'* section of some Kelabit leaders had, by the late 1980s, become much bigger than those of other longhouse inhabitants. The extra *tawa'* area was divided into a number of sleeping rooms for guests. This advertised the (status-generating) fact that guests are accommodated by this hearth-group in large numbers. However, this did not happen in all longhouses – for example it did not happen in Pa' Dalih – although prominent hearth-groups tended to have more *télong*, or individual rooms, in order to accommodate guests.

The Kelabit longhouse changed radically between the Second World War and the late 1980s when I arrived in Pa' Dalih. Before the war, the *dalim* and *tawa'* had been in one building, as illustrated in **Figure 2**. By the late 1980s, however, they were housed in two long parallel buildings joined by bridges, one bridge for each hearth-group, as illustrated in **Figure 3**. Each hearth-group built and owned a section of the *dalim* and a section of the *tawa'*, with the sections belonging to different hearth-groups joined together at each side.

Whereas it appears that the pre-Second World War Kelabit longhouse was fairly standard in structure between communities, by the late 1980s there were quite radical differences between longhouses, although the reasons for this are not entirely clear. For example, some longhouses in the Bario area had their *dalim* areas on the ground and their *tawa'* areas on stilts. While all longhouses had now begun to build small rooms for storage and sleeping (*télong*) between the *tawa'* and *dalim*, some have attached these to the *tawa'* and some to the *dalim*.[14] In Pa' Dalih they were part of the *tawa'* building.

The *tawa'* area was, before the Second World War, an open gallery with a platform along the outer side for visitors and unmarried men to sleep on (**Pl. 15**). It was also used for socialising, particularly in the evening. There was a row of hearths (without the framework built over it – the *raran* (**Fig. 2**) – for the storage of firewood which the hearths in the *dalim* have and had then too) along the inner wall of the *tawa'* which were used for warmth and to cook snack foods.

By the late 1980s, what remained of this open gallery was much less used and there were no hearths. Men sometimes used the gallery for craftwork; **Plate 70** shows a man making a fishing net (*pukat*) in the *tawa* area in Pa' Dalih. Almost everyone slept in *télong* rooms, which occupied an intermediate position between *dalim* and *tawa'*, although, in Pa' Dalih, they were actually in the *tawa'* building. Informants in Pa' Dalih told me that these changes to the *tawa'* section of the longhouse were made in order to be able to store valuables away from the smoke from fires. Thus, they built the *tawa'* separate from the *dalim* because of the *télong* it contained, where things are stored. However, it is interesting to note that in Bario longhouses it was common for *télong* to be built between the two parallel structures which constituted the *tawa'* and *dalim*, as separate structures, and Talla says that the *télong* were part of the *dalim* building in Pa' Ramapoh (Talla 1979). This would mean that, in longhouses constructed in this way in Bario, there is no clear reason for not having hearths in the *tawa'*, since they would not affect valuables stored in the *télong*.

A socially significant effect of not having hearths in the *tawa'* is that social activity shifted its focus into the *dalim*, since the lack of any heating in the *tawa'* made it uncomfortable in the evening (it gets chilly at night at 3,500 ft above sea level, even in the tropics). This means that men and women almost always socialised together, whereas they might well have socialised separately more often in the past, when the men spent more time on the *tawa'*. It also meant that visitors were almost always entertained in the 'inner' part of the longhouse, although they slept in one of the *télong*. The *télong* are not a significant place for social interaction; I found that although people sometimes sat inside *télong*, this – in Pa' Dalih at least – was rare and was somewhat frowned upon by others because it meant that people were engaging in private, and thus potentially suspect, conversation.

A striking feature of the Kelabit longhouse has always been that, at least until the 1960s, the *dalim*, the 'inner' area, was not divided up physically. In all Kelabit longhouses until the 1960s, and in some longhouses in the late 1980s – including the two in Pa' Dalih – the only division between hearth-group areas was very low protruding walls between hearths on the outer wall of the *dalim* longitudinally, extending only about 3ft from the outside wall. In Bario the divisions between hearth-group areas were, in the late 1980s, becoming more substantial but still did not completely separate them. The lack of physical barriers means that the *dalim* of a Kelabit longhouse is a very public place, where everything that happens can be clearly seen all the way down the longhouse. It means that the 'community of voices', as Helliwell describes the Lahanan longhouse (Helliwell 1993), is a community of gestures and movement too. All the evidence suggests that Kelabit longhouses have always been open-plan like this (Lian-Saging 1976/77; Schneeberger 1979).

The hearth at which the rice meal is cooked, the *tetal* (**Pl. 14**, **Fig. 4**), is the focus of the Kelabit *dalim* – and, indeed, of the apartment. In Pa' Dalih, the hearth was set a few feet from the outer longitudinal wall of the *dalim*, so that the

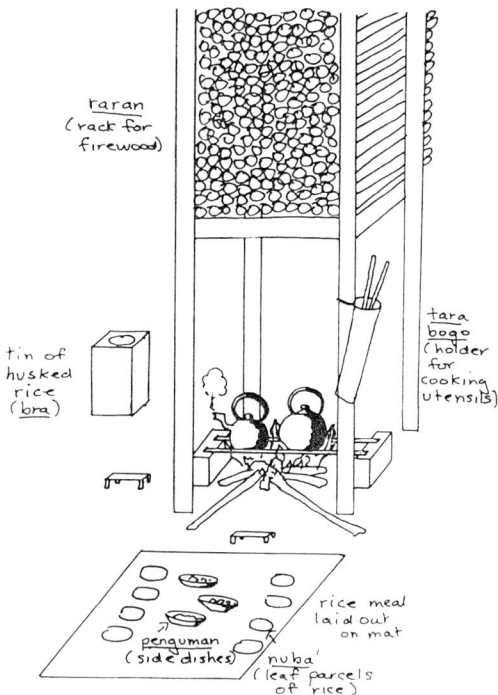

Figure 4 A Kelabit hearth (*tetal*) and rice meal (*kuman nuba'*)

hunting or had been to their fields to gather cassava or maize cobs that day. Rice was not eaten on these occasions. The *tawa'*, then, served in the past as a neutral area, not so heavily imbued with membership of a hearth-group as the *dalim*. However, it must be pointed out that the few hearths on the *tawa'* would have been built by specific hearth-groups, who may have been seen as hosting other people at such sessions. In the late 1980s, evening sessions were hosted at one of the hearths in the *dalim*. These hearths seemed to change their character in the evening, to lose to some extent their close association with the hearth-group. Snack foods eaten on these occasions were similar to what was eaten on the *tawa'* in the past, except for the addition of fried foods (mainly cassava and sweet potato chips).

In the past, during and just after after the Second World War, I was told that visitors entered through the *tawa'*. In the late 1980s in Pa' Dalih, though, visitors usually normally entered through the *dalim*. Each hearth- group had a door behind its hearth leading outside the longhouse, and Kelabit visitors entered through the door belonging to the hearth-group to which they were most closely related. In Kelabit longhouses, visitors who are not Kelabit usually enter through the official, government-appointed headman's door.

In Pa' Dalih in 1986-88, each hearth-group had its own water supply. In the 1960s and 1970s each Kelabit longhouse constructed a system to bring piped water from streams above the longhouse, with assistance from the government which supplied the PVC pipes; Pa' Dalih got its system in 1975 (Talla 1979: 411). In Pa' Dalih in 1986-88, pipes went along the back of the *dalim*, and each hearth-group had a tap inside the longhouse for washing dishes and another in a bathroom area. This might be inside the longhouse, accessed either from inside or from outside, or in a separate cubicle. Here, people washed by pouring water over themselves using dippers filled from buckets, themselves filled from the tap. Each hearth-group also had a pour-flush toilet at the back of the longhouse, which was flushed using a bucket filled at the tap in the bathroom area. However, the water supply sometimes failed because of siltage in the inlet of the pipe, and until this was cleared people resorted to the old system of bringing water from the river to the longhouse in containers made of segments of the large bamboo, *bulu' betong*, which are known as *tabang pa'* (BM160, SM33; **Pl. 17**).

small walls between hearth-group apartments marked a symbolic although not a visual boundary between them. The area immediately around the hearth was the only area belonging to the hearth-group that was not freely utilised by members of other hearth-groups, since the other side of the *dalim*, on the side closest to the *tawa'*, was used as a passageway by all and sundry. The close association of the hearth with hearth-group members was particularly marked when a rice meal was taking place, and although passers by were always asked to sit down and join in, they did not accept. However, since hearth-groups usually ate their separate rice meals at the same time, such a situation did not arise often.

The *dalim* was, until the 1960s or 1970s, used as a sleeping place by the married couple heading a household and their small children up to the age of about 12. This emphasises the close association between the couple and the hearth itself as the place where the rice meal is produced and eaten. Teenage girls slept in an attic over the *dalim* area, while teenage boys slept in the *tawa'*. Until after the Second World War at least, the need to be near a fire for warmth in the cold highland nights meant that everyone slept either by a fire in the *tawa'* (unmarried men and visitors), by the cooking hearth in the *dalim* (married couples and young children) or over the hearth area in the attic (unmarried girls). By the late 1980s, however, people used town-bought blankets and slept in the *télong* rooms.

The *tawa'* is an area which, unlike the *dalim*, is not associated with the separateness of hearth-groups. Until the rebuilding of the longhouse in Pa' Dalih in the 1960s, when the new longhouses were built without hearths on the *tawa'*, it was the place where people, especially men, would spend time in the evening socialising and working at handicrafts. Hearths on the *tawa'* provided necessary warmth, and snacks were cooked at them. Such snacks included roast meat, boiled cassava and boiled maize cobs. These were provided by any hearth-group whose members had been

The fabric of the longhouse

Before the Second World War and for some time afterwards, there were few iron tools in the Highlands, and no mechanical tools. Because longhouses were moved frequently and because of the difficulty of felling and cutting up wood, people only used wood when they had to or in order to emphasise status. Other materials were generally used where possible for building, because they were easier to obtain. The most important of these was bamboo. Using different varieties of bamboo – but mainly that described as *bulu' betong*, which is the largest variety – an entire house can be built. Bamboo can be used for the stilts and beams, split and spread out it can be used for flooring and walls (**Pls 18, 52**), and split in two it can be used for roofing (for which leaf thatch can also be used). A bamboo building of this kind is bound together with rattan. Other materials that were used included palm and other leaves for thatch and tree bark for walls. Where wood was used, less durable and more easily cut varieties were often used.

Bamboo, leaves and tree bark are not durable materials, and while they are actually good for walls, because they allow ventilation, and acceptable for roofs, wood is much better for floors, being flatter and more stable, and is also very good as roofing, in the form of tiles. Higher status hearth groups tended even in the past to use more wood in their longhouse apartment, and all hearth-groups tried to make planks to floor their apartment. These were used again when the longhouse was moved. Wooden planks made before chainsaws were available still made up a good part of the floor of the two Pa' Dalih longhouses in the late 1980s (Pl. 1). Higher status hearth groups would also make and use wooden tiles for their part of the longhouse. The making of planks and roofing tiles would show that male hearth group members were hard-working (being hard-working is very important in the generation and maintenance of status among the Kelabit). It was often accomplished, I was told by informants in Pa' Dalih, through the hosting of communal work groups whose labour was repaid through a lavish meal, in the same way as major agricultural tasks are accomplished nowadays through *kerja sama* work groups organized through the SIB Church parish. This would require considerable means, since not only was food provided, but rice beer too.

The two longhouses in Pa' Dalih in the late 1980s had been built in the 1960s. Building at that time would have been using axes (*uai*), locally made or imported; but by the late 1980s, a handful of hearth-groups in Pa' Dalih owned chainsaws and other hearth groups could borrow or hire them. However, the petrol necessary to operate them was very expensive because it had to be brought up by charter plane (MAS, the national carrier, will not transport petrol) and then carried to Pa' Dalih. Chain saws were used to make more planks as necessary for repairs to the longhouse.

Roofs were, when the longhouses in Pa' Dalih were built in the 1960s, made of corrugated metal sheeting; these metal roofs made the interior of the longhouse quite hot and uncomfortable during the middle of the day. A good deal of this was sheeting left behind by the British Army after the so-called Confrontation period in the mid-1960s, when the British became involved in the undeclared war between Malaysia and Indonesia; during this period, a good deal of fighting took place in the interior, including the Kelabit Highlands and Kerayan Highlands areas.

Only at the back of the longhouse, behind the hearth, was some bamboo still used when the longhouses in Pa' Dalih were rebuilt. Even in the late 1980s, sheds, bathrooms and doors at the back of the longhouse were often made partly or wholly of bamboo. Access ladders made of rough logs or notched bamboo (*chan*) were often used, although some hearth groups had wooden stairs leading up to their doors. These same ladders were also used to allow easy access down the riverbank to the river (Pl.19).

The furniture of the longhouse
Although in Bario in the late 1980s many hearth-groups owned beds, tables, benches and chairs, these were quite unusual in Pa' Dalih. In Pa' Dalih, only one hearth-group owned a table and benches while I was living there, and a few owned beds, although they rarely used them; people normally sat and slept on the floor. In the *dalim* area near the hearth, people sat or lay on mats. There were three types of mat: *ugam*, *tarub* and *pin ue*. *Ugam* (BM155, SM95; Pl. 1), made of a coarse type of grass, were purchased from the nearby Kelabit community of Remudu, three hours' walk away (see Map 2). Remudu has access to the grass (*berpah*) for these mats, which grows nearby. *Tarub*, made of finer *siar* grass (BM157–159, SM96–98), were made in Pa' Dalih (Pl. 108). A few hearth-groups had rattan mats (*pin ue*; BM156; Pls 20, 86) of a type made in the Kelabit community of Long Lellang (and also by Kenyah and Kayan groups living nearby). The rattan used for these mats, which is called *ue (*rattan*) tak*, does not grow in the Highlands. Long Lellang is outside the Kelabit Highlands, on the other side of the Tama Abo range of mountains which separates the Kelabit Highlands from the rest of Sarawak on the western side (see Map 1). These mats from Long Lellang were expensive and difficult to bring in and it was relatively prestigious to own one of them in Pa' Dalih.

A common practice when I lived in Pa' Dalih was for smaller *tarub* to be placed on top of bigger *ugam* (Pl. 90) to sit on, since they were of a finer texture and more comfortable to sit on. Often, *ugam* were left out all the time except when all the members of a hearth-group were away for a period of time. *Tarub* were spread out when people were actually sitting by the hearth, especially if visitors came and sat down. They were often made more decorative by dying some of the pieces of grass before weaving to create a pattern. All of those in the two collections are patterned in this way.

Some hearth-groups had linoleum which they laid on the floor of their *dalim*. However, people did not sit on this, but on mats on top of it. This seemed to be because it was not considered comfortable to sit on linoleum, although it was prestigious to own it.

As well as mats, people also sat on low stools, *laan* (SM23, BM103, 105; Pls 1, 67, 73, 96), particularly when they were cooking at the hearth. *Laan* were also used to support the head while lying on the mat chatting or resting (Pl. 16). There were even special *laan* that were specifically made with rounded edges to be used as head supports, which were described as 'head stools' – *laan oloh* (BM104, SM24).

Most people slept either on fine *tarub* mats or on thin mattresses brought up from town. Everyone slept under mosquito nets brought up from town; there were mosquitoes in the *télong* whereas when people slept by the fire in the *dalim*, as they did until the 1960s, the smoke kept the mosquitoes away and mosquito nets were not so necessary.

Babies and children slept with their parents during the night. During the day, babies and toddlers slept in *royo'*. A *royo'* is a metal triangle on a spring which hangs from a beam and from which a *tekip* (a length of cloth sewn together at the ends, normally worn as a kind of skirt; in Malay, it is described as a *sarong*) is slung, opened out at the bottom so that the child can be placed inside it. The *royo'* would be bounced up and down to put the child to sleep, and could be draped with another cloth to protect the child from insects if necessary. *Royo'* were usually hung in the *dalim* area of the longhouse, near the hearth, since that was where most people spent most of their time, and it was common to see a number of them hanging down the length of the open-plan longhouse (**Pls 1**, **96**).

Storage

Those things that could be damaged by the fire and its smoke were kept in the *télong*, and usually hung on hooks on the walls. Some people had shelves, and a small number had cupboards made by male members of the hearth group. Valued possessions were kept inside *uyut* baskets (BM51–56, 58, SM84; **Pls 5**, **86**, **104**) and *gawang* baskets (BM57, 78, SM86). These were not only used inside the longhouse, but also on visits to other longhouses and to town (**Pls 5**, **21**). *Uyut* in particular were highly valued, especially if they were well made. The best ones were considered to be made by the Penan hunter-gatherers who lived in the highland area. Although some Kelabit women knew how to make them, none, as far as I know, were as skilled as the Penan.

There was, in Pa' Dalih, a serious problem with cockroaches, which had become much more numerous, I was told, since the government started spraying the community with DDT regularly; they, unlike other living things, seemed to be resistant to DDT. Cockroaches infested, and ate, many of the things stored in *télong*. They were also quite happy, however, in the smokey atmosphere of the *dalim*.

Storage containers, also used for serving foods such as fruit, included bamboo containers without lids – *boko'* (BM63) and *a'ab* (BM82–84, SM74, 75, 77; **Pls 32**, **90**, **105**). These were often lined with *ubir* (BM143, SM102), the inside of the bark of the *ubir* tree mixed with water, which made them nearly waterproof and proof against small bits of whatever is being stored in them falling through the gaps between the bamboo strips. *Ubir* was also used to line *ra'ing* and *bu'an* baskets (see below). In the past, rice had, I was told, been stored in a container made from the *tabuh* gourd, *orong bua' tabuh* (SM27). Smaller *tabuh* gourds were also used for storage (SM58). By the late 1980s, tins brought up from town, particularly big cracker tins, were being used for storage, particularly for rice. They were valued because they are cockroach-proof. Plastic tubs, bottles and bags were also used. These were used until they fell to pieces, and even then the pieces were re-used where possible, e.g. for reinforcing containers. There was very little litter deriving from town-bought items in Pa' Dalih when I was living there.

Music-making in the longhouse

By the late 1980s, music-making in Pa' Dalih was focused on hymn singing. Although everyone enjoyed singing hymns in church, unmarried youngsters, both boys and girls, also sang hymns for their own entertainment, usually in mixed groups. Hymns were accompanied, as they were in church, by guitars purchased in town. These were played by both boys and girls, although more often by boys.

Young people's music-making took place in private rooms, *télong*, not in the *dalim* area (**Pl. 22**). This was undoubtedly related to the fact that these youngsters were not yet *lun merar* and therefore they had no role in leading a hearth-group, or in being in charge of a hearth and a hearth-group, and so the area around the hearth, in the *dalim*, was not their proper place. Married men sometimes played and sang with a group of youngsters in *télong*. Married women never did, though, underlining their easier adoption of the role of *lun merar*.

Before the Second World War, a range of musical instruments had been in use in Pa' Dalih, mostly made of bamboo and rattan, including flutes and a variety of stringed instruments. By the late 1980s, locally made musical instruments were little used in the Kelabit Highlands but examples of them still existed and some individuals still made and played them in 1986-88. In the collection there are examples of flutes, both *selingut*, played by mouth (BM43–44, SM30) and *kelingut*, played by nose (BM42, SM31; **Pl. 23**). There are also examples of stringed instruments, whose strings are either plucked (*sape*: BM39, SM32; *lotong*: BM40–41, SM28; **Pl. 24**) or tapped with a bamboo stick (*pagang*: BM38, SM29). *Lotong* and *pagang* have strings cut out of the bamboo of which the instrument is made, while *sape* have metal strings bought in town. All of these instruments are made out of bamboo except the *sape*, which is made of wood.

Learning skills

The children in Pa' Dalih were keenly interested in adult activities. This included both physical activities and adult conversation. They would sit quietly and listen at adult meetings, and they often sat and watched adults engaged in household activities and craftwork. They were also interested in learning hunting and gathering skills, going out of the longhouse with same-sex adults and then with peers to hunt and gather from a young age. When they returned, they liked to cook what they had brought back themselves for the family rice meal. Rice-growing, on the other hand, was not something which children imitated so readily, although girls did involve themselves in helping in it once they were teenagers. Rice-growing was classed as *lema'ud*, a word best translated as 'work', and was something that confers more 'grown-up' status but was not considered to be fun. Hunting, gathering and handicraft work, on the other hand, were considered enjoyable, and children were keen to engage in and become skilled in these.

Children learnt craftwork by watching and through active adult guidance. I frequently saw children intently observing a same-sex adult working at handicrafts (**Frontispiece**, **Pls 70**, **92**). Children would then themselves begin to practise the skill, under adult supervision, with peers or alone. At what age they began to practise depended to some extent on the individual but also on the materials. Some materials were easily obtainable as a gift from an adult – for example a chunk of wood for carving a top or a small boat. Others required gathering skills or even money – for example, nylon thread had to be purchased to make a fishing net. Only once a boy reached his teens was he likely to be able to negotiate with other members of his hearth-group to obtain nylon thread (**Pl. 111**). Even as adults, individuals were very interested in the handicraft skills of others and often watched these being practised. This helped them to improve their own skills.

I found that there was a significant degree of

specialisation in different handicraft skills within Pa' Dalih. There was, firstly, a broad differentiation in specialisation between men and women; all handicraft items were either made by women or by men, never by either one or the other interchangeably. This was in contrast to agriculture and cooking, where although there were tasks which were mainly done by one sex, they could also be done by the other. In addition, there was specialisation on the part of certain individuals in making certain items. Certain items were regularly made on commission by one member of the community for other members or other hearth-groups. This is not to say that others in the community were not able to make these items, but that certain individuals were considered particularly good at making them. Items made on commission could be paid for with money, through barter for something else or with labour. Certain other items, however, were practically never made for members of other hearth-groups. This particularly applied to the furniture of the hearth – cooking utensils and utensils for use at the fire. This may well be linked to the very private and 'inner' (dalim) nature of what happens at the hearth (see Chapt. 9).

All individuals had the opportunity to learn to make all types of handicraft item through observation, since the open plan of the longhouse made handicraft work visible to everyone. However, there seemed to be a tendency for a high level of expertise in a certain handicraft skill to be passed on more frequently from parent to child, since a child has the opportunity not only to watch his parent but to be explicitly guided in due course.

Play

Inside the longhouse, children at play were always visible. While children over the age of about five played outside a good deal, they also played inside the longhouse, which is a huge and complex playground for them. Groups of children of mixed ages were always to be seen roaming around playing games, cooking things, and watching adults doing things. My daughter Molly (aged between 1 and 3 during our stay in 86–88) spent her time with these groups of children and roamed all over the longhouse just as the other children did, under the supervision of the older children in a given group, who would bring her back if there was any problem.

I found that for the Kelabit of Pa' Dalih the conceptual boundary between 'work' (lema'ud) and 'play' (raut) did not fall between livelihood-related activities and 'useless' activities, as it does in English. While lema'ud referred primarily to rice-growing activities, in which adults spent more and more of their time as they grow older, raut was used to refer to activities which were considered enjoyable and which people had an instinctive desire to engage in, whether or not they contributed to livelihoods. Despite the growing importance of lema'ud as an individual becomes an adult, raut was not confined to children, but was something engaged in by people of all ages – although as an individual grew older, and particularly as he or she attained the status of lun merar, and headed a hearth-group, activities classed as raut were less frequently engaged in. However, there were certain activities which even the most mature adult engaged in regularly or occasionally which were classified as raut – hunting, fishing and gathering, which were considered enjoyable even though they are certainly strenuous.[15]

Raut activities might well be very significant in terms of household livelihoods. However, some raut activities were considered enjoyable but did not contribute to livelihoods – and were thus parallel to the notion of 'play' in Euro-American society. These included games, and also play with toys which were not copies of adult tools and implements. The main such toy was the top, gaing (BM109–110), which appeared to have no function except enjoyment (although in some parts of South-East Asia tops have a cosmological function there is no evidence that the roots of top playing in the Kelabit Highlands lie in any cosmological role which they may have or have had). Tops were often made by young men and were, in fact, more associated with them than with small children.

As well as referring to enjoyable activities, whether or not they contribute to the household livelihood, raut was also used to refer to activities in which children engaged as learners, where they were imitating grownups. In this meaning of the word, Kelabit children often 'played' at grownup activities and their toys were sometimes difficult to distinguish from the real thing except in size. Small-scale kalang and bekang baskets (BM74–76) were used by children for the same carrying purposes for which big ones were intended. Children also proudly used full-size baskets and other containers and tools, once they were (just about) big enough (**Pl. 45**). Some toys, of course, could not be used as small versions of the real thing; toy boats, alud raut anak (BM111, SM53), for example, cannot be used 'for real'; they are too small to transport anything and were used only in 'make-believe' play. I also saw toy blowpipes, (put) (**Pl. 25**), made of bamboo, which did work though obviously they are less effective than full-scale wooden ones and it was not clear whether they were ever used for hunting.

The outside world in the Kelabit longhouse

In 1986-88, the Kelabit Highlands was no longer a 'World Within', as Harrisson described it as having been at the time of the Second World War when he was parachuted in (Harrisson 1959). Not only was a large proportion of the Kelabit population living in town, but the people of Pa' Dalih, like those of all other Kelabit communities, were part of the broader Malaysian world through their identity cards, their use of the health clinic in the community and the attendance of their children at the primary school in Pa' Dalih. They were in regular contact with relatives living outside the Kelabit Highlands through letter, radiophone and regular visits, and all of them had spent time in town visiting relatives or working, some having spent years outside the Highlands. The outside world was also tangibly present in physical form through the presence of many items and substances made in town. The Kelabit world of the longhouse was also present in Kelabit houses in town; many town Kelabit, perhaps most, were keen to preserve their ethnic identity and one way in which this was done is by bringing things from the Highlands down to town.

Before 1945, most people in Pa' Dalih did not belong to networks which linked them to places beyond the highland area, and while they did have some (prestige) possessions from the outside world, only some people had these. Iron (*belawan*) was an important import but one that until the 20th century was probably still rare and valuable; in the late 19th century Kelabit tools were often still made of stone (see Harrisson 1959: 334; Hose and McDougall 1912: 194 and pl. 107; **Pl. 78**). However, Harrisson suggests that the iron age began in this area well before AD 1000, because it is clear that metal points were used in many of the megalithic structures in the Kelabit Highlands which he classes as 'Pre', i.e. of unknown, but considerable, antiquity (Harrisson 1958b: 695).

Before the Second World War, there would have been, as there was in the late 1980s and early 1990s, some specialisation on the part of different communities in the processing of certain forest substances which grow better in some places than others, and so some everyday items may well have come from other communities, as they did when I lived in Pa' Dalih. However, it is only since the opening of the air strip in Bario in 1961 that everyday items began to come from or be made of materials from outside the immediate area.

For the people of Pa' Dalih, even in the late 1980s, things which derived from outside the Kelabit Highlands were desirable *per se*. It is of course true that some of the things and substances brought up from town, particularly things made of plastic, were extremely useful. However, the desirability of objects from outside also seemed to be due at least partly to the fact that these things had been made using processes that the people of Pa' Dalih did not understand, and this gave them status. The Kelabit seem to associate the European/American/Australian ability to make things using processes that they do not know themselves, particularly if the thing concerned is able to perform wonderful feats (like aeroplanes or cars) with the possession of *lalud* (potency or life force) deriving from adherence to Christianity. By implication, it seems that for the Kelabit, the making of something is believed to imbue it with *lalud*, deriving from the maker. The more mysterious and wonderful the process used and/or the more wonderful the feats the object can perform the greater the *lalud* which the object possesses. The desire to acquire the *lalud* to make highly sophisticated machines is, I would suggest, one of the reasons for the Kelabit adoption of Christianity.

After the Second World War, contact with the outside world and the first things that began to flow into the Highlands from the outside world were associated with Tom Harrisson, who had spent many months with the Kelabit during the war and continued to maintain a very great interest in the Kelabit after he settled in Kuching as Curator of the Sarawak Museum. These things came in by air, rather than overland as before the war, and were therefore regarded as all the more wonderful, since most of the Kelabit had still, at that point, not left the Highlands. Songs were composed about the wonder of Tom Harrisson's arrival by parachute in the Highlands, which was described in the same way as was the usual method of arrival – also dropping down from the sky – of heroes of the song-stories told by the Kelabit (Rubenstein 1973: 789-792). In the 1960s, with the Confrontation with Indonesia, British soldiers were based in the Kelabit Highlands, and they also brought many things, consumable and non-consumable, with them. Many were given to the Kelabit, either immediately or after the soldiers

left. In Pa' Dalih in the late 1980s there were still numerous reminders of the Confrontation, including metal rods used as supports for pots on all hearths in the two longhouses; metal strips used to construct bridges; and ammunition boxes used as stools. There were also memories in the shape of numerous children's names borrowed from British soldiers, remembered and still being bestowed on children in the 1980s. Because of their contact with Tom Harrisson and what seem to have been very good relations with British military men in the 1960s, the Kelabit of Pa' Dalih had a positive and affectionate attitude towards the British.

Although staple foods in Pa' Dalih are produced locally, there are certain things made outside the Highlands which have, since the 1960s, come to be considered vital to normal everyday life. This includes cotton clothing, matches, petrol – and of course money itself, which is used as currency within the Highlands now instead of the salt packets used up to the Second World War. All hearth-groups had to get hold of these things, and managed to do so, although sometimes with difficulty. Practically all hearth-groups had members who were working in town, temporarily or permanently, and it seemed that money was occasionally sent up by them, although people did not like to reveal details of this. It was very difficult to sell anything produced in Pa' Dalih, however, because of the long walk to Bario, and this was not a normal source of cash for people in Pa' Dalih. Longhouses in the northern part of the Highlands nearer Bario (Pa' Ukat, Pa' Umor and Pa' Lungan) were able to get fairly regular income by selling meat in Bario, but Pa' Dalih people very rarely did this. Despite the difficulty of getting hold of money, however, especially for some hearth-groups, everyone managed to get the very basic necessities from town. Hearth-groups which had a regular cash income – those of the teachers at the primary school in Pa' Dalih and of the 'dresser', the medical officer stationed in Pa' Dalih – were quite well-off, since salaries went far when almost everything could be produced locally.

By the 1980s, the people of Pa' Dalih all went to town occasionally, and they tried to buy most things which they wanted from town themselves personally (**Pl. 26**). However, there was a small number of entrepreneurs, almost all Kelabit, who brought things and materials in and sold them through small shops. Most of these were in Bario. In Pa' Dalih, there was in 1986-88 one man and one woman who ran small shops. These sold only a very limited variety of goods. Soap, soap powder for washing clothes and matches were the items which found the readiest market at the inflated prices which were charged once goods reached Pa' Dalih, because these were, by the time I lived there, seen as essentials.

Most things which were being imported from town to Pa' Dalih in the late 1980s were everyday items. Items made of plastic and nylon probably made up the largest proportion of these; they are relatively cheap, and are light to transport (all items coming in from outside Pa' Dalih had to be carried on someone's back for 10 hours through the forest). These included buckets and basins (**Pl. 19**), flexible pipes to carry water from streams into the longhouse and plastic bags. Paper items – books, notebooks, schoolbooks – fulfilled a role which did not exist before literacy came to the

Highlands in the 1960s.[16] Clothing made of cotton was a very important import from town, replacing bark cloth. Some cotton cloth – the deep blue, black and red cloth which has been described as 'trade cloth' – was brought into the Highlands from at least the 19th century, and was used both for clothing and for trimming certain items, e.g. rain capes (*samit*). However, there was a continuing reliance on bark cloth until the Second World War. After this, cotton quickly replaced bark cloth and no bark cloth has been worn since the 1960s. In the late 1960s, plastic sandals and rubber football shoes were an important import, though some older people still went barefoot as they did until the 1960s. Blankets were essential now that people slept in *télong*, individual rooms in the *tawa'* part of the longhouse (**Fig. 4**), rather than by the cooking hearth in the *dalim*. Metal tools and cooking implements were a very important import. Metal cooking pots had replaced locally made earthenware pots almost entirely by the late 1980s (**Pl. 27**). China plates had been a prestige import for a long time, but in the late 1980s and early 1990s china, metal and plastic plates were being brought up to Pa' Dalih in much greater numbers than before the Second World War; although leaves were used for wrapping rice, and were also used as 'plates' for eating *nuba' laya*, 'soft rice' (see below), china, metal or plastic plates were used for serving side dishes and for eating 'hard rice', *nuba' to'a*, in other words rice cooked with the grains separate.

Other important imports in the late 1980s and early 1990s included machines: rice husking 'mills' (one was shared by the whole community in Pa' Dalih), chainsaws, torches, solar and diesel generators (the school had a diesel generator and two households had solar generators in 1986–88). These things lighten existing tasks and/or fulfil new tasks. The purchase and possession of town-bought machines carried status as well as making tasks easier, and most machines were clearly imported either partly or largely because of their prestige . The small number of motorbikes and televisions which had at that time been imported into Bario (not into Pa' Dalih, which had less cash and no road system) were particularly prestigious. The import of beads also falls into the category of prestige imports. Although most beads bought while I was living in Pa' Dalih were the old ones brought across from the Kerayan and Ba Rian areas in Kalimantan Timur by Lun Bawang, some new beads were being bought in town.[17] Small glass beads for beadwork, strands of coloured wool and sequins were also brought up from town for making 'house decorations' (*bunga ruma'*), which also had associations with prestige.

I found that by the time I went to live in Pa' Dalih clocks and watches had introduced a definite notion of accurate measurement of time into life in Pa' Dalih. The significance of this could be seen particularly in two areas of life: cooperative work in the rice fields, and the SIB Church. Some (not all) kinds of cooperative agricultural work were now regulated by the clock, so that the exchange of labour was based on doing the same amount of time in each participant's field. The Church held services at specific times, and these were adhered to fairly accurately

Kelabit life had, between the 1950s and 1980s, become, in general, much healthier. The Christian missionaries of the Borneo Evangelical Mission brought to Kelabit attention the significance of clean water, disposal of toilet waste and lack of contact with animal faeces in ensuring health. The Kelabit took this up eagerly, introducing the penning of pigs and excluding dogs from inside the longhouse, and this, together with the introduction of piped water from small streams instead of using water from the river, the boiling of all drinking water, and the building of toilets, have meant that there was little, if any, water-borne illness in Pa' Dalih while I was there.

Some town-bought items and substances have been integrated together with forest materials into handicraft work. In particular, nylon has come to be used widely for string (*nopar*), with raw hanks of sheet nylon being twisted into cord as are natural substances like bark and pineapple fibre.

Town-bought items were very important in storage. The majority of containers were, by then, made of plastic and were bought ready-made in town. The most important exception was the container for bundles of cooked soft rice (*nuba' laya'*), the *belalong nuba* (BM80, SM26; **Pl. 32**), which continued to be made of bamboo and rattan. This kind of container has good insulating qualities while allowing the escape of steam better than a plastic container. Buckets, basins and bowls made of plastic had been found to be better for water (for storage, washing etc.) than their equivalents made of internodes of bamboo, partly because plastic is longer lasting and the shapes available are much more varied. However, internodes of giant bamboo (*bulu' betong*), which are called *tabang pa'* (BM160, SM33), were still being used to carry water from the river to the longhouse if the piped water supply failed due to silting up, because they enabled a larger quantity to be carried at a time with less trouble. This is because *tabang pa'* were carried propped on the shoulder rather than hanging from the hand, a method which distributes the weight more evenly on the body and is much better balanced so that spillage is less likely.

Many of the kitchen utensils being used in Pa' Dalih in the late '80s were made of plastic. Spoons, ladles and plates were the most important of these. Seed pod ladles (**Pl. 40**) had been very largely displaced by metal and plastic ones. Plastic (as well as china) bowls were found very useful for serving the soupy side dishes that the Kelabit still favoured, despite the advent of fried foods. There was, in fact, nothing comparable to plastic bowls that the Kelabit could muster up out of their environment, although very serviceable plates could, and were, made out of leaves. The same thing was true of spoons. Folded leaves were still sometimes used, but spoons are much more convenient, and folded leaves were only used in the forest.

Plastic bags were of considerable importance. They were re-used many times – not because people could not afford them easily (they were given away free on the coast) but because they were relatively rare in the Highlands since they had to be brought in and did not have a long life. First of all they were used for carrying and keeping a wide range of things. As they fell to pieces, pieces of plastic bag were used for other purposes such as patching up holes. There was very little plastic rubbish lying around in Pa' Dalih, although there was some in Bario, where there was easier access to plastic from town. Along paths between settlements a little plastic rubbish was to be seen; but the most significant category of rubbish at places where people regularly stopped along paths was discarded leaves that had been used to wrap rice and other foods.

There was, in fact, very little waste derived from any of the items and substances from town in Pa' Dalih, although rotting remains of items made of forest materials were to be seen frequently. Substances were almost always recycled and used in various ways until they disentegrated to the point that they were quite useless. Containers in which town-bought substances and items were sold were particularly valued in Pa' Dalih and were always re-used. This included plastic jars and boxes, plastic bags and metal containers of all kinds. Metal tins in which crackers had been purchased were particularly valued, especially for storing husked rice in the kitchen area ready for cooking, because they were more or less insect proof. Like plastic, most containers went through a number of re-incarnations as they got older – for example, pieces of metal tin, after having been used to store rice, were used to stop rats getting up the 'stilts' of rice storage huts.

The Kelabit longhouse in the outside world

Not only were there many things from town in the Kelabit longhouse; there were also things from the Kelabit longhouse in Kelabit houses in town. One very important export from the Highlands to Kelabit houses in town was rice. People in Kelabit households in town tried to eat only rice from the Highlands, preferably from their own natal hearth-group – thus maintaining, in effect, their membership of that hearth-group (see Janowski forthcoming c). Kelabit in town also maintained their ethnic identity by displaying Kelabit handicrafts in their houses in town. Certain Kelabit handicraft items had acquired a special status, that of being used as *bunga ruma'*, or 'house decorations'. The making of these items was considered to require special skill, and the labour invested in them was valued more highly than other types of work. These items served as ethnic markers. They were displayed both in Kelabit houses in town, and in those longhouses in the Highlands which had a significant number of visitors who were not Kelabit (most importantly the longhouse of Ulung

Palang in Bario, where the Kelabit *penghulu*, Ngimat Aio', lived; the son of the *wakil penghulu*, who is from Long Dano, also displayed Kelabit handicrafts in Long Dano although there were far fewer outside visitors there).

It seems that not only did such ethnic marker items underline Kelabit ethnic identity, but also, since they cost money, they displayed status (Janowski 1997a). They were put up, usually on the wall, in places where guests were hosted. In the Kelabit Highlands, this was in the *tawa'* area (the *penghulu* and the *wakil penghulu* had built specially extended *tawa'* sections to accommodate guests). In town, such items were displayed in sitting rooms, where guests were hosted. *Bunga ruma'* included necklaces made of tiny beads (BM115–116); sun hats with beaded centres, *ra'ong* (BM46; **Pl. 29**); *uyut* baskets with beaded decorations (BM58, 60); and decorated quivers for blowpipe darts, *selongan* (BM8). I found that items made to be *bunga ruma'* were often commissioned. Commissioned items included those which involved beading with the tiny beads bought in town, the making of dancing, dancing skirts (*kelebong pakai ngarang*) (BM113), and the making of *uyut* baskets. Quite high prices would often be paid for these items: the dancing skirt in the collection (BM 113) for example, cost 180 Malaysian ringgit, about £35 in 1988.

Beaded necklaces might also be commissioned by parishes holding money-raising events to be distributed to the major sponsors, *penaung*, of the event, and this underlines their prestige associations. An example is the *pesta memotong kek*, 'cake-cutting party', of which I attended a number. Here, the major sponsors, who contributed the most, were given beaded necklaces, *bane*, of the kind worn a good deal by men until the '60s or '70s (BM115–116; **Pls 13, 99**); my husband, Kaz, was a sponsor at one of these and he received a necklace which is in the British Museum collection (BM115). Such necklaces often ended up as *bunga ruma'*. This illustrates the status associated with beading work.

It seemed in 1988 that the earthenware pots which used to be made in the Highlands, *kudin* and *tuning*, were about to become *bunga ruma'*. Kelabit living in town visiting the Highlands were showing an interest in buying old pots made in the Highlands (BM125, 128, SM36; **Pl. 119**), particularly the large *kudin* pots. These would presumably then be displayed in their houses in town, although I did not see this when I visited for the second time in 1992/93.

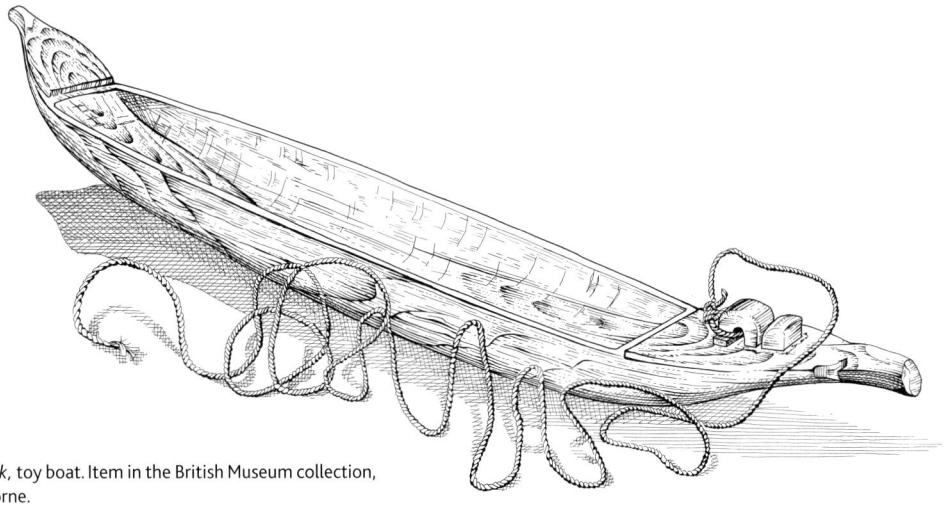

BM111 *Alud raut anak,* toy boat. Item in the British Museum collection, drawing by Claire Thorne.

4 The Kelabit Hearth

The cooking hearth, or *tetal*, occupied the central position in the *dalim* area of each hearth-group apartment in Pa' Dalih, and the line of hearths was the most prominent feature of the interior of the *dalim* part of the longhouse. All everyday activities by members of the hearth-group pivoted around the *tetal*. The *tetal* in Pa' Dalih, as in other Kelabit longhouses, was a big structure, about 6-8 feet square at the base and rising to the roof (**Pls. 14, 96, Fig. 4**). It consisted of an earthen base which sat on a platform below the level of the wooden floor, and a framework over the hearth, the *raran*, which was used for storing firewood, drying foods and keeping things dry (such as salt cakes made in the Highlands – BM106–107, SM12; **Pl. 34**). On the earthen base, practically all hearths in Pa' Dalih had a pair of iron rods supported at each end, at each side of the hearth, by a heavy piece of wood; these rods had been salvaged from the scrap that the British Army left behind after the Confrontation in the 1960s. The cooking fire was made under the middle of these rods, and metal cooking pots were placed on top of them. In the past, when only earthenware pots were used, they were not placed on the fire but ranged around it, their rounded bases propped up by stones.

The fire in a *tetal* was made using damar tree resin, *natang* (BM139, SM103; **Pl. 31**). Split pieces of wood about 3ft long were used in the fire. These were stored above the fire in the *raran*. Three or four pieces of wood were placed with their ends meeting under the middle of the metal rods, and resin was placed under these ends. A match was then applied to the resin, which burns very easily. A bamboo tube called a *iop apui* (BM101, SM15; **Pl. 31**) was used to blow on the fire to cause the wood to catch alight. In earlier times, before matches became available after the Second World War, a tinder box, *tik* (BM35; **Pl. 31**), was used to make fire. By the late 1980s, this was no longer used in the Kelabit Highlands although I was told that older people in the Kerayan area across the border with Kalimantan still used them at that time. The example in the collection is from Long Layu in the Kerayan.

Men brought wood for the fire. Women did not normally handle firewood except in taking it from the *raran* above the fire (although in 1986–88 there was one old lady in Pa' Dalih who regularly brought back firewood from the forest herself). I found that it was usually women who made the fire in the morning, since they rose first, at about 4 a.m., to cook rice, but later in the day any member of the hearth-group would make a fire if they wished to cook. Fire tongs (*pit apui*) made of bamboo (BM22–23, SM13–14, **Pl. 31**) were used to move the ends of the pieces of firewood inwards as they burnt, and to manipulate cooking pots on to and off the fire. The hearth fire was never allowed to go out while there was a member of the hearth-group in the longhouse.

The hearth area was kept clean using brooms (*upoh*) made of rice stalks, *rongoh pade* (BM 98–100, SM17–18; **Pl. 31**). Brooms made of young unopened sago palm leaves, *kenangan* (BM161, SM22), which are longer, were used to sweep the rest of the *dalim*. Brooms were bound with rattan or with nylon string (*nopar*).

In Pa' Dalih there was, in the late 1980s, no mains electricity, and this is still the case in 2002. The primary school owned a generator in 1988 which they used if they had petrol for it, and this provided light for the teachers' houses and for the children's dormitories. A couple of hearth-groups had solar panels that powered neon tubes. The rest of the hearth-groups relied on brass lamps without shades, said by informants to have been brought from Brunei, which were filled with petrol; some had other kinds of lamp bought in town. Until the 1960s or 1970s, people burned resin (*natang*) on bamboo stands, *dawan natang* (BM102, SM25; **Pls 31, 95**) for light. While we were there we used one of these, not having a 'Brunei lamp', and a couple of other hearth-groups began to use them too, for a while.

The rice meal

There were two main contexts in which food was eaten in Pa' Dalih: rice meals and snacks. Both were important nutritionally; but only the rice meal was marked as a significant eating event. At everyday rice meals, people consumed only rice produced by their own hearth group; where people ate rice produced by other hearth-groups, this implied lower status and dependancy, since provision of rice for others is the basis of social differentiation (see Chapter 9 below and Janowski 1995). Only at *irau* feasts did people willingly eat other people's rice, and the generation of status for the providers here was reciprocated when those provided for held their own *irau*. The morning and evening meals were eaten beside the hearth in the longhouse, together with other members of the hearth-group (**Fig. 4**). There were few people left in the longhouse during the day, and most people ate the midday meal in a field hut (*daan*) in the rice fields or, in the case of men out hunting, in the forest. In these circumstances, people belonging to different hearth-groups often ate together. However, they still consumed their own rice. In the rice fields, people often worked in exchange labour groups, and when this was the case they were hosted at lunch time in the field hut, or *daan*, by the hearth-group for whom the group was working. In this situation, the host hearth-group provided the side dishes but members of other hearth-group brought their own rice (**Pl. 33**). Back at the longhouse, people would often share rice meals with members of another hearth-group rather than eat alone – but they would always eat their own rice, sharing only side dishes.

Rice in the form in which it is eaten at rice meals is called *nuba'*. In Pa' Dalih, as in other parts of the Kelabit Highlands, two kinds of *nuba'* are made: hard (*to'a*) and soft (*laya'*). Hard *nuba'* is rice with separate grains, as it is eaten by most peoples. Soft *nuba'*, on the other hand, is cooked for several hours with a good deal of water and then beaten until it turns into a formless paste which is spooned into leaves and allowed to grow cold before it is eaten. The Kelabit prefer soft *nuba'* and this is the kind which is usually eaten (**Pls 32, 35, 37**). Only the varieties of rice called *pade adan* and *pade dari*, which are grown exclusively in wet rice fields, are cooked as *nuba' to'a*. This is usually when visitors are present and more rice needs to be cooked quickly.

Together with *nuba'*, side dishes are eaten. In Pa' Dalih, these were normally referred to during my stay as *nok penguman* (literally 'something to eat with [rice]').[18] They included vegetables (*krid*), and meat (*belabo*), which are classified as wild ('living on their own', *mulun sebulang*). They were treated differently from rice in that they were freely shared between hearth-groups. The provision of side dishes for other hearth-groups, as occurred regularly at exchange labour meals, was not, I found, treated as anything very significant. It was seen as a courtesy rather than of great social value, and it did not generate prestige for the giver as does the giving of rice. Within the longhouse, hearth groups frequently share out vegetables and meat for side dishes, in both raw and cooked form, if they have too much of something or it is something that others particularly like.

In Pa' Dalih, vegetables for side dishes were usually prepared using the small-bladed, long-handled locally made knives called *io* (BM 9c, 152–154, SM19–20; **Pls 13, 65**), which sometimes have beautifully carved handles (BM152). They were normally made for right-handed people, but left-handed varieties existed too (BM154). Vegetables were peeled and cut using the *reno* (BM88–91, SM67–69; **Pl. 50**) to hold the parings and pieces; the primary use of *reno* is as winnowing trays for rice (**Pl. 51**), but they were, I found, used as a receptable in various contexts including handicraft work (**Pl. 93**). Before being cooked, vegetables were sometimes pounded using a hardwood pestle (*totok*) and mortar (*longing*) (BM29a and b, SM52). These were made in Pa' Dalih, using the *uai tetad*, an adze made in the Kelabit Highlands (BM2; **Pl. 77**). However, few hearth-groups possessed them and they were likely to be borrowed by neighbours.

Vegetables were usually boiled, although they might sometimes be fried in a *wok*, a Chinese-style frying pan. Until after the Second World War, cooking could only be done in earthenware pots ranged around the fire. Because of the lack of iron pots, animal fat could not be rendered to make lard in which to fry food, and access to town, where vegetable oil could be obtained (not to mention the money to buy it) was very limited. Coconut trees, from whose fruit coconut oil could be extracted, do not grow successfully at the altitude at which most settlements in the Kelabit Highlands are situated (the exception is Remudu, which has some coconut trees).

While rice was always cooked without salt (*tusu'*), side dishes were always cooked with it, underlining the distinction between the two categories of the meal. There is only one Kelabit term for tasty, salty and sugary – *main*. Side dishes eaten with rice (*nok penguman*) should be *main*. Salt (*tusu'*), was the main flavouring substance which the Kelabit of Pa' Dalih used for side dishes. They almost always used the salt made in the Highlands, which contains many minerals besides salt itself and which was considered much tastier than town-bought salt. Very few other flavourings were used. No onions, garlic or ginger were grown in Pa' Dalih. Salt, I found, was considered something tasty in itself, equivalent to sweet titbits, and I was told that in earlier days it was sometimes given to children in Pa' Dalih to suck as though it were a sweet. The salt used by the Kelabit (BM106–107, SM12; **Pl. 34**) is made by boiling down brine from salt springs, which are common both in the Kelabit Highlands and across the border in the Kerayan. By the late 1980s, however, the people of Pa' Dalih did not do this themselves (although there is a salt spring not far from Pa' Dalih – see **Map 3**), but bought their salt from people in the Kerayan. Before the Second World War, salt-making was an activity which supplied not only salt for cooking but also generated a valuable commodity. Salt was traded, both within the Highlands (as the people from the Kerayan still trade it to the Kelabit) and also outside the tableland, to other interior peoples who valued the salt from springs in the Highlands for its flavour; it contains iodine as well as other minerals, which means that enlarged goitres do not occur in the Highlands. It was, in the late 1980s and early 1990s, still sometimes used as a currency between Kelabit in Pa' Dalih. Salt made from brine springs is stored in solid cakes wrapped in leaves, made by pouring the thick brine into bamboo internodes, drying it and then removing it from the bamboo, wrapping it in leaves and finally binding it up with rattan cord. The size of salt packets is standardised. There are two basic sizes: about 10in long and 1½in in diameter and about 15in long and 3in in diameter. This of course facilitates its sale and its use as a currency, and it is quite probable that this is the reason for the standardization in size.

In addition to salt, the Kelabit used to use pounded leaves called *epa'*, which are said to enhance the flavour of side dishes. By the 1980s, monosodium glutamate brought up from town was usually used in Pa' Dalih instead, and was considered equivalent to *epa'*; indeed it was referred to by the same word.

When the rice meal was eaten in the longhouse, it was eaten by the hearth itself, in the *dalim*, with the members of the hearth-group sitting in a circle on a mat (**Fig. 4, Pl. 35**). Side dishes were served in china or plastic bowls, usually using town-bought utensils. Until the 1960s, ladles (*bak*) made of gourds or seed pods, with wooden or bamboo handles, were used (BM27, 30, SM4; **Pl. 40**), and I was able to collect specimens of these, which were no longer in use. Rice was made twice a day (early in the morning and in the late afternoon) and at the meal it was already ready-packed in leaves. The leaf packets were simply taken out of the *belalong nuba'* (BM 80, SM 26; **Pl. 32**) with the hands. Some were ranged in a circle around the side dishes in the centre, one or two per person depending on the number each person is known usually to consume. It is a matter of pride to eat as many packets as possible. *Nuba'*, being a paste, is an uncountable substance, but because of the way it is packaged it becomes countable, with one packet of rice being 'one *nuba*'; I found that people were always aware of how many of these they had eaten at a given meal. Grace was said by one of members of the hearth-group, usually a senior member, and then people unwrapped a packet of rice and broke the rice – now in a solid form – in two lengthways. They then used their hands to eat pieces broken off the chunk of rice inside their packet, dipping these into the side dishes and picking up pieces of meat. Metal spoons bought in town were used to eat more liquid foods – the liquid in stewed meat and vegetables, and rice porridge (*kikid*), which was sometimes served as a side dish. Before the use of spoons became widespread, it was, I was told, usual to use a piece of leaf for this purpose.

People did not drink at rice meals, although they might drink afterwards. They drank boiled water between meals if they were thirsty[19] and very sweet tea and coffee in social contexts; in pre-Christian times, however, rice beer (*borak*) was the usual drink, both within the hearth-group and as a drink provided for members of other hearth-groups in various contexts. By the late 1980s, it had been replaced by sweet tea and coffee, which were served at naming feasts (*irau mekaa ngadan*) (see Chapter 8), at co-operative work group meals, and sometimes in the evenings for simple hospitality, when people were gathered chatting and eating snacks. Rice beer is no longer made since the Kelabit became fully evangelical Christians in the early 1970s. When tea and coffee were distributed at feasts, this was done following ritualised procedures which used to be followed in the past in the distribution of rice beer (**Pl. 36**). There was, indeed, a sense that providing tea and coffee generated status for the provider as the provision of rice beer did in the past; nevertheless, there was a strong sense that there was something significant missing from the occasion. Rice beer used to be made in the huge Chinese jars (*belanai*) that the Kelabit owned, and valued highly (**Pl. 51**). These were, by the late 1980s, not in evidence any more; most seemed to have been thrown away or were stored out of sight. Tea and coffee were made in aluminium kettles bought in town. In the past, people drank rice beer through straws out of the jar. Drinking vessels (*obe* – BM34) made of bamboo were also used, but probably not for rice beer.

Snack foods

There is no distinct Kelabit term for snacks; however I found that there is a clear distinction in the Kelabit mind between the rice meal and other contexts in which food is eaten, and I use the English term 'snacks' to describe the latter. I found in Pa' Dalih that while rice meals were silent and formal, and included only members of the hearth-group, snacks were eaten with a good deal of talking and enjoyment and might include anyone. Snack foods in Pa' Dalih during my stay included fruit, cassava, maize and roast meat. The amounts of each of these depended a good deal on availability, which varied. A good deal of the wild fruit comes in season. While it was available, it might be eaten in very large quantities, both near the tree and in the longhouse. Roast meat as a snack was eaten during periods when there were many pigs migrating through the southern part of the Highlands; at

other times it was mainly eaten as part of the rice meal. Maize in its fresh form was only available for a relatively short period, although it was also dried and some was eaten as popcorn throughout the year.

Snacks were, in Pa' Dalih, freely given away and accepted by members of different hearth-groups. To give away snack foods did not seem to generate status for the giver as was the case with rice and with tea and coffee. While roast meat was the best liked of snack foods, cassava was the most versatile. It might be simply boiled in pieces or deep fried as chips. It might also be grated, using a town-bought grater, and made into fried cakes, and it might be made into cassava crisps by a thin layer being laid out to dry in the sun and then pieces of this being deep fried. Grated cassava was put through a sifter especially for cassava (*agag ubi kayuh* – BM87, SM70; **Pl. 105**), with bigger holes than sifters made for rice. Maize was usually boiled and eaten as 'corn on the cob'. It might also be taken off the ear, made into a mash and packed in leaves as rice was, making *nuba' dele*. In fact, *nuba'*, the word used for cooked rice but which also referred to the form it took as 'soft', mashed rice, can, I was told, apparently be made out of any starch food, indicating that this is a description of a way of preparing rice rather than a term for rice. These other types of *nuba'* were, however, never eaten at the rice meal in place of rice but only as snacks.

Cooking and serving implements

By the late 1980s, metal cooking pots bought in town were used for most cooking. These included the Chinese *wok*, which was used for frying side dishes for the rice meal and fried snack foods. A few hearth-groups in Pa' Dalih still used the old-style earthenware cooking pots made in the Highlands for cooking certain food – particularly rice porridge made with fish, peanuts or vegetables, which is called *kikid*. Before the Second World War, all food was cooked in these round-bottomed earthenware pots. The biggest pots, *kudin* (BM125, 128, SM36) were used for cooking rice, while the smaller pots, *tuning* (BM120–124, BM126–130, SM37–45) were used to cook side dishes for the rice meal – vegetables (*krid*) and meat (*belabo*). *Tuning* were still, in 1986–88, sometimes used for making *kikid*, which is eaten as a side dish to rice (**Pl. 119**). I commissioned a batch of *tuning* in 1987 from Na'an Tenan of Pa' Dalih (see Appendix 2 Section 3).

In Pa' Dalih, the rice meal, consisting of rice and side dishes, was eaten three times a day: at about 7.00 a.m., 12.30 p.m. and 7.00 p.m. Morning and evening rice meals were shared by members of the hearth-group only, unless it had visitors from outside the longhouse. At lunch, rice meals were often eaten in a *daan*, either that of the hearth-group or, if working in a cooperative work group, in another *daan*. However rice was taken from home; this was not shared with other work group members. One of the women of the hearth-group prepared the rice meal, usually the female member of the leading couple. 'Soft rice', *nuba' laya'*, (see above) was spooned out in standard-sized dollops and packed in leaves (**Pl. 37**). The leaves used were a variety called *da'un isip* which were cultivated (**Pl. 106**). They were also used for wrapping other foods for journeys and for thatching (**Pls 52**, **107**). Once wrapped in leaves, the rice was packed into a basket specifically made to hold bundles of *nuba'*, which is called *belalong nuba'* (BM80, SM26). After the soft rice was cooked, the rice adhering to the pot was scraped out using a locally forged tool called a *gayut* (BM138, SM11). This crusty rice was considered a delicacy and was usually given to children to eat straight away, although it might be packed in leaves and kept for the rice meal. 'Soft' rice (*nuba' laya'*) packed in leaves was taken to the fields or into the forest for the midday meal. For *irau* feasts, it was made in larger packets, about four times the usual size, and distributed to visitors (**Pl. 38**). The size of the leaf packets emphasized the significance of the event and the generosity of the host hearth-group.

Rice was stirred and beaten in the pot using a flat-ended spoon called a *bogo* (BM13–19, 24–26, SM1–3, 5–10; **Pls 39**, **93**). This was usually carved out of a piece of the largest type of bamboo, called *bulu' betong*. It might, however, also be made of wood (SM1). *Bogo*, some of which have carved handles (**Pl. 39**), came in different sizes used for different sized pots. They were kept in a container called *tara bogo* (BM31–33, SM16, **Pls 39**, **94**), which was also made out of a piece of *betong* bamboo. The *bogo* was also used for stirring side dishes being boiled in water, including *kikid*, although *kikid* might also be stirred using a special implement called a *bogo kikid* (BM21). Tongs made of bamboo (*pit karid* 'tongs for vegetables' *or pit naak* 'tongs for cooking') (BM20; **Pl. 31**) were used for frying in *wok*.

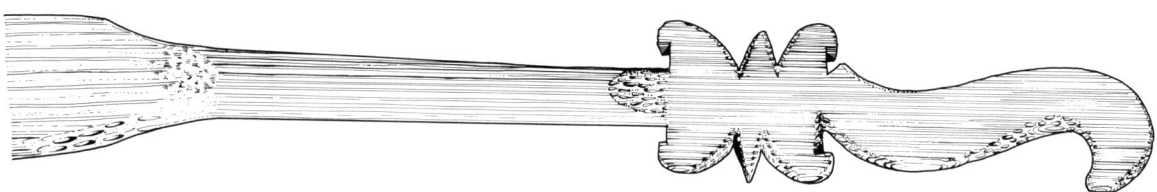

BM14 Carved handle of a *bogo*, an implement for stirring food while cooking. Item in the British Museum collection, drawing by Claire Thorne.

5 Kelabit Agriculture

The people of the Kelabit Highlands make both wet and dry fields, and have done so as far back as oral history reaches. It seems that the type of soil and terrain has been the main factor dictating the balance between the two types of agriculture in a given community. Some parts of the Kelabit Highlands, and in particular the area now known as Bario, have extensive flat areas with peaty, frequently-flooded soil which are suitable for wet rice and not for dry cultivation. Many other parts of the Highlands appear to have been used only for dry cultivation until the 1970s.

Whichever type of field, wet or dry, is made, the main crop in both types of field is rice; in dry fields other crops are also grown. It is the needs of the rice that are paramount, though, and other crops have to fit in with these. Rice is weeded; other crops benefit or not depending on whether they happen to be near rice plants. They are very much secondary cultivars.

Although the animals which the people of Pa' Dalih keep (pigs, buffaloes and chickens; and in the past deer and some goats) are predominantly kept for meat (and eggs, in the case of chickens), buffaloes have, since the 1960s, been let into wet rice fields to trample them before they are planted. In Pa' Dalih while I was there, buffalo and pigs were killed at *irau* feasts (see Chapter 8), while chickens were slaughtered only when guests visited the longhouse. Until the last century, when buffalo began to be traded up from the coast, the Kelabit trapped and fattened deer for feasts (Talla 1979: 383; Harrisson 1949a); there were still a few deer being kept in Pa' Dalih in 1986–88. Buffalo were always owned by individual hearth-groups, and were very valuable. Some were kept tethered and were moved around to ensure that they got enough grass, while others were allowed to wander wild in the surrounding area. Around the settlement of Pa' Dalih, as around other Kelabit settlements, an area of park-like grass has developed, due to grazing by buffalo. Until the coming of Christianity after the Second World War, when new hygienic principles were brought in together with new beliefs, pigs used to be allowed to wander around under the longhouse eating rubbish and excrement, but pigs are now kept in pens where they are fed cassava, taro, cooked rice and rice husks, and dogs are no longer allowed into the longhouse.

Before the Second World War, the people of the Kelabit Highlands followed a bird calendar, linked to lunar cycles, in their rice-growing. The bird calendar was related to the arrival, settling in and departure of the yellow wagtail, the brown shrike, the Japanese sparrow-hawk and the pallid thrush (Harrisson 1959: 68). By the early 1960s, however, they had abandoned this calendar. In Pa' Dalih in the late 1980s and early 1990s calendrical months were used to determine the initiation of stages of the rice year.

The history of rice cultivation in the Kelabit Highlands and in Pa' Dalih

Although many Apo Duat peoples related to the Kelabit grow dry rice too, wet rice agriculture is a distinctive feature of Apo Duat peoples of the interior tableland, including the Kelabit, and may be quite ancient here (Janowski 2001a). A shortage of iron tools in this area, and the possibly widespread use of stone tools in the past (see Harrisson 1959: 334; Hose and McDougall 1912: 194, pl. 107; **Pl. 78**) may have been instrumental in causing the people of flat, badly-drained valleys, including those in the Kelabit Highlands, to adopt wet rice agriculture, where the land was suitable, rather than practice dry swidden cultivation – dry swidden requires the annual felling of trees, difficult without iron tools (Padoch 1983). Wet rice cultivation as practised in the highlands in swampy areas did not necessarily involve the moving of earth and could be done with simple tools, stone as well as iron.

Before the Second World War, different systems of wet rice cultivation were practised in different parts of the tableland. In the Kerayan headwaters fields appear to have been more permanent and to have involved some investment in the moving of earth and the building of substantial earth bunds. In the Bario area, in the headwaters of the Baram, less permanent fields were made, which did not involve substantial moving of earth. These were used for about seven years before being abandoned (Lian-Saging and Bulan 1989: 110). They could be made on irregular land, using a system of mini-bunds made of rotting vegetation, which directed water around the whole of the field (Harrisson 1960). Although the fields themselves may be said to have been a form of shifting cultivation, the main bunds and channels which served them did involve moving earth and would be repaired and re-used when the area was once again used for wet rice fields.

It is not possible to say, at the moment, when wet rice agriculture in the highlands began. According to the Kelabit (and according to informants in the Kerayan too – see Sellato 1997), it is ancient, although not all communities practised it before the 1960s. The people of Pa' Dalih in the southern part of the Kelabit Highlands, for example, where I carried out fieldwork, say that they cultivated only dry rice until recently.[20] In the southern part of the Kelabit Highlands, which does not have extensive flat areas – it is, in fact, at the very edge of the highland area as outlined by Schneeberger (Schneeberger 1979: map 2) – both wet and dry fields were made by some communities in the past, as is now the practice in Pa' Dalih. Dry fields enable other crops besides rice to be grown, and may in the past have been preferred for this reason. Nowadays, however, there is a greater interest in wet rice cultivation.

Wet rice cultivation has remained central to the lives of Apo Duat peoples like the Kelabit living in the highland areas, but it has changed radically since the 1950s. Once metal tools became easily available after the war, terraced wet rice fields were constructed, with large bunds and ditches. From the 1960s onwards, even communities without much flat land or the potential for good irrigation were nevertheless investing a lot of labour in extending small flat areas and tapping what are often unreliable water sources to make wet rice fields (**Pl. 46**). The Kelabit of Pa' Dalih told me that wet rice fields are, once they are made and in operation, less work than swidden. However, I calculated the amount of time put into wet and dry fields in 1986 and it seemed that the relationship between labour input and rice produced was not very different between wet and dry fields; also, many new wet fields, particularly if there is not a reliable source of water, do not turn out successfully, and the labour invested is therefore wasted. The explanation for the effort being invested in making wet fields seems likely to be related to the prestige associated with making marks on the landscape, and past Kelabit megalithic activity at *irau/borak* feasts (see Chapter 8 and Janowski 1988).

Until the 1970s the people of the southern part of the Kelabit Highlands appear to have relied largely on dry cultivation. According to informants in Pa' Dalih, the people of that community and of the smaller communities which preceded it in the immediate area practised only dry cultivation of rice, shifting their fields every year to maintain soil fertility and reduce erosion. However, there were traces of wet field systems at Ra'an Baa near Batu Patong, about an hour and a half's walk away from Pa' Dalih (these old wet fields were, in the 1990s, being brought into cultivation again by immigrants from the Kerayan), and it would seem that in Remudu, three hours' walk away from Pa' Dalih, the people practised some wet rice cultivation in the early part of the 20th century (Douglas 1912). By the middle of the century these wet rice fields had fallen into disuse, and the people of the communities in the southern part of the Highlands relied entirely on dry cultivation. It was only in the 1970s that the people of Pa' Dalih, Remudu and Long Dano, the three remaining settlements in the southern part of the Highlands, began to make wet rice fields again, in the hope of being able to export rice by air to town. In the late 1980s and 1990s, the Kelabit of Pa' Dalih practised both shifting dry cultivation and permanent (or what they hoped would be permanent) wet cultivation of rice (Janowski 2001a).[21]

The term *late'* refers to a field in which rice is the only or most important crop. *Late' baa'*, literally 'wet' *late'*, is the term used for wet rice fields (**Pls 46-47**), and *late' luun*, literally 'surface' *late'*, is that used for dry rice fields (**Pl. 41**). While *late' baa'* are used only for rice, *late' luun* are used for other crops too, interspersed with the rice, but at least two-thirds of the surface area, and almost all human attention and care, is devoted to the rice.

Dry swidden (shifting) fields (*late' luun*)

In Pa' Dalih, since there was plenty of land available, land was left fallow for many years, usually at least 20, before it was used again for a *late' luun*; however land might continue to be used for other crops, particularly tree crops, if it was

flat, fertile land. The people of Pa' Dalih told me that they preferred to make *late' luun* in 'big' forest, since there were fewer weeds to contend with (and Talla confirms the preference for using this type of forest for *late' luun* among the people of Pa' Ramapoh in Bario, who originated in parts of the Highlands where dry cultivation was the norm – Talla 1979: 362). However most fields were not made in really 'big' forest, but in areas which had been cultivated previously.

It was usual for *late' luun* to be made in blocks, with a number of hearth-groups making them next to each other. I was told that this reduced pest attack and it also allowed for easier exchange of labour between hearth-groups. Choice of area in which to make swiddens was a matter of some negotiation, although this was not carried out formally. Rather, certain hearth-groups put up markers showing that they intended to use a certain area, while others waited to see which area would be eventually chosen. Hearth-groups that put up markers were usually the leading hearth-groups in the community, whose focal couple was considered particularly skilful in rice cultivation. This made it more likely that others would follow them. However, it was often the case that there was some rivalry, with different areas being proposed by different leading hearth-groups. A battle of wills and for leadership, largely invisible from the outside, led to the final consensus as to which area would be cultivated by most hearth-groups in a given year.

In Pa' Dalih in 1986-88, when I lived there (and worked in the fields with the people of the community), the rice cultivation year began in May, when work began on clearing the undergrowth (*lemidik*) and felling trees (*nepung kayuh*) in *late' luun*. The vegetation was burnt off (*nutud*) in late July, immediately followed by dibbling (*no'an and mra*). The harvest was in January and February.

The criteria used for selecting a site for a *late' luun* included the slope of the land, the quality of the soil and access to a water source. These are similar to the criteria which Talla lists as used by the people of Pa' Ramapoh in making *late' luun* (Talla 1979: 365-6). The area most favoured was that termed *patar*, a flat, fertile area close to a river or stream. *Patar* are the areas most likely to be used after rice has been harvested, for other crops. In the story of Tukad Rini, the Kelabit are described as the people of Luun Atar (*atar* is interchangeable with *patar* in meaning), with the implication that this is the proper, and best, place for people to live (Rubenstein 1973: 967).

In order to make *late' luun*, trees had to be felled (*nepung*) and their branches cut off (*ngarik*). The men belonging to a hearth group were responsible for this, using chainsaws. Until the 1960s or 1970s, they used locally-made axes (*uai bara'*, BM3; **Pl. 77**) or, more recently, town-bought axes. The metal for locally-made axes was forged in the Highlands, as that for bush knives (*tongol*) still was in the late 1980s (**Pls 75, 76**), and a *uai* was bound on to a wooden handle using rattan and latex from the *mat* tree. By that time chainsaws were almost invariably used for felling trees, both for firewood and wood for construction and in the making of *late' luun*. It was always men who owned chainsaws and felled trees (and who made *uai bara'* in the past).

After waiting a few weeks for the wood to dry off, it was gathered into piles (*temo'a*) and burnt (*nutud bupun*). After this, men and women working together in co-operative work groups planted the rice. Cultivation of rice in *late' luun* followed the usual pattern in Borneo, with a dibbling stick being used to make holes in the ground (*no'an*) into which seed rice is dropped (*mera*). Seed rice was carried around in the field in various containers, but most frequently in the type of basket called *ra'ing* (BM61–62, 64–65, SM89–90, 93; **Pl. 44**). BM64 is 'pointed', *bodok*; this is the way the Kelabit used to make *ra'ing* and also *bu'an*, the larger baskets of the same kind used to transport rice to the longhouse (BM66 and SM91–92; **Pls 45, 91, 112**). The making of pointed baskets may be related to the predominance of *late' luun* in this part of the Kelabit Highlands; in a *late' luun* there is little flat ground and a pointed basket is easier to prop up on slopes and against trees and stumps. Seed rice might also be carried in a gourd from the *tabuh* plant (*be'ong bua' tabuh*).

While I was living there, the people of Pa' Dalih grew many crops other than rice, including a number of vegetables, sugar cane, cassava (*ubi*), sweet potatoes (*ubi sia'*), taro (*opa'*) (grown only so that the leaves could be fed to pigs), bananas (*ba'ong*), and several different fruit trees. Most of these were grown in *late' luun* with the rice or in fields which had been previously been used as *late' luun*. The only crop sometimes grown in wet rice fields was taro (**Pl. 46**), although *Ipomoea aquatica* (known as *kangkong* by the Kelabit) and the fruit tree *Psidium guajava* (*bua' libu* in Kelabit) are grown on the borders of wet fields. Broadly, there were three categories of non-rice cultivar: those eaten as accompaniments to rice at the rice meal; fruit; and starchy plants including grains and root crops. The latter two categories were eaten as snack foods, the first raw and the second cooked. There was some overlap between the category of plants eaten as side dishes at the rice meal and fruit, since some kinds of fruit were prepared as side dishes when they were unripe.

The most important of the other grains grown in *late' luun* in terms of quantity was maize (*ea mays*, Linn.; *dele* in Kelabit). Others were millet (*Setaria italica*, Beauv; *bua' lenamud* in Kelabit) Job's tears (*Coix lachryma-jobi*, Linn; *dele arur* in Kelabit), sorghum (*Sorghum bicolor*; *kuloi* in Kelabit) and a grain which the people of Pa' Dalih called *bua' lengoh*, which I was unable to identify. Of these, only maize was planted in any significant quantity. It was planted separately from the rice and a bit later but usually throughout the *late' luun*. Millet and Job's tears, on the other hand, were planted at the same time as the rice, around the edges of the *late' luun*. Sorghum, where it was cultivated, was planted mixed with the rice, the seed intermingled.

The two most important sources of starchy snack food in Pa' Dalih were maize and cassava. The other grains were rarely eaten. I was told that before the Second World War more of these grains were planted and that they were used to make beer. It is possible that they were cultivated so that they could be used for this purpose if there was insufficient rice. Other root crops grown for consumption as snacks included Irish potatoes and sweet potatoes. Sugar cane and cultivated fruits were also eaten as snacks.

While in Pa' Dalih crops other than rice were mainly grown in *late' luun* together with the rice, in Bario they were grown in gardens called *ira*, which were smaller than *late' luun* and were not used for growing rice. In Pa' Dalih, *ira* were rare. Although gardens were made which did not contain rice but only other crops, this was generally only after the land has been used once for rice as *late' luun*. Where a piece of land was flat and known to be fertile, this was usual. Such gardens were known as *atar*. Finally, there was a type of garden known as *kebun*, made from about the 1970s onwards in both Bario and Pa' Dalih. *Kebun* were used for newly introduced exotic vegetable crops, such as cabbage, which have a high cash value in the Highlands. Such vegetables were sold rather than given away as most vegetables are. In Bario, most were sold to the secondary school or the primary school there, although some were sold to individuals since there was a shortage of vegetables in Bario due to the high population density and the making of wet rather than swidden rice fields (vegetables cannot be grown in wet fields). In Pa' Dalih, the only client for these vegetables was the primary school. The school had fixed prices for different foods which it paid to villagers, and the prices for these vegetables was much higher than that for other vegetables. The type of vegetables grown in *kebun* were not liked particularly, and they were not usually bought by other people in Pa' Dalih.

Vegetables grown in *late' luun* were planted by making a small hole in the ground with the hand and dropping the seed into it, and then covering it up. This was done on the day after the cleared shrubs and trees were burnt off, a few days before the rice, in mid-August. Rice was harvested in January and February, but vegetables were harvested when they were ripe; for some crops this meant before the rice, for some after. Other crops might be planted in a *late' luun* that was on flat land, including fruit trees (which establish a lien on the land), after the harvest, making it into an *atar* (a dry field in which there is no rice) for the subsequent year. Rice was never grown two years in succession in the same plot because of the thick growth of grassy weeds in the second year, which are difficult to remove. The rice harvest was also considered to be less good after the first year.

While the rice was growing in a *late' luun*, it was weeded (*ramamo*) regularly both in co-operative work groups and by members of the hearth-group which made the *late' luun* working on their own. Women did much more weeding than men. They used a weeding tool called *belu'ing* (BM1, SM60; **Pl. 77**). Once the rice was big enough for it to be vulnerable to wild animals, fences (*taa*) were made to protect the crop. It was also sometimes protected by bird-scaring systems as described below for wet rice.

Rice harvesting (*raneh*) in *late luun* was in January and February. Individual panicles were removed from the plant using a small knife, the *io peraneh* (**Pl. 42**). This is a method of harvesting common throughout South East Asia, and such knifes are often called 'finger knives'. In Pa' Dalih in the late 1980s, some *io peraneh* were made of sharpened bamboo (BM12, SM59), but by this time most were small metal knives bought in town. The long-handled *io* (BM9c, 152–154, SM19–20; **Pl. 65**) which was used in the forest and in preparing food, was never used in harvesting. Each harvester carried a *ra'ing* basket (BM61–62, 64–65, SM89–90, 93; **Pl. 44**) in which panicles of rice were placed. As *ra'ing* filled up, they were emptied into *bu'an* baskets

(BM66, 68, SM86, 91–92; **Pls 43, 91**) that stood at the edge of the field (**Pl. 45**). The amount to be harvested by a co-operative work group was calculated as a certain number of *bu'an*. The *bu'an* were then carried by men either to the hearth-group's field hut (*daan*) (where members of the hearth-group ate and slept while working in the fields) or directly to their rice barn (*lepo pade*) near the longhouse.

Harvesting of crops other than rice, as they ripened, was mostly done by women, sometimes with friends invited to gather for their own use, using either a *ra'ing* basket or a *kalang* basket (BM69–70, SM88; **Pl. 103**). The latter was used for root vegetables and maize. *Kalang* were also made in small sizes to allow little girls to help their mothers (BM76).

Wet rice agriculture nowadays in Pa' Dalih

From the 1960s and 1970s onwards, there was an increasing interest in making permanent wet rice fields (*late' baa'*) in the Kelabit Highlands, including in communities in the southern part of the Highlands such as Pa' Dalih. This was at least partly due to the hope that it would be possible to sell this rice, if the Pa' Dalih Mission airstrip was eventually lengthened sufficiently for planes to land. Certain varieties described locally as *pade adan* and *pade dari*, which can only, I was told, be grown in wet fields, are popular in town and fetch high prices there. The neighbouring community of Long Dano had an ex-Mission airstrip which was – just – able to take a charter plane, and the son of the deputy *penghulu*, Peter Aran, who was from Long Dano, occasionally brought in a charter plane to Long Dano while I was living in Pa' Dalih, to take out rice to sell in town. In the late 1980s the people of Pa' Dalih spent a good deal of time extending their ex-Mission airstrip in the hope that it might be able to take a charter plane. Unfortunately by the turn of the century it had still not proved possible to send rice to town by air from Pa' Dalih. It is too far to carry significant amounts of rice to Bario and the airstrip in Pa' Dalih was still too short to take a charter plane. Nevertheless the people of the community continued to make wet fields and to grow the varieties of rice which are popular in town, *pade adan* and *pade dari*, even though they could not sell rice.

The underlying reason for the construction of permanent wet rice fields after the Second World War appears to have been the generation of status. Status is generated both through the cash generated through the sale and through the actual possession of successful *late' baa'*, wet rice fields (Janowski 1988). Although some cash was used to buy necessities, a very large proportion of cash was, in the '80s and '90s, being used to fund big status-enhancing *irau* feasts and to buy new prestige possessions in town.

In Pa' Dalih, a great deal of work has been put into moving earth to make these *late' baa'*. Some are made in the beds of streams; others are made where there are springs; yet others rely entirely on rainwater. While I was living in the community, the making of new *late' baa'* and the improvement and enlargement of others was a major element of the work-load for the year for almost all hearth-groups. One hearth-group or a couple of related hearth-groups usually concentrated on developing *late' baa'* in a particular spot, for example where there was reasonably level land along a stream.

In enlarging a *late' baa'* in Pa' Dalih, earth was dug using spades and *cangkol* (a hoe-like implement) bought in town. It was transported using the *bakol tana'*, an open-weave tray-type basket (BM92, SM76). Dugout boats (*alud*) (**Pls 71-72**) were used to move earth from one part of the field to another (there is a child's toy boat, *alud raut anak*, in each of the two collections – BM111, SM53).

Wet rice cultivation in the Kelabit Highlands in the late 20th century involved the making of nursery beds and transplanting.[22] When I was in Pa' Dalih, the year began in June, when seeds were put to soak and sprout (*ngepo*). They were planted out in nursery beds (*samai*) at the end of the month, and transplanted (*nibu*) in mid-August. The harvest took place, as in *late' luun*, in January and February (see Talla 1979: 354-356 for a timetable of the sequence of wet field activities in Bario after 1968; Christensen says that the harvest in *late' luun* takes place in March in Pa' Dalih, but this is not my experience). In Pa' Dalih in the late 1980s, rice seed was sprouted at the longhouse, using a variety of containers including baskets of various kinds and plastic basins. This process was the responsibility of women and it was a matter of great pride for those women whose rice sprouted first, since they were said to have strong *ulun* (human life force, see Chapter 9). Once the rice sprouted it was sown (*ngotad*) in a nursery bed (*samai*), a part of the *late' baa'* which had been carefully levelled and which did not have deep water but a very thin layer of water over the mud.

Once the rice reached the height of about 12in, it was considered ready for transplanting (*nibu*). It was carefully taken from the ground and, in bundles, transported to the place where it was to be planted. If this was some distance from the nursery bed, in a different field, then the seedlings were transported from one place to another in a basket before transplanting (**Pl. 47**).

Great care was taken to avoid birds eating the ripening rice in wet fields (less care was taken in dry fields). During the latter stages of ripening, a member of the hearth-group which had made the *late baa'* was always present to mind the rice (*moro*) and to scare away birds. This was done using a system of strings, bits of cloth, old tins, anything which will either flutter or make a noise when the rattan strings are pulled (**Pl. 48**). Harrisson describes a similar system in Bario in the 1940s and 1950s (Harrisson 1959: 78-79); at that time bamboo clappers and windmills played a big part in the system, while in Pa' Dalih in the late 1980s ex-cracker tins, brought up from town, were the most important element. Fences (*taa*) are also made to protect the crop from animals entering the fields.

Harvesting of rice (*raneh*) in *late' baa'* in Pa' Dalih was done in the same way as in *late' luun* (see above) although of course the harvesting experience was very different because in a wet field the work is done in water. The rice was also planted closer together in wet fields and consequently it takes longer to harvest a given area.

Storage and husking of rice

In Pa' Dalih rice was stored in the *lepo*, the rice barn (**Pl. 49**), belonging to the hearth-group which had grown it, until it was husked. In the late 1980s it seemed to be mainly stored on the stalk, as *rongo'*. It seems from informants that by the end of the 20th century this had changed and it was mainly being stored as loose grain, threshed and dried on mats outside the *lepo* before storage.[23] Rice was not, while I was living in Pa' Dalih, husked before storage; husking was carried out every week or so. Each hearth group had its own *lepo*. In one case in Pa' Dalih where two couples were sharing a hearth but farming separately (something which was said to be improper, since the rice cultivation and rice consumption group should be the same) they stored their rice in separate *lepo*. Before Christianity was introduced after the Second World War, I was told that people often kept a charm in the *lepo* that was believed to make the amount of rice stored in it increase. The most popular charm, of which there were still several around in the late 1980s – although I was told that they are no longer kept in *lepo* – was what is called a 'thunder stone' (*batuh pera'it*) or 'rice stone' (*batuh pade*) (BM144–145).[24] The keeping of stones in rice granaries in the belief that this will attract the blessings of the rice goddess also exists among the Kenyah (Sellato 1996).

The *lepo pade* (**Pl. 49**) – storage hut for rice – which each hearth-group in Pa' Dalih owned was a permanent and important building, which makes sense given the focal significance of rice. Although the Kelabit do not build grandiose rice barns as do some peoples in South-East Asia such as the Toraja of Sulawesi, the married couple leading each Pa' Dalih hearth-group put a lot of effort into ensuring that their *lepo* was a durable and well-built structure. *Lepo* were built on stilts, with metal discs at the top of the stilts (made out of old metal tins brought from town) to stop rats from getting in. By the late 1980s, they were built of planks and wooden beams with a roof of corrugated metal. Inside, there were no compartments; mats were used to separate different varieties of rice.

In Pa' Dalih, there was one group of *lepo pade* which were built like longhouse apartments, in a row. This was apparently the usual practice in the early part of this century (Douglas 1907). This seems to make sense if one takes into account the fact that there is a symbolic sense in which the whole longhouse produces rice together, under the leadership of the leading couple (Janowski 1995). It was a group of closely related hearth groups which built the row of *lepo pade* in Pa' Dalih, just as closely related hearth groups would build their apartments adjoining in the longhouse, and this can be seen as reflecting lines of fission which potentially exist within the longhouse and which could lead to the establishment of separate longhouses eventually, led by different couples (Janowski 2003).

Until the 1970s when they bought, as a community, their first generator-powered rice-husking 'mill', the Kelabit of Pa' Dalih used to pound rice to remove the hull, using a large pestle (*aluh*) and mortar (*iung*). This was done standing, by one woman or by two women working together, each holding a pestle and hitting the rice with it alternately. During my stay, the generator-powered mill which the community of Pa' Dalih owned broke down a number of times and it became necessary to pound rice to hull it. When rice flour was needed, the same pestles and mortars were used for pounding rice to powder. In the late 1980s, not

every hearth group owned a pestle and mortar for pounding rice, and those that did own them would lend theirs to others when asked. Pestles and mortars were made using the *uai tetad* (BM2; **Pl. 77**), an adze made in the Kelabit Highlands that was also used for making dugout boats (*alud*).

After pounding or mechanical husking, rice had to be winnowed. This was done in *reno* trays (BM88–91, SM67–69), made of bamboo with a rattan frame, sometimes with a pattern woven into them (**Pl. 50**, of BM89–90). Outside, usually under a rice storage hut (*lepo pade*) near the longhouse, the *reno* would be tossed with the flat side away from the user, so that the rice flew into the air and then fell again, while the wind carried the chaff away (**Pl. 51**). *Reno* were lined with *ubir* (BM143, SM102), made from the inside of the bark of the *ubir* tree mixed with water, to prevent rice slipping through the cracks. Rice was eventually sifted to ensure its absolute cleanliness using an *agag bera* (BM85–86, SM71; **Pl. 105**). Only a small amount of rice was milled and cleaned at a time, and this was stored in cracker tins (originally brought up from town full of crackers for distribution to guests at *irau* feasts) in the hearth area.

Mini-hearth group apartments in the fields – *daan*

When the members of a Pa' Dalih hearth group made a rice field, they built a *daan* hut nearby (**Pls 52, 53**). This was a version of the *dalim*, the kitchen and living area of the longhouse apartment (see Chapter 3), with a hearth for cooking rice (**Pl. 112**). Like the longhouse, a *daan* was built on stilts with a ladder (*chan*) (**Pl. 19**) for access. It was used for preparing the midday meal during the day, and occasionally for sleeping. Some hearth groups had only one *daan*, if their wet and their dry fields were close to each other; others had two, one near their wet and one near their dry fields.

Most *daan* in Pa' Daan were still built of bamboo and other short-lived materials in the late 1980s; they were not intended to be permanent. The people of Pa' Dalih made only dry swidden fields until the 1960s and a permanent *daan* would not have been relevant to their needs. However, since making wet rice fields a handful of hearth groups have now built *daan* made of wooden planks with corrugated metal roofing near these fields, which are intended to be permanent. To build such *daan* was expensive and prestigious, since this involved expenditure of money on petrol for chainsaws to cut planks and on roofing. However, despite their prestige, such *daan* were not as comfortable as buildings built with bamboo or wooden roofs and walls made of bamboo, since they became very hot due to the lack of air circulation and the concentration of heat through the metal roof. Thus, comfort was sacrificed for the sake of permanence and prestige.

Cooperation in growing crops

The people of Pa' Dalih were highly cooperative in rice agriculture, although the rice, when finally harvested, was owned by separate hearth groups. Other crops, on the other hand, were not produced cooperatively – and they were not treated as though they were owned by the hearth-group which grew them.

Cooperative labour could be used for most rice-growing

activities: However, it was usually used for activities which involved a considerable investment of time and which had to be done all at once. They were also, however, those activities considered least likely to fail. Activities which are considered likely to fail, for reasons either of skill or because they necessitate prayer (Christian prayer, by the late 1980s) were carried out by members of the hearth-group which was making the rice-field. These all involved wet rice fields: *naro' samai* (making of nursery beds), *ngepo* (putting rice seed to soak) and *ngotad* (sowing of sprouted seed in nurseries). All of these activities were much more likely to be carried out, or at least supervised, by a woman than by a man. *Moro* (guarding the ripening rice against attack by birds) was also always done by members of the hearth-group making the rice-field, but not only by women.

Planting and harvesting of rice in both dry and wet fields were always organized overwhelmingly through exchange of labour with other hearth-groups, usually through direct exchange labour with a group of other hearth-groups, through a system called *baya'* (**Pl. 48**). *Baya'* was always carefully accounted for. Less frequently, a system organized through the SIB Church called *kerja sama*[25] was used. Each hearth-group had the opportunity of using *kerja sama*, contributing a sum of money to the Church and receiving in exchange the labour of one member of each hearth-group in the community on a given day. No reciprocal work was due when *kerja sama* was used.[26]

Those participating in exchange labour usually ate their midday rice meal in the field hut (*daan*) of the host hearth-group, which supplied side dishes to eat with rice; the participants supplied their own rice. The host hearth-group also provided snacks. During harvesting, however, the hosts did give rice to participants. This was in the form of *senape*, leaf packets of rice steamed in the leaves. These were distributed and eaten in the rice fields. Sometimes, especially at *kerja sama* events, the hosts provided cooked rice, *nuba'*, at the midday meal. I had the strong impression both that the hosts derived status from providing rice in this way. When it was provided it seemed to be sprung on participants in the *kerja sama* when they returned from the fields for the meal, and they gave me the impression of being uneasy, even annoyed, at having to accept it. I believe that this may be because acceptance puts them in a dependant position *vis-à-vis* the hosts, who are providing them with rice as dependants within the hearth-group are normally provided with rice. This also happens at *irau* – but whereas at *irau* this seems to be accepted, this did not seem to be entirely the case at *kerja sama* rice meals, perhaps because the status of this whole event is a little unclear. *Kerja sama* seemed to have some elements of the method of organizing labour in pre-Christian times called *ngerupan* (Talla 1979:305-6). This means literally 'drinking event', and the work done by the participants was reciprocated by a big rice meal and lots of rice beer. The rice was served in the large bundles in which it is still served at *irau*, and it is likely that the event was status-generating for the hosts, being seen as a mini-*irau* (see Chapter 8). However, *kerja sama* are also associated with the SIB Church, and as such should not be associated with status differentiation, which the Church opposes. Hence, perhaps, the ambivalent attitude towards

accepting cooked rice at *kerja sama* rice meals.

While rice was produced according to a strict timetable and much work was done cooperatively, other crops were planted and harvested in a much looser fashion. They were not really considered to be owned, as rice is; often members of other hearth-groups were invited to come and pick some of the vegetables or other crops belonging to a given hearth-group, for their own use, without there being any sense of obligation to reciprocate except through common politeness. Since they were simply planted and then left until they were harvested, crops other than rice were, in effect, treated in a way little different to wild plants. This was particularly true of vegetables eaten as accompaniments to rice; members of other households were often invited to go on expeditions to pick these, much as women invited other women to go gathering wild plants with them. Starchy foods other than rice – mainly cassava and maize, but also the minor grain crops grown – were more definitely owned, but these too might be given away to neighbours and kin.

Women, men and rice-growing

I found in Pa' Dalih that rice was in a paradoxical position in relation to gender. While most of the work involved in growing crops other than rice was done by women, rice was produced through the labour of both men and women. However, women were much more closely associated with rice, and they spent more time in the rice fields while men spent time in the forest hunting (see Chapter 9). It was women who were almost always responsible for seed selection and for decisions about which varieties to plant each year, and, for wet rice cultivation, they put the seed to soak (*ngepo*) and sowed the sprouted seed in the nursery beds, considered a tricky manoeuvre.

Apart from the initial sprouting and broadcasting of the sprouted seed, men participated in all the work in wet fields. Wherever there was a job which was done in a cooperative group, this almost invariably involved both men and women. Generally, they did the same tasks – except that in dry fields it was usual for men to use the dibbling stick and make holes, while women dropped the rice seed into the holes. Even here, though, where there was an imbalance in the numbers of men and women it was considered quite acceptable for women to dibble or for men to drop the seed in.

Men carried out the heavier labour in both dry and wet fields, although women would usually also participate in fairly heavy work. In wet fields, most of the heavy work was related to enlarging and maintaining the fields, which involved digging and moving earth. In making dry fields, where an area of forest had to be cleared at the beginning of the year, both men and women worked on the clearing, but men cut down the bigger trees while women were involved in *lemidik* (clearing the undergrowth). The only phase in the making of dry fields in which women were not involved was the firing of the trees which had been cut down for a swidden field, once they were dry. Quite possibly because of the association with destruction and death (of trees and of small creatures which are in the area) and also with the forest, this was a male job.

6 Kelabit Use of the Wild

The 'wild' – where plants and animals 'grow on their own'
In English, the word 'wild' is used colloquially to describe living things which are unmanaged by humans. This is a cultural notion, and arriving at a full definition of its meaning in an anthropological sense means unpacking what any given group of people using the English word actually mean when they say that a resource is 'wild' and not managed; it may well be that humans have affected the resource but this may be disregarded by the culture concerned. However, the word 'wild' has also been adopted as a scientific notion, so that the word is used in describing places which are believed truly never to have been affected by human activity. This has confused the use of the word and it is important to clarify what is meant in using it here.

I am using the word 'wild' in this book to gloss a Kelabit way of describing most living things (*mulun sebulang*, literally 'growing on its/their own') This is used to describe plants and animals which do not need human help to grow, although they may be encouraged to grow in certain places rather than others and may be given assistance in their growth. I have heard the description used by people in Pa' Dalih to refer both to forest plants and animals and to domesticated plants and animals other than rice. It is not that the Kelabit do not consider that they affect the growth of these plants and animals; the point is that they are capable of growing without human help. Rice, on the other hand, is considered by the Kelabit not to be able to grow without human assistance; 'Rice is the one essential item in Kelabit life which cannot come, go or grow of itself naturally. It has to be farmed or cultivated' as two Kelabit writers have said (Lian-Saging and Bulan 1989:102).

Thus the 'wild' referred to in this book is not the 'wild' as it is defined by scientists. It is a cultural concept, rather than a scientific one. It refers primarily to the forest, 'big' or 'little'; but ultimately all living things except rice are 'wild' in the sense that they are seen as 'growing on their own'. Clearly, much of the forest around a settlement like Pa' Dalih has been affected and continues to be affected by human actions; nevertheless, for the Kelabit, it 'grows on its own'.

Using the forest
For the people of Pa' Dalih in the late 20th century, the *polong* (forest) was the source of almost all of the raw materials for handicrafts, of everyday meat, and of large quantities of vegetable food,[25] as well as being the domain of spirits and the place where the dead were placed. The people of Pa' Dalih differentiated *polong* according to the degree of influence which humans had had upon it, mainly through agriculture. Many people, and most men, were able to immediately say how recently forest was cut and began to regrow. This was because they knew in detail the

agricultural history of the area, and also because they knew which species succeed which as forest becomes 'big' (*raya*, *merar*). By contrast, forest which had recently succeeded agricultural use was described as 'little forest' (*polong i'it*).[28]

While both men and women gathered wild resources, the 'bigger' the forest the more likely it was that men would be the ones who exploited it for handicraft materials and bringing in wild food. Women normally only entered 'big forest' if they were travelling between settlements on well-trodden paths, and they almost always went in groups, not alone. They told me that they were afraid of the spirits (*ada'*) in the forest, who were believed to be much more numerous in 'big forest'. Men, on the other hand, professed not to be afraid of spirits. Indeed some men had relationships with forest spirits (see Chapter 7).

Men hunted, felled trees for firewood, collected resin (*natang*) (BM36, SM103; **Pl. 31**)[29] and gathered handicraft materials in both 'big' and 'little' forest. Women were active in 'little forest' areas, where they gathered wild plants and fungi for side dishes for the rice meal (**Pl. 57**), as well as handicraft materials. Sometimes women would gather materials usually gathered by men, and there was one woman from Remudu who used regularly to enter the 'big forest' to get wood and handicraft materials, but I know of no woman who ever entered the forest to hunt.

Within the 'little forest' there were well-established routes (*dalan*) which people followed to get to agricultural areas, which were scattered within the forest. Within the 'big forest' there were routes which went from settlement to settlement, and which women did not normally leave. All of these were kept in good condition, with responsibility for those in 'little forest' areas near a given settlement being the responsibility of that settlement and those in 'big forest' areas being the responsibility of more than one settlement, with an understood demarcation between the parts which were within the areas of different settlements. An important part of these routes were bridges (*apir*) over streams and rivers. Those over small streams were simply logs, sometimes with handrails (**Pl. 55**); those over rivers were suspension bridges. These were made of bamboo lashed with rattan. Some were made of metal cables and metal pieces left behind by the British Army in the 1960s. Responsibility for maintaining routes and bridges rested with the *sidang* – parish – of the SIB Church. Maintenance work was organized through the parish, through *kerja sama* parties in which all men were supposed to participate.

The Kelabit and the Penan
Although the people of Pa' Dalih were competent in utilizing forest resources they considered that the Penan had better forest skills than they did. The Penan were, for them, people

of the forest. This is because they do not (at least not by inclination, only through encouragement from the government) make fields to push the forest back and make any significant human space, as do agriculturalists like the Kelabit.

Particularly from the 1970s onwards, the Penan were encouraged by the government to make rice fields. This was supported by the agriculturalist groups, who appeared to consider that this would be civilising. There were, in the late 1980s, two semi-settled Penan settlements in the Kelabit Highlands, Pa' Tik and Pa' Berang. The Penan did not pass through Pa' Dalih regularly, and were rarely seen there during my stay, but those living in Pa' Berang, in the southern part of the Highlands, passed regularly through the community of Remudu, three hours' walk from Pa' Dalih.

The Kelabit attitude to the Penan was, I found, a complex one. On the one hand, the Kelabit seemed to see the Penan as equivalent to children, in that they are not able to generate relative social status because they do not grow rice, the epitome of human control of the natural environment (Janowski 1997). It seems a reasonable hypothesis that it was in order to enable social structure and hierarchy – proper human society, in Kelabit eyes – to come into being that the Penan were encouraged to settle and grow rice.

On the other hand, the Penan were respected, particularly by men, for their forest skills and their ability to craft forest materials, and also iron. Penan-made handicrafts were generally more highly valued than Kelabit-made handicrafts, and the people of Pa' Dalih traded with the Penan to get them, giving rice or cash in exchange. The Penan are particularly skilled at forging metal and at basket-making, and many of the knives and high-quality baskets in the two collections were made by Penan (e.g. BM56–57, SM62, 86).

The Kelabit attitude to the Penan reflects their attitude to the forest. Just as there is a reluctance to openly declare that the forest is profoundly important to Kelabit life yet men are, in fact, very proud of being able to manage in the forest, the Penan are talked of as though they were worthless, 'even less than a slave' (Harrisson 1959: 133), but the Kelabit are, at the same time, rather in awe of their skills in the forest – and by implication of their ability to manage its *lalud* or life force (see Chapter 7).

Gathering wild vegetables (*merin*)

Gathering wild vegetables (*merin*) (**Pls 56, 57**) was a predominantly female activity. It was mostly done in the 'little forest' near the longhouse (**Map 3**). Gathering provided around 40% of the vegetable foods eaten at the rice meal in Pa' Dalih in the 1990s (Christensen 2000). It was therefore a very important activity nutritionally and economically. However it was also an activity that was regarded as very enjoyable, and was considered an excursion. Women on a gathering expedition might go

Map 3 Pa' Dalih and Batu Patong showing hunting areas and main gathering areas 1987, derived from a map made by a group of young men from Pa' Dalih

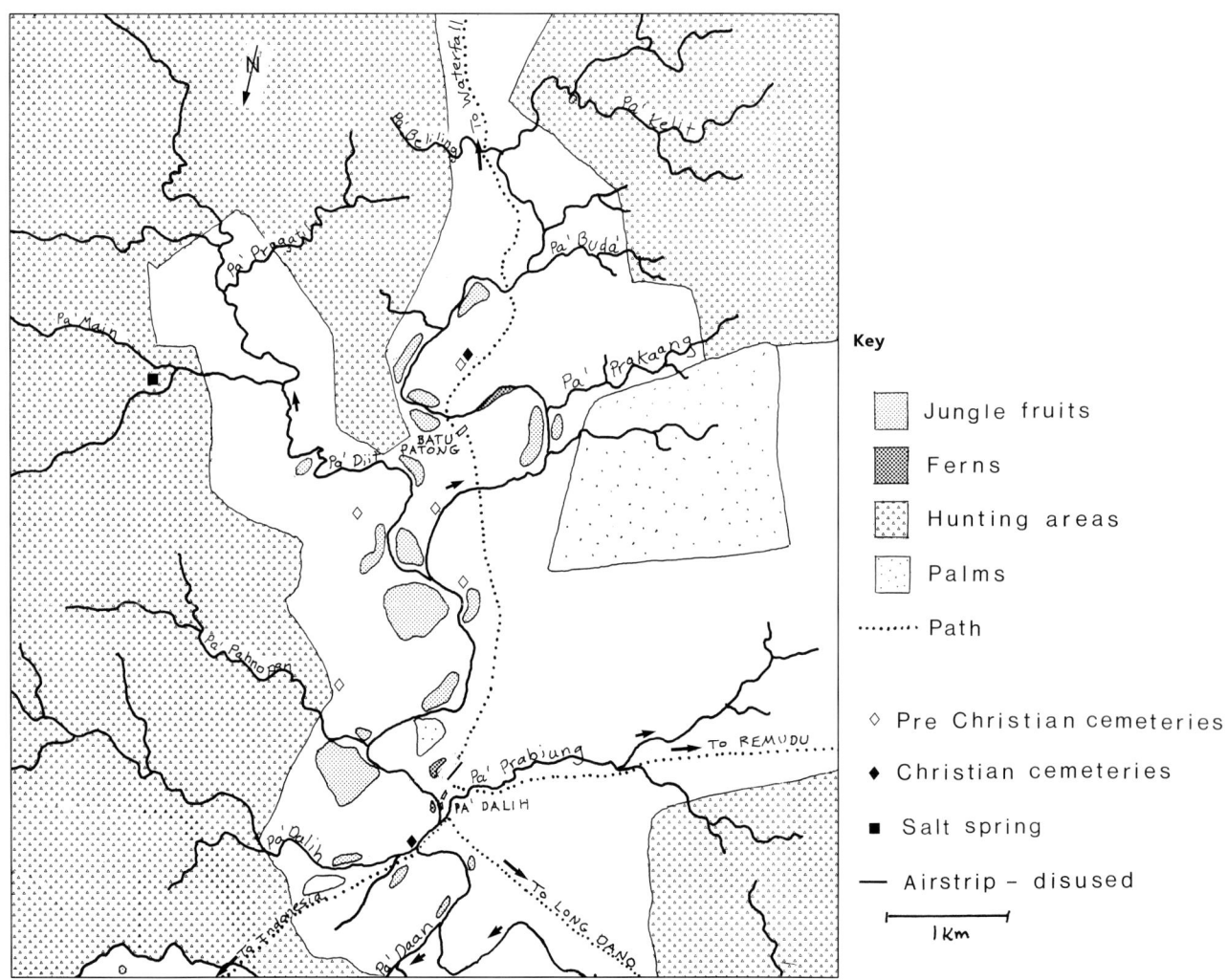

alone, but they would often go in the company of one or more other women, as an outing. Only women went on expeditions which were specifically aimed at gathering vegetables. Men only gathered vegetables if they came across them in the course of other activities.

What was brought back from a gathering expedition was shared around friends, neighbours and kin (including my family, while we were living there) if more was brought back than the gatherer's hearth-group could consume that day. Wild vegetables were not considered to be owned in the way that rice was. As with all the food consumed in side dishes for the rice meal, vegetables were treated as something to be shared freely with others.

The table on page 37 shows the wild plants which I recorded as being gathered in Pa' Dalih for consumption at rice meals in 1986-88.[30]

Wild plants eaten as side dishes at rice meals in Pa' Dalih, as recorded by Monica Janowski in 1986-88

Kelabit name	English name	Botanical name	Plant part collected & consumed
ubud kenangan	Sago	Eugeissonia utilis	Shoots
ubud poo'	Wild banana	Musa sp. 5 (0086); Musa	Shoots
ubud ue	Species of rattan	Calamus pogonacanthus	Shoots
ubud derma	Species of rattan	Arenga brevipes	Shoots
ubud bua' salah		Etlingera elatior	Shoots
ubud nanong		Unidentified	Shoots
ubud bua' tubu' tana'		Etlingera punicea	Shoots
ubud lekwa		Sp. (0155, 0723); Laur.	Shoots
ubud kawit		Unidentified	Shoots
kulat berak	'pig mushroom'[31]	Amanita sp. 1 – Lentinus sp.	Fruiting body
kulat berangan	'bear mushroom'	Russula virescens	Fruiting body
kulat pra	mushroom	Russula sp.	Fruiting body
kulat item	'black mushroom'	Unidentified	Fruiting body
kulat buda'	'white mushroom'	Russula sp.	Fruiting body
kulat laam	'sour mushroom'	Gymnopilus sp. 1: Cort.	Fruiting body
kulat belu'an	mushroom	Lentinus sajor-caju – L. sp. 1	Fruiting body
kulat long	mushroom	Unidentified	Fruiting body
kulat laping	mushroom	Sp. 1; Cort	Fruiting body
kulat tetadiw	mushroom	Unidentified	Fruiting body
kulat udang	'prawn mushroom'	Hygrocybe sp. 2; Hygr	Fruiting body
kulat aleng	mushroom	Pleurotus djamor	Fruiting body
kulat kerubau	'buffalo mushroom'	Macropeliota procera	Fruiting body
kulat ulub	'white bead mushroom'	Amanita hemibapha (Berk. & Br.) Sacc. vel aff.; Aman.	Fruiting body
kulat paduk	mushroom	Unidentified	Fruiting body
pa'o payah	'swamp fern'	Stenochlaena palustris	Leaves
pa'o pa'	'water fern'	Diplazium esculentum – D. asperum	Leaves
tangayan	creeper	Hyrtanandra hirta	Leaves
abang		martini Setaria palmifolia (Koenig) Stapf (0092, 1739)	Shoots
lanau		Commelina paludosa vel aff.	Stem
da'un bekeriup		Unidentified	Leaves
bua' payang		Pangium edule	Fruit
bua' ludu (flower of bua' sala)		Etlingera elatior	Flower
bua' kiran		Artocarpus sp.	Unripe fruit (also eaten ripe as snack)
dore		Pseuderanthemun borneense-Rungia sp.	Leaves
bua' ulim		Solanum torvum	Fruit

Wild and semi-wild tree fruit, eaten as snack food in Pa' Dalih, as recorded by Monica Janowski in 1986-88

Kelabit name	English name	Botanical name
bua' bupu		Dimocarpus longan
bua' lengaat	langsat	Lansium domesticum
bua' rambutan	rambutan	Nephelium lappaceum
bua' mermitem		species of Nephelium
bua' sia'	'red fruit'	species of Nephelium
bua' metot		species of Nephelium
bua' pangin		Mangifera pajang
bua' kiran		Species of Artocarpus
bua' laam	horse mango	Mangifera foetida (Lour.)
bua' keramut	mango	species of Mangifera
bua' dato' alo'	soursop, Dutch durian	Annona muricata
bua' dato'	durian	Durio zibethinus
bua' medela		probably species of Durio
bua' badok	jackfruit	Artocarpus integra (Merr.)
bua' iyau		unidentified
bua' lupi		Mangifera indica L. vel aff.; Anar.
bua' itan		Species of Elaeocarpus
bua' kesi		Species of Garcinia
bua' ario		unidentified
bua' terbak		unidentified
bua' neput		unidentified
bua' puak		Baccaurea edulis Merr.: Euph
bua' kelopa		Syzygium malaccense (L.) Merr. & Perry; Myrt.
bua' ubir		unidentified
bua' pao		unidentified (Christensen gives a number of different species as types of Bua' pao; Christensen 2002: 377.

Gathering wild fruit (*ngalap bua'*)

The people of Pa' Dalih also gathered (*ngalap*) many wild and semi- wild tree fruits (semi-wild in the sense that the trees were originally planted in cultivated areas), which were eaten as snack food between rice meals. These fruits mainly came from 'little forest' areas. Both women and men gathered these, often in large communal groups, when the fruit was in season.

The table on page 37 shows the main wild fruit which I recorded as being gathered in Pa' Dalih in 1986-88.

Hunting (*ngeraad*)

Hunting was definitely a male-only activity. Men in Pa' Dalih very much enjoyed hunting. Most men went hunting regularly, at least every couple of days, and young men went almost daily.[32] Both primary and secondary forest were used for hunting. Most hunting was done within an hour or two's walk from Pa' Dalih (**Map 3**) but sometimes parties of men would go off for a few days to a more distant hunting ground (**Pl. 58**). All everyday meat was from hunted animals; meat from domestic animals was only eaten if guests from outside the longhouse were present (when a chicken was likely to be killed) or at *irau* naming feasts (when pigs and sometimes buffalo were slaughtered). It has been estimated that 83% of meat eaten in Pa' Dalih in 1997-8, overall (presumably including at *irau*) was from wild animals (Christensen 2000). This means that hunting was, like gathering wild vegetables, of considerable nutritional and economic importance, as well as being enjoyable.

The most commonly hunted game in Pa' Dalih in the late 1980s was the wild pig (*Sus barbatus*, S. Muller and other varieties of *sus*, Linn; *baka* in Kelabit). The wild pig migrated through the Kelabit Highlands regularly in search of the acorns that are its staple food. However, because they are migratory, there were sometimes no pigs to be had, and the main game then became deer. Three kinds of deer were hunted: the sambhur deer (*Cervus unicolor* var. *equinus*, Cuvier, *payo* in Kelabit); the barking deer (*Cervulus muntjac*, Lydekker, *tela'o* in Kelabit); and the mousedeer (*Tragulus ravus*, Miller, *planok* in Kelabit). Besides pigs and deer, almost any animal might be occasionally hunted, although many people would not eat meat other than from pigs and deer.[33] Women in particular tended to be squeamish about strange kinds of meat, and this relates to the attitude which women had to the *polong* from which meat comes, which is that it was alien and frightening. Some people, both men and women, said that they 'didn't eat' certain sorts of meat, although no consequences were stated of eating them nor did I ever manage to get an elaboration of the reason for this.

A man going into the forest always carried two things: his bush knife, *tongol* (BM5a, 9a, SM62; **Pl. 65**), and his forest carrying basket, *bekang* (BM73a, b, SM78–79; **Pls 59, 62**). If he was hunting he would also carry either a gun or a spear (*boso*) (BM6, SM65, **Pls 61, 66**); if he was hunting with a spear he would go with his dogs (*muit oko'*, literally 'taking along dogs'). The *bekang* is an expandable basket made of rattan and wood with a tongue at the front and a small grass mat (*liling*) inside to hold the contents. It comes in two varieties: the *bekang dela'ih* (BM73a, b, SM78–79; **Pl. 59**) for men and *bekang dechur* (BM71a, b, BM72a, b, SM80–81; **Pl.**

60) for women. These differ only in size and quality of materials – the *bekang dechur* was more carefully made, using finer materials, and was sometimes carved. *Bekang¸* which were made of rattan, were made by men. A man might make a *bekang* for any woman on commission; but I was told that he was more likely to make a beautiful one when he was making it for his wife or a female relative. Thus, the carving and craftsmanship were not done for money. Women used their *bekang* for transporting loads through the forest between settlements; men used theirs both for this and (much more often) for hunting and gathering materials in the primary forest. There were also children's *bekang*, with tiny *liling* mats to go with them (BM74a, b, 75a, b, SM82–83), so that little girls could help to carry things between settlements and little boys could help with the carrying and begin to go hunting with their fathers.

When men wore loincloths (they were no longer worn by the 1980s), they could not comfortably sit down in the forest because their bottoms were bare. Therefore, when going into the forest a man would wear a small mat on his behind, tied around his waist, which he could sit on, called a *tabir puet* (BM114). Informants in Pa' Dalih told me that other tribal groups wore such sitting mats too. These were often made of animal hide. A man's forest equipment, in the late 1980s, often included a rain cape, *samit* (BM50, SM66; **Pls 63-64**), made of the leaves of a palm called *ilad* (*Licuala valida*). These were often bought from people in the Kerayan, who specialise in making them.

The bush knife, *tongol* (BM5a, 9a, SM62; **Pl. 65**), was the most essential piece of equipment for the primary forest. Although a woman might use a *tongol* occasionally, she would never carry one at her waist as a permanent piece of equipment; this reflects the fact that it is basically a male tool. *Tongol* were often forged and made in Pa' Dalih, but blades, handles or other parts of the ensemble were sometimes bought from other Kelabit, from people in the Kerayan, or from Penan.[34] A *tongol* was kept in a wooden sheath, *binan tongol* (BM5b, 9b, SM62), which was worn hanging from the waist on a plaited rattan cord. Bound to the *binan tongol* was a small sheath (*labuh io*) made of the bark of a plant (*anit reman belabo*) for the *io* (BM9c), a small longhandled knife, which was also used in preparing food in the longhouse. These two knives constituted a very versatile tool kit, enabling a man to chop down bushes and small saplings, to blaze trees to make a trail, to kill snakes and to butcher animals, to carry out minor repairs to his equipment and to make a temporary shelter and hearth. They were sharpened using a sharpening stone, *batuh pian* (BM10, SM61; **Pl. 98**).

Hunting in the Kelabit Highlands was, in the late 1980s and 1990s, carried out either with the help of dogs and using a spear, *boso* (BM6, SM65, **Pls 61, 66**), made of locally forged iron with a wooden handle fixed to the handle with rattan and latex from the *mat* tree, or using a shotgun. The Kelabit have had shotguns since the 1950s. By the end of the 1980s, it had become impossible to get a licence to purchase new ones, so existing ones were prized; new handles were made for them when necessary. The blowpipe was no longer used in Pa' Dalih when I lived there; it seems that it had fallen out of use by the 1970s. Across the border in the Kerayan and Ba

Rian areas there were far fewer shotguns and the blowpipe, *put* (BM7, SM64), was still used in the late 1980s, together with a quiver, *selongan* (BM8, SM63), filled with darts, *langan* (**Pls 66, 67**). Attached to the quiver would be a small gourd, *bua' tabuh kre*, which held flights (*ra'o*) made of wild sago (*kenangan*) pith. The darts were tipped with poison from the *parir* tree (*Antiaris toxicaria*) (BM11).

Once an animal was shot or speared, it would be butchered in the forest, using the *tongol* and *io* knives. Bits that were not wanted were fed to the dogs or left behind. The rest of the animal was packed into the *bekang* basket (as in **Pl. 66**) and taken back to the longhouse.

Meat from hunted animals was almost always, like gathered vegetables, distributed among relatives, neighbours and friends, and no money would change hands. This distribution was, in fact, an important way in which networks of kin and alliance were generated, furthered and underlined. However very occasionally relatively uncommon meat which was considered particularly tasty, for example from the mousedeer, was sold. When this happened it tended to be done quietly since it was not felt to be right to sell meat.[35]

Men might hunt alone; this was usual, in fact, in the case of married men. Young men, though, often hunted in pairs or threesomes. There was only one situation in which a large group of men would go hunting together. This was when a communal meal (*kuman peroyong*, literally 'eating together') was planned. *Kuman peroyong* were held at the end of the rice harvest and when visitors were present from outside the longhouse for reasons other than an *irau pekaa ngadan* (a name-changing feast – see Chapter 8). This would happen when religious travellers (*pelawat*) came visiting and also when a community hosted other communities for Easter or Christmas, as Pa' Dalih did at Christmas 1992/93. For these meals, a large group of men, often just the young men, would go hunting and bring back as many pigs as possible. If there were no pigs, the feast would have to be cancelled – so there was often some anxiety about the success of the hunting party.

Fishing and snail collecting

In Pa' Dalih, both men and women fished, but while men fished in rivers, women gathered snails (*akap*, literally 'shells') and small fish in streams and wet rice fields (**Pl. 69**). Snails were collected by hand; women collected fish either by hand or using framed nets, *iap* (BM94–95, SM72; **Pl. 68**). Both snails and fish were placed in gourds, *be'ong*, hung from the waist or around the head (BM93, SM94, **Pl. 40**). *Iap* were made of string made of bark or cotton; if the latter, it was bought in town. The frame was made of a creeper called *uar bekar* (*uar* means 'creeper'). The net was bound on to the frame using bark or nylon string (*nopar*).

While women fished for tiny fish in small streams, men fished for larger fish in the Kelapang river, although in fact none of the fish in the river where it flows through Pa' Dalih were larger than about 18 inches long. I did not identify any of the fish which were fished by either men or women. Certain men tended to specialise in fishing, although all men could turn their hand to it. They fished using throw nets, *pukat* (BM96, SM73), made of nylon, or traps, *bubuh*

(BM112, SM57; **Pl. 102**), made of bamboo and rattan. Nets began to be used from the 1960s onwards, when nylon became easily available. Although the nylon for *pukat* was bought in town, the nets were made in Pa' Dalih (**Pls 70, 111**). Traps were conical and contain a double trap so that the fish could not easily escape. Fish were taken out via a small door near the pointed end.

In Pa' Dalih the larger fish from the river were highly valued as food, both because they were uncommon and because they were considered very tasty. In the late 1980s, large fish, because they were valued, were sometimes sold. However, fish were distributed among neighbours and relatives in the longhouse when they were caught in large quantities.

The boats (*alud*) used for fishing were dugout boats made by men (**Pl. 72**). In the highland area, individuals who were considered particularly skilled sometimes traveled to other communities to hire themselves out to make boats. In 1987, a relative from the Kerayan came to Pa' Dalih to make a boat for the headman there, Lawe Padan (**Pl. 71**). To make a boat, a suitable tree, of a common wood such as *kayuh labakan*, would be cut down and the inside gouged out using the *uai tetad*, an adze (BM2). Fire was used to harden the wood. The sides were built up using planks if the tree is of a small diameter. Boats were moved along by paddling, using a wooden paddle (*besai alud*; **Pl. 73**).

Alud were also used to transport harvested rice across the river if there was no convenient bridge (**Pl. 74**), and to transport earth from the middle of the field to the edge in the making and enlargement of wet rice fields. However their major use was in fishing and, sometimes, for crossing the river. The river was not deep enough at Pa' Dalih to enable transport by boat to be of much significance, since there were few navigable areas.

Bringing in wood

Before the 1970s when chainsaws came to be widely owned in the Kelabit Highlands, locally-made axes, *uai bara'*, (BM3; **Pl. 77**) made in the Highlands, were used to fell trees. By the 1980s, chainsaws were, as far as I know, always used in Pa' Dalih to fell trees; those who did not own a chainsaw would borrow one. Trees were cut into logs about four feet long which were left in the forest for a few weeks to dry out. After this the wood would be brought back to the longhouse, almost always by men, in *bekang* baskets (BM73a, b, SM78–79; **Pl. 59**) and split, using a modern axe (*uai*), outside the longhouse. The wood would then be stored in the *raran* above the hearth (**Fig. 4**) ready for use. Firewood was burnt from one end, with a large log at the back and a fan of long pieces of wood sticking out of the fire at the front. Although many different kinds of wood (*kayuh*) were used for firewood, some quite soft and quick-burning, the preferred wood for this purpose was a heavy, hard wood called *belaban*. There did not appear to be a preference for quick burning woods, even for rapid cooking.

Wood was also necessary for many other purposes. It was used very widely in handicrafts, when specific woods were often preferred, and it was used in building. Woods used for handicraft and building included those described by the Kelabit as *labakan, tara', menubun, tai'la'al* (literally 'chicken shit'), *pul, matah, mata loang* (literally 'fish eye'), *bua' bupu'* (the wood of a fruit tree), *ketong, nato', seboko* and *ore*. When planks were being made it was usual for a camp to be set up in the forest where trees were brought and made into planks by the person who needed them. He might employ others to help him. In Pa' Dalih in the late 1980s, men from across the border in the Kerayan were sometimes employed. It was, however, most common for men to make their own planks for building. In Bario, however, where there was more money, wealthier individuals were more likely to hire labour.

Gathering handicraft material

A wide variety of materials, besides wood, were brought in from the wild for use in handicrafts. These included bamboo, rattan, leaves, grasses, tree bark, and the sap from various trees. The materials to be used for handicrafts were almost always gathered by the individual who planned to use them, whether this was a man or a woman. Sometimes groups of individuals would go out together to gather materials, but usually individuals went alone. The exception was where it had been agreed that cooperative labour would be used to carry out a certain task involving the use of handicraft skills, such as building a field hut (*daan*). This was done through the SIB Church parish (*sidang*) with the benefitting hearth-group paying a sum of money to the Church, and providing side dishes for a midday meal (and sometimes the rice too) for the workers.

The cooperative work group would be made of men or women or both depending on the task. If the task was, for example, to build a *daan*, then men would be involved since this was considered men's work. They would not only make the *daan* but would usually be involved in gathering some of the materials for it, where this could be done close by immediately before the job was done. The rattan would already have been gathered from the primary forest by the man of the benefitting hearth-group; the bamboo, which comes from secondary forest, would be gathered by the cooperative group in this case.

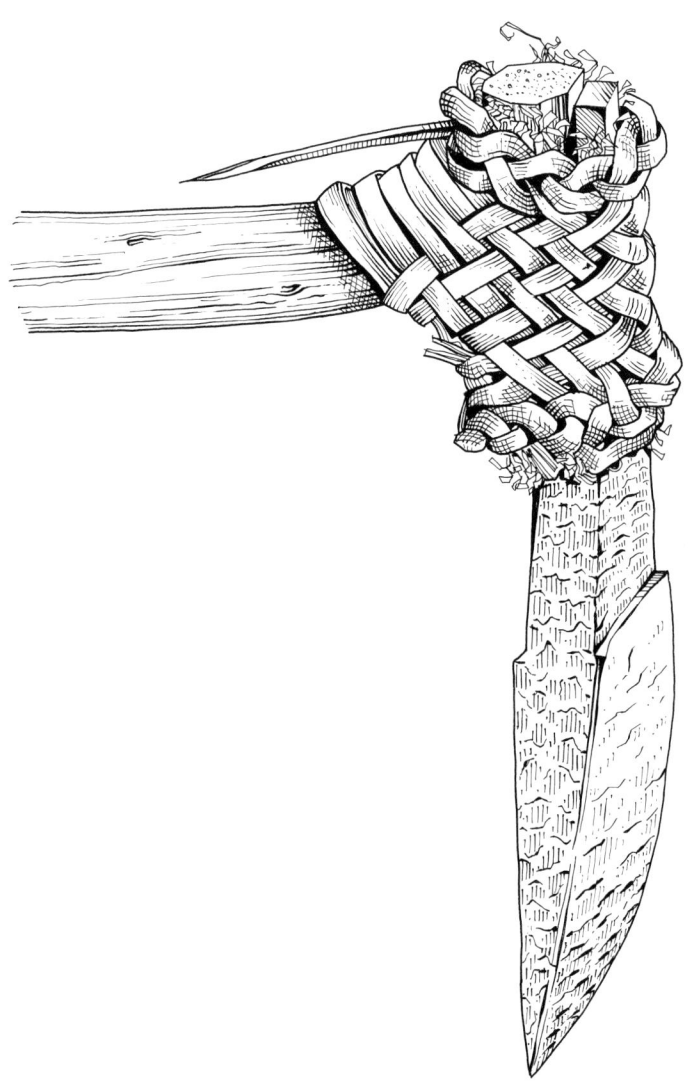

BM2 *Uai tetad*, adze. Item in the British Museum collection, drawing by Claire Thorne.

7 Life Force from the Wild: *Lalud*

Lalud (sometimes the Malay translation *kuasa* is used) is a central Kelabit concept. It is the force which drives and makes possible all life. It is a wild and potentially dangerous force, not by its nature under human control but susceptible to management by humans, giving temporal as well as spiritual power to those who learn to manage it. I was told in Pa' Dalih that it comes ultimately from God (*Tuhan*), conflated with the pre-Christian creator deity by older informants. A force of this kind is believed in by peoples throughout the Malayo-Polynesian world. It has been described as 'power' or 'primordial essence' (Anderson 1972), as 'charisma' (Geertz 1980) and as 'potency' (Errington 1989 and 1990), and it may be equated with the concept of *mana* in Polynesia (Geertz 1980: 106).

The people of Pa' Dalih in the late 1980s and early 1990s certainly saw *lalud* as being present in the natural environment, although this was much less evident then than it would have been before the Kelabit became Christian and gained access to the power (also described as *lalud*) of modern medicines, modern sources of power and modern machinery. I found that *lalud* was believed to be present in all living things, plant and animal. Certain plants and animals were considered to have particularly high levels of it, especially big, strong animals and animals which I was told were present in the forest only as *ada'* or spirits (such as the tiger – *balang* – which does not, at least nowadays, exist in the flesh in Borneo). Plants used to cure and to kill were believed to have higher levels of *lalud* than other plants.

The people of Pa' Dalih possess a general knowledge of many medicinal plants to cure both human and animal diseases (see Christensen 2002: 96-108), although nowadays they resort first of all, for the treatment of humans, to the government clinic in the community. Both medicines of all kinds (traditional and modern) and other plants which have the power (*lalud*) to effect other kinds of changes (such as cinnamon bark, *tabat borak*, used in the past to flavour rice wine, *borak*), are called by the same term, *tabat*. Until a few decades ago the people of Pa' Dalih used a variety of poisons (see Christensen 2002: 109-112 for a full list of these), but predominantly *parir*, the sap of *Antiaris toxicaria*, to kill game with blowpipes. Some people were able to show me small quantities of this poison; close relatives from over the border in the Kerayan area continued to use blowpipes. Such poisons are considered to have very high levels of *lalud*. This is unstable, however; I was told that *parir* had to be kept carefully, away from strong smells and preferably in a rice storage hunt, to ensure that it remained potent. There is a belief among the Kelabit that it is possible to use certain plants which have the power to counter curses, *pub* (for details of the plants used, see Christensen 2002: 143-4). However, it was, in Pa' Dalih, more common to resort to prayer to Jesus for this purpose in the late 1980s.

The topological character of the environment seemed to contribute to the level of *lalud* which it was believed to possess. The Kelabit Highlands is a relatively flat area with low mountains within it but encircled by higher mountain ranges. These mountain ranges (*apad*), and particularly certain peaks, are very significant elements of the wild natural landscape. They have a powerful spiritual significance, and seem to possess strong *lalud*, particularly Batu Lawi, the most important of the mountains in the area to the Kelabit, Lun Bawang and Lun Dayeh people, and Mount Murud, the highest mountain in Sarawak. Even now that they are Christians, the Kelabit still pray on mountains (see Chapter 9).

Lalud and places not under human control – the wild (see page 35) – were conceived of as being both life-giving and dangerous – forest spirits were feared as being able to eat human spirits. The dead were, in pre-Christian belief, considered to reside in the forest after death. Kelabit graveyards were still in the forest in the late 20th century, as they had been in pre-Christian times, although the souls of the dead were believed to go to heaven. Before the 1960s megalithic memorials to the dead were placed in the forest or on mountain ranges. The role of the forest seems to suggest a cyclical relationship between life and death, with the place of death also being the source of fertility and life (Bloch and Parry 1982).

Mountains and stone seem to be closely associated in the Kelabit mind, and it seems that the Kelabit believe that *lalud* is often located in stone. All mountains are associated with *lalud*, but craggy, rocky ones (where the stone – *batuh* – is visible) are considered particularly potent. Batu Lawi consists of twin peaks of stone, one smaller than the other, which were said by informants to be male and female (**Pl. 81**) and which were, until the Second World War, often mirrored in the erection, in the forest, of pairs of menhirs (*batuh senupid*) at death feasts. A part of the Tama Abo mountain range which runs between Sarawak and Kalimantan, visible from Pa' Dalih, was called the stone longhouse (*ruma' batuh*) by the people of Pa' Dalih (**cover photo**). Informants said that it had been turned to stone when someone in it laughed at an animal;[36] petrification is said to have been, at least in pre-Christian times, the result of making fun of animals, illustrating the dangerous nature of *lalud* associated with stone.

The importance of craggy, stony mountains is related to the special role of stone in the Kelabit Highlands. This is undoubtedly rooted in the high value attached to permanence in the tropical environment. The tropical rainforest is, of course, subject to very rapid decay. Even iron, which is smelted in some parts of Borneo, rusts away to nothing relatively quickly. The sharp awareness of perishability has profound significance for the way in which material objects are experienced in this environment. Everything created out of forest products, however skilfully, will perish or deteriorate very significantly within the lifetime of its maker. This prompts a need – and an ability – to move on, to make afresh. Baskets, mats, implements – even houses – are all made in the awareness that they have a limited life and more will need to be made. Until the Second World War, the awareness of perishability was coupled with regular physical mobility, with longhouses being abandoned every few years and new ones being established in another site. Agriculture too was transient: not only dry fields but wet ones too were used briefly (one year for dry fields, a few years for wet fields) and then abandoned for many years.

This awareness of the transience of almost everything has made the Kelabit, probably in common with other rainforest peoples, acutely aware of those few things that do not decay. The Kelabit show an interest, and associate high status, with substances and objects which do not decay, and attribute potency and life force to them. These include the heirloom objects which are passed down from generation to generation and which serve to mark the status of 'very good people' (*lun doo' to'oh*), leaders of longhouses and groups of longhouses. Before the war these included old jars (*belanai ma'on*) (Pl. **51**) and plates, brass gongs, and glass and beads. The Kelabit see beads, like stone, as being repositories of life force, *lalud* – expressed in the belief in Pa' Dalih that beads exist in male and female forms, implying that they reproduce. It is possible that this is based not only on a belief in their natural possession of *lalud* but also on the belief that their makers had, through their skill, concentrated the *lalud* of the raw material in the forms of the beads; and on the fact that beads have, if they are very old, been owned by a succession of high-status people with high levels of potency (Janowski 1998).

Even in the late 20th century, despite growing contact with the outside world, stone was the most common non-perishable substance in the Kelabit environment. It represented permanence in both a positive and a negative way. Thus although people who misbehaved in certain ways, such as laughing at animals, were said to turn into stone, it was also believed to carry potency and life force (*lalud*). 'Thunder stones' or *batuh perahit* – also known as *batuh pade*, 'rice stones' (BM144–145) – were, until about the 1960s, placed in rice stores, since they were believed to have the power to increase the quantity of rice (see note 24). It also seems that, like the Kenyah, at least some Kelabit longhouses in the past had powerful stones which were the property of the whole community or its leader (Rubenstein 1990: 897), and which were dipped in water used to sprinkle heads taken in war. In Pa' Dalih in the late 1980s some men collected strange stones or 'crystals', as they called them, in the forest (which they were not willing to show, however). They believed these gave them *lalud* and would make them successful in their enterprises.

Managing contact with *lalud*

The Kelabit believe that humans need *lalud*. Without it, they (like all other living things) cannot live; it is the force which makes life possible. However, because it is potentially dangerous, it needs to be channelled and controlled; if this is successful, *ulun*, a form of life which only humans are described as having, becomes possible. Therefore, relations with the source of *lalud* need to be managed. This applies both to the relations of living humans with that source, and to the way in which the dead, and their *lalud*, are dealt with. This applies to Christian as well as to pre-Christian contact with the source of *lalud*.

Within pre-Christian Kelabit cosmology/theology as it was explained to me in Pa' Dalih, *lalud* derived ultimately from Baru, said to be the Creator Deity.[37] The means of accessing *lalud* was through wild areas: forest and mountains. Until the Kelabit became Christian, the procedure called *ngelua'*, which involved smearing with blood from a slaughtered pig, seems to have been an important part of the management of relations with the wild and with *lalud*. Talla describes this procedure as 'blood purification' (Talla 1979: 250). He says that it was used where someone had had a bad dream (which was believed to carry a message from the spirit world) or where a whole longhouse had to be put under a 'taboo', presumably because of potentially dangerous contact with the spirit world (ibid: 291). *Ngelua'* appears to have been used to manage contact between the wild, spirit world and the human world. It was also used on a child and his or her relatives at the initiation of the child into proper human life at *borak ngelua' anak* feasts (see Chapter 8), and upon their return from the graveyard in the forest on those men who had deposited the dead person's remains there at secondary funerals (Talla 1979: 250, Lian-Saging 1976/77: 147).

The animal slaughtered for *ngelua'* was always a domestic pig. Pigs seem to have a special symbolic role for the Kelabit. They were still essential at naming feasts, *irau mekaa ngadan*, in the late 1980s and early 1990s, which as a minimum always involved the slaughter of one or two pigs. Although buffaloes might also be killed at *irau mekaa ngadan* (and in the past, deer had been killed at *borak* feasts), these were purely associated with status. Pigs, on the other hand, seem to be closely associated with humans, to have something in common with them. Puntumid, the most important forest spirit for the people of Pa' Dalih, was said by some informants there to hunt humans as we hunt pigs. Domestic pigs are fed the same food as humans eat – rice. This used to be emphasised in the prayer recited before pigs were killed for the *ngelua'* ceremony, for example at *borak ngelua' anak* (Talla 1979: 208, 292). It was also emphasised in epic tales such as that of Agan (Rubenstein 1973: 898). Having been fed rice seems to make pigs peculiarly close to humans. It also seems to make them peculiarly suitable for effecting the transition between the *lalud*-laden forest and the world of people.

It is important, then, to maintain and manage a distinction, a semi-permeable barrier, between humans and wild *lalud*; *lalud* is essential but it must only make contact with the controlled human world in specific contexts and in specific ways. These are managed by men. The most important way in which *lalud* is managed is through killing, both of domestic animals – in particular pigs – and of wild, hunted animals in the forest.

The most regular way in which *lalud* is brought into a Kelabit longhouse is in the form of hunted meat. Like dead humans, dead animals carry *lalud*, particularly when the animal is large and powerful. I would suggest that killing dead animals is perceived by the Kelabit to release their *lalud*, and eating them means taking their *lalud* into one's body. However, now that the Kelabit are Christian, this is not explicit; it is difficult to know whether it was in pre-Christian times, since there is a reluctance to discuss pre-Christian beliefs in any detail.

In pre-Christian times, *lalud* was also channelled and utilized through certain men who had special friendships with forest spirits, and especially with Puntumid, 'Grandfather Heel'. Puntumid was a very major spirit for the people in the southern Kelabit area, and also in the Kerayan area across the border, before they became Christian, so important that many informants in Pa' Dalih had clearly spent time trying to work out how to categorize him and conceive of him within the Christian belief system. For example, I was told by one (male) informant (who told me that he had himself been approached by Puntumid with a view to a friendship some years previously) that Puntumid was one of the fallen angels who left heaven with Lucifer. Puntumid, according to many informants in Pa' Dalih with whom I discussed him, was a spirit who originally belonged to the group of beings, the *lun rabada',* which came before humans – proto-humans, one might call them[38] – who were the ancestors of present-day humans but were different from them in that they had greater *lalud*. They were bigger and could accomplish feats which humans now cannot. The fact that these proto-humans were said to be responsible for some of the more impressive megaliths in the Kelabit Highlands reflects the fact that working stone is associated with *lalud*; this was also illustrated by the remark on the part of an informant in Pa' Dalih, quoted on page 52, that men's possession of *lalud* was exemplified by their working of stone.

Relationships between Puntumid and Kelabit men appear to have been fairly common before the Kelabit became Christian and contact with him does, I was told, still occur. Many people said that they had heard him in the forest, even while sitting in Pa' Dalih itself, and there were three men in Pa' Dalih who said that they had had contact with this spirit, two of them since Christianity was introduced. However only one of these three had had a protracted friendship with Puntumid, when he was a young man. He told me that Puntumid gave him powerful substances, called *tabat* (the same word used for modern medicine) which enabled him to kill and to cure – which gave him the power over life and death.

I was told Puntumid's story a number of times while I was in Pa' Dalih, and it varied little. He was said to have gone hunting with other young men from his group, and to have hurt his foot in the forest. He told the others to return without him, since he intended to remain in the forest and to hunt the 'hairless ones' (humans), while humans continued to hunt the 'hairy ones' (pigs). Since then, he has been a source of fear because he is said to eat your *ada'* (soul), but he has also been a source of *lalud* which is controlled and can be utilized by humans. This is through his relationships with certain men, whom he chooses. It seems that these men are generally considered to use the *lalud* which they get from Puntumid for good, mainly to cure sickness, although I was told that it is also possible to use it to kill. Thus relations with Puntumid were seen by my informants as having been beneficial, even though nowadays these have been abandoned because people are Christian and access *lalud* through Christ.

Headhunting and *lalud*

The Kelabit hunted human heads in the past, as did many other peoples in Borneo, and indeed throughout the region (see Watson Andaya 2003 for an overview). However, although head-hunting scares have occurred in Borneo right up to the present (including during ethnic clashes in Kalimantan between transmigrants and local groups at the end of the 20th century), the Kelabit themselves do not seem to have been involved in head-hunting since before the Second World War, and may have given it up by the early 20th century. The Brooke Rajahs discouraged head-hunting and succeeded in reducing its incidence and in many areas they eliminated it as early as the 19th century.

Head-hunting is proclaimed and celebrated in the victory songs (*kuyab aki*) recorded by Rubenstein in 1972 from older people who remembered their recitation (Rubenstein 1973). According to Yahya Talla, head-hunting expeditions were organised after an elderly aristocrat was sent to the cemetery after having been kept in the longhouse until all the flesh had rotted from the body (Talla 1979: 191). Talla says that initiation rites for young children, both boys and girls (*borak ngelua' anak* – see Chapter 8) were held immediately after such expeditions, although it is likely that old skulls were sometimes used instead of fresh ones for such initiation rites if a head-hunting expedition had not taken place (ibid: 191-202). Where a child whose parents and grandparents were of high status was being initiated, an *ulung* or 'monument log', was erected at the *borak ngelua' anak*, which according to Lian-Saging was decorated with human skulls (Lian-Saging 1976/77: 138-40, drawing after p. 148).

The fact that head-hunting was carried out after the death of a high-status individual, which meant the loss of someone whose life force was strong, and also the fact that human heads were used in the initiation of new human beings, both imply that heads were believed to carry life force, *lalud*. Indeed, the association between taking heads and bringing fertility (for both crops and humans) into the community is evident in many parts of South East Asia (Watson Andaya 2003; Hoskins 1996). Human heads were clearly seen as very potent. It is suggestive that, in Kelabit *kuyab aki* (victory songs), there are parallels between the taking of human heads and the taking of the heads of powerful animals with high levels of *lalud* (some, like the tiger, explicitly said to be spirits, and hence particularly powerful); most of the *kuyab* talk of bringing back human heads, but some talk of the heads of tigers and crocodiles too:

> Stand up, all you clever young people, let us fish in the lake.
> Let us fish in the fishpond, the big clearing made in the land –
> to catch and kill the crocodile,
> to catch and kill the tiger with striped skin and long fangs.
> Their fresh heads will wait for us on the sand,
> will wait on the verandah made of hard bamboo.

The two heads will have their brains emptied out,
the brains will be emptied out of all the heads we bring back.
Later we will climb the fence and take down the heads we dried;
we will take them back to our house
to our people who live along the big river.
Di-ah!' (Rubeinstein 1973: 769)

It was almost impossible to persuade Kelabit in the 1980s and 1990s to talk about the hunting of human heads, which was, for them, strongly associated with the pre-Christian past. There were clearly still strong feelings about the practice, but it was difficult to find out much in detail about it; it was surrounded by an atmosphere of fear and mystery, and was spoken of, it at all, in hushed tones. When, shortly after our arrival in Pa' Dalih in 1987, my husband and I celebrated Halloween by making a hollowed out pumpkin with eyes, nose and mouth cut in it and a candle inside (as is customary in Europe), we engendered a powerful sense of shock and fear in the whole longhouse; it had (perhaps surprisingly) simply not occurred to us beforehand what we were doing. The strength of the feelings about it which remained in the late 1980s seemed indicative of the symbolic importance of head-hunting in the past.

Head-hunting appears to have been central to Kelabit pre-Christian notions of cosmic causality, in relation to what one might describe as the flow of wild life force, which involved the bringing in of life force, harvested from other living things. Like the hunting of animals, the hunting of human heads brought in *lalud*, but in much greater quantities than everyday hunting. Humans were equated with powerful, spirit animals in terms of the levels of *lalud* which their heads brought into the community. There is a clear link between headhunting and masculinity, as there is between hunting of animals for meat and masculinity.

There is also a strong link between head-hunting and high status; leadership and success in war expeditions which brought back human heads are closely associated with high-status young men in the song-stories of Balang Lipang, Agan and Tukad Rini (Rubenstein 1973).

Birds as messengers from the spirit world and the supreme deity

The Kelabit believed, until they adopted Christianity, that messages from the spirit world and from the supreme deity came through birds. This is nothing unusual in Borneo, where birds have a special role as omen birds, often associated with ancestors, for many peoples (Harrisson 1960a).

The spider hunter, *ngae'* (literally 'helper') was, for the Kelabit, the usual bird through whom messages came from the supreme deity, and such messages were actively sought through prayers (*tatang*) before important undertakings to ensure success (Talla: 263-4). Another very important bird in Kelabit pre-Christian belief and practice (and for many other Borneo peoples – see Harrisson 1960a: 23) was the eagle known in English as the Brahminy Kite, called by the Kelabit *kaniu* or *kaniu balang* ('tiger eagle'). The *kaniu* was, in Kelabit pre-Christian belief and practice, called (*nawar*) when *ngelua'* (the smearing of blood from a domestic pig – see above) was performed at *irau* feasts and when someone had had a bad dream. Talla and Rubenstein both give examples of prayers to call the *kaniu* (Talla 1979: 192 and 288; Rubenstein 1973: 779). Here is an extract from one of the *nawar kaniu* prayers as translated by Talla:

Oui, friend of mine, 'tiger' eagle,
Oui, friend of mine, the 'striped' eagle,
Soar into the sky, take to the heights,
Wherever you are, wherever you may be, over there, perhaps you are under Batu Lawi, maybe you are under the jagged mountain peaks...
We call you to be our saviour, to be the life-giver in this family...
(Talla 1979: 289).

Since *ngelua'* was performed in contexts where contact with the spirit world was managed, it seems clear that the *kaniu*, called in conjunction with *ngelua'*, was believed to come to humans from the spirit world. The fact that the *kaniu* was described as a 'tiger' is also significant in this context, since the tiger, which is not present physically in Borneo, is by definition a spirit. Both *ngae'*, the link with the supreme deity, and *kaniu* were addressed in prayers as inhabiting high mountains and cliffs, and prayers to the *ngae'* were recited in the forest. The association of these birds with the wild and with the *lalud* of the spirit world is quite clear. In Kelabit pre-Christian belief, they brought messages and *lalud* from spirits and the supreme deity, located in the wild, into the human world.

BM152 Part of the carved handle of a *io tonan narit*, small long-handled knife. Item in the British Museum collection, drawing by Claire Thorne.

8 Irau Feasts: Statements of Status, Rice-growing Success and Potency

Rice and social status

Harrisson wrote in the 1940s and 1950s that: 'Rice is the one *essential* in Bario life which cannot come, go or grow of itself naturally...' (Harrisson 1959: 70). One could say the same of Pa' Dalih in the late 1980s. It is debatable whether the Kelabit – or indeed many other peoples living in the Borneo rain forest – believe rice to derive from the wild at all. As far as they are concerned, it cannot grow by itself and is entirely dependant on humans for its survival. However, not only is it dependant on humans; humans are dependant on it as well. For the Kelabit living in the Highlands, rice is the pivot of life and the basis of social structure, kinship and social status. In pre-Christian times it was regarded as kin to the Kelabit (Talla 1979: 327). It had to be treated very carefully and respectfully; it was considered to be susceptible to positive and negative influences which were capable of leading to a decrease or increase in its quantity as it was being harvested and once it was stored (Talla 1979: 320, 325, 327-329). This was still to some extent believed to be the case in Pa' Dalih in the late 1980s.

Daily life and the annual cycle of work in Pa' Dalih revolved around the production and consumption of rice, and work in the rice fields always had priority over all other work. The rice meal was eaten three times a day, and it was essential for the couple heading each hearth-group to produce enough rice to feed their children and any other dependants. They also had to produce enough spare rice to allow them to contribute towards *kuman peroyong* ('eating together') when the whole of the community ate a rice meal together at certain important points in the rice-growing and the Christian calendars, and when important guests visited the community. Finally they had to produce enough to enable them to hold an *irau* feast once in their productive lifetimes, for the naming of their first co-resident grandchild.[39]

An important reason for the emphasis on production of rice and particularly on providing rice for others is that rice was the basis of status differentiation. Basic standing in Pa' Dalih was predicated on being able to provide rice for dependants within one's own hearth-group. High status was associated with leadership, particularly in rice cultivation, and in being able to provide lavishly in various contexts for members of other hearth-groups, as well as for visitors. Before the Second World War, other members of a Kelabit longhouse were conceived of literally as the 'children' (*anak*) of the leading couple of the community. This reflects the way in which hierarchical status was conceived, which was in terms of the relationship between parents and children within a hearth-group (Janowski 1995).

Irau feasts were one of the most important contexts in which rice meals were provided for others; at *irau*, not only members of the same longhouse community but visitors from other longhouse communities were fed. Before the Second World War, high status couples displayed their rice wealth and their ability to provide for others through truly enormous *irau* which lasted days and involved the consumption of very large amounts of rice beer as well as a series of rice meals (Janowski forthcoming b). However, even with the coming of Christianity after the war, rice remained the basis of wealth and status, both through provision for others and through its sale in town. One of the major ways in which rice was used to display status in the 1980s and 1990s was still through *irau*, not only directly through the consumption of rice but indirectly through the purchase of animals for slaughter and the distribution of town-bought snacks, drinks and gifts to guests.

Kelabit stratification and leadership

The Kelabit are not a hierarchically stratified group as are some Central Borneo groups such as the Kayan. However, differences in status are profoundly important in their social structure, and these are conceived of as being inherited. In Pa' Dalih in the late 1980s, differences in status were expressed in terms of how 'good' (*doo'*) or 'big' (*merar*) a person was said to be. Being *doo*, 'good', at the basic hearth-group level was clearly mapped on to being *merar*, 'big'; if you were one you were also the other. All adult couples leading a hearth-group were described as *doo*. This meant that they were considered to possess the fundamental ability to be *merar*. Being *lun merar* at this basic level meant two things: having children and then grandchildren; and being able to provide these dependants with the rice meal.

It is very probable that the Kayan/Kenyah system of three named classes (Whittier 1973: 109-110; Rousseau 1979) and the Kelabit system are related in their logic to the Kelabit system, although I have not heard Kelabit refer to each other as belonging to any named class, as would occur among the Kayan or Kenyah. Some Kelabit writing about their own people have argued that the Kelabit were clearly stratified, at least until the Second World War. Talla, Lian-Saging and Bulan all say that there were terms which referred to separate social classes (Talla 1979: 76-90; Lian-Saging 1976/77: 115-125; Bulan n.d.). However, they disagree as to what these terms were and how they were used. This lack of clarity in terminology reflects, I would suggest, the fact that many of the terms concerned may not be Kelabit terms but may have been borrowed from the Kayan and Kenyah and that they could be seen as attempts to project the Kelabit system, which was actually more fluid, in a way that would make sense to other tribes. The fact that the terms *doo'* and *merar,* on the other hand, are fundamental to the Kelabit system of status differentiation is reflected in the prominence of these words among the terms mentioned by Talla, Lian-Saging and Bulan as referring to social classes.

The concept of *lun merar* relates both to the notion of leadership and to that of adulthood. On an everyday basis, the term was used in Pa' Dalih to refer to all those who were married and led a hearth-group with their spouse. However, a 'really big person', *lun merar to'oh*, was a leader of what can be described as a higher-level hearth-group – a bigger group of people who may be considered, in certain contexts and in certain ways, to produce rice as a group and to be commensal in relation to the rice meal. This may be the longhouse itself or a group of longhouses.

At least in theory, only the leaders of longhouses (described in the past as *la'ih raya*, literally 'big man', and now as *ketua ruma'*, using the Malay government term) and their immediate relatives are 'really' *lun merar – lun merar to'oh*.[40] Leaders are also considered somehow more adult, to belong to a higher generation level than their age merits. This was reflected, even in the 1970s, through the use of parental and grandparental terminology in addressing them and referring to them (Talla 1979: 152). However, this was no longer the practice in Pa' Dalih in the late 1980s.

Being *lun doo to'oh*, 'really good', and *lun merar to'oh*, 'really big' was, in the minds of the people of Pa' Dalih, closely tied up not only with leadership but also with provision for others within the group led. Before the Second World War, this meant leading a longhouse or group of longhouses, which was, at a higher level, equivalent to leading a hearth-group; the leading couple of a longhouse was seen, ultimately, as having 'children', *anak katu* (as his followers, who make up the longhouse he leads, were called up to about the 1960s), and as being responsible for feeding them (Talla 1979: 85). In theory, leadership should be clear and uncontested in this way. In fact, of course, things were not, and still are not, as clearcut as this. Contests for leadership clearly occurred before the Second World War, and have become even more common since then (see below). Before the war, these contests could be expressed through the splitting of longhouse communities and the forming of new ones under different leaders. This became less easy with increasing sedentarization after the 1960s.

Until 1902, when the first Kelabit *penghulu* were appointed, each longhouse had a *la'ih raya* and groups of longhouses might be under an overall *la'ih raya*, with others in the area subordinate to him. After 1902, *penghulu* were appointed by the Brooke government, two within the Kelabit Highlands, one for the Southern Kelabit (*lun pela'ud*) and one for the Northern Kelabit (*lun pedayeh*), and two more for Kelabit communities outside the Highlands (Talla 1979: 104-127). These were distinct from the *la'ih raya* of each longhouse community, but, like them, were *lun doo to'oh*. After the Second World War, the government became even more involved in the appointment of leaders, appointing not only *penghulu* but also taking a role, together with the *penghulu*, in the appointment of leaders of longhouse communities, who became known as *ketua ruma'*, 'house heads', using Malay terminology.

With growing government involvement in the appointment of leaders, both at chiefly and at longhouse level, leaders were selected who might not have held these positions otherwise. Also, the more sedentary residence patterns which developed with a desire to have access to government services are likely to have meant that communities did not reform around new leaders as regularly as they would have done previously. This all meant that *de jure* leaders, by the late 1980s, were not always the only *de facto* leaders. Thus the labels of *lun merar* within a longhouse community and of *lun merar to'oh* at a higher, chiefly level were not clearly and unequivocally attached only to the *de jure* leaders.

I did not find in Pa' Dalih that the longhouse community clearly accepted only their headman, their *ketua ruma'* appointed by the government, as the uncontested and only *lun merar to'oh* in the community. There were other individuals who were also respected and might compete for the title of 'the' *lun merar to'oh* of the longhouse. This was partly rooted in the fact that the inhabitants of Pa' Dalih in the late 1980s derived from a number of earlier, pre-war communities and each of these had their own *lun merar*, as well as originating in the fossilization of current residence and land-use patterns which meant that the community was not likely to split and follow more than one leader. Undeclared contests for leadership simmered constantly under the surface while I was living there. There were various individuals who appeared to be in competition for leadership. Each had claims to *lun doo do'oh* ancestry, which would fit them for leadership. Whether they were accepted by others as *lun merar to'oh* depended on the effectiveness of their actual leadership, and this was something they struggled to assert (Janowski 2003).

Asserting status through success in rice cultivation

Despite the belief that *doo*-ness is inherited, Kelabit leaders had always, it would seem, to regularly prove that they were still *doo to'oh*, through effective leadership and through wealth. Before the Second World War, and still in a community like Pa' Dalih in the late 1980s, this was based on success in rice cultivation.

Success in cultivating rice on the part of leaders was expressed in two ways: in the fields cultivated by their own hearth-groups, and through leading the rest of the community in communal decisions. This included, for example, choosing appropriate sites for dry rice fields each year, and selecting the best time to burn and to plant. Effective leadership in rice cultivation made it possible for leaders of a longhouse community to guarantee that all members of the community would have enough rice to eat. If necessary, they would take very unsuccessful hearth-groups, who did not have enough rice, into their own hearth-groups as dependants, as *anak*, where they would lose their independent status as *lun merar* in their own right, but would be fed.

Personal rice-growing success was never as easy for Kelabit leaders as for Kenyah and Kayan 'aristocrats' (*paran* and *maren*) since while the latter had slaves and commoners to do the work in the fields, Kelabit leaders had to do most of their own agricultural work even before the Second World War; while some *lun merar to'oh* had slaves at that time (never as many as major Kayan and Kenyah leaders), they did not have assistance from other longhouse members, as

Kenyah and Kayan leaders did. Thus, rice-growing success on the part of Kelabit leaders was an expression of personal skill.

In Pa' Dalih while I was there, skill in rice-growing was much admired and was a basic prerequisite for respect and leadership. An individual who did not take an adequate interest in rice-growing or who could not make a success in it was disparaged and not respected, even if he was successful in other respects. Respected leaders, those whose opinions were listened to at meetings, who hosted visitors and who were prominent members of the SIB Church, were always very successful in rice-growing.

Megalithic activity and *irau* feasts: marking and memorializing status and *lalud*

Kelabit leaders before the Second World War proved and memorialized their position, status and the fact that they were indeed *doo to'oh* and *merar to'oh* through holding *irau* feasts and through making marks on the landscape. Marking the landscape was done in a variety of ways, including through megalithic monuments, right up to the late 1950s.[41] After this, with the coming of Christianity, *irau* were still held, but they did not usually involve marking the landscape. However, it can be argued that status is still being marked on the landscape through the construction of permanent wet rice fields (Janowski 1988), although the work involved in this is rarely, now, accomplished at *irau*.

Irau, both in pre-Christian and Christian times, act to justify the status of *lun merar* and *lun doo*. To a large extent this is through an advertisement of rice-growing success. They were, before the Second World War, and still were in the 1980s and 1990s, focused on the consumption of rice, as cooked rice eaten with meat at huge rice meals shared by all guests, and, before the Kelabit became Christian, as *borak*, rice beer. Indeed so much *borak* was consumed at *irau* before the Second World War that the events were usually called *borak*. The production of huge quantities of rice has always been the cornerstone of *irau*. This was true before the Second World War and it remained true even after the Kelabit had given up making *borak*. Even though *borak* – which consumed the majority of the rice used at *irau* before the war – no longer needed to be made in the late 1980s in Pa' Dalih, large quantities of rice had to be sold to generate money to buy the town-bought elements of *irau*, including sugar, tea, coffee, biscuits and gifts for guests.

Besides being celebrations of rice-growing success, however, pre-Christian *irau* also emphasised the possession of *lalud*, potency/life force, on the part of the feast giver and the person being commemorated. This was made clear through the slaughter of powerful large animals, through the manipulation, and sometimes the carving, of stone, a potent substance; and through the placing of the high-status dead in coffins made in the shape of potent wild animals. The highest-status male leaders were buried in 'tiger coffins' (*lungun balang*) (Talla 1979: 226); the tiger, which does not exist in material form in Borneo but only, the Kelabit say, as a spirit, is the animal considered to have the highest level of *lalud*.

The *irau/borak* feasts at which these marks on the landscape were made were held at the secondary funerals of leaders. Throughout the Apo Duat highland area such death feasts (*borak ate* – literally 'rice beer of death') were held by the heir or heirs of the dead person up to the middle of the 20th century (Banks 1937b; Harrisson 1958b; Schneeberger 1979). At *borak ate* it was the male guests who made the mark on the landscape, thus acknowledging the status of their host. They were 'paid' by being fed and watered well over the period of the *irau*. The mark memorialized the event and the individual for which it was held, and confirmed his high status and that of his descendants. Marks included menhirs (*batuh senupid*), stone carvings (*batuh narit*)(**Pl. 79**), stone bridges (*apir batuh*), ditches (*nabang*) and notches in mountain ridges (*kawang*). Tom Harrisson has recorded many of these in the Kelabit Highlands (**Pl. 80**) (e.g. see Harrisson 1958a, Harrisson 1958b). Some were associated with the disposal of the dead, with the dead being placed under stone slabs erected for that purpose (Talla 1979: 249). Talla tells us that the method of 'registering the death of a person on the landscape' was determined by stated preference of the person concerned; by family tradition; by the means of the family; by the local topography; by rice-growing requirements (a channel might be needed to facilitate irrigation, for example); by the weather; by omens and dreams; and by recent trends among families of similar status (Talla 1979: 242-243). In general, however, marking the landscape, particularly through stone, is believed by the Kelabit to express potency, *lalud*; this is expressed in the remark quoted on page 52.

Batuh senupid, the most common memorial at *irau ate*, were often erected in pairs, considered male and female (Harrisson 1962: 380; Labang 1962), just as Batu Lawi, the great mountain north of Bario, has two peaks, which are, according to informants in Pa' Dalih, male and female (**Pl. 81**). This reflects the fact that it was, in many cases, apparently not just a male leader who was being memorialized, but his wife as well. There is a considerable emphasis on the male + female married couple in Kelabit thinking, and it is only as a member of married couple that an individual can, in fact, become a longhouse leader.

However, it is notable that the actual work of marking the landscape, expressing the *lalud* of the feast-giver, was always carried out by men. Female guests remained at the longhouse to help prepare the rice meal which was the complement of the landscape mark, as well as representing payment for the workers/guests. It was and continues to be men's work to enter the forest and make a human mark on it; just as men clear forest at the turn of the century, as they have since time immemorial as far as the Kelabit are concerned, they also made notches in ridges and erected megaliths until the 1950s. This expresses the association between men and *lalud*, which I will discuss further in the next chapter.

Some of the marks on the landscape in the Highland area are associated with *irau* known to have been held for a particular individual in the past, but I was told by informants in Pa' Dalih that others had been made by the ancestors of the Kelabit at unknown times in the past, or by their earlier ancestors the *lun seluyah* (see note 38). There was a series of different death feasts for a deceased person, after the secondary funeral, and at each one a different mark might be made (Lian-Saging 1976/77; Talla 1979).

By the late 1980s it was difficult to get people in Pa' Dalih to talk in much detail about death in the past, because this was associated with pagan belief. However, it is clear that secondary funerals were not held for all the dead. All the dead were put in either a wooden coffin or a jar[42] (both coffin and jar are described as *lungun* when used for this purpose although the usual term for a jar is *belanai*) after death and a small feast was held for those assisting in making the coffin. I was told that a certain kind of (not very valuable) bead, the 'red bead' (*ba'o sia'*) was attached to the wrist or toe of dead people before they were put in the coffin; Talla however says that valuable beads were used for this purpose, particularly for leaders (Talla 1979: 224). He tells us that in the case of ordinary people the coffin was kept for ten days in the *dalim* (kitchen/living area) of the hearth-group to which the person had belonged. Items associated with the gender of the deceased (such as a basket for men, a hoe (*belu'ing*) and an earthenware pot (*tuning*) for women) were also put in the coffin (ibid). After this, ordinary people were taken to the cemetery in the forest, where the coffin or jar was left.[43]

The bodies of those of high status, of leaders of communities, were kept in the *dalim* for at least a year, after which a secondary funeral was held (Talla 1979: 232, Lian-Saging 1976/77: 146). I was told in Pa' Dalih that at the secondary funeral certain of the bones – the skull and certain other bones including the big toe bones – were transferred to a smaller jar; however, Talla says that transfer to another jar only took place if the person had come originally from another community (Talla 1979: 248). It is clear from the pre-Christian cemetery near Pa' Dalih that smaller jars, made of stone, were not uncommon in the past, since there are a number there. Talla tells us that the reason for keeping the bodies of the dead in the longhouse for so long was that if a dead leader were sent straight to the cemetery, there would be insufficient rice for the community, thus clearly associating rice with high status and leadership (Talla 1979: 234).

By the late 1960s death feasts were no longer held, because the Kelabit had converted to Christianity and such feasts were considered un-Christian. This was partly because of their reputation as drunken debauchs, partly because they explicitly glorifed status differentiation, something which the missionaries wished to discourage, and partly because they had an association with pre-Christian belief. In Pa' Dalih in the 1980s and 1990s, the dead were disposed of immediately.

I witnessed a funeral in Pa' Dalih in January 1993. Because the death, of an old lady originally from the Kerayan called Pun Ngelipo, occurred at the same time as an *irau pekaa ngadan* (a naming feast) was going on in the community, it is possible that the funeral was less elaborate than it might have been otherwise – but even so, drinks, crackers and a rice meal (with hunted meat rather than valuable domestic meat, however, and therefore not status-generating) was served to the mourners. A rough coffin made of planks originally made for house building was constructed within hours. Pun Ngelipo was placed in this, keened over all night by close relatives, and then buried in

the cemetery (*tanem*) across the river in the forest. The burial was carried out by men, who are associated more closely with death. Only three women went to the cemetery; women are afraid to go to cemeteries, which are associated with spirits.

Although megaliliths are no longer erected at *irau*, marks on the landscape continued to be made in the form of wet fields even after the Kelabit became Christian. Innovation has always been considered appropriate in marking the landscape. Harrisson recorded that the placing of a plaque on top of the mountain Batu Lawi counted as *irau* 'work' (Harrisson 1958b: 699) (**Pls 81**, **82**). Thus, the notion that earth-moving associated with making wet rice fields – to bund them and to make ditches to carry water to them and away from them – is a derivative of the marks on the landscape made at *irau ate* in the past is not, I think, far-fetched. *Irau* were still held in the 1980s and 1990s, although not at secondary funerals, and guests at an *irau* were still sometimes asked to participate in an earth-moving task related to rice agriculture. Talla says that in the 1970s it was usual to ask the guests at an *irau* to contribute some form of labour to the family holding the *irau*, including work in the rice fields such as digging drains and making bunds (Talla 1979: 307).

Name-changing *irau* in the 1980s and 1990s: competitive attempts to generate status

At some point shortly after the Second World War, *irau* began to be held after the birth of the first child of a young couple. To a large extent, these seem to derive from *borak ate*, but they also derive from the pre- Christian *borak ngelua' anak*, when children and new parents were introduced to the community (see below). Unlike the *borak ngelua' anak*, however, they were, at least in the late 1980s, held by all hearth-groups. They are known as *irau mekaa ngadaan* ('name-changing *irau*') or *irau naro' ngadan* ('name-making *irau*).

In Pa' Dalih in the late 1980s, *irau mekaa ngadan* acted as statements of the success of the hosts (who were the parents of one of the two partners) as *lun merar*, as successful leaders of their hearth-group, successful at producing children and grandchildren, and successful at providing for them through regular rice meals. The young couple receiving parental names were just beginning to be *lun merar*; the older couple, their parents/parents-in-law (depending on whether they lived with the wife's or the husband's natal hearth-group; the Kelabit were about equally likely to be virilocal or uxorilocal), who were taking grandparental names at the *irau*, were proclaiming the peak of their achievement as *lun merar*.

There were considerable variations in the scale of *irau pekaa ngadan* in the late 1980s. This reflected the fact that although every young couple was introduced to adult life through such an *irau*, not every hearth-group had the same means or commanded the same respect. To a certain extent, I would suggest that all of the *irau* I witnessed in the late 1980s were status- generating, like *borak ate* (and, as we shall see, to some extent parallel to *borak ngelua' anak*), being attempts to project the host *lun merar*, the older couple, as being, temporarily, *lun merar* of the entire group of guests. By definition, all Kelabit, and all who attended, were kin and many of these declared themselves to be so by renewing (*ngebru*) their grandparental names or even by taking new ones. By doing this, and accepting a (lavish) rice meal from the hosts, they were putting themselves, at least for the period of the *irau*, in a dependant position *vis-à-vis* the hosts, declaring themselves, by eating the rice meal, to be 'children' (*anak*) of the hosts.

Particularly in the case of the very grand *irau* held in the 1980s and 1990s by very high-status couples, to which it is hoped all Kelabit will come, it can be argued, I think, that *irau mekaa ngadan* were attempts to project the host *lun merar* couple as *lun merar to'oh*, as leaders of a higher-level group than just their own hearth-group, thus generating status and enhancing their position as *lun merar*. By giving gifts to them if they do this, the hosts of *irau* encouraged guests to declare their relatedness, and thus to enhance the position of the hosts, through renewing or changing their grandparental names. The gifts given to guests who renewed or changed their grandparental names at *irau mekaa ngadan* in the 1980s and 1990s were bought in town. They were often clothing, particularly *sarong* (Malay; Kelabit *tekip*); before the Second World War, informants told me that they were usually salt made in the Highlands (*tusuh* – BM106–107, SM12; **Pls 32, 34**) and large earthenware pots (*kudin* – BM125, 128, SM36).

While increasing proportions of what is provided at *irau* are not rice-based, it is notable that almost all derive from the sale of rice; thus, *irau mekaa ngadan* continue to emphasise rice-growing success as the basis of status.

The possibility of selling rice to town by air from 1961 onwards, when the airstrip in Bario was opened, was the basis for a growing potential for social mobility. Undoubtedly, mobility has always taken place, but before the Second World War it was much harder to achieve because of limited means to build up cash (Janowski 2003). The SIB Church itself also provided the means for social mobility since it provided what was to a large extent an alternative hierarchy, and the opportunity for lower-class members of society to train to became pastors (*gembala*) and to build up status through becoming *pelayan* (deacons).

Rapidly accumulated money was, in the late 1980s, being used in bids for upward mobility, mainly occurring in Bario where the cash was concentrated because rice grown in wet fields there could easily be sent to town by air. Bids were made partly through the purchase of prestige objects, including ancient beads (*ba'o ma'on*), gold jewellery, televisions, motor bikes and other consumer goods. Money was mainly used, however, to hold *irau mekaa ngadan* which were as lavish as possible, with hosts competing to give the best spread and the best (town-bought) presents to those guests who 'renewed' their names (and enhanced the 'name' (*ngadan*) of the hosts).

Bids for social mobility are part of the resurgence of an emphasis on social differentiation in the Kelabit Highlands. The SIB Church, influenced by the Australian, British and American missionaries who founded its predecessor the Borneo Evangelical Mission, has preached against status differentiation, and SIB leaders have periodically made efforts to discourage the symbolic expression of such differentiation. During the 1970s, after the Revival, they discouraged the wearing of heirloom beads, a traditional mark of inherited status. However this practice had crept back by the mid-1980s, with active and widespread purchase of these beads both in Bario and to some extent also in communities like Pa' Dalih, by those making upward bids. In Pa' Dalih between 1986 and 1988, letters were sometimes sent by SIB Church leaders to be read out in church, which called upon people not to advertise status.

It seemed from the somewhat puzzled response to these in Pa' Dalih that the Kelabit did not really understand why they should not emphasise status and success. Status was, for them, a good thing, earned through hard work, accepted by others, and leading to a better life not only for the individual and his or her hearth-group but also for other members of his longhouse, who were (or would, it was hoped, become) his accepted dependants. Indeed, this is reflected in the adjectives used to describe those of high status ('good', *doo'*) and low status ('bad', *da'at*). However, although 'good'-ness was believed to be inherited and not acquired, it was supposed to be demonstrated through hard work. By the late 1980s, there was a problem with this. Access to the means of production had begun to be unequal in Bario[44] and a good deal of labour from the Baa Rian area across the border was used in the rice fields. This meant that rice-growing success could be achieved without personal hard work. In the late 1980s this had not yet begun to seriously affect the view that being of high status and being wealthy were the same thing as being 'good', but it seems likely that this may happen soon.

Lalud and name-changing *irau*

Lalud continues to be central to *irau* now that the Kelabit are Christian. However this is no longer through emphasis on powerful wild animals and on the working of stone, as in pre-Christian *irau ate*. It is achieved through prayer, and contact with Jesus Christ (*Iesus*) and, through him, directly with God (*Tuhan*). *Irau* have at their centre very long prayers. These are recited by prominent individuals as well as by *gembala* (pastors). An important distinction between pre-Christian and Christian *irau* is that there is, nowadays, an emphasis not on the possession of *lalud* by the hosts, but on their ability to access it. All the guests participate fervently in these prayers, which are passionate monologues. In church, each member of the congregation prays, aloud, individually; even in *irau*, there are often individual mutterings on the part of guests. All present are deeply concerned with what is achieved through prayer, and in participating in this. All guests are involved, in effect, in helping to access the *lalud* of God through *Iesus*.

I will say a little more about the nature of Christian *lalud* in the next chapter. I would just say here that although there is a sense in which Kelabit Christianity clearly differentiates between the *lalud* of the forest, accessed through animals and expressed through such things as the working of stone, and the *lalud* of the Christian God, there is also a sense in which there is a continuity between the two. Thus, present-day naming *irau* may be seen as expressing not just a continuing concern with expressing social status through rice-growing but also a continuity in the concern with possession of *lalud*.

Borak ngelua' anak in pre-Christian times: initiating children and marking status

Naming *irau* in the period after the Second World War derive from two sources: *irau ate* on the one hand and the feasts held before the war to celebrate the initiation of a child on the other hand, *borak ngelua' anak* ('*borak* drinking at which a child is smeared with blood').[45] While a major, and arguably the primary function, of *borak ate* was to memorialize the status of the dead person or couple, and to generate status for his/her descendants (particularly the host of the feast), the primary function of *borak ngelua' anak* was the ritual initiation of the child into social life and of its parents and grandparents to their new roles within the hearth-group and the community, in relation to their changed roles as *lun merar*.[46] Naming was a way of marking this transition; both Talla and Lian-Saging say that at such feasts the child of the hosts, the parents and the grandparents, and close relatives all took names.[47] *Borak ngelua' anak* were not held by all hearth-groups, only by better-off hearth-groups. However, it seems likely, from what Talla and Lian-Saging say, that all children did go

through initiation and their parents and grandparents had the opportunity of changing their names, since less well-off, lower-status hearth-groups could participate in ceremonies held by others, changing their own names and those of their children (Lian-Saging 1976/77:141; Talla 1979: 198-206). *Borak ngelua' anak* might also be shared by a few hearth-groups, to reduce the cost.

Although *borak ngelua' anak* were not primarily intended to raise status, they were certainly used as a means of enhancing status, and the fact that not all hearth-groups could hold them underlines this. The highest-status hearth-groups raised an *ulung*, a wooden or bamboo post surmounted with valuable items such as gongs, jars and hornbill casques, at these feasts. Talla tells us that this was intended to raise the status of the hosts (Talla 1979: 206). Thus, the proclamation of parental and grandparental status, as *lun merar*, has always been associated with generating status, both through *borak ngelua' anak* and through *irau mekaa ngadan* carried out from the 1950s or 1960s onwards.

Lungun balang (tiger coffin) used for high-status dead in pre-Christian times (after Talla 1976: 226)

9 Rice and the Wild: Gender, the Rice Meal and the Generation of *Ulun*

I found that the attitude which the people of Pa' Dalih had to rice as being not only their staple but also their focal food had a close bearing on the relationship which they had with the wild (see page 35). Rice on the one hand and foods conceived of as wild on the other had, I would suggest, complementary symbolic roles in pre-Christian Kelabit cosmology, and to some extent even after the Kelabit became Christian. Through the bringing together of rice and *lalud*, the rice meal, and proper human life, *ulun*, becomes possible. This process of bringing together rice and wild foods is mediated through gender; although men, in the 1980s, were involved in rice-growing, and women gathered wild foods, rice was nevertheless associated more with women and wild foods more with men. In this chapter I want to explore the symbolic role of rice and of wild foods in generating *ulun*, and to look at the significance of gender in achieving this. *Ulun* was generated, at least in pre-Christian times, and, implicitly, now as well, through what might describe as the correct cosmological relationship between male and female, between rice and wild life force (*lalud*), expressed through the rice meal, *kuman nuba'* and the way in which *ulun* is generated through the rice meal provides, I suggest, the basic structure of Kelabit kinship. I want to explore this cosmological relationship, and at the end of the chapter, I will look at the impact of Christianity on notions of *ulun* and *lalud*.

Rice was, for the people of Pa' Dalih in the late 1980s and early 1990s, categorically opposed to forest products, both meat and handicraft materials. It was, in fact, the antithesis of forest products, because it can *only* grow in the tropical forest if people plant it, whereas forest products grow on their own (*mulun sebulang*). The Kelabit, then, as self-conscious rice growers, are making a statement about their *non*-reliance on the forest. However, at another level it is clear that in the Kelabit Highlands in the late 20th century there continued to be a profound reliance on the forest – and perhaps also to some extent, despite Kelabit Christianity, also a spiritual dependence on the wild life force, the *lalud*, which derived from the forest and was consumed most importantly through meat. Although the importance of meat on an everyday level was not played up – indeed it was freely shared – its importance could be clearly seen at *irau* feasts, where meat was given explicit monetary value through the slaughter of valuable domestic animals (Janowski 1995).

Kelabit rice-based kinship

In the Highlands, and to a large extent even in town, rice continued, in the 1980s and 1990s, to be the foundation of Kelabit kinship. The focal significance of rice had an effect on the way in which the people of Pa' Dalih conceived of their relations with others. Ties with other people were based on rice – whether you ate another person's rice or whether he or she ate yours was fundamentally important in setting up the kind of relationship which you had with that person. I therefore describe Kelabit kinship as 'rice-based kinship' (Janowski 1998b).

In Pa' Dalih, a kin relationship described in affinal terms was said to exist with anyone with whom one had regular contact. It would have been rude to declare that you were not related in any way to someone with whom you had social relations. The implied assumption was that, if two people had social relations with each other, at some time in the past someone related to one person must have married someone related to the other. The Kelabit term for kin of any kind is *lun royong*, literally 'people together'; in other words, being together generates kinship. Although the closeness of kinship varies, then, its existence cannot be questioned among those who are *royong*, together.

The closeness of kinship was said to depend to some extent on actual biological relatedness. However, beyond the closest biological ties, the activation of ties seemed in fact to depend on choice. The kin links that were considered most significant were those that had been kept active through feeding – of rice, at the rice meal (see Carsten 1997 for a similar construction of kin ties through feeding in Langkawi). This in turn related to belonging to the same hearth-group and to the same longhouse, since these were conceived of as entities within which feeding of rice meals takes place. Their existence was also the basis of being 'people together', *lun royong*.

Kelabit kin relations are hierarchical. Those who feed are of higher status, both genealogically and in terms of standing within the longhouse, than those who are fed. In a Kelabit community like Pa' Dalih, status, being *lun doo'* (a 'good person'), was based on success in maintaining a separate hearth-group, and in particular on being at the head of a longhouse or group of longhouses, which meant being the focal couple of the longhouse as a higher-order entity of the same type as the hearth-group itself (Janowski 1991; Janowski 1995). Both within the hearth-group in its basic form and at the level of the longhouse, it is the sharing of rice meals that held people together, and those who do the feeding are of higher status. Those considered leaders in Pa' Dalih were also the leaders in rice cultivation. Leaders are conceived of as feeding others, and this is the basis of their status. Rice, then, both organizes Kelabit kinship and makes it hierarchical. It is the glue that holds a community together and which to a large extent dictates the roles which people take vis-à-vis each other.

Women and rice; men and *lalud*

The rice meal restates, three times a day, the importance of the male and female roles in constructing rice-based kinship. In its most essential form, as at *irau* feasts, the meal consists of just two components: rice and meat. These are associated respectively with women and men, and express their complementary roles in generating rice-based kinship. The married couple is the basic unit of Kelabit society, and it is seen as proper that they should be very closely tied to each other.

For the people of Pa' Dalih rice, and the generation of what might be described as 'proper human life' (*ulun*) was more closely associated with women than with women; while the wild, and the life force (*lalud*) which derives from it, was associated with men. This remained true even though Christianity, with its emphasis on access to Christ, appeared to have increased women's direct contact with *lalud*. Direct contact with *lalud* seems in pre-Christian times to have been through wild places and men. This was expressed through song-stories like the story of Tukad Rini and that of Agan, from which I will quote later.

This association between women and rice and men and the wild, from which the wild meat eaten at the daily rice meal still derived in Pa' Dalih in the late 20th century, is, I believe, rooted in the essential complementarity of male and female within the Kelabit married couple; the rice meal, consisting of wild foods and rice, associated with male and female respectively, symbolises the bringing together of wild *lalud*, or life force, from the forest (male), with the organizing, and humanizing principle which is rice. At another level, however, the couple are associated together with the production of rice, and work together to ensure that their dependants with the hearth-group have enough rice to eat at every meal.

Among the Kelabit of Pa' Dalih, as among the majority of other South East Asian people, there was no strict separation between men and women in everyday life; this is linked to the 'togetherness' of the married couple, particularly in the growing of rice. However, there were places and jobs that were generally associated with one gender or the other, and these underlined the association of women with the 'inside' – the hearth, the longhouse and the rice fields – and of men with what is the antithesis of 'inside' – the forest and mountains in which men hunt and like to spend time.

In general, the longhouse – especially the hearth – and the rice fields were associated with women, while wild areas outside human control (*polong*, forest and *apad*, mountains) were associated with men. This did not mean that men might not be found cooking at the hearth or that they did not work in the rice fields, and it did not mean that women never went into the primary forest, even on their own. But the closer a place was to the *dalim*, literally 'inside', the innermost part of the longhouse and particularly the area around the hearth where the rice meal is cooked – and the more it has been shaped by humans – tamed, as it were – the more female was the place or task associated with it. Conversely, the further a place was from the 'inside' and the less affected by human activity, the more the place or task carried out in it was male.

Women in Pa' Dalih were closely associated with the production, processing and cooking of rice. Both men and women informants considered that women knew more about rice-growing than men. With Christianity, the spiritual aspect of this knowledge has become less significant; but before the Kelabit became Christian, informants told me that women had a special relationship with the female deity associated with rice, whom they called Deraya (now also translated as 'luck').[48] Prayers to the rice spirits, the *ada' pade*, make it clear that there were two women, who existed on a spirit plane, called Una and Sina Ure, who were responsible for the rice spirits (Talla 1979: 281-284; Rubenstein 1973:797-8). According to Matthew Amster's informants, Kelabit women in pre-Christian times owned secret and potent plants associated with success in rice cultivation, which they kept in a small rattan container, the *bi'ut*, which was kept above the hearth (itself associated with rice and the rice meal) (Amster 1998: 298).

The association of women with rice associates them with the power to domesticate nature, since rice was regarded as the most 'tamed' crop; by contrast, men were associated with untamed areas – the big, wild forest – and with *lalud*, expressed through the strong male association with meat (*belabo*). Men, according to Matthew Amster's informants in Pa' Ukat, kept secret and potent objects in a rattan basket, the *poren*, objects which linked them with the wild and with killing – a special knife and other metal objects used to create ritual incisions in animals before they were slaughtered (Amster 1998: 298). In 1993, I was told by Balang Pelaba, a (male) informant in Pa' Dalih aged about 60, that *Dela'ih tupu inan lalud, dechur na'am te lalud to'oh* (Only men have *lalud*, women don't have real *lalud*). This was in the context of a discussion about the *batuh kalabit*, a stone in the mountains near Pa' Dalih which has the spreadeagled figure of a human carved in relief on it and which I had visited with him a few days before (**Pl. 79**) (a photograph of this is provided by Tom Harrisson in Harrisson 1958: pl. XVI), and Balang Pelaba said that their lack of *lalud* was the reason why women could not have carved the stone; he went on to say that male *lalud* was associated with going into (literally 'running in') the forest, and with carving stone there, while women made rice beer and cooked rice (*Lalud kami – me upun lam polong. Decur naro' borak, naro' nuba'*) – the implication being that transforming rice into food and rice beer was in some sense parallel to male *lalud*-related activities in the forest.

Men and women in Pa' Dalih gradually developed, as they grew out of childhood, their associations with meat and rice respectively. Although young men in Pa' Dalih went hunting more often than older men, fat (*lemak*), which was considered the most potent part of the animal, was considered to be particularly associated with older men, and younger men were not always very keen on it (**Pl. 53**). At *irau* feasts, meat was cooked by men outside the longhouse, and meat was distributed by young men and fat by older men (**Pl. 83**), while rice was cooked and distributed by women (**Pl. 38**).[49] Fat-eating competitions were organised for older men at some *irau* I attended (**Pl. 84**), with lumps of boiled fat strung on strings and the idea being to finish all the lumps on one's string first. It was pretty much compulsory for older men to participate. In Pa' Dalih in 1987, our neighbour Balang Pelaba, felt unable to refuse to participate in such a competition despite the fact that he did not like boiled fat.

It was considered inappropriate, even dangerous, for women to eat fat. They were free to express their unwillingness to eat it, unlike men (**Pl. 85**). The attitude to women eating fat was illustrated at one *irau* when I witnessed a mother become quite concerned when she saw her daughter eating some of the chunks of fat which are distributed at *irau*, although she did not mind her son eating them. Although the mother concerned was not able to explain why she felt this way except to say that girls should not eat fat, I would suggest that it is because fat is the 'meatiest' part of the meat and therefore carries a very potent dose of wild *lalud* from the forest, of which women are afraid, as they are of entering the primary forest on their own. Chunks of fat distributed at *irau* were usually taken home by women to be rendered into lard, which they then used in frying food for side dishes for the rice meal and for snack foods. Interestingly, it did not seem to be a problem for women to consume food cooked in lard – possibly because the fat had been processed and its potency distributed through the food.

This association between forest and men and more domesticated areas and women was carried through to handicrafts; this remained true in the late 1980s. Materials from the 'big forest' (*polong raya*) were gathered and generally worked by men in Pa' Dalih. Those from secondary growth areas near the longhouse, however, (*polong i'it*) might be gathered and worked by either men or women. This distinction is particularly clear if one looks at rattan and bamboo. Rattan, which is from the 'big' forest, was always prepared and worked by men (**Pls 86–89, 109**), but bamboo, gathered in areas of secondary growth, was often worked by women, particularly where complex work was necessary. Some baskets were made entirely of rattan, and men made these (**Pls 88–89**). Others were made of bamboo and were made by women (**Pl. 90**).

In the making of *bekang* baskets (BM73a, b, SM78–79; **Pls 59–60**) and *bu'an* baskets (BM66–68, SM87, 91–92; **Pl. 91**), which are made of both bamboo and rattan, a women would make the body (*burur*) out of bamboo and afterwards her husband would bind the edges with rattan (**Pls 92, 112**).

Men bound wooden tools and knives with rattan (**Frontispiece** and **Pl. 110**). They made solid objects out of bamboo, including cooking implements (*bogo*) (BM13–19, 24–26; SM1–3, 5–10; **Pl. 93**), holders for these (*tara bogo*) (BM31–33, SM16; **Pl. 94**) and stands for burning damar resin to provide light (*dawan natang*) (BM102, SM25; **Pls 31, 95**). Wood, which appeared to have become more important in the 1970s and 1980s because it became much easier to obtain and to work due to the greater number of metal tools and particularly with the availability of chainsaws, was cut from the 'big forest' and was always worked and carved by men (**Pls 13, 73**).

Mats, which were made from grasses gathered in open areas of secondary growth, were always made by women (**Pls 96, 108**). Other items made of grass were also made by women (**Pl. 97**). Knives and agricultural tools, made of locally forged iron with wooden handles bound with rattan and with the blades fixed using latex from the *mat* tree, were made exclusively by men.

Clay pots, made of clay from rice fields until the 1970s, were made by women (**Pls 113-118**). When I commissioned a set of these pots in 1987, the damar resin which sealed them, from a forest tree, was applied by the husband of the female maker.

Iron, which was used to make agricultural tools and knives, is a material that was always worked by men, who made and sharpened iron tools (**Pls 75-76, 98**). Iron was always brought from far away – before the Second World War it was not smelted in the immediate area, and after the war it came from town – and perhaps this is related to its being worked by men, who are associated with the 'outside', while women are associated with the 'inside'.

The fact that iron is primarily used in destruction and killing is probably also relevant to the fact that in Pa' Dalih men worked it and sharpened tools. Although women did gather snails and small fish by hand in rice fields and streams using *iap* nets (BM94–95, SM72; **Pl. 68**) and *be'ong* gourds (BM93, SM94, **Pl. 40**) they did not kill them but allowed them to die; by contrast, men actually killed animals which they hunted and the larger fish which they caught using traps, *bubuh* (BM112, SM57; **Pl. 102**) and nets. *Bubuh* were made of rattan, by men. Throw fishing nets, *pukat* (BM96, SM73), were made of nylon thread brought up from town, and were also made by men (**Pls 70, 111**). *Iap* used by women, were made of bark or cotton, and were made by women; but their frames, made of rattan, were added by men.

Men did all construction work in Pa' Dalih, building longhouse apartments, *da'an* (field huts near rice fields for resting during the day) and *lepo pade* (rice storage huts) for their hearth group. This involved working in wood, bark, bamboo and rattan. Chainsaws were used for making planks.

Techniques used in craftwork were gender-specific. Weaving mats and baskets using bamboo, clay pot-making and making string (*nopar*) from bark, pineapple leaf fibre or nylon were all women's work. Carving, whether of hornbill ivory, of wood or of bamboo, binding things together and plaiting – probably because the substance plaited was almost always rattan – and working with iron were all men's work.

The male association with the primary forest and with *lalud* was expressed most strongly in their working of, and wearing, materials from animals, particularly those which are considered to possess high levels of *lalud*. By the end of the 1980s, the Kelabit used no animal material in crafts except a little goatskin, brought in from outside the Highlands. Animal materials used in the past were worked by men and used for male personal clothing and ornamentation. They included the skin of domestic goats (*Capra aegagrus*; Kelabit/Malay *kambing*), sometimes used to decorate the sheaths of *tongol* knives (BM5a, 9a, SM62; **Pls 65, 99**); the skin of the sun bear (*Helarctos malayanos*; Kelabit *beruang*) for sitting mats, *tabir puet* (also sometimes made of rattan – BM114); the tail feathers of the rhinoceros hornbill (*Buceros rhinoceros borneoensis*; Kelabit *manangan*) and sometimes the helmeted hornbill (*Rhinoplax vigil*;

Kelabit *manangan*) to decorate headdresses used for dancing; the skins of clouded leopards (*Neofelis nebulosa*; Kelabit *kuer*) as cloaks; the fangs of clouded leopards worn through holes in the upper ears; and the carved casques of helmeted hornbills worn as ear pendants (**Pls 5-6**; see Chapter 2). The only animal material sometimes used by women is hornbill feathers, which were still sometimes used in making dancing fans in the late 1980s.

Male and female as viewed through Kelabit epic tales

Before the Second World War, and to some extent for a decade or two after that, the Kelabit possessed a rich variety of songs and tales which were told in various contexts – mainly while working in rice fields and sitting around a fire in the evening in the longhouse. Some of these were long song-stories which told of culture heroes – the tales of Tukad Rini, of Balang Lipang and of Agan. These were known well only by certain individuals. By the end of the 1980s, these song-stories had been almost forgotten, since the individuals who knew them were growing older or had died.

These long song-stories illustrate what it meant to be an ideal Kelabit man and woman – as demonstrated in the high-status (*doo' to'oh* or 'very good') heroes of the stories – as well as the relationship of men with the wild and of women with rice. To some extent the characteristics of the heroes of the stories can still be said to exemplify ideal Kelabit virtues. Most of the heroes of the stories are male, and success in war is a major focus of the stories, but there are enough female heroes to be able to get a picture of what an ideal Kelabit high-status woman should be like. The ability to grow ample rice and prepare lavish rice meals and plenty of rice beer come out clearly as central virtues for such a woman, as well as quietness and the ability to string valuable beads. For both men and women, the ability to consume plenty of *borak* is an important virtue.

The story of Tukad Rini has many variants. I collected one version from Balang Pelaba in Pa' Dalih in 1987; a longer version has been collected by Carol Rubenstein, an American poet who collected poems, tales and epics of a number of different ethnic groups in Sarawak at the beginning of the 1970s. Carol Rubenstein also collected versions of the story (*Adi'*) of Agan and the story of Balang Lipang (Rubenstein 1973).

The heroes of the story of Tukad Rini live in this world (described as *Luun Atar*, 'literally on the flat place') but possess a level of *lalud* not possessed by ordinary Kelabit men. They travel beyond *luun atar* to wild areas which are an extreme variant of the forest and mountains which the Kelabit are actually surrounded by; to the far corners of the universe, to caves within the earth, to the sky, even to the moon. Here, they do battle with other male heroes, also imbued with high levels of *lalud*, performing incredible feats, such as leaping over mountains, in the process. Eventually, they are victorious.

The strong association between animal materials, maleness and potency is underlined in the stories told about Agan, Balang Lipang and Tukad Rini, whose beauty and strength are expressed and displayed through the animal materials which they wear, in particular the skin and teeth of tigers (*balang*) (Rubenstein 1973). Since there are no tigers in Borneo, the *balang* is a mythical, spirit creature (*ada'*) for the Kelabit, possessing very high levels of *lalud*. The fact that Agan, Balang Lipang and Tukad Rini were said to wear *balang* teeth and *balang* skin cloaks and caps (with the face of the tiger on top of the head) are strong statements of what it means to be as male as can be: possession of the *lalud* of the tiger. In the story of Agan, he is said to be in control of the spirit which rules the tiger skin cloak he wears, *Ada' Akang* (Rubenstein 1973: 868). Male grandparental names both in the past and now often include 'Balang', expressing the boastful expression of possession of high levels of *lalud* (Janowski 2000).

An extract from the song or *Adi'* of Agan, recorded by Rubenstein, describes how the hero prepares himself for a trip into the wild (Agan says modestly that he is just going hunting, but in fact he is going to fight with an enemy who has sent word asking him to come). The association between high-status men and animals which have high levels of *lalud*, such as the tiger, as well as with spirits, is explicit:

> Agan puts on his tiger-skin cloak
> with beautiful feathers attached to it.
> He places on his head his headdress,
> the cap of which is the face of a tiger,
> its face stretched so that its nostrils are big,
> its eyes gleaming,
> its great fangs overhanging above and below;
> His headdress with tall manangang (sic) feathers, standing
> ten tall and five short feathers.
> The young man is white,
> white as the shell fastened to the front of his cloak,
> the shell which is as big as both his arms outspread.
> It gleams below his knees,
> the shell gleaming also beyond both sides of his ribs.
> Carrying his spear and his shield,
> Agan strides along the verandah,
> and following along with him is the calling sound
> of Ada' Akang, the spirit that rules the tiger-skin cloak,
> following along with Agan. (Rubenstein 1973: 884)

Another extract from a Kelabit song, that of Tukad Rini as recorded by Rubenstein, describes how one of the male heroes expresses his power, and how it makes him capable of what are normally impossible feats, performed in mountainous, wild areas:

> Iya' Utul Aling Bulan…looks straight up into the Highest Sky and
> begins to draw power to himself as he sings his Nadadir song:
> > 'Running, I jump and leap up high,
> > high my leap,
> > climbing in height, lifted into the air until I fly –
> > running above the tops of the ripa trees,
> > soaring far over the highest of the mountains.
> > I go floating through the clouds,
> > the great still clouds,
> > and from there carry in my arms a cloud
> > big as a baby deer, a baby deer raised as a pet,
> > and kept within the enclosure made of green bamboo.
> > I draw together all my breath
> > for my next leap through space – I rest in air;
> > then I drop down,
> > landing among people on the mountainside…' (Rubenstein 1973: 1001)

The heroes return to their longhouses to hold huge *borak/irau* feasts. The rice meals, and especially the *borak* (rice beer) are prepared by the high-status women of *Luun Atar*, who are the wives of the male heroes. The association of these women with rice, particularly with *borak* (rice beer), and with the longhouse and the 'inside', as opposed to the wild 'outside' in which the men do battle, is quite clear. This is illustrated in the following extract from the story of Tukad Rini as recorded by Rubenstein, in which Aruring Salud Bulan (who has come from the Moon to marry Iya' Utul Uling Bulan) sings a *Nadadir* song, but not about war and wonderful feats – the topic of the *Nadadir* of the male heroes – but about making *borak*: Just as the male heroes can perform impossible physical feats in the wild, she is also able to perform the impossible, producing *borak* instantly without going through the usual process of making it which she nevertheless describes in her song.[50]

> Standing, she goes to get some borak to drink. She brings one tiny jarlet the size of the egg of the pirit bird. Tasting the borak, she becomes a little bit giddy. Then she takes one deep great container and splashes within it the contents of her tiny container of borak. She shakes the great container and at once it becomes completely filled.
> She hands the drink upwards to Iya' Utul Aling Bulan. Then, gazing up at Iya' Utul Aling Bulan, and drawing power to herself, she begins singing her Nadadir song:
>> 'Your name is Iya' Utul Pakaling Riung, Pakaling Kuman all talk about,
>> the man with the bun of magic hair used to kill,
>> used to lure the fish in the river...
>> This is the borak, which I made
>> with powdered yeast of old lakuwa root,
>> made with the powdered yeast of the new lakuwa root.
>> We drink it at our feasting in the center of the longhouse,
>> the place at the middle door,[51]
>> at the midpoint time when the moon is fullest.
>> The borak is put into old jars,
>> jars tied against the walls from corner to corner. They are set on planks that are hard and strong, planks that are very big.
>> The borak is drawn from the jars through tubes of batung bamboo,
>> drawn through the bones of the baby lagung deer.
>> The borak goes into the bu'ung gourd containers, gourds strung
>> with old beads, special guest kaduwit gourds
>> covered with old lapudun beads that cross each other
>> in a sieve against coarse particles.
>> Please take this, please take this drink into your body –
>> the drink will pass through your mouth into areas between your ears,
>> and behind your ears, and beneath your great earrings.
>> The drink will pass along your spine of bones like notched steps,
>> so that you feel like the charging wild boar in the jungle.'
> (Rubenstein 1973: 1021)

Lalud and the relationship between men and women

Both men's association with the wild and their ability to kill makes them attractive to Kelabit women. Kelabit men are always responsible for killing; women are extremely reluctant to kill even a chicken. On an everyday basis, life in the Kelabit Highlands has always involved the killing of animals; occasionally, in the past, other humans were also killed. Small-scale wars between groups of longhouses with different leaders were not uncommon until the middle of the 20th century, and especially before the *Pax Brookiana* imposed by the Rajah Brookes in this area from the early part of the century. Occasionally, heads were taken, although the Kelabit never went in for head-hunting on a large scale. Heads were necessary for the rituals initiating children at *borak ngelua' anak*.

Kelabit song-stories clearly associate high status in men with success in war and in killing. The heroes of these stories

are also described as beautiful and attractive to women, and their exploits in places outside *Luun Atar*, the Kelabit world, are described, where they do battle and kill many people. The association between beauty and battle is clear in this extract from the story of Balang Lipang, quoted by Rubenstein:

> His face is beautiful and red – it is very bright...
> So bright are his eyes they shine
> as if the flame of a damar lamp burns within them.
> So well shaped are his arms they are as if carved
> his ear ornaments of tiger teeth big and beautiful...
> See how like a cleared path,
> a clearing made on the side of a steep incline,
> is the top part of his cheek where the hair is removed,
> as if his lover had rubbed it smooth...
> When the young lord returned from battle,
> from burning the longhouses of the emeny to ashes,
> he freshly shaved parts of his head. (Rubenstein 1973:809-810)

When the heroes go to do battle with other peoples, the heads they bring back, carrying the *lalud* of the dead, are given to their wives or girlfriends, as in this extract from the song of Agan:

> Dayang receives the heads from him (Agan) and strikes them, crying along the high victory cry...
> Eight times they parade around the verandah with the heads,
> Marching, singing kuyab victory songs, and dancing.
> (Rubenstein 1973: 896-897)

In the late 20th century, Kelabit men no longer killed other people, but they did kill wild animals in the forest. This too made them attractive to women. Other women in Pa' Dalih often joked with me about the attractiveness of men returning from the forest, with the smell of it still on them.

It would seem that the relationship between men and women has a link with killing and with men's activities in the forest, that the *lalud* which men bring back from the forest and from killing – whether other humans or wild animals – is something that women desire from their men, and perhaps even that the transfer of *lalud* from men to women is part of the reproductive relationship between them.

It is tempting to make a parallel between this and the relationship between the male and female components of the Kelabit rice meal. The rice meal constructs rice-based kinship on the basis of feeding male and female foods (rice and meat carrying *lalud*); the physical relationship between the man and woman who are responsible for providing the rice meal constructs kinship on a biological basis, bringing women together with men and their *lalud*.

However, it should be noted that the two types of kinship are not coterminous since members of a hearth-group are not always the children of the couple which heads it. There is, in fact, a tension between rice-based kinship and biological kinship: people who have been adopted are *supposed* to belong to the adopting hearth-group, according to what people say, but *in fact* they feel a strong pull towards their natal hearth-group and biological parents. People in Pa' Dalih said to me often that adoptive parents tried to prevent their children from finding out that they were adopted, but that in the end they always found out and that children often returned to their biological parents when this happened, even though this was strongly disapproved of by others.

Lalud, ulun and Christianity

Lalud (wild life force) and *ulun* ('proper human life') continue, at the turn of the century, to have significance in the context of the Kelabit conversion to Christianity. This is both through the continued centrality of the rice meal, within which *lalud*, meat and men are associated on the one hand and rice and women are associated on the other; and through fresh, Christian interpretations of the two concepts.

In Pa' Dalih in the late 1980s, there continued to be an association of provision of the rice meal for dependants with possession of *ulun* on the part of the couple providing it. The symbolic role of male and female and of rice and wild foods, particularly meat, in the rice meal is particularly clearly stated at *irau* feasts, where the male association with meat and with killing on the one hand, and the female association with rice on the other, are emphasised through the mode of preparation and serving of the rice meal around which the whole event is focused. However, there is also an emphasis at present-day *irau* on accessing *lalud* from God. However, there is no longer any overt emphasis on the *lalud* of the animals slaughtered, and there are no *lalud*-expressing feats accomplished by male guests. There is a strong emphasis on *ulun* at all rice meals, through prayers said at the beginning of the meal which usually contain requests that Jesus 'give *ulun*' (*bre ulun*), and this is particularly true at *irau* feasts, which always involve lengthy prayers of this sort.

Kelabit Christian prayer, as I observed it, mainly consisted of attempts to access the *lalud* of God in order to draw down *ulun* from the deity. Kelabit prayer is not silent; each individual prays individually, on an impromptu basis, at the church services which take place every day in each community. Thus it is possible (though not always easy, given the noise of everyone else praying as well) to identify what each individual is praying for. At *irau*, the main officiants pray loudly and clearly on their own. There was very frequent mention of both *lalud* and *ulun* in prayers, both at *irau* and at church services, with individuals referring to the *lalud* of *Iesus* and *Tuhan* very often, and asking for *ulun*. In Kelabit Christianity, there is a very great emphasis on *ulun*. This is sometimes explicitly said to be *ulun bru*, 'new life', and I was told that this was always implied. Very large proportions of parental and grandparental names taken during the period after the Kelabit became Christian include the word *ulun*, proclaiming, I was told, the individual's and the couple's adherence to Christianity and reliance on life from God.

Clearly, then, Kelabit Christianity has not abandoned the importance of *ulun* or of *lalud,* although the concepts have shifted their meanings somewhat. While *ulun* was still considered, in Pa' Dalih in the late 20th century, to be expressed through the ability to grow rice successfully and to provide the rice meal, this was interpreted as being due to a good relationship with God, through effective communication with him via prayer. It is through access to the *lalud* of God that strong *ulun* (*kail ulun*) is believed to be possible. *Ulun*, then, is, in the Christian interpretation, still due to access to *lalud*; but this is accessed direct from God. *Lalud*, on the other hand, is no longer overtly associated with individual men but is associated with God (often using the term *kuasa*, the Malay translation of *lalud*). Humans

draw on it to assist in generating *ulun* but individual men do not, as they did in pre-Christian times, make claim to possess it individually (at least, not overtly or publicly; however, men do refer to the male gender possessing it – see quote on page 52).

The intermediary through whom access to the *lalud* of God is achieved is now believed to be Jesus Christ. Jesus is considered to be a much more effective intermediary than the spirits (*ada'*) of the forest, such as Puntumid, through whom *lalud* was accessed in pre-Christian times. Although there is a sense in which the Kelabit have been persuaded by the missionaries that the spirits of the forest are evil, *seitan*, not all informants were convinced that a spirit such as Puntumid was evil. Rather, he was believed to be ineffective, relative to Jesus.

Even within Kelabit Christianity, there are indications that *lalud* still has an association with wild places. This is expressed in the habit of praying on forested mountains and hills. Pilgrimages are organized regularly to major mountains in the area, which bring together both the Kelabit and the related Lun Bawang and Lun Dayeh living in the Fifth Division of Sarawak (**Pl. 101**).[52] There is now an annual pilgrimage to Mt. Murud, and a church was constructed on the summit in 1992 which has a capacity of 1200 (Amster 1998: 305). Not only highland-dwelling but also urban Kelabit participate in these pilgrimages.[53] It is not entirely clear whether the official view of the SIB Church, which has gone along with all of this, is that God can be reached from these places. However, it would seem likely that in the view of most of the congregation, praying in the forest has the advantage of conflating the pre-Christian and Christian sources of *ulun*.

The Kelabit emphasis on the importance of controlled access to *lalud* in the pre-Christian context (see Chapter 7) is also evident in accessing *lalud* from God via Christ. There is a tendency towards charismatic Christianity among the Kelabit, which is evident particularly in the Kelabit Highlands itself but was also present among Kelabit in Miri, involving speaking in tongues, altered states of consciousness and faith healing. However, this was a source of worry among many of my informants, who believed that it was dangerous because it was potentially uncontrolled. What I was told by many informants in Pa' Dalih, where charismatic events were quite common while I was living there, was that Satan (*seitan*) may be unwittingly contacted rather than God. In Miri, there are now five SIB Church congregations and one has distanced itself from charismatic practices (Amster 1998: 307). The Kelabit did not have a concept of an entity equivalent to Satan in their pre-Christian cosmology, and there does not seem to be a pre-Christian tradition of two different sources of *lalud*, one good and one evil. I discussed this with informants in Pa' Dalih; while some, using a clearly Christian analysis, did talk of the existence of good and evil, older informants in particular were reluctant to draw a distinction between different sources of *lalud*. Thus, I would suggest that the worry that was being expressed about charismatic Christianity may have had its source rather in a fear of uncontrolled contact with the source of *lalud*.

Conclusion: Crafting a Human World

'me tau kerja lam late' Tuhan'
'Let's go to work in the garden of the Lord' –
from a Kelabit/Lun Dayeh Christian hymn

The use of forest materials for craftwork in the community of Pa' Dalih in the late 1980s and 1990s was part of a broader relationship which the people of the community had with the forest which surrounded them. This relationship involved utilizing what came from the natural environment - 'God's garden' (*late' Tuhan*) in the words of a Christian hymn often sung in Pa' Dalih during my time there – in order to craft a world which was, in their view, peculiarly human. Areas which were not under any human control were conceptually opposed to areas which were fully under human control, and the latter was conceived of as being created out of the former. Rice, the rice meal, and the hearth at which it was cooked, epitomized human control; the forest and all that was in it epitomized both a vital resource which was the basis of human life, and lack of human control. Pa' Dalih craftspeople were, in their enjoyment of their work, expressing a fundamental Kelabit interest in taking a substance in its natural form and making it into something human. Human society should be ordered and controlled: in it, men and women, old and young, should be interconnected in defined, ordered ways. Substances and objects must have specific uses and functions.

In all living things, for the Kelabit of Pa' Dalih, there is a powerful life force, which they call *lalud*. Gathering and using plant materials for craftwork, and gathering of plants and the hunting of animals for food, means coming into contact with the *lalud* of the forest with its fecund chaos, harvesting it and harnessing it. At the other end of a continuum from *lalud*, but complementary to it, is rice. Rice is treated quite differently from other plants, even from other crops. It has a special role in defining and creating human culture, and it is closely associated with a distinct kind of life which only humans have, *ulun*. Creating *ulun* is achieved through control of nature, expressed in cultivating rice, which, unlike all other plants, is believed to be unable to grow on its own. One could perhaps say that, for the people of Pa' Dalih, as God generates *ulun* in cultivating and managing the entire natural world, so humans create much more limited amounts of *ulun* in cultivating their rice fields. Humans, then, are closer to God than other creatures since only humans generate *ulun*.

The Kelabit eat rice three times a day at the rice meal, *kuman nuba'*. In Pa' Dalih in the 1980s and 1990s, rice was always eaten with foods which were wild or treated at wild – so that the meal brought rice together with wild life force, *lalud*. Through this, *ulun* was made possible, and so was proper human kinship. The rice meal is the only context in which the structure of Kelabit society, based on hearth-groups which eat together, is clear. It is the foundation of kinship, which I have called 'rice-based kinship', and which is based on hierarchical relationships between parents and their children set up through rice meals.

At the end of the 20th century, Pa' Dalih men hunted in the forest and worked materials from both the 'big' and the 'little' forest (see note 28), while women were primarily responsible for rice-growing, gathered in 'little' forest and agricultural areas, and worked materials from the same areas. This meant that women were relatively more associated with the 'inside', with the hearth, the longhouse and with rice-growing and preparation; while men were relatively more associated with the forest and with contact with *lalud*. In pre-Christian times, men's closer contact with *lalud* was expressed through their working of stone in making megalithic monuments at *irau* feasts, and through their working and wearing of animal materials, particularly from animals like the clouded leopard and the hornbill; most importantly, it was expressed through head hunting. The higher the status of a man, the more *lalud* he was considered to have; the highest status leaders were buried in coffins in the form of the *balang*, the spirit tiger, the most potent animal believed to exist. Now that the Kelabit are Christian, men continue to have a much closer relationship with the forest than women, hunting and bringing in materials for craftwork from the biggest forest, full of *lalud* and spirits, a forest which women still fear and men bravely say they do not.

There are complexities in the relationship of men and women with *lalud*. The fact that both are involved in craftsmanship illustrates this. Kelabit material culture in a community like Pa' Dalih means, in effect, channelling a flow of *lalud* from the forest, through the skill of craftspeople, into made objects. I found that women were, as one might expect, cautious of those that carried a high level of *lalud*, such as those made of iron (especially knives and spears) and substances of animal origin, and did not usually own them. However, skill itself was also a factor in channelling *lalud*, and all made objects, because they had the power to *do* something, had *lalud*. This means that both men and women were involved in the process of channelling *lalud*, through their skill, to make useful objects. Women, then, were both afraid of *lalud* and were involved in managing it. This complex, and situationally constructed, relationship with *lalud* may be seen as an illustration of the situationality of the construction of gender, recognized by many scholars both throughout the world (e.g. Moore 1994: 56, Strathern 1988) and specifically in South East Asia (e.g. Howell 1995). When women are doing craftwork, perhaps they are being less female and are a little bit male; while when men cook (as they quite often do) they are less male and are a little bit female. Most of the time, though, men have attitudes, and do things, which are masculine, and which are to do with managing *lalud*; while women have attitudes, and do things, which are feminine, and related to rice cultivation and processing.

It seems that the Kelabit believe that the processing of something from natural substances to make an object, wherever this is done and whoever does it, involves the harnessing of *lalud* of the raw material. They seem always to have been very interested in objects and substances manufactured elsewhere. This was evident before the Second World War, when they had little contact with peoples other than other forest-based agriculturalists and hunter-gatherers, and it was still true in the late 1980s. Before the war the most important things made elsewhere which the people of the Kelabit Highlands possessed were heirloom items – beads, gongs and ceramics. These were considered to have high levels of *lalud*, and it seems that this was at least partly due to the fact that these striking objects, which the Kelabit themselves were not able to make, were assumed to have been made by peoples with high levels of skill, who had the ability to harness the *lalud* of raw materials to make them. After the war, many of the objects made by Europeans, Americans and Australians, particularly machines like aeroplanes, appeared amazing to the Kelabit. They were also considered to possess high levels of *lalud* which were exhibited in the feats they could accomplish; and, as an illustration of a very strong link between their (largely Christian) makers and God, the source of *lalud*, to be a good argument for converting to Christianity. The people of Pa' Dalih continued, in the 1980s and 1990s, to have a fascination with things manufactured elsewhere, especially if they can *do* clever things (and therefore, by implication, carry *lalud*).

After conversion to Christianity, the Kelabit relationship with wild, forested areas not under the control of humans continues, at the turn of the century, to have both practical and spiritual significance. On a practical level, control over what derives from the wild, exercised through both crafts and through gathering and hunting of foods from the forest, continues to be vitally important, particularly in a community like Pa' Dalih that still has limited access to cash and to the means to bring in town-bought goods, materials

and food. In any case, it would be impossible to replace many – perhaps most – of the items which are discussed here by going on a spending spree in town, since there is no need for most of them in town and they are simply not manufactured.

On a spiritual level, *ulun* and *lalud* continue to be central concepts in Kelabit Christianity, although they have changed and become Christianized. The association of *lalud* with the wild areas from which so much of their physical sustenance comes, and hence the role of those wild areas as source of spiritual sustenance too, has not vanished; wild forested and mountainous areas continue to have a role as a source of *lalud*, although this is now seen as deriving from God via Christ. The Kelabit pray, as Christians, on forested mountains (**Pl. 101**). The forest and mountains remain a place of mystery, fascination and some fear, a potential source of *lalud* and a necessary source of food and craft materials, but also associated with danger and death. The coming of Christianity seems to have cast a brighter light on the negative and dangerous aspects of the spiritual significance of the wild, and has emphasised the importance of controlling the *lalud* which is believed to come through it, since this is now believed to come, potentially, from evil sources as well as from God. Christianity is also changing the gender relationship with the source of *lalud*, since women are now in direct contact, through prayer (sometimes on forested mountains, conflating the pre-Christian and Christian conduits of *lalud*), with this source – God, through Christ – in a way in which they were not in pre-Christian times.

The complex and many-faceted nature of the significance of the forest to a people like the Kelabit, who have lived in its midst for so long, means that its loss, which is fast approaching with the beginning of logging in the Highlands in the late 1990s, will undoubtedly have a profound effect on them. Although success in education and employment outside the Highlands have become vitally important at the turn of the century, work in 'God's garden', transforming the raw materials of nature and crafting a human way of life, remain vitally important. The link to the natural world in the Kelabit Highlands is also important in constructing Kelabit identity, not only in Pa' Dalih but also for Kelabit in town. Losing the link to that natural world could mean the eventual loss of that distinctive identity.

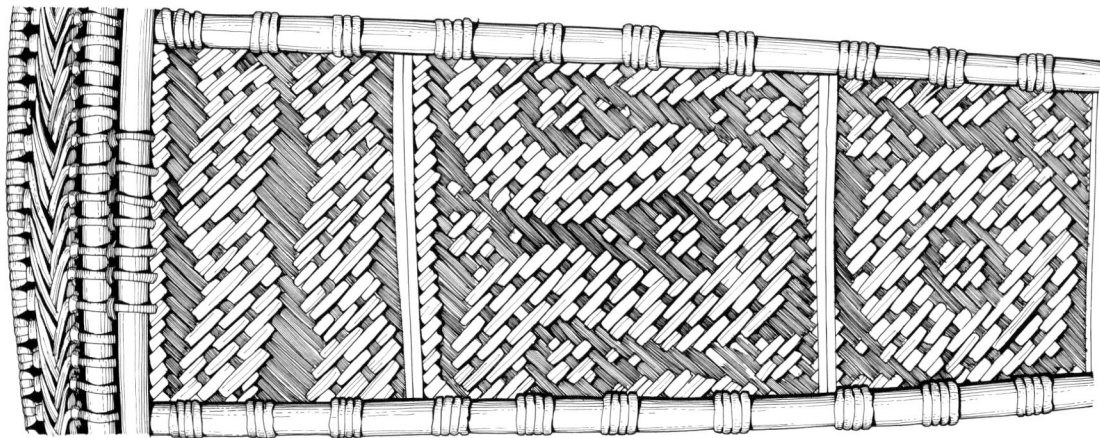

BM66 Decorative weaving on a *bu'an bodok barit*, large rigid basket for carrying rice. Item in the British Museum collection, drawing by Claire Thorne.

Plate 1 Inside the longhouse, Pa' Dalih, 1987. Lawe Padan, headman of Pa' Dalih, sitting at his hearth in the *dalim* part of the longhouse with his grandchild Balan and a neighbour, Lugun Bala. They are sitting on a coarse grass mat, *ugam* (BM155, SM95). Lugun Bala is sitting on a stool, *laan* (SM23, BM103, 105) and Lawe Padan is sitting on a piece of cloth as a substitute for a *laan*. He is wearing football trousers and the bun of his traditional hair style is clearly visible. On the left can be seen the framework (*raran*) above the hearth, containing firewood. An empty *royo* (a *sarong - tekip* in Kelabit - on on a spring) for a baby to sleep in during the day is visible in the distance by another hearth. The floorboards are handmade, and very wide; they are older than this longhouse. Along the right can be seen windows, and doors which lead across bridges, one for each hearth-group, to the parallel *tawa'* part of the longhouse.

Plate 2 Tom Harrisson with Negri Besar ('Big country' in Malay), an upper-class Kelabit, in 1945. Both Harrisson and Negri Besar have chosen a style of dress mixing the traditional Kelabit and the modern European: Harrisson is wearing Kelabit beads and a *sarong* with a modern cap, a watch and a t-shirt and is barefoot while Negri Besar has long ears, shell bracelets and clouded leopard's fangs with beaded decorations in his ears, and is wearing a loincloth together with a t shirt and boots. Photographer unknown but possibly Junaidi bin Bolhassan. Photo © Sarawak Museum; accession number unknown. Reproduced as the frontispiece of Harrisson's book *World Within* (1959).

Plate 3 Church collection basket (*uyut ruma' tebupun*) (BM59, BM60) in use in the Remudu church three hours' walk from Pa' Dalih (**see Map 2**), 1987. On the floor are *ugam* mats (BM155, SM95).

Plate 4 Line of women dancing at an *irau* naming feast at Bario Asal longhouse, 1987. They are wearing what are locally described as 'uniforms', *sarong kebaya* in the Malay style made especially for this occasion, and valuable beads as necklaces (*bane*) and caps (*petaa*).

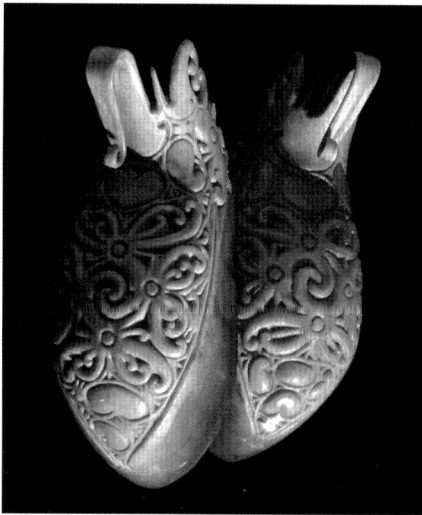

Plate 6 A pair of the carved hornbill ivory ear pendants worn by some men in the Kelabit Highlands until the Second World War, and occasionally still worn. A gift from a Kelabit friend to Kaz Janowski in 1990. Made of the casques of helmeted hornbills (*Rhinoplax vigil*; Kelabit *manangan*).

Plate 5 An older man at an *irau* naming feast at Bario Asal longhouse in Bario, 1987. He is wearing a mixture of new and old: a *batik* shirt and trousers; and a necklace of valuable old beads (*bane ba'o*), with a knot of tiny shop-bought beads wound around a wooden core at the base of the necklace, as well as clouded leopard fangs in his ears, hornbill ivory ear pendants and a *topi* (*orang*) *ulu* hat (BM97). On each side of him is an *uyut* basket; one is his with probably his personal belongings in it. He is sitting on a rattan mat (*pin ue*; BM156). The other man visible in the photograph has elongated ears but is not wearing ear pendants.

Plate 7 Women at an *irau* naming feast in Bario Asal longhouse, Bario, 1987. All are wearing necklaces made of valuable old beads (*bane ba'o*), and three are wearing bead caps (*petaa*) also made of old beads. One of the women is also wearing a gold chain. Two of the women are wearing brass ear pendants (*abe*). They are sitting on a rattan mat (*pin ue*; BM156; **see Pl. 20**).

Plate 8 Esther of Remudu in 1987. Esther was, as far as I know, the last child in the southern part of the Kelabit Highlands to have long ears and to wear ear pendants.

Plate 9 Balang Muned of Pa' Dalih holding a little girl, 1986. He is wearing brass earrings (*abe tawak*) (BM148-149). The longer of the two longhouses can be seen in the background.

Plate 10 A young Kelabit girl called Muda Mathu in 1962, probably at Bario Asal longhouse, holding a baby. She is wearing a simple bead headdress made of what are probably *alai*, some of the most valuable beads in Kelabit eyes, and a necklace (*bane*) made up of strings of tiny beads, twisted around a wooden core, and larger beads, possibly also *alai*. She is wearing the earrings known as *abe ringgit* (BM146-147), which were the most usual type of earrings for women at that time. In the background another woman can be seen wearing a full bead cap (*petaa*). Photographer unknown but possibly Tom Harrisson. Photo © Sarawak Museum; accession number KE32.

Plate 11 Mata Bulat of Remudu in 1987, wearing her bead cap, *petaa*, of *alai* beads. These are among the most valuable beads the Kelabit have and her cap would have been worth the equivalent of about £20,000 at that time. She is also wearing a necklace of valuable old beads (*bane ba'o*) and brass earrings (*abe*). One of her ears was damaged as a child and had to be re-pierced, which is why her ears are of different lengths.

Plate 12 Judin Lu'un Aio, a young unmarried man, with his hearth-group's buffalo, Pa' Dalih, in 1987. He is wearing a necklace of old beads (*bane ba'o*) including some considered ancient (*ma'on*) but not currently in fashion.

Plate 13 Anyi Perak, a talented Kelabit woodcarver from Pa' Bengar, at work in 1949 on the handle of a bush knife (*tongol*) (BM5, BM9; SM 62). He is using a long-handled *io* knife (BM152-154, SM19-20), holding the handle in his armpit as is usual with this kind of knife to achieve stability. He wears Kelabit male dress of the time: a loincloth (*chawat*), a Kelabit male haircut, leopards' teeth in his ears, heavy brass ear pendants (*abe tawak*) (BM148-149), bead necklaces (*bane*) and *unus* bands around his legs. He also has a touch of the modern world: a pair of small extra ear studs and metal bracelets probably bought in town. Photographer unknown, possibly Tom Harrisson. Photo © Sarawak Museum; accession number unknown.

Plate 14 The hearth-group headed by Monica and Kaz Janowski in Pa' Dalih between 1986 and 1988, with their hearth behind, taken in 1987. Because of the fact that we had a daughter, Molly, born in 1985, we were not able to join another hearth-group; it was considered by the people of Pa' Dalih to be essential for our own (newly adult, due to Molly) dignity that we should have a separate hearth-group. A small feast was held shortly after we arrived in Pa' Dalih in 1986 to give us parental names, by which we were then known for the whole of our stay in the Kelabit Highlands. Photographer Sally Greenhill, © Sally and Richard Greehill.

Plate 15 The interior of the *tawa'* section of Bario Asal longhouse in 1962, showing the raised platform on which bachelors and guests slept and the line of hearths, used only for warmth and cooking snacks, never for cooking rice meals. Photographer unknown but possibly Tom Harrisson or Junaidi bin Bolhassan. Photo © Sarawak Museum; accession number KC/19.

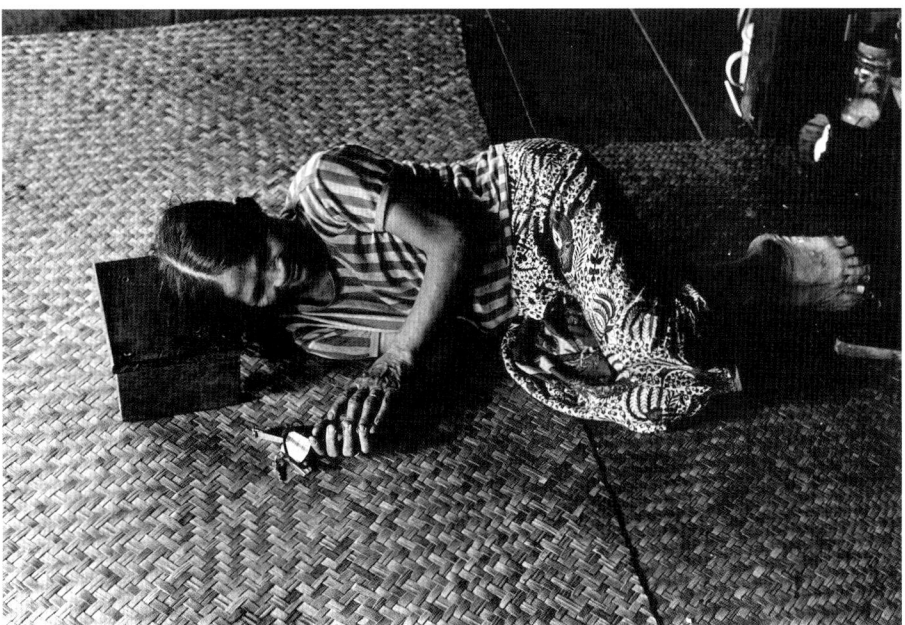

Plate 16 Laba Awa of Pa' Dalih, relaxing near her hearth, 1987. She is lying on a *tarub* mat (BM157-159, SM96-98), with her head on a wooden stool/headrest (*laan oloh*) (BM104, SM24). She is holding the keys to her hearth-group's sleeping/storage room (*télong*).

Plate 17 Women carrying water in *tabang pa'* bamboo carriers (BM160, SM33) along the side of a wet rice field in 1947. They are wearing bead necklaces (*bane*), and, although it would not have been long since these became easily available in Bario, *sarong* (Malay; Kelabit *tekip*) and blouses rather than wearing bark skirts as was the custom until about 1945. Photographer unknown; possibly Tom Harrisson. Photo © Sarawak Museum; accession number Ka 146 (10).

Plate 18 Lugun Bala of Pa' Dalih splitting open giant bamboo (*bulu betong*) for flooring for his hearth-group's field hut (*daan*), using an axe (*uai*) bought in town, 1986. The walling of the *daan*, to his right, is also made of opened-out giant bamboo, as is the roof. He is carrying his bush knife (*tongol*) (BM5a, BM9a, SM62; **see Pl. 65**) at his waist.

Plate 19 A young girl descending the log ladder (*chan*) from the longhouses in Pa' Dalih to wash clothes in the river, the Pa' Kelapang, 1987. She is carrying the clothes in a plastic bucket, an item which has no full equivalent in the traditional repertoire of items which are locally made. A bamboo fence (*taa*) is visible behind her.

Plate 20 Rattan mat (*pin ue*). Rolled up, with cut surface laid on floor visible. Item in the British Museum collection, BM 156.

Plate 21 A group at an *irau* naming feast in Bario Asal longhouse in Bario, 1987. One of the two women is wearing a bead cap (*petaa*) made of valuable old beads, a bunch of ear rings (*abe ringgit*) made of white metal and a necklace of old beads, *bane ba'o*. The other woman is wearing a gold necklace. She and the man have had their previously extended ear lobes cut off and their ears stitched up. The group is sitting on a rattan mat (*pin ue*; BM156; **see Pl. 20**). Both women have an *uyut* basket with them to hold their personal belongings.

Plate 22 A group of boys playing the guitar and singing hymns in Pa' Dalih in 1988. They are sitting in a *télong* belonging to the hearth-group of one of them; young people usually gather in the *télong* rather than near a hearth.

Plate 23 Balang Pelaba of Pa' Dalih playing a bamboo nose-flute (*kelingut*) (BM43, 44, SM30) 1988.

Plate 24 Ra'an Kerayan of Pa' Dalih playing the *sape*, a stringed instrument made of wood (BM39, SM32) 1988.

Plate 25 Lian Balang Pelaba of Pa' Dalih testing out (inside the longhouse!) a toy blowpipe (*put*) made of bamboo, watched by his younger brother Morgan.

Plate 26 Women with town-bought goods loaded into *bekang* baskets (BM73a, b, SM78-79), ready for carrying to other longhouses through the forest in 1987. The woman in the foreground has tattooed arms.

Plate 27 Na'an Tenan of Pa' Dalih scrubbing an iron, town-bought cooking pot with leaves by the Pa' Kelapang river in Pa' Dalih in 1986, to remove the soot which accumulates on the underside of pots through cooking over an open fire.

Plate 28 A barbering session outside the longhouse in Pa' Dalih, 1987. Baye Ripug of Pa' Dalih shaves the side of the head of Balang Muned, to maintain the traditional hairdo for men, where the hair is shaved off the front and sides and kept long at the back. Balang Muned, squatting, is wearing brass ear pendants, *abe tawak* (BM148-149). Baye Ripug, standing, has extended ear lobes but is not wearing ear pendants. The knife being used for shaving is a factory-made knife bought in town.

Plate 29 Sun hat (*ra'ong*), made in Pa' Dalih. Item in the British Museum collection, BM 46.

Plate 30 Sinah Mekat Balang making the beaded centre for a sunhat (like those on BM46-47) in 1962, probably in Bario. She is wearing a necklace (*bane*) of old beads, probably including *alai*, one of the most valuable types in Kelabit eyes. Her tattooed legs can be seen. She is wearing a blouse and *sarong* (Malay; Kelabit *tekip*). Photographer unknown; possibly Tom Harrisson or Junaidi bin Bolhassan. Photo © Sarawak Museum; accession number KF85.

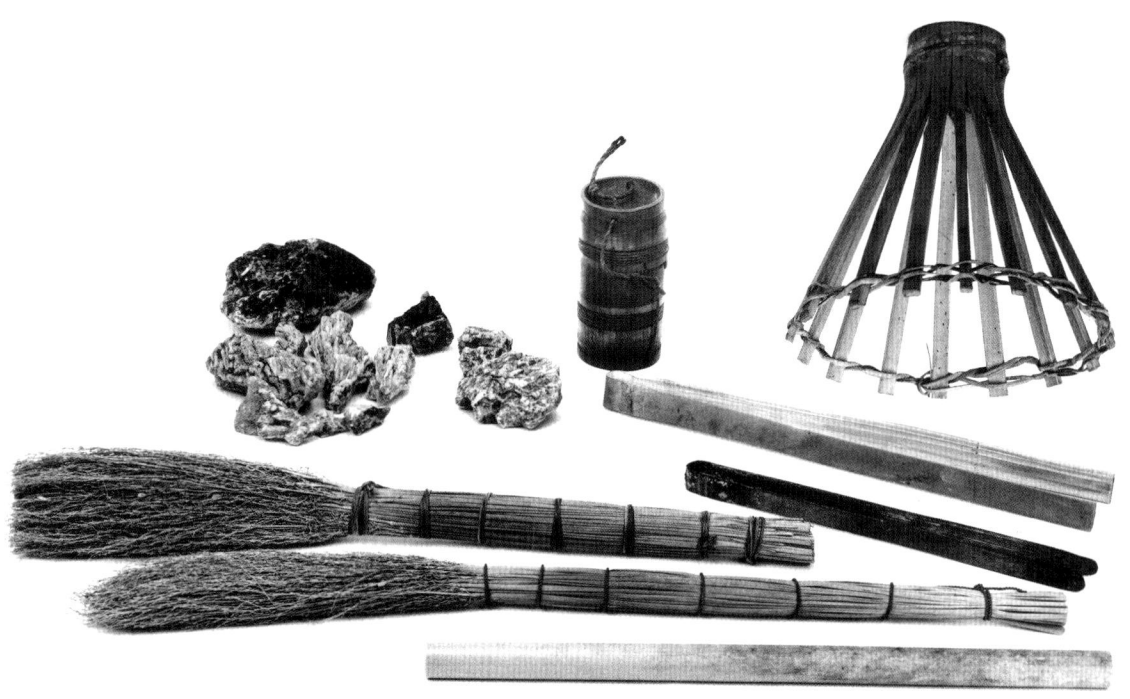

Plate 31 Back row left to right: damar resin (BM 36) (*natang*), container for fire-making equipment (*tik*) (BM 35), prop for burning damar for light (*dawan natang*) (BM 102); from front to back: blow tube for fire (*iop*) (BM101), hearth brooms made of rice stalks (*apoh rongo pade*)(BM 98, BM 100), bamboo tongs for cooking vegetables (*pit krid*) (BM 20), bamboo tongs for fire (*pit apui*) (BM 23). Items in the British Museum collection.

Plate 32 Breakfast in Bario Asal longhouse, 1962. The lady in the middle is Sinah Raja Umong, wife of the chief of the southern Kelabit at that time, Penghulu Miri. She and one of the other ladies is wearing *abe ringgit* earrings (BM 146-147). They are eating soft rice (*nuba' laya'*) from leaves and the side dishes (*nok penguman*) are presented in metal dishes. A container for cooked rice (*belalong nuba'*) (BM 80, SM26) is visible on one side. Photographer possibly Tom Harrisson or Junaidi bin Bolhassan. Photo © Sarawak Museum; accession number KF77.

Plate 33 A rice meal in a *daan* field hut during a cooperative work group day, 1986. Members of different hearth groups eat their own rice, but share side dishes provided by their host.

Plate 34 Packets of salt (*tusu'*) boiled down from brine springs in the forest, wrapped in leaves, bound with rattan (BM 106 (left), BM 107 (right)). Items in the British Museum collection.

Plate 35 A breakfast rice meal (*kuman nuba'*) being eaten near their hearth in the longhouse by the members of the hearth-group headed by Lawe Padan, the headman of Pa' Dalih, and his wife Laba Awa, 1993. Present are three generations: Lawe Padan, his son and daughter in law, and three grandchildren. The two boys are in school uniform, since they are about to leave for the Pa' Dalih primary school. Soft rice (*nuba laya'*) packed in leaves is visible in front of each person, and the side dishes (*nok penguman*), consisting of vegetables and meat, are in the middle, in plastic and china bowls.

Plate 36 A man dispensing sweet tea or coffee at an *irau* in Pa' Dalih in August 1987, wearing a cloth on his head as would have been worn when dispensing rice beer, *borak*, at feasts (*irau borak*) in the past.

Plate 37 Laba Awa of Pa' Dalih by her hearth-group's hearth in 1987, putting dollops of soft rice (*nuba laya'*) into leaves to be wrapped and put aside for eating at a rice meal (*kuman nuba'*).

Plate 38 *Irau* naming feast at Bario Asal longhouse in Bario, 1987. A woman distributes large leaf packets of cooked rice (*nuba'*) to all guests, from a *ra'ing* basket (BM61-62, BM64-65, SM89-90, SM93; **see Pl. 44**); such a basket would also be used for harvesting rice. She is wearing a bunch of heavy ear rings, *abe semera'* (BM 147). Another woman on her left is wearing a bead cap (*petaa*) made of valuable old beads.

Plate 39 At back: holder for cooking implements (BM 31) (*tara bogo*); at front, cooking implements (*bogo*) (BM13-19 and BM24). Items in the British Museum collection.

Plate 40 From left to right: gourds (*be'ong bua' tabuh*) for collecting fish (BM 93) and for seeds (BM37); seed pod ladle (*bak bua' payang*) (BM30); seed pod used in making mats (*bua' payang*) (BM151). Items in the British Museum collection.

Plate 41 *Late' luun* swidden field and forest near Pa' Dalih, 1987. View from the top of one *late' luun*, which is on a steep slope, down over it and *daan* field huts, with another *late' luun* visible in the forest in the background with another *daan*.

Plate 42 Mariar Aran of Pa' Dalih harvesting rice in 1987, using a finger knife. She is wearing a sunhat (*ra'ong*) made in the Ba Rian area at the headwaters of the Kerayan river in Kalimantan (Indonesia) (BM48, SM56) and has on a long-sleeved shirt and gloves to protect her from scratches from the rice stalks and from the sun.

Plate 43 Sinah Ngimat Ulun of Pa' Dalih empties harvested rice from her *ra'ing* basket into the larger *bu'an* basket on Sinah Belan Paran's back during the 1987 rice harvest in Pa' Dalih.

Plate 44 Baskets for harvesting rice and gathering vegetables (*ra'ing*) (BM61 (left), BM64 (right)). Items in the British Museum collection.

Plate 45 Morgan Balang Pelaba of Pa' Dalih at the 1987 rice harvest with a *bu'an* basket (BM66,BM 68, SM86, 91-92) on his back, at the side of a wet rice field. There is a headstrap of grass attached to the *bu'an*, which is an old-fashioned *bu'an bodok* ('pointed *bu'an*'). Other *bu'an* are visible, of the flat-bottomed variety which is more common nowadays.

Plate 46 A wet rice field (*late baa*) near Pa' Dalih just after planting (*nibu*), showing terracing. The field has been made by extending the bed of a stream. Taro (*opa'*) is growing at the edges of one of the terraces.

Plate 47 A young boy carrying young rice shoots in a *bu'an* basket from the nursery bed to the wet field where they will be transplanted, Pa' Dalih 1986. Behind him terraced wet rice fields (*late' baa'*) can be seen.

Plate 48 Harvesting scene in a wet rice field, Pa' Dalih, 1986. The rice is being harvested by a *baya'* cooperative work group. There is a bird-scaring system in the field consisting of lines of rattan with old cracker tins at the corners of the fields.

Plate 49 Group of children in Remudu village, 1987. A rice storage hut (*lepo pade*) made of bark, wood and bamboo with a corrugated metal roof, and a bamboo fence (*taa*) are visible in the background. The children are wearing various pieces of town-bought jewellery made of plastic and metal.

Plate 50 Rice winnowing trays (*reno*) (BM89 (right), BM90 (left)). Items in the British Museum collection.

Plate 51 Sinah Da'on of Bario winnowing rice in 1962, using a winnowing tray (*reno*) (BM88-91, SM67-69). She is wearing a blouse and a *sarong* (Malay; Kelabit *tekip*). In the picture can be seen a row of old Chinese jars, *belanai ma'on*, which at that time were still regarded as very valuable; by the late 1980s, in Pa' Dalih, there was little interest shown in them, perhaps because no more rice beer – made in these jars in the past – was being made by that time with the increasing impact of Christianity. Photographer unknown; possibly Tom Harrisson or Junaidi bin Bolhassan, photographer at the Sarawak Museum. Photo © Sarawak Museum; accession number KF44.

Plate 52 Man with basket for transporting chickens (*belalong la'al*) (BM79) on the entrance platform of a field hut (*daan*) near Pa' Dalih; the walls, floor and roof are of split *betong* bamboo and leaves (*da'un isip*), and the man has an *uyut* basket (BM51-56, BM58, SM84) on his back.

Plate 53 Pa' Dalih men eating boiled meat in a *daan* (field hut) after a night-time hunting trip, 1987. One older man is pressing a piece of fat on a younger man, who seems reluctant to eat it. An *ugam* mat (BM155, SM95) is on the floor.

Plate 54 Harvesting rice in 1987, Pa' Dalih. The women are harvesting while the man is collecting harvested rice from them in a large *bu'an* basket (BM66, 68, SM86, SM91-92). Two of the women are wearing locally made sunhats (*ra'ong*) - one (showing strips of cloth) made in the Kelabit Highlands (BM46-47, SM54-55) and the other made in the Ba Rian area at the headwaters of the Kerayan river in Kalimantan (Indonesia) (BM48, SM56). All are wearing long-sleeved shirts to protect them from scratches from the rice stalks and from the sun.

Plate 55 Monica Janowski with friends from Pa' Dalih crossing a log bridge (*apir*) in the forest between Remudu and Pa' Dalih, 1987. Photographer: Sally Greenhill. Photo © Sally and Richard Greenhill.

Plate 56 Sinah Paran To'oh of Pa' Dalih gathering pineapple shoots (*ubud bua' rosan*) from an abandoned *ira* vegetable and fruit garden, to be eaten as a side dish with rice at the rice meal, 1987. She is putting the shoots into an *uyut* basket (BM51-56, BM58, SM84), visible in the background.

Plate 57 *Ra'ing* basket (BM61-62, BM64-65, SM89-90, SM 93) with wild vegetables gathered for making side dishes (*nok penguman*) for the rice meal, including ferns, wild gingers and mushrooms. A bundle of the leaves which are cultivated for a number of purposes including wrapping rice and other food, *da'un isip*, is also shown. Two types of mat are also visible, the coarser *ugam* (BM155, SM95) underneath and the finer *tarub* (BM157-159, SM96-98) on top.

Plate 58 Two young men from Pa' Dalih returning from a hunting trip in the primary forest stop to rest at the base of a damar tree (*kayuh tomoh*) and a spectacular strangler fig, 1987. One man's carrying basket (*bekang*) (BM73a, b, SM78-79) contains a fish trap (*bubuh*) (BM12, SM57) and bundles of rattan.

Plate 59 Man's carrying basket (*bekang*) and mat for use in the forest and for carrying things from settlement to settlement through the forest (BM73 a and b). Items in the British Museum collection.

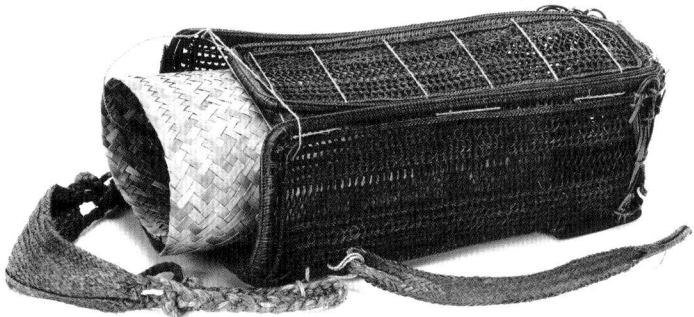

Plate 60 Woman's carrying basket (*bekang*) and mat for use in carrying things from settlement to settlement through the forest (BM72 a and b). Items in the British Museum collection.

Plate 61 A young Pa' Dalih man ready to go hunting, carrying a spear (*boso*) (BM6, SM65), with his *bekang* basket (BM73a, b, SM78-79) on his back.

Plate 62 Ribuh Ulun of Pa' Dalih about to go hunting, 1986. He has his *bekang* basket (BM73a, b, SM78-79) on his back, and his bush knife (*tongol*) (BM5a, BM9a, SM62) is visible in it. In the background is the longer of the two Pa' Dalih longhouses.

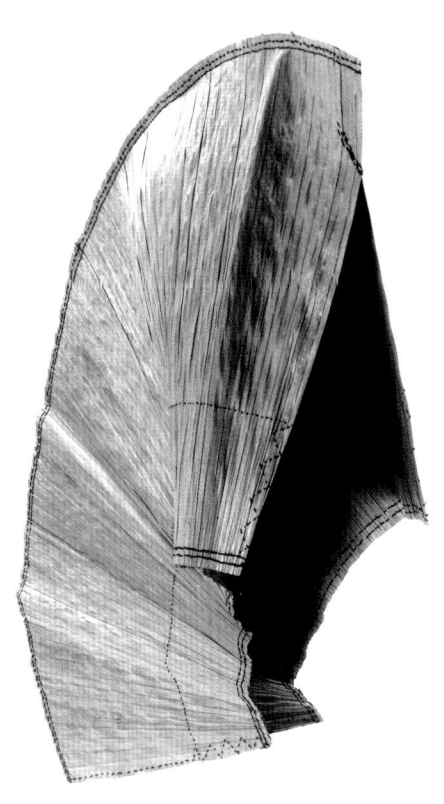

Plate 63 Kelabit boy under a rain cape (*samit*) (BM50) made of *ilad* leaves, 1987.

Plate 64 Rain cape made of leaves (*samit*). BM50. Items in the British Museum collection.

Plate 65 Bush knives (*tongol*) and small-bladed, long-handled knives (*io*), with sheaths, string for hanging around waist and sharpening stone. Back to front: BM 9 a, b, c; BM 5 a, b., with sharpening stone (BM 10) in middle. Items in the British Museum collection.

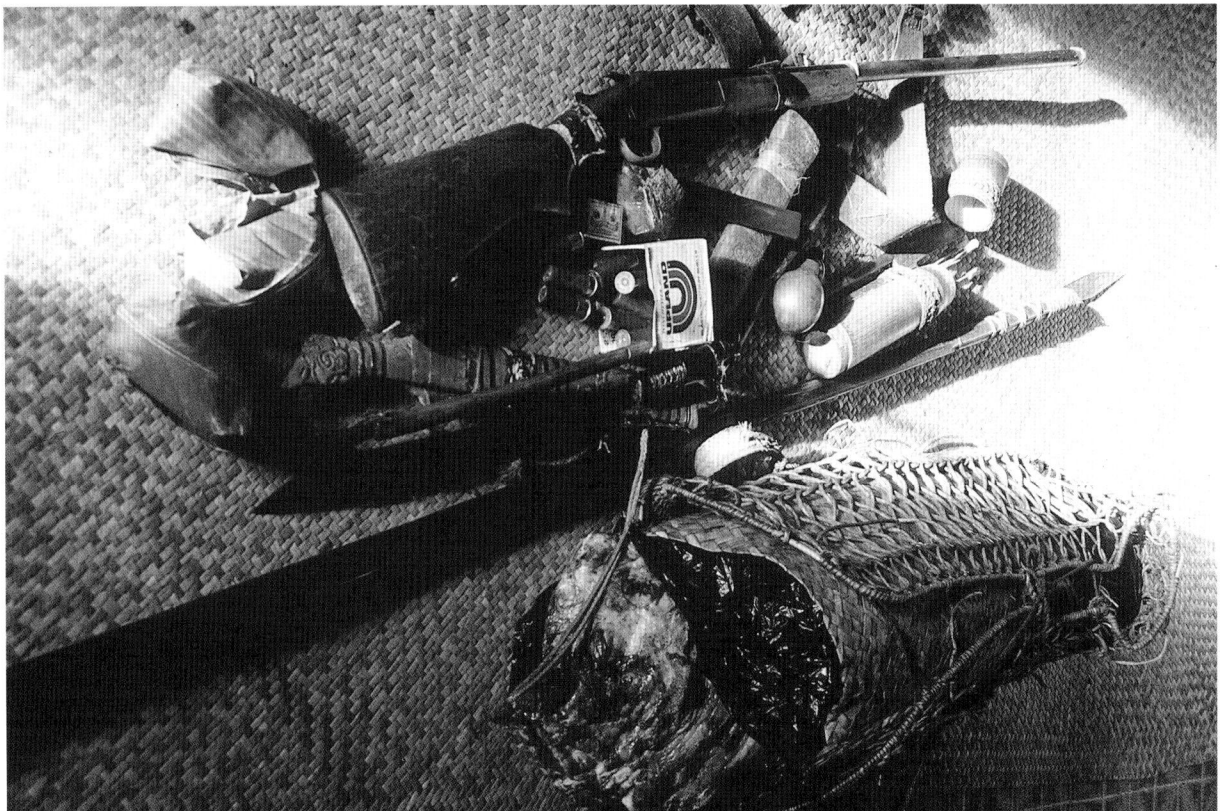

Plate 66 Hunted wild boar meat in a *bekang* basket (BM73a, b, SM78-79) with assorted hunting equipment including shotgun; shotgun cartridges; quiver - *selongan* (BM8, SM63) - filled with darts, *langan*, for use with a blowpipe (*put*); a small gourd, *bua' tabuh kre*, which holds flights (*ra'o*) made of wild sago (*kenangan*) pith for use with blowpipe darts; damar resin for making fires; and a pigspear. A bundle of rice wrapped in a *da'un isip* leaf is also shown, which would be eaten in the forest. Photograph taken in 1993.

Plate 67 Balan, a visitor from the Kerayan area over the border in Kalimantan, making bamboo blowpipe darts in 1987. His quiver, *selongan* (BM8, SM63), filled with darts, *langan*, is beside him. Attached to the quiver is a small gourd, *bua' tabuh kre*, which holds flights (*ra'o*) made of wild sago (*kenangan*) pith. He is sitting on a wooden stool, *laan* (SM23, BM103, BM105), on an *ugam* mat (BM155, SM95).

Plate 68 Sina' Ulit of Bario in 1962 gathering fish in a wet rice field, using a *iap* net (BM94-95, SM72). She is wearing *abe ringgit* earrings (BM146-147). Photographer unknown; possibly Tom Harrisson or Junaidi bin Bolhassan, photographer at the Sarawak Museum. Photo © Sarawak Museum; accession number KF119.

Plate 69 Women collecting snails (*akap*) in a stream near Pa' Dalih in 1986.

Plate 70 Balang Pelaba of Pa' Dalih mending a fishing net (*pukat*) (BM96, SM73) in the *tawa'* part of the main longhouse in 1987, watched by three young boys, who are also doing their homework. The plank walls between the open part of the *tawa'* and the individual rooms (*télong*) are on the right-hand side of the photograph.

Plate 71 Apui Jau, a kinsman from across the border in the Kerayan area of Kalimantan Timur who is particularly skilled at making boats, in 1987, using a town-bought axe (*uai*) to hollow out a log to make a dugout boat (*alud*) for the headman of Pa' Dalih, Lawe Padan.

Plate 72 Three children playing in a dugout boat (*alud*) on the shores of the Kelapang river at Pa' Dalih, 1986. The boat has a seat of split bamboo, as well as smaller seats of planks of wood.

Plate 73 Ribuh Ulun of Pa' Dalih making a paddle (*besai alud*) for a dugout boat (*alud*) sitting on a wooden stool (*laan*) (SM23, BM103, BM105), on an *ugam* mat (BM155, SM95), 1987. A bush knife (*tongol)* (BM5a, BM9a, SM62; **see Pl. 65**), and small long-handled knife (*io*) (BM152-154, SM19-20) are on the mat beside him, as well as another paddle.

Plate 74 Group of people crossing the Pa' Kelapang river near Pa' Dalih in a dugout boat (*alud*) with *bu'an* baskets (BM66, 68, SM86, 91-92) on their backs, on their way to harvest rice in an exchange labour (*kerja baja*) group, 1986.

Plate 75 Baye Ripug of Pa' Dalih preparing to forge the blade of a bush knife (*tongol*) (BM5a, BM9a, SM62; see **Pl. 65**), under a rice storage hut (*lepo pade*), 1987. He is using a Chinese horizontal bellows of the type used nowadays in the Highlands.

Plate 76 Baye Ripug using a town-bought hammer to forge the blade of a bush knife (tongol) on a large stone. He is sitting on a wooden stool (laan) (SM23, BM103, BM105).

Plate 77 Group of tools, all with metal blades. Front to back: boat-making adze (BM2), weeding tool (BM1), tree-felling tool (BM3), model tree-felling tool (BM4). Items in the British Museum collection.

Plate 78 A unidentified Kelabit man using a stone hammer in 1962, probably in Bario, to forge the blade of a bush knife (*tongol*). A bamboo fence (*taa*) can be seen in the background, and the posts of the longhouse under which he is working. Photographer unknown; possibly Tom Harrisson or Junaidi bin Bolhassan, photographer at the Sarawak Museum. Photo © Sarawak Museum; accession number KD/36.

Plate 79 Balang Pelaba and Lawe Padan of Pa' Dalih in the forest, by a stone carving of a human being, 1987. This is believed by the Kelabit to have been made by their ancestors at an undetermined time in the past, at a death *irau/borak* for a prominent individual.

Plate 80 Tom Harrisson with Kelabit men in 1962 inspecting a megalith known as the Batuh Ritung, in the Kelabit Highlands. Harrisson was very interested in the Kelabit megalithic tradition and gathered information on hundreds of megaliths in the highland area, some of which he published in the Sarawak Museum Journal but much of which was never published. Photographer unknown but possibly Junaidi bin Bolhassan. Photo © Sarawak Museum; accession number KH1.

Plate 81 Batu Lawi, north of Bario. This mountain has two peaks, one higher than the other, which are considered to be `male' and `female' respectively and were, in pre-Christian times, paralleled in the erection of paired megaliths in the forest for leading couples at huge *irau* feasts. Photographer unknown. Photo © Sarawak Museum; accession number KH 150.

Plate 82 The plaque erected on top of Batu Lawi by Tom Harrisson to commemorate the success of the Semut I operation against the Japanese, photographed before it was taken up to Batu Lawi. The erection of this plaque in 1946 by Kelabit and Tom Harrisson on the 'female' peak counted as 'irau work' as far as the Kelabit were concerned, equivalent to the erection of megaliths. Semut I involved Harrisson and a party of men from Australia, New Zealand and the UK being dropped into the Kelabit Highlands to organize resistance against the Japanese 'from the inside out'. The Kelabit and other interior tribes living in the highland area were very cooperative and the plaque pays tribute to their bravery. Photographer unknown but possibly Junaidi bin Bolhassan, photographer for the Sarawak Museum. Photo © Sarawak Museum; accession number CH 201

Plate 83 Two young men distributing bamboo skewers of boiled meat at an *irau* naming feast in Bario Asal longhouse in Bario in 1987, from a *ra'ing* basket (BM61-62, BM64-65, SM89-90, SM93, **see Pl. 44**).

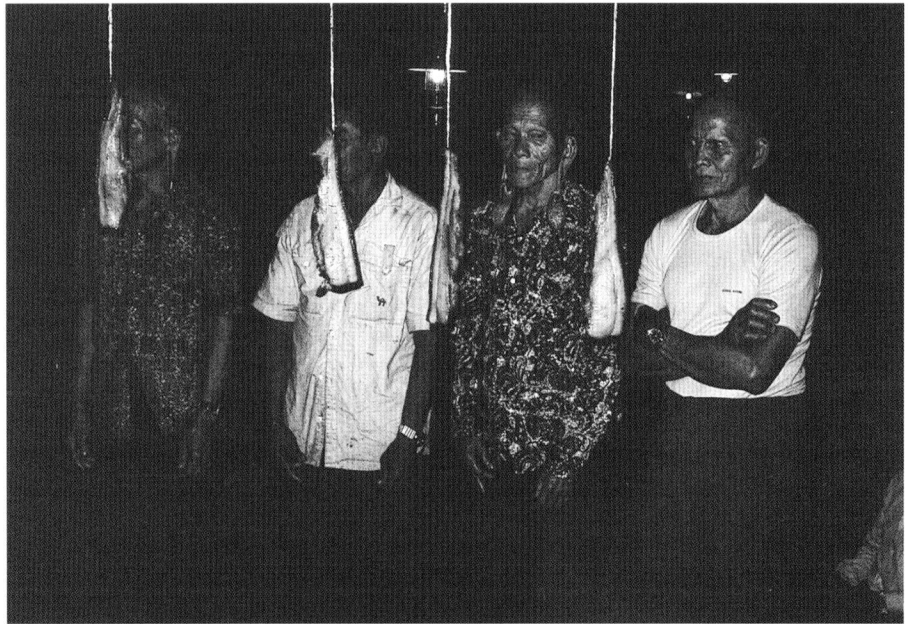

Plate 84 A fat-eating competition at an *irau* in Pa' Dalih in August 1987. The fat is hanging on strings in front of the contestants, who have to eat all the fat on their string as fast as they can. All of the contestants are middle aged or older men.

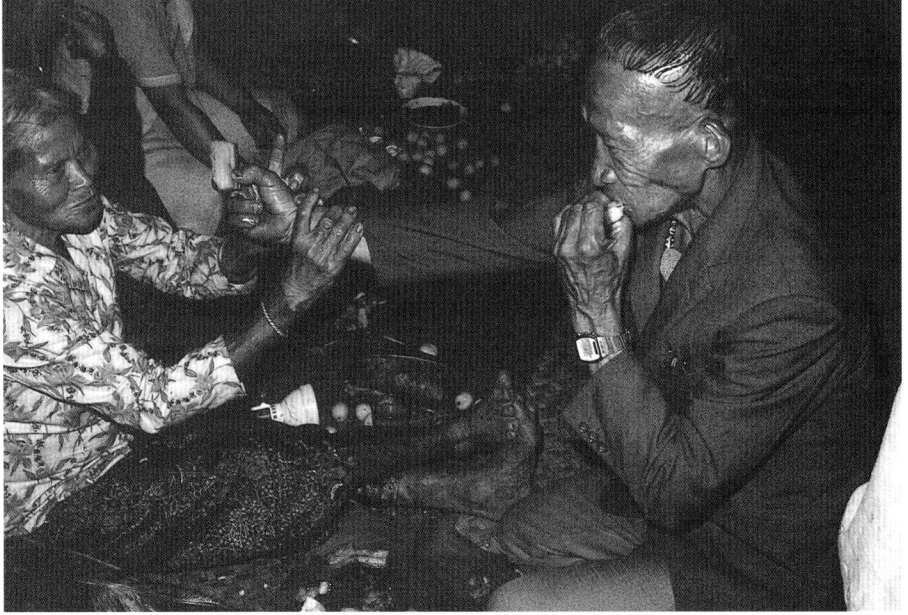

Plate 85 A man and a woman feeding each other fat at *irau* in Pa' Dalih in August 1987. The man is eating the fat but the woman is pushing it away, showing the reluctance of women to eat solid fat.

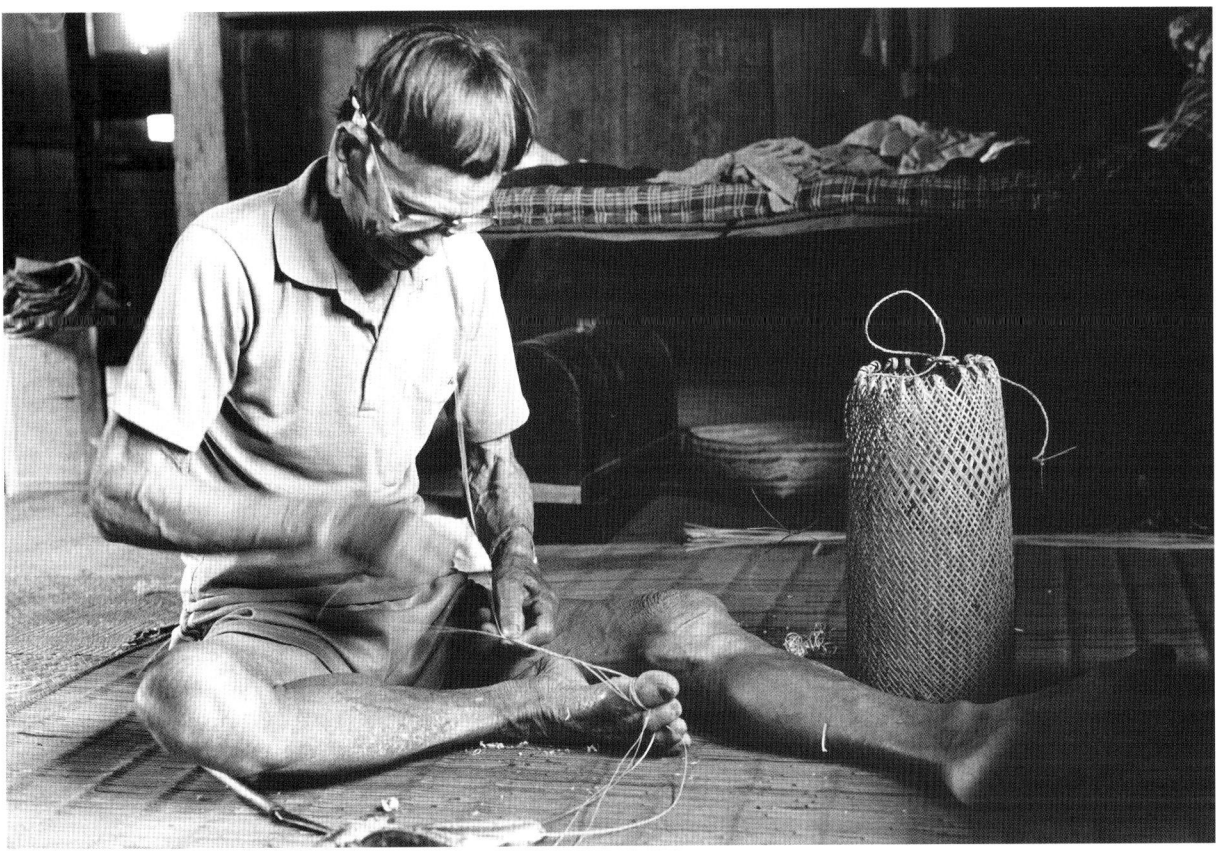

Plate 86 Riwed Bala of Batu Patong preparing strips of rattan (*ue*) for a plaited cord for an *uyut rawang* (SM85, BM58), using a small knife (*io*) (BM152-154, SM19-20), 1987; the *uyut* itself is also visible. He is sitting on a rattan mat (*pin ue*; BM156; **see Pl. 20**). Behind him the floor is covered with other types of mats, *ugam* (BM155, SM95) and *tarub* (BM157-159, SM96-98). Also behind him is his bed, with a bamboo storage container (*a'ab*) (BM82-84, SM74-75, SM77) visible under it, as well as a town-bought sewing machine.

Plate 87 Ra'an Kerayan of Pa' Dalih stripping rattan (*ue*) for craftwork near the longhouses in Pa' Dalih, 1987. He is using a *io* knife (BM152-154, SM19-20). In the background can be seen a pig pen (on the right) and a rice storage hut (*lepo pade*) (on the left).

Plate 88 Balang Pelaba of Pa' Dalih making the base of a rattan basket for transporting chickens (*belalong la'al*) (BM79), 1988. A wooden stool (*laan*) (SM23, BM103, BM105) is visible in the foreground.

Plate 89 Balang Pelaba of Pa' Dalih nearing completion of a rattan basket for transporting chickens (*belalong la'al*) (BM79), 1988. His knife (*io*) (BM152-154, SM19-20) is beside him.

Plate 90 Doo Paran of Pa' Dalih making a bamboo storage container (*a'ab*) (BM82-84, SM74-75, 77), 1987. She is sitting and working on a *tarub* mat placed on top of an *ugam* mat (BM155), and a small *uyut* basket (BM51-56, BM58, SM84) is visible.

Plate 91 Basket for transporting rice from the fields, of the old-fashioned 'pointed' type (*bu'an bodok*) (BM66). It has named patterns on it. Item in the British Museum collection.

Plate 92 Ra'an Kerayan of Pa' Dalih working on the back part of a *bekang* basket (BM73a-b, SM78-79; **see Pl. 59**), watched by his son-in-law Lugun Bala and grandson Michael, 1988.

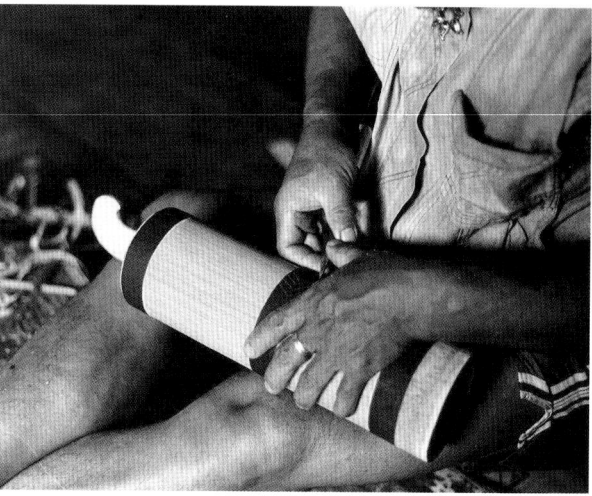

Plate 93 Ribuh Ulun of Pa' Dalih making a bamboo cooking implement (*bogo*) (BM13-19, BM24-26, SM1-3, SM5-10), 1988. He is using a *reno* tray, whose primary use is for winnowing rice, to collect the shavings.

Plate 94 Ribuh Ulun of Pa' Dalih making a holder for bamboo cooking implements (*tara bogo*) (BM31-33, SM16), 1988. He is using a *io* knife (BM152-154, SM19-20).

Plate 95 Lawe Padan, headman of Pa' Dalih, making a bamboo stand (*dawan natang*) (BM102, SM25) for burning tree resin (*natang*) as a lamp, 1988.

Plate 96 Interior of the main longhouse in Pa' Dalih, 1987. Laba Awa, the headman's wife, is sitting in front of her hearth, processing *siar* grass for making *tarub* mats (BM157-159, SM96-98). She is sitting on a wooden stool (*laan*) (SM23, BM103, BM105) on an *ugam* mat (BM155, SM95). Suspended near her hearth is a *royo'* (*tekip* cloth on a spring) in which her grandchild Balan is sleeping. A brass lamp for burning petrol (bought in Brunei) is visible at her hearth. A small hearth broom (*apoh*) made of rice stalks, *rongoh pade* (BM 98-100, SM17-18; **see Pl. 31**) is hanging on the hearth. A *bu'an* basket can be seen suspended upside-down opposite another hearth, on the right-hand side of the photograph, and a *gaweng* basket (BM57, BM78, SM86) is hanging from the short wall which protrudes from the outer wall of the longhouse between Laba Awa's hearth and her neighbour's. A *tarub* mat (BM157-159, SM96-98) is visible rolled up in the distance.

Plate 97 Laba Awa, wife of the headman of Pa' Dalih, making the grass cap (*oloh*) of a sunhat (*ra'ong*) (BM46-47, SM54-55; **see Pl. 29**), 1986.

Plate 98 Balang Pelaba of Pa' Dalih sharpening a weeding tool, *belu'ing* (BM1, SM60; **see Pl. 77**, on left) on the bridge between his hearth group's sections of the *dalim* and the *tawa'* of the main longhouse in Pa' Dalih, 1987. He is using a sharpening stone, *batuh pian* (BM10, SM61).

Plate 99 Kelabit Penghulu Deta' Bala and his son in the Sarawak Museum grounds in Kuching in 1955. Both have the Kelabit male haircut, wear the loincloth (*chawat*) and have bead necklaces (*bane*) and heavy earrings (*abe*). Deta' Bala has shell bracelets (*leko' olo' akap*) (BM150) leg bands (*unus*) and a bush knife (*tongol*) in a beautiful ornate sheath (*binan*) both decorated with goat's hair (BM5, BM9; SM62 includes less ornate examples of *tongol* and *binan*). Photographer Junaidi Bin Bolhassan. Photo © Sarawak Museum; accession number KA 12.

Plate 100 One of the church deacons (*pelayan*) in Pa' Dalih, Ra'an Kerayan, beating a bamboo gong (BM85, SM34) to announce that a church service is about to start.

Plate 101 Kelabit praying on Batu Lawi during the pilgrimage in 1987 to the mountain.

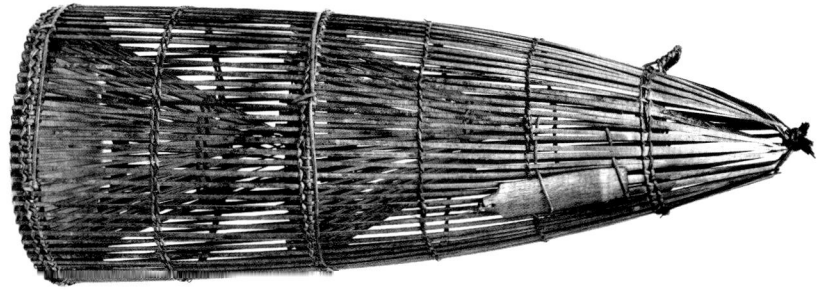

Plate 102 Fish trap made of rattan (*bubuh*). The fish swim in at one end and cannot get out because of the double row of spikes (BM112). Item in the British Museum collection.

Plate 103 Basket for carrying fruit, vegetables or firewood (*kalang*) (BM 70). Item in the British Museum collection.

Plate 104 Baskets for personal possessions (*uyut*) (BM55-56 and BM58). Items in the British Museum collection.

Plate 105 Clockwise from bottom left: 2 baskets for serving and storing food (*a'ab*), rice sifter (*agag bera*), cassava sifter (*agag ubi kayu*) (BM 82, 83, 85, 87). Items in the British Museum collection

Plate 106 Tse Aran of Pa' Dalih gathering *da'un isip* leaves, which are cultivated for many purposes including wrapping rice and food.

Plate 107 Ra'an Kerayan of Pa' Dalih loading up leaf thatch made of *ilad* leaves in a *bekang* carrying basket (*bekang*) (BM73a, b, SM78-79; **see Pl. 59**) for use in roofing his hearth-group's field hut (*daan*), after drying above his hearth-group's hearth in the longhouse. The line of hearths of the *dalim* area of the longhouse are visible at the right-hand side of the photograph.

Plate 108 Tse Aran of Pa' Dalih making a *tarub* mat (BM157-159, SM96-98). The seed pod of the *payang* tree (*bua' payang*) which she is using to smooth out the strips as she weaves them is visible. A roll of *ugam* mats is visible in the background, and cracker tins used to store rice.

Plate 109 Visitor to Pa' Dalih from the Kerayan area in Indonesia plaiting rattan (*ue*) to make a shoulder strap for a basket, sitting on an *ugam* mat (BM155, SM95). His hair is cut in the traditional male style.

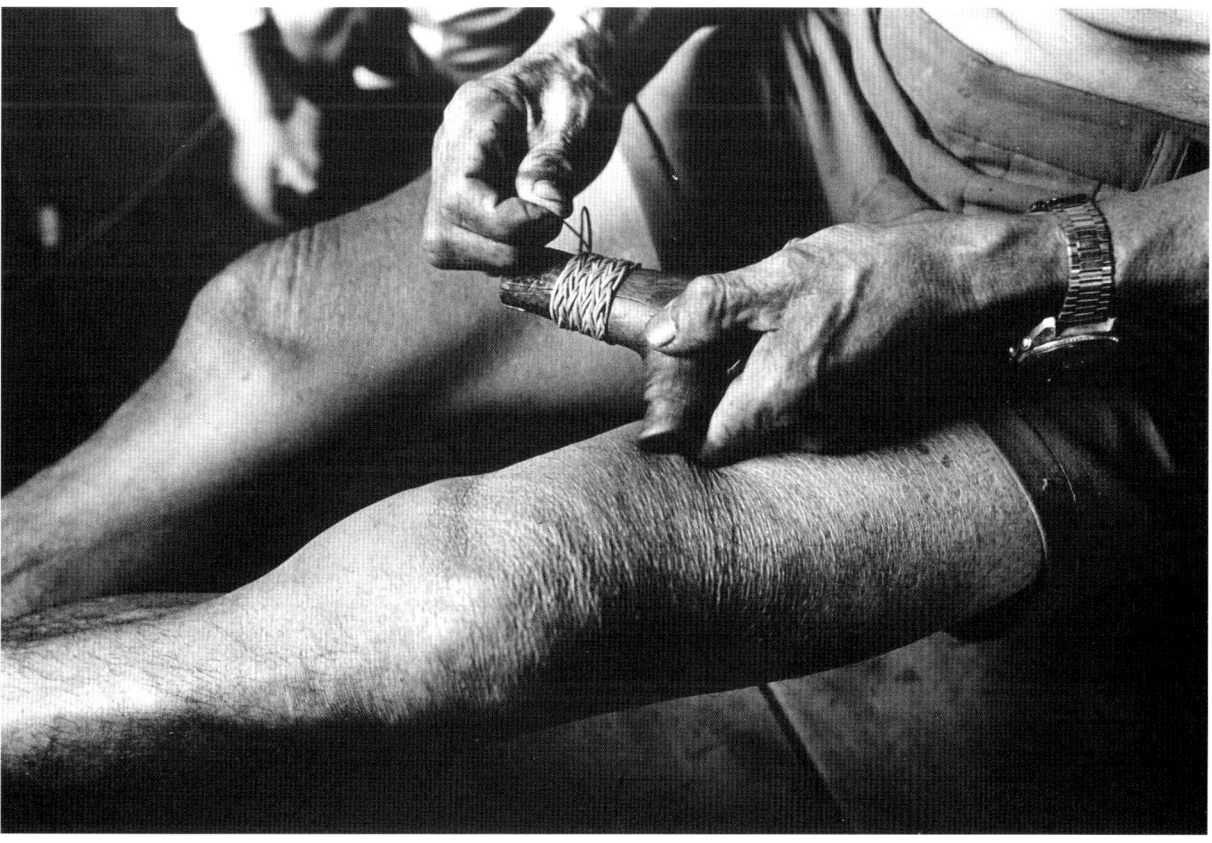

Plate 110 Close up of Balang Pelaba of Pa' Dalih putting new rattan binding on to the wooden handle of a bush knife (*tongol*) (BM5a, BM9a, SM62; **see Pl. 65**).

Plate 111 Young boy making a throw fishing net (*pukat*) in the *dalim* area of one of the two Pa' Dalih longhouses 1986. He is wearing a string of old beads (*ba'o*).

Plate 112 Bala Ukung of Pa' Dalih repairing the end of a 'pointed' *bu'an* basket (*bu'an bodok*) (BM64) with rattan strips 1988. The *ubir* (BM143, SM102) which has been smeared on the outside of the *bu'an* to seal it can be clearly seen. In the background can be seen earthenware pots (*tuning*) made by his wife Na'an Tenan, drying over the fire preparatory to firing. Bala Ukung's ears are extended through the wearing of heavy ear pendants although he no longer wears these.

Plate 113 Na'an Tenan of Pa' Dalih gathering clay from her wet rice field (*late' baa'*) for use in making a batch of earthenware pots (*tuning*) (BM117-121, SM41-44). She is wearing a gold chain; gold is now an important marker of status.

Plate 114 Na'an Tenan pounding clay to make earthenware pots using the heavy *topah tana'* stick (BM132, SM50). She is working on an old *tarub* mat (BM157-159, SM96-98), inside her hearth-group's field hut (*daan*).

Plate 115 Na'an Tenan paddling clay around the *topah tana'* stick to begin to form a pot. The paddles (*pepe'*) (BM134-135, SM47-48) are criss-crossed with an incised pattern.

Plate 116 *Tuning* pots made by Na'an Tenan of Pa' Dalih, drying by the fire in her hearth-group's field hut (*daan*) before final shaping. The *topah tana'* stick, paddles (*pepe'*) and stones for shaping the pots (*batuh tuning*) (BM136, SM46) can be seen. The pots are sitting on an old *tarub* mat on rattan circlets. An old *ugam* mat can be seen in the background.

Plate 117 After drying the pots, Na'an Tenan shapes the lip of a pot using a partially split piece of bamboo, sitting under her hearth-group's field hut (*daan*). She has already shaped the body of the pot by inserting a rounded *batuh tuning* and holding this against the inside of the pot while hitting the pot from the outside with the *pepe'* paddles, finishing with a paddle without an incised pattern to achieve a smooth finish. Other pots, as yet rough and unfinished, lie on the ground.

Plate 118 The tuning pots made by Na'an Tenan of Pa' Dalih being fired on top of the newly-lit bonfire (*taa* - literally 'fence').

Plate 119 Earthenware cooking pots (*tuning*) (left to right, BM125, BM128, BM127, BM130, BM120). BM120 is new, and is part of a batch commissioned in 1987 by Monica Janowski. Items in the British Museum collection.

Glossary of Important Words and Expressions used in the Text

Note on phonemic transcription

While significant vocabularies of Kelabit have been recorded by Blust (Blust 1993) and Amster (Amster, 1998), these are of what Blust terms 'Bario Kelabit' and of what is spoken in Pa' Ukat respectively. The dialect spoken in Pa' Dalih has not previously been recorded, although a few words were recorded by Hudson of the variety of Kelabit spoken in Batu Patong, which is very similar, in the 1970s (Hudson, 1977).

It seems that within the Kelabit Highlands there has been a historic distinction between a southern and a northern grouping of communities, which had different leaders until after the Second World War (when the Government instituted one chief for the whole of the Kelabit Highlands, based in Bario). These two groupings have, and presumably have had for some time, distinct dialects. Nowadays, the three remaining southern communities, Remudu, Long Dano and Pa' Dalih (Batu Patong, although it has a few inhabitants, may be considered part of Pa' Dalih for all practical purposes), appear (at least to my ear, admittedly not trained to recognize subtle differences) the same dialect. This is significantly different from the northern dialect, as recorded by Blust and Amster. However it should be noted that the majority of the inhabitants of Bario are from communities outside Bario, mainly in the south of the Highlands, either displaced at Confrontation or voluntary migrants. I suspect that the variety recorded by Blust may not be the variety spoken by everyone in Bario, particularly by older people who have come from the southern part of the Highlands. However this remains to be investigated.

For what he calls Bario Kelabit, Blust (1993) lists six vowels: a, e (shwa), é (mid-frontal), i, o, and u; and 20 consonants: b, b(h), d, d(h), g, g(h), h, j, k, l, m, n, ŋ, p, ʔ (glottal stop), r, s, t, w and y. He notes that in word-final position the neutral vowel 'shwa' does not occur, so he has transcribed the mid-front vowel as e here. Blust notes the existence of phonemes which begin voiced and end voiceless in Bario Kelabit: b(h), d(h) and g(h), and he suggests that these correspond to p, s and k respectively in Pa' Dalih/Batu Patong.[54]

I would suggest that, for southern Kelabit as I recorded it in Pa' Dalih, the same vowel phonemes exist, but many instances of u in Bario Kelabit are o in Pa' Dalih (e.g. puluŋ in Bario Kelabit is poloŋ– which I transcribe as polong for ease of reading on the part of the non-specialist reader – in Pa' Dalih); a number of instances of e (shwa) in Bario Kelabit are a in Pa' Dalih Kelabit (e.g. da?et in Bario is da?at – which I transcribe as da'at) in Pa Dalih, some instances of e (shwa) in Bario Kelabit are i in Pa' Dalih Kelabit (e.g. kuden in Bario is kudin in Pa' Dalih); and some instances of i in Bario Kelabit are é in Pa' Dalih Kelabit (e.g. lati? in Bario is late? – which I transcribe as late' – in Pa' Dalih). However, I am not able, as a non-specialist, to analyse any pattern whereby this occurs.

As far as consonants are concerned, the only differences are the three phonemes which Blust writes as b(h), d(h) and g(h) for Bario Kelabit. While I agree that Bario b(h) is the Pa' Dalih p, and that Bario g(h) is Pa' Dalih k, I would suggest that d(h) is not s in Pa' Dalih but the sound which I shall transcribe as ch.

I have followed Blust's transcription system – apart from the differences I point out above – including writing final é as e.

I have included words which appear to have been taken into Kelabit as loan words, but not those Malay words which are used but which appear still to be considered to be Malay and not part of the Kelabit language (although clearly the point at which a loan word enters a language and is considered to be part of that language is difficult to pinpoint). Where I have used such words in the text I have indicated that these words are Malay.

Where place names are concerned, I have used the usual spelling of these and not attempted to reconcile this with the phonetic transcription I am using.

Word list

A'ab	open basket for serving food
Abe	ear pendants
Abe tawak	brass ear pendants
Abit /nopar	string twisted from nylon, bark or pineapple leaf fibre
Ada'	spirit
Agag bera	rice sifter
Akap	shell, snail
Alai	valuable variety of old bead
Alud	dugout boat (may have plank sides)
Alud raut anak	children's toy dugout boat
Aluh	pestle
Anak	child
Anit	bark or plant skin
Anit kayuh kilid	bark of the *kilid* tree
Anit kayuh rababar	bark of the *rababar* tree
Anit reman belabo	outer skin of the *reman belabo* plant
Apir	bridge
Apoh	broom
Apui	fire
Atar	flat (fertile) piece of land, used for growing other crops after growing rice for one year
Ba'o	bead
Ba'o bata'	variety of bead ('blue/green bead')
Ba'o burur	variety of bead (cornelian); fashionable and valuable in early 20th century
Ba'o ma'on	bead considered 'ancient' (*ma'on*)
Ba'o rawir	valuable variety of bead normally used in

	late 20th century for bead caps (*petaa*)
Bak	ladle
Baka	wild pig
Bakol tana'	basket for carrying earth
Balang	tiger (mythical, and therefore considered to be a spirit – *ada'* – in Borneo)
Bane ba'o	necklace of beads
Batuh	stone
Batuh pade	'rice stone'; also described as *batuh pera'it* – 'thunder stone'. In pre-Christian times, kept in rice barn (*lepo*) to increase amount of rice stored. *Batuh pade* are probably neolithic tools (see Harrisson 1951; Sellato 1996)
Batuh pian	whetstone
Batuh senupid	monolith or menhir
Batuh tuning	stone used in making clay pots
Bawang	settlement
Barit	patterned, coloured
Baya'	system for exchanging ricefield labour between hearth-groups
Be'ong	gourd
Be'ong bua'tabuh	gourd made from the *tabuh'* fruit
Bekang	basket used for carrying in the forest
Belabo	meat
Belalong nuba'	basket for keeping wrapped parcels of cooked 'soft' rice (*nuba'laya'*) until they are eaten
Belu'ing	weeding tool
Beruang	sun bear
Besai alud	paddle for dugout
Bi'ut	women's basket for keeping sacred plants used in pre-Christian times (vocabulary item collected by Matthew Amster in the Kelabit community of Pa' Ukat; see Amster 1998: 298)
Binan tongol	sheath for the *tongol* knife
Bodok	pointed
Bogo	bamboo or wooden flat spoon for stirring food while cooking
Boko'	small bamboo storage container
Borak	rice beer/feast at which a lot of borak is drunk (such a feast may also be described as *irau*)
Borak ate	feast held to memorialize a high-status person in pre-Christian times
Borak ngelua'anak	feast held to initiate a child into social life, at which the child (*anak*) is smeared (*ngelua'*) with the blood of a sacrificed pig
Boso	spear
Brit	beaded belt
Bu'an	large basket for carrying rice
Bua'	fruit
Bua'lenamud	millet
Bua'lengoh	unidentified grain sometimes grown in small quantities by the Kelabit
Bua'payang	a fruit eaten as a vegetable at the rice meal. The seed pod when dry is used as a tool in mat-making and as a ladle.
Bua'tabuh	a gourd
Bua'tabuh kre	small gourd used for holding flights for use with a blowpipe
Bua'tepang	a fruit, the seeds of which, when boiled, are used to make a red dye for use in mat-making

Bubuh	fish trap
Buda'	white
Bulu'	bamboo
Bunga'ruma'	house decorations (*bunga'* literally means 'flower', and is a Malay loan word)
Burur	body
Cangkul	a hoe-like implement (Malay loan word)
Chan	notched piece of wood used as a ladder
Chawat	loincloth
Da'at	bad
Da'un	leaf (also used to refer to grasses)
Da'un berpah	a variety of grass used in making fine quality mats
Daan	field hut, used to prepare meals, to keep tools and sometimes to sleep overnight
Dalan	path
Dalim	hearth area of the longhouse; literally, 'inside'
Dawan natang	bamboo prop for burning damar resin as a lamp
Dechur	female
Dela'ih	male
Dele	maize
Dele arur	Job's tears; literally 'stream maize'
Di'id	split stick to hold *tuning* and *kudin* clay pots while glazing with damar resin
Doo'	good
Gaing	top
Gawang	basket for carrying personal possessions
Iap	small hand-held net for catching fish
Ilad	fan palm (*Licuala valida*), used in many handicrafts
Ilong	seed
Io	knife
Io perane	harvesting knife
Ira	a dry, shifting field used only for crops other than rice
Irau	feast
Irau ate	see *borak ate*
Irau mekaa ngadan	feast held to name a couple's first child or children, at which they and the child's grandparents also change their names
Item/mitem	black
Iung	mortar
Iop apui	bamboo tube for blowing on a fire to build it up
Kail	strong
Kalang	loose-weave basket (literally 'net'), for carrying vegetables
Kambing	goat (probably a Malay loan word)
Kaum bapa	'fathers' circle', an SIB Church-based group in each parish (*sidang*) (Malay loan term)
Kaum ibu	'mothers' circle, an SIB Church-based group in each parish (*sidang*) (Malay loan term)
Kayuh	wood
Kebun	garden used to grow exotic vegetables, mainly for sale (Malay loan word)
Kelebong	piece of clothing
Kelebong pakai ngarang	skirt worn in dancing
Kelingut	nose flute
Kenangan	sago
Kerja sama	a work party to carry out ricefield labour

	organized through the SIB Church (Malay loan term)
Kerubau	buffalo (loan word, possibly from Malay)
Kikid	porridge made with rice and vegetables/fish/meat
Krid	vegetables to eat with the rice meal
Kudin	large clay cooking pot
Kuer	clouded leopard (*Neofelis nebulosa*)
Kulat	mushroom
Kuloi	sorghum
Kuman	to eat
Kuman nuba'	rice meal (literally 'eat cooked rice')
Kuman peroyong	rice meal shared by all members of a longhouse community, for which all participants provide rice and meat; literally 'eat together'
Laam	sour
Laan	low stool
Laan oloh	low stool for resting the head on
Labuh io	sheath for small knife *(io)*
Lalud	life force (sometimes the Malay translation *kuasa* is used for this concept)
Langan	blowpipe darts
Late'	field in which rice is grown (not necessarily on its own)
Late' baa'	wet rice field
Late' luun	dry, shifting field used for rice and other crops (literally 'field on the surface')
Leko' olo' akap	shell bangle
Lema'ud	work in rice fields
Lemak	animal fat
Lemidik	to clear undergrowth
Lemulun	people (alternative to *lun*)
Lepo pade	storage hut for rice
Let	variety of bead
Liling	small mat to put inside bekang basket to keep the contents in
Lobang ruma'	literally, 'house-cavity'; a term used for the hearth-group or household
Lotong	musical instrument
Lun	person/people (alternative to *lemulun*)
Lun doo	respectable person/people, of good standing in the community (literally 'good person/people')
Lun doo' to'oh	high status person/people (literally 'really good person/people'); also used to refer to leader/leading couple of a group of communities
Lun merar	adult person/people; the leaders/elders of a community
Lun merar to'oh	high status person/people (literally 'really big person/people'); the leader/leading couple of a group of communities
Lun royong	relatives (literally 'people together')
Luun atar	the Earth as referred to in the Song-Story of Tukad Rini (literally 'on the flat place')
Ma'on	very old/ancient
Manangan	hornbill (helmeted and rhinoceros)
Mat	latex used as glue in craftwork
Maya'	to follow
Mera	to drop rice into a dibbled hole in a dry swidden field
Merar	big
Merin	to gather wild vegetables
Moro	to mind ripening rice to prevent pests (mainly birds) from eating it
Mulun	to live
Mulun sebulang	to live alone (used to refer to plants which can grow without human help*)*
Nabang	channel dug in the past as a mark on the landscape at an *irau ate*, or death feast
Naro' samai	to make a nursery bed for wet rice
Natang	tree resin from the *tumuh* or *obong* trees, used to make fire, to burn for light on the *dawan natang*, and to glaze earthenware pots
Nenganoh	to weave bamboo in basket-making
Nepung	to fell a tree
Ngalap	to gather up (used to refer to fruit)
Ngarang	to dance
Ngarik	to cut branches off trees which have been felled
Ngebru	to renew
Ngepo	to soak
Ngeraad	to hunt
Ngotad	to sow sprouted rice in wet fields
Nibu	to transplant rice seedlings in a wet field
No'an	to dibble a hole for rice in a dry swidden field
Nok penguman	side dishes for the rice meal (literally 'something to eat with [rice]')
Nopar	string made of twisted strands of nylon, pineapple leaf fibre or bark fibre
Nuba'	cooked rice
Nuba' laya'	rice cooked as the Kelabit usually eat it, with a great deal of water for a long time and then beaten and packed in leaves, to be eaten warm or cold (literally 'soft rice')
Nuba' to'a	rice cooked so that the grains are separate (literally 'hard rice'*)*
Nutud bupun	to burn off the trees felled in a swidden field, after they have been left to dry and piled up
Okat	stick used in making earthenware pots
Ole buatikan	beeswax
Oloh	head
Orong bua' tabuh	container made from a gourd from the *tabuh* plant
Pa'	water
Pade	rice growing in the field
Pagang	bamboo musical instrument played by tapping with a stick
Parir	poison used with blowpipe
Payah	swamp
Payo	sambhur deer
Pelawat	religious traveller
Pelayan	deacon (Malay loan word)
Penaung	sponsor at a fund-raising event (possibly a loan word but if so origin unclear)
Penghulu	chief (Malay loan word)
Pepe'	paddle used in making earthenware pots
Pesta memotong kek	fund raising event where cakes are sold and auctioned (literally 'cake-cutting party'; Malay loan phrase)
Petaa	cap made of valuable old beads
Pin ue	bamboo mat
Pit apui	tongs for using in the fire

Planok	mousedeer
Polong	forest
Polong i'it	young secondary growth forest (literally 'small forest')
Polong raya	old secondary growth or primary forest (literally 'big forest')
Poren	man's basket holding secret metal objects including knives (vocabulary item collected by Matthew Amster in the Kelabit community of Pa' Ukat; see Amster 1998: 298)
Pra	fragments of old earthenware pots used in making new ones
Pru ue	rattan grater
Pukat	throw net for catching fish (Malay loan word)
Put	blowpipe
Ra'ing	small basket for use in harvesting rice or in gathering vegetables
Ra'o	blowpipe dart flights made of sago pith
Ra'ong	sun hat used in the fields
Ramamo	to weed
Rane	to harvest rice
Raran	wooden framework over the hearth at which rice is cooked, for storing wood, smoking food and storage
Raut	to play or enjoy oneself
Raya	big
Reno	winnowing tray, also used for preparing vegetables
Rongoh pade	rice stalks
Royo'	cloth cradle on a spring in which small children sleep during the day
Ruma' kadang	longhouse
Ruma' rawir	longhouse
Ruma' sebulang	house on its own (separate house, as distinct from a longhouse which contains many hearth-group apartments, also known as houses, *ruma'*)
Samai	nursery bed
Samit	rain cape made of fan palm leaves
Sape	stringed musical instrument
Seitan	Satan, spirit (*ada'*) interpreted under Christianity to be evil (Malay or English loan word)
Selingut	bamboo flute
Selongon	quiver for blowpipe darts
Senape	rice steamed in leaves, eaten as a snack in the fields during harvest
Sengoloh	headstrap for carrying baskets
Sidang	parish of the SIB Church (Malay loan word)
Taa	fence (also used to refer to bonfire on which earthenware pots are fired)
Tabang pa'	bamboo container for carrying water
Tabat	modern or traditional medicine/powerful substance given by spirits to certain men in pre-Christian times
Tabir puet	mat for sitting on in the forest, worn attached to waist before the 1950s
Tana'	earth
Tanem	cemetery (Christian)
Tang	territory belonging to a Kelabit settlement or *bawang*
Tara bogo	bamboo container for keeping *bogo* cooking implements
Tarub	fine mat for sitting on
Tawa'	the 'gallery' section of the longhouse
Tekip	piece of cloth with ends sewn together, worn wrapped around the waist as a skirt (Malay: *sarong*)
Tela'o	barking deer
Temo'a	to gather up dry branches in swidden fields for firing
Tetal	hearth; group of people who use one hearth (hearth-group or household)
Télong	individual rooms for sleeping and storage, built as part of the *tawa'* since the 1960s
Tik	tinder box, used to make fire before matches were available
Tobong	bamboo gong, used to summon people to church
Tongol	large knife used in the forest to clear undergrowth, to fell small trees, and to butcher animals
Topah tana'	heavy stick used to pound clay in making earthenware pots
Topi ulu	bamboo hat worn by men on formal occasions, short for *topi orang Ulu*, literally 'hat of the people of the interior' (Malay loan term)
Tuning	small earthenware pot
Tusuh	salt
Tutok	hammer
Uai	axe
Uai bara'	locally made axe used for felling trees
Uai tetad	locally made adze
Uang	flesh, inside
Uang ruma'	'flesh/inside of the house'; a term used for the hearth-group or household
Uar	creeper
Uat	root
Ubir	substance from inside the bark of the *ubir* tree used to seal any cracks in baskets
Ubud	shoots of plants
Udang	prawn (probably a Malay loan word)
Ue	rattan
Ugam	coarse mat for sitting on
Ulun	human life
Uyut	soft basket for carrying personal possessions

Appendix 2
Materials and Techniques Used in Craftwork

The intention of this appendix is to provide more detailed information about the items in the collection, since these are only referred to but not described in any detail in the main text. It includes descriptions of the structure, making and function of the most important items in Pa' Dalih in the late 1980s, information about the different forest materials used in making the items in the collection, and details of the techniques used in working them.

Section 1 – Major categories of items

Baskets
In Pa' Dalih, baskets were the main means of transporting goods, some were used for temporary storage, and they were sometimes used for decoration of houses in town as *bunga ruma*' (house decorations), in which case they were usually made using bamboo which had been dyed or painted.

Baskets were carried using either a headstrap (*sengoloh*), shoulder straps (*kela'e*) or both, if the basket was heavy. Women almost always used a headstrap, but men did so less often. When not in use, baskets were stored hanging upside down to prevent anything accumulating or living inside. The cord for the shoulder straps, which passes under the basket, was usually used for this purpose. Baskets that did not have shoulder straps were usually provided with a rattan loop at the bottom so that they could be hung upside down (BM65).

Ra'ing
Ra'ing (BM61-62, 64-65, SM89-90, 93, **Pl. 44**) were used for harvesting rice in the fields (**Pl. 43**), attached to the waist, and for gathering wild and cultivated vegetables. They might be used for sundry other purposes, such as distributing meat at an *irau* (**Pl. 38**). When used for harvesting rice, they were regularly emptied into *bu'an* baskets (BM66-68, SM87, 91-92; **Pls. 43, 45, 54, 91**), the larger baskets used for the transportation of rice from the fields to rice barns (*lepo pade*). From the 1970s onwards, *ra'ing* were normally made with flat bottoms (BM61-62, BM65, SM89-90, SM93) but it would appear that this is copied from the style made by the related people living in the Ba Rian area across the border in Kalimantan (see below, section on *buan* baskets). Until about the 1960s the Kelabit made *ra'ing* (and *bu'an*) with pointed bottoms; there is an example of a *ra'ing* with a pointed bottom in the British Museum collection (BM64; **Pl. 91**). *Ra'ing* were usually made with headstraps only, used when the basket was used for gathering vegetables, and sometimes used to tie the basket to the waist when harvesting. However BM62, a particularly large example, has shoulder straps too. *Ra'ing* were made in a variety of sizes and shoulder straps were considered necessary, in addition to the headstrap, when carrying a heavier load.

Ra'ing were made principally of bamboo and rattan; the bamboo body (described literally as 'body', as for a human being, using the term *burur*) was made first, by women, and the rattan frame, binding and base were added afterwards by men. Headstraps, made of grass, were made by women. *Ra'ing* were, before use, smeared inside with *ubir* (BM143, SM102) in order to seal them and stop any small holes. BM62 and BM65, however, have no *ubir* inside them. BM65 is as yet unused, and it would have been smeared with *ubir* before being used. BM62, which is made of painted strips of bamboo, appears to have been intended for display purposes as a house decoration (*bunga ruma*') (see Chapter 3) and for this reason *ubir* has not been applied.

Bu'an
Bu'an (BM66-68, SM87, 91-92; **Pls 45, 91**) were used only for harvesting rice. They were used not only for the transportation of the grain to rice barns from the fields, but also as units of measure. A tally was kept of how many baskets of rice had been harvested from a given field, of a given variety of rice, and of how many baskets had been carried by people working in the cooperative work exchange system from the fields to the rice barns. This means that all *bu'an* needed to be of uniform or nearly uniform size. *Bu'an*, like *ra'ing*, were, until about the 1960s, made with pointed bottoms – and were described as 'pointed' (*bodok*). Examples of *bu'an* with pointed bottoms are BM66 and BM67 and SM91 and SM92 (**Pls 45, 91**). From the 1970s, however, they were made with flat bottoms, a style which was probably copied from that usual among the people living in Ba Rian area across the border with Kalimantan. It is probable that the 'pointed' *bu'an* were more suitable for sloping dry fields which were the norm in Pa' Dalih until recently, while wet fields, with flatter land around the edges, have been made for much longer in the Rian river area. Example of *bu'an* with flat bottoms are BM68 and SM87. BM68 was actually made in Ba Rian area in 1960 and bought from there by a Kelabit woman of Pa' Dalih at that time. It is a particularly fine example of a *bu'an* of this type, made as it is with the highly valued rattan called *ue tak* rather than the more usual *ue pa'it*. *Bu'an* were carried using both a headstrap and shoulderstraps, in order to distribute the weight as much as possible over different weight bearing parts of the body. BM67 has no headstrap but it would probably have been used with one. Some 'pointed' *bu'an*, such as BM66 and SM91, were decorated (*barit*) with patterns that have names (**Pl. 91**). These are said by informants to have only descriptive significance. However, the name of one of the patterns refers to spirits, *ada*', and another to the pre-Christian ceremony of *lua*' or *ngelua*'

(smearing with pig's blood).

As with ra'ing, *bu'an* were made principally of bamboo and rattan; the bamboo body was made first by women and the rattan frame, binding, base and lip were added afterwards by men. Shoulder straps were made of rattan, by men. Headstraps were made of grass, by women. Like *ra'ing*, *bu'an* were smeared with *ubir* (BM143, SM102) inside before use in order to seal them and stop any small holes, and all the *bu'an* in the collection are used ones which have had *ubir* applied. In the case of BM66 (**Pl. 91**), the matt inside and shiny exterior of the bamboo has been used to create the pattern by reversing the strips. The shiny exterior of the bamboo has not taken the *ubir*, which does not adhere to the slippery surface, and this makes the pattern particularly clear. Perhaps because the *ubir* has not taken everywhere, *ubir* has in this basket been applied both to the inside and to the outside of the basket. On the outside, it has adhered to the places where it has not adhered inside, thus ensuring that all areas are smeared with *ubir*, either inside the basket or outside. Some *buan'* baskets have an outer casing made of strips of rattan (BM68).

Kalang

Kalang (BM69-70, 76 and SM88; **Pl. 103**) are simple baskets normally used by women and girls (but made by men, since they are made of rattan, and sometimes used by them) when gathering wild or cultivated fruit or vegetables. They could also be used for carrying firewood, although bringing in firewood is a task that men usually carried out and they used *bekang* baskets for this. The word *kalang* literally means net, and these baskets are open-weave, and quite quickly made. In the two collections there are four examples of *kalang*. Two are made of split rattan in a simple horizontal and criss-cross pattern (BM69 and SM88), another is made in the same style but for a child in a smaller size (BM76), and one is made of whole rattan in a looping interwoven style (BM70). *Kalang* might be used with either a headstrap or shoulder straps or both, if wished; BM69, 76 and SM88 have shoulder straps and BM70 has a headstrap. They were usually used with a small mat (*liling*) inside to keep the contents from falling through the holes; BM69 has a *liling* mat to go with it.

Bekang

Men used *bekang* in hunting – to carry back the meat – and in bringing back firewood. Both men and women used *bekang* to transport goods between settlements, particularly town-bought goods. There was no other way of transporting goods out of Pa' Dalih in the late 1980s since there was no road. They were also used for personal items and food for the journey.

There were different styles of *bekang* for men and women: while men's (BM73, SM78-79; **Pl. 59**) are open at the front, relying on the small mat used inside (*liling*) to hold things in, women's (BM 71-72, SM80-81; **Pl. 60**) have a flap at the front to assist in holding things in, though they also have a *liling*. The significance of the difference is probably in the fact that without a front flap, men's *bekang* were more versatile in what shapes they could carry, which relates to the fact that men used them for carrying pieces of animal. Men's *bekang* were about 6 inches longer than women's.

Women's *bekang* were more ornate although no less functional, and more carefully made; men's tended to be purely functional. There was a pretty standard size for *bekang*, with little variation. There was also little variation in the structure of them, although some are more beautifully executed than others; of the two women's *bekang* in the collection, BM71 is more finely made than BM72 (**Pl. 60**).

Bekang were made of two basic pieces, with a third piece for women's. The first is the back, which consists of a strong rectangular rattan frame with rattan woven across it and wooden board at the bottom to strengthen it. The second is a much longer rectangular rattan frame with rattan also woven across it, which is curved round to follow the back piece to form the sides and bottom of the basket, and which is held together at the front with strong string (*nopar*) made of rattan or nylon. In women's *bekang*, a further rectangular frame of rattan with rattan woven within it attached at the bottom forms a front to the basket. At the bottom of the *bekang* there is a coiled piece of rattan to provide support for the contents and protection from the ground.

Bekang, which are entirely made of rattan, were made by men, although the *liling* mat inside would be made of grass by women. Men almost always carried *bekang* using shoulder straps only; women often used headstraps as well as shoulder straps.

Bekang were made for children too, and the kinds for girls and boys follow the same structure as those for their elders (BM 74-75, SM82-83).

Gawang and uyut

These were used for interchangeable purposes although they are somewhat different in structure. Both kinds of basket were made of a variety of rattan called *ue tak*, which does not grow in the highland forest and had to be brought from lower altitudes. While *uyut* (BM51-56, 58, SM84; **Pls 21, 56, 86, 104**) have drawstrings at the top and a pattern woven into them, *gawang* (BM57, BM78, SM86) do not have drawstrings and are not decorated with patterns. However, they were often woven using both plain rattan and rattan which has been dyed black, so that the crossing over of the two colours makes a kind of blanket pattern. Both types of basket were considered the speciality of the Penan hunter gatherers, although other tribes could make them too. Some Kelabit knew how to make them, but they were never as skilled as Penan or as the Kenyah. This was, I was told, true even of Kelabit like those of Long Lellang who live at lower altitudes where they can get *ue tak*. Kelabit often buy these baskets from the Penan.

Both *uyut* and *gawang* were used to carry personal possessions. The craftmanship in them was much admired if they were well made and they were quite highly prized if they were good examples. They were bought and sold for high prices, particularly if they were made by Penan. Both types of basket came in a wide variety of sizes, and this is represented in the collection. The Kelabit themselves often made *uyut* baskets to give as gifts to each other and such baskets might be decorated with beads and usually carried messages woven into them, often Christian messages (BM51-53, BM55). Such baskets were also given as prizes at school, for example for achievements in sports (BM54). Small *uyut* baskets were made, carrying Christian messages, to be used as baskets for collecting money in church; in the collection are those which were being used until 1988 in the parishes of Pa' Dalih and nearby Remudu (BM59-60; **Pl. 3**). There is another variety of *uyut* which is open weave and which is therefore more quickly made called *uyut rawang*, of which there is an example in the collection which I commissioned for the collection from Riwed Bala of Batu Patong near Pa' Dalih (BM58; **Pl. 86**).

A'ab

These are broad, open baskets of different sizes (BM82-84, SM74-75, 77; **Pls 90, 105**), with flat bases made of bamboo with a rattan frame, lined with *ubir* (BM143, SM102) in order to seal them. They were used for storage and serving of fruit and sometimes cooked rice parcels (*nuba'*). They were usually plain, but were sometimes made with a pattern woven in using dyed bamboo (BM84) and some were painted using paint bought in town (SM77).

Agag

This is a basket which is slightly concave and which is woven loosely of bamboo with a rattan frame. The loose weave is so as to leave holes between the strips of bamboo to enable the basket to be used for sifting. There are two types of *agag* in the collection: the *agag bera*, which is for sifting uncooked but husked rice (BM 85-86, SM71), and the *agag ubi kayuh*, for sifting grated cassava (BM87, SM70; **Pl. 105**). The difference between them is purely in the size of the holes, bigger for cassava than for rice.

Belalong

This is a lidded basket that is taller than it is wide. There are two types of *belalong*: that used for storing cooked rice packets (*nuba'*) until they are eaten, *belalong nuba'* (BM80, SM26; **Pl. 32**), and that used for keeping hens with baby chicks, *belalong la'al* (BM79; **Pl. 52**). The *belalong nuba'* is made of tightly woven bamboo, with a rattan frame. It has a square body that closes in at the top to a round neck, with a tightly fitting lid of bamboo held on to the body of the basket with a rattan carrying handle. The *belalong la'al* is made of rattan and is roughly the same shape as the *belalong nuba'* but is very loosely woven, with big holes between the strips of rattan of which it is made. It has a simple lid closing the hole at the top, also made of strips of rattan, and a carrying handle of rattan.

Rain capes (samit)

Rain capes, *samit* (BM30, SM66; **Pls 63-64**) are made in a fan shape, using a double thickness of the leaf of the fan palm, *ilad*, which is also used for wrapping food. The two pieces are sewn together – the examples in the collections have been sewn using wool purchased in town to achieve a decorative effect – so as to make it possible to place the cape over the head with one end open in the front and the rest over the head and hanging over the back. This means that any basket carried on the back will also be covered. People in Pa' Dalih normally bought rain capes in the Kerayan area, since the fan palm *ilad* (*Licuala valida*) used in making them does not grow near Pa' Dalih. However, I was told that *samit*

were sometimes made in Pa' Dalih, although I did not see any that were.

Mats

Three types of mat were made and used in the Kelabit Highlands in the late 1980s and 1990s: firstly *ugam*, (BM155, SM95; **Pl. 1**) which are quickly made mats of the coarse *berpah* grass, secondly *liling*, (BM69b, 71b, 72b, 73b, 74b, 77, SM99; **Pl. 59**), which are small mats also made of *berpah* grass used to line *bekang* and *kalang* baskets and to sit on in the forest, and thirdly *tarub* (BM157-159, SM96-98) which are finer mats made of *siar* grass, often weaving some green and red dyed grass into the mat to create a pattern (**Pl. 108**). While the red dye used is natural, made using the seeds of a fruit, the *bua' tepang*, which is pounded in a pestle and mortar, mixed with water and then boiled in bamboo, the green dye was purchased in town. *Ugam* are everyday mats which were used in front of every hearth and were often left out, but hearth-groups tended to possess fewer *tarub*, and they were prized and cared for, being carefully rolled up when not in use.

Women made mats, and most women in Pa' Dalih could make *ugam*, although they usually bought them from the nearby community of Remudu which has lots of *berpah* grass. However, only certain women were considered skilled in making *tarub*, and they made such mats for others for payment.

There is another type of mat of which there were a few in Pa' Dalih but which were not made there: the rattan mat, *pin ue* (BM156; **Pl. 20**). Since this is made of *ue tak*, a variety of rattan which does not grow in the Highlands, such mats were not made in the Highlands. While *ugam* and *tarub* were woven using a plaiting technique across the body of the mat, *pin ue* were made by laying carefully split strips of rattan with the outside, shiny side up next to each other and then joining these together by passing cord (made of nylon nowadays) through the strips. The sides of the mat were bound together by finer strips of rattan woven down the side. *Pin ue* were made by Kenyah and Kayan people, and also by Kelabit living in communities outside the Highlands. They were much prized. They were also used by Kelabit living in town as floor covering, although not often to sit on since in town Kelabit sit on chairs.

Boats (alud)

The Kelabit in Pa' Dalih made dugout boats (**Pl. 72**) using a tree trunk, sometimes adding plank sides to build them up a bit. These were used for fishing on the river and were also used for transporting earth in wet rice fields when these were being extended. There was expertise in Pa' Dalih in making *alud*. However, in Pa' Dalih when I was there in 1986-88 it was usual to ask a man called Apui Jau living in a community in the Kerayan area over the border in Kalimantan, related to the people in Pa' Dalih, who was considered particularly expert in boat-making. The person who commissioned the boat would assist the expert in the work of making the boat, carrying the selected tree from the forest, seasoning it by roasting over a fire and digging out the centre of the tree using a locally-made adze (*uai tetad –* BM2; **Pl. 71**).

Toy boats (*alud raut anak*) were one of the few toys that children in Pa' Dalih had. There is one in each of the collections (BM111, SM53).

Section 2 – Materials used in handicraft work

A wide range of materials from both secondary and primary forest are used in craftwork in Pa' Dalih, and are present in the items in the collection. In Appendix 3 I have listed all the species which I recorded as being in use for craftwork in Pa' Dalih in 1986-88. The identifications are mostly based on Christensen's work (Christensen 2002). Christensen recorded a more exhaustive lists of species used in craftwork than I did, on the basis of her discussions with informants in Pa' Dalih in the early 1990s. Although many of the species which she recorded were undoubtedly only used on rare occasions, it should be noted that, as can be seen in the catalogues, I did not always record the species used (this particularly applies to types of wood), and in such cases these may well include some of those which Christensen has listed as used.

The majority of the species listed are wild. I would categorise the rest as semi-wild. Christensen lists some of the species as cultivated, explaining that she uses this term to indicate that a species receives attention throughout its life.. However, she admits that the distinction between 'cultivated' and the category she also uses, 'semi-managed', is not always clear-cut (Christensen 2002: 50). My own observations are that species used in craftwork receive little attention. Christensen does not say whether the species she lists as 'cultivated' exist in the wild in the area, and I am not able to comment on this for sure, but it seems likely that they have in fact been brought in from the wild (if not in the Kelabit Highlands then from the forest in another part of Borneo). Insofar as the Kelabit attitude to whether they are wild or not is concerned (and this is arguably more important than whether they are actually wild or cultivated), I have discussed in Chapter 4 (in the section on the the rice meal) the fact that the Kelabit see plants other than rice as being capable of 'growing by themselves' (*mulun sebulang*), and as needing minimal attention; thus it could be argued that they categorise all plants except rice as wild.

Forest materials used for handicrafts and building

Bamboo (*bulu'*)

Many varieties of bamboo were used, selected for size and working characteristics. The walls of the largest-bore bamboo (*bulu' betong*), were used as a solid substance – to make, for example cooking implements, *bogo*, fire and cooking tongs (*pit*), the handles of small knives (*io*) and lice combs (*kasib*). *Bulu' betong* was used whole where a large container was required, such as for the *tara bogo* used for holding cooking implements, gongs (*tobong*), water carriers (*tabang pa'*), bamboo stands for burning damar resin (*dawan natang*) and for the musical instruments *lotong* and *pagang*. Sometimes young *bulu' betong* was used for containers, such as drinking vessels, *obe*. *Bulu' bayuh*, a smaller bamboo, was also used to make objects requiring a smaller bore – harvesting knives (*io peraneh*) and the tube for blowing up the fire (*iop apui*), are made of this bamboo.

Another smaller bamboo, *bulu' poran*, was used for making into strips for weaving into the bodies of baskets (*ra'ing, bu'an, belalong nuba', a'ab, agag, reno*), the inner caps of sun hats and *topi (orang) ulu* hats. A medium sized bamboo, *bulu' telang*, was used to make containers such as the tinder box (*tik*), the quiver for blowpipe darts (*selongan*), nose flutes (*kelingut*) and mouth flutes (*selingut*). Large-bore *bulu' betong* could be used to make floors and walls, split and opened out; in the late 1980s it was used for floors in temporary buildings like field huts (*daan*). It was also used for making suspension bridges over rivers and streams, together with rattan for binding it together. Bamboo was also used to make fences (*taa*), bound together with rattan (**Pls 19, 49**).

Rattan (*ue*)

Rattan from the primary forest (**Pl. 58**) was extensively used for binding parts of things together – brooms, baskets to their frames, parts of fish traps, spear blades to handles, blades of knives to their handles, agricultural tools and axes to their handles, bridges, fences. *Ue kusah, ue lengan, ue tak* and *ue pa'it* are the Kelabit terms for the varieties used for binding. *Ue kusah*, which is a thicker rattan, was used for the frames of bamboo baskets (*ra'ing, bu'an, a'ab, belalong nuba', agag, reno*). *Ue rabun* was usually used for the lips of *ra'ing* and *bu'an* baskets.

Rattan was also used for weaving mats and baskets. One type of mat (*pin ue*) and *uyut* and *gawang* baskets were made of *ue tak*, which was considered a high-quality rattan; but, since it does not grow in the Highlands, it was rarely used in Pa' Dalih. *Ue kusah* was used, made into strips, for making *kalang* baskets of the most common type. Some *kalang* baskets were made using the whole rattan; BM70 is made of *ue repit* for the frame and *ue rabun* for the body. *Bekang* baskets were made of *ue rabun* or sometimes *ue kusah* or *ue lengan*. Until about the 1960s, rattan was used to bind together the materials used in the construction of longhouses, and in the late 1980s it was still used to bind together the parts of field huts (*daan*).

Wood (*kayuh*)

Many varieties of wood were used, varying from very hard to quite soft, and deriving from both old and young forest. The hardest, and therefore the best and longest-lasting, was considered to be that which the Kelabit called *belaban*. There are two varieties of *belaban*: *belaban sia'* ('red belaban') and *belaban buda'* ('white belaban'). Wood was used for pig spears and blow pipes, musical instruments (*sape*), for the handles of knives (*tongol* always have wooden handles; *io* sometimes do), axes and weeding tools, for ladles (*bak*), for boats, for *bogo* cooking utensils, for pestles and mortars, for the bases of *bekang* baskets, for stools, for toys (toy boat, tops), for sticks and paddles for pot-making and for replacement handles of shotguns. It was used for notched log ladders (*chan*) at the entrances to the longhouse, which were also used to get over fences or down slopes, such as down to the river in Pa' Dalih (**Pl. 19**). After chain saws made their appearance from the 1970s onwards, it had become much easier to work wood and the floor and walls of longhouses were in the '80s and '90s always made of wood.

The fact that corrugated metal was used for longhouse roofs was because of its prestige value; also, making wooden tiles, which were used very widely until the 1960s, is very time consuming, since modern tools cannot easily be used. Planks and posts are, if they are made of good quality, hard wood, inherited from generation to generation (**Pl. 1**). In the past, only the longhouse itself ever had wooden floors or roof; field huts (*daan*) and rice barns (*lepo pade*) were made of bamboo, rattan and grass. In the 1980s, even *daan* and *lepo* were often made partially of wood, particularly if they were built near wet rice fields which were intended to be permanent.

Clay (*tana'*)

This comes from certain spots in wet rice fields (**Pl. 113**). It was used until the mid-1970s to make earthenware pots.

Tree bark (*anit kayuh*)

The bark of two trees was used in the late 1980s in Pa' Dalih: that of the *kilid* tree (*anit kayuh kilid*) (BM140-141, SM101) and that of the *rababar* tree (*anit kayuh rababar*) (BM142, SM100). The bark from the *talun* tree (which appears to be called a *kilid* tree when it is young) was used until the Second World War to make bark cloth for skirts for women, loin cloths for men, and short jackets worn when it was cold. It would appear that even before the Second World War some cloth was traded up to the Highlands and people wore a good deal of this, although in the form of traditional short skirts and loincloths. During the war it became harder to get cloth and it would appear that people reverted to some extent to using bark cloth. However after the Second World War cloth became available again – it is, of course, one of the easiest things to trade, being light and therefore easy to carry long distances – and it seems that the Kelabit very quickly began to wear cloth after the war in the form of 'Western' clothes as well as Malay *sarong*. Bark cloth was no longer made in the 1980s nor did there appear to be any left in Pa' Dalih.

The principle use of bark in the late 1980s was to make string (*abit*) for binding and tying things together. It is more flexible but weaker than rattan. However, it was often replaced with nylon string (*nopar*), which is very strong.

Bark was also used in the forest for flooring for shelters for the night.

Creeper (*uar*)

Creeper was used for binding things together and for making cord. It fulfilled a similar function to bark string. By the late 1980s, it was often replaced with nylon string (*nopar*). Three varieties were recorded as being used during fieldwork and are used in the collections: *uar bekar*, *uar ubu* and *uar reman*.

Leaves and grasses (*da'un*)

Leaves were widely used for wrapping food or anything else that needed to be enclosed, carried or stored in a protected way. They were also used for wrapping salt cakes made at brine springs in the forest (**Pl. 34**). Although when in the forest any largish leaf might be used, for example for wrapping hunted meat, the people in Pa' Dalih cultivated, in small plantations, a variety of leaf which they called *da'un isip*, and which they used for wrapping rice (**Pls 38, 57, 106**). This is a very large leaf that grows on a long stalk straight out of the ground. They also made significant use of the leaf of a palm that they call *ilad* (*Licuala valida*). It is *da'un ilad* that was used for wrapping salt. It was also used for making sun hats (*ra'ong*) and, since it is waterproof, for rain capes (*samit*) and for thatching. The leaf of the sago palm (*kenangan*) was used for making brooms, *apoh*.

Grasses (described as types of leaf [*da'un*] by the people of Pa' Dalih) were used for making most mats (*ugam* and *tarub*), the inner caps (*oloh*) of sunhats and the sunhats (*ra'ong*) themselves, headstraps (*sengoloh*) for baskets (*ra'ing, bu'an*), and for binding. For headstraps *da'un tamar* grass was normally used. Coarse mats, including *liling* used inside *bekang* and *kalang* baskets and *ugam* used for sitting, were made of a grass known as *da'un berpah*. The finer *tarub* mats were made of *da'un siar*. *Da'un tamar* was often used for binding. Finally, rice straw, which is of course a type of grass too, was used for making hearth brooms (BM99, 100, SM17, 18; **Pl. 96**)

Tree resin (*natang*)

Resin (BM139, SM103; **Pl. 31**) was used from two trees: the *tomoh* tree and the *obong* tree. The *tomoh* tree (**Pl. 58**) provides a hard resin (*damar*) which was used for fire-making in the 1980s and and was previously used for burning on bamboo stands to make a kind of lamp (*dawan natang* – BM102, SM25; **Pls 31, 95**). The *obong* tree provides a softer resin which was used, mixed with oil, to caulk dugout boats (*alud*), which often had sides made of planks which needed to be joined to the dugout base. Until the 1970s, resin from the *obong* tree was also used to glaze earthenware cooking pots; it was used to glaze the pots which were commissioned for the collection (BM117-121, SM41-44).

Ubir

Ubir is a black sticky substance (BM143, SM102; **Pl. 112**) that was applied to the inside of bamboo baskets (*ra'ing, bu'an, belalong nuba', a'ab, agag, reno*) to seal any cracks. It was made from the inside of the bark of the *ubir* tree, which was mixed with water to make a paste. After *ubir* was applied, the basket was put to dry in the sun.

Dyes

Black dye was, I was told, made by pounding shoots of the *takarau* tree and the leaves of a fruit tree called *bua' meritem* and then boiling these with mud. It was used for dyeing strips of bamboo used in some types of basket (*ra'ing, bu'an, a'ab, reno*.[55]

Red dye was, I was told, used for dyeing mats such as BM157. It was made by pounding the seeds of a fruit called the *bua' tepang* with pestle and mortar, mixing with water, then boiling in *bulu telang*, a medium bore bamboo.[56]

Tree latex used as glue (Kelabit: *mat*; species unidentified)

This was used to fix the blades of knives (*io, tongol*) and of weeding tools (*belu'ing*) and the shafts of axes and adzes (*uai*) into their handles. It was made from the sap of the *mat* tree.

Beeswax (*ole buatikan*)

This was put on the handles of knives to stop them splitting, and was used for stops on *sape*, a musical instrument.

Blowpipe poison (*parir*)

This was smeared on the ends of blowpipe darts. It was made from the sap of the *parir* tree (*Antiaris toxicaria*), mixed with water from an unspecified creeper (*uar*) and boiled, and was described as *parir*. It was said to be very vulnerable to losing its power (*lalud*) if it were stored in the wrong place, particularly in places where there were strong smells. I was told by one informant that it was good to keep *parir* in a rice storage hut, where there was no smell but that of the rice.

Materials from outside the Kelabit Highlands

Iron (*belawan*)

The Kelabit of Pa' Dalih had the forging skills to make iron blades for bush knives (*tongol*), small knives (*io*), weeding tools (*belu'ing*) and axes and adzes (*uai*) of various kinds. These were bound on to wooden handles using rattan. Forging was a male activity, and there were certain men who were specialists in this work. Even in the 1980s and 1990s, *tongol, io* and *belu'ing* were still forged in Pa' Dalih (**Pls 75-76**), although the bellows used were the Chinese, town-bought horizontal bellows which had replaced the Southeast Asia/Madagascar wood/bamboo vertical bellows, as it was made and used by the Kelabit in the earlier part of this century. Iron was bought in town, and I was told that old car springs were often used. Other metal tools, including modern axes and chain saws, were bought in town.

The Kelabit appear never to have mined or smelted iron, although the technology for doing this using local iron ore and simple pit methods is widely distributed in Borneo, including in the interior, and produces a high quality of iron (Christie and King 1988)

There were no substitutes for *tongol* and *belu'ing*, the knives used in the forest, and these were made in Pa' Dalih or bought from Penan who made them using the same technology as the Kelabit. However, town-bought knives were used instead of *io* within the house and might also be used for harvesting rice. In the kitchen, ready-made iron and steel utensils had become extremely important by the 1980s. Earthenware pots (*tuning* and *kudin*), no longer made by then, had been replaced by metal pots and *wok* (Chinese frying pans). Metal utensils – cutlery, ladles, *wok* utensils and so on – were widely used. Seed pod ladles had been displaced almost entirely by metal and plastic utensils. However, bamboo tongs were still widely used for frying.

While until the 1970s corrugated metal for longhouse roofs was that left behind by the British after Confrontation, by the 1980s new sheets of metal – mainly zinc – were brought in from the coast at considerable expense and with some difficulty, particularly where a longhouse like Pa' Dalih was concerned, because the sheets had to be carried through the forest from Bario. Such roofs were longer lasting than grass or bamboo, although probably less lasting than the hardwood tiles which were the high-status roofing material before the Second World War. After the war, corrugated metal became the prestige roofing material, even though it has the disadvantage of making the interior of the house very hot because of the accumulation of soot on its underside due to the lack of chimneys.

Suspension bridges over rivers and streams were very common in the Highlands. Only the smallest ditches were crossed by a log; to cross others on main tracks, suspension bridges were constructed. Before the Second World War these were made entirely of bamboo and rattan, and this was still the case in the late 1980s in the southern part of the Kelabit Highlands near Pa' Dalih. However, some bridges, particularly in the Bario area, were made of metal left behind by the British Army after the Confrontation in the 1960s. This included woven metal ropes and perforated metal sheets, which were used respectively for the suspension cords of the bridge and its flooring. Metal suspension bridges are longer lasting than bamboo ones but are more difficult to make since the materials are very heavy to manipulate. I know of no bridges made of metal brought up for this purpose since the 1960s, and new bridges in the 1980s and 1990s seemed always to be made of bamboo and rattan.

Nylon

By the 1980s, nylon was extremely important for making string. For this purpose, it was bought in town in hanks of extremely long strips that have been scrunched up. These were then made into string (*nopar*) using the same process used with bark, which involves rolling strands around each other on the thigh so that they wind themselves together in the other direction and stay together. This string was then used for all sorts of purposes including the string on all sorts of baskets.

Section 3 – Some important techniques used in handicraft work

Weaving (*nenganoh*)

This is a technique used for mats, *ra'ing, bu'an, reno* and *a'ab* baskets, rattan binding for lips of baskets, edges of rattan mats (*pin ue*), knife, axe and spear handles. When mats were being made, a seed pod (BM151) or other rounded object was used to smooth out the strands, which were then folded over and brought back in the other direction (**Pl. 108**). In weaving bamboo, strands were not folded over and the ends were held together by the rattan frame.

Plaiting

This is a technique used for making headstraps out of grass, and shoulder straps for baskets out of rattan. In plaiting, the strap is held by the foot while it is being worked with the hands (**Pl. 109**).

Carving and tool and knife making

The big bush knife, *tongol*, was used in cutting down bamboo and small trees, and for cutting these up into smaller pieces. The smaller *io* knife was used for carving and working small items of wood and bamboo (**Pls 13, 73, 87, 89, 94**). The modern axe was used in working large items such as mortars, stools and boats, together with the *uai tetad* (BM2), an adze made in the Kelabit Highlands.

Blades of all kinds were fixed to their handles using two steps, both of which act to hold the blade in place: putting latex from the *mat* tree in the socket, and binding the top of the handle, within which the blade is fixed, with woven rattan (**Pl. 110**). Axe blades, which are very heavy, were fixed at an angle to the shaft, which was then fixed into the handle using *mat*. The blade was bound to the shaft using woven rattan and a piece of leather or gunny sack was wrapped around the blade to present a springier, more easily gripped, and less damaging, surface to the rattan which binds it in.

Forging of metal

Although the Kelabit do not mine or smelt iron, they did forge it in Pa' Dalih, mainly to make knife blades and spear heads but also to make weeding tools. Metal was heated until it was white hot with a bamboo or town-bought bellows that blows air into a charcoal fire. If the bellows was bamboo, this was placed vertically to the ground and feathers were attached to a plunger which was used to expel air out of the bottom. This was directed through a thin bamboo tube to the fire. After heating up, the metal was beaten into the correct shape using a *tutok*, a hammer (**Pls 75-76**). Blades for *io, tongol*, weeding tools (*belu'ing*), axe and adze blades (*uai*) and spear heads (*boso*) were all made in this way.

String and cord making using bark, creeper, nylon, pineapple fibre and grass

While grass (described using the same word as that for leaf, *da'un*) was used as it is to wrap packets which did not require a strong cord – such as leaf packets of food – creeper (*uar*) and bark (*anit kayuh*) were usually twisted together to make a stronger cord. This was done by rolling strands of the bark or creeper around each other tightly and then allowing it to unwind, after which it stays together as a twisted cord. This technique was also used with strands of nylon, bought in hanks, which takes the form of a broad, very long piece which has been scrunched into a kind of string. Either nylon or fibre from pineapple leaves (*da'un rusan*) rolled in the same way was used to make cord (*nopar*) to thread beads on.

Making of nylon throw fishing nets (pukat) and hand fishing nets (iap)

This was done by knotting the cord being used, which is nylon wire for *pukat*, and cotton cord, nylon cord or bark string (*nopar kilid*) for *iap*. The net was then tied to a hook on the wall and the maker gradually moved away from the origin point as the net grew bigger (**Pls 70, 111**). This technique was also sometimes used to make nets (*kalang*) to go around the necks of baskets to hold the contents in. An example of a a basket with such a net is BM55.

Working rattan

Rattan was used either whole or split into strips. In either case it was always wetted before being worked since this made it more pliable. Once rattan dries it remains in the shape into which it has been worked. It was often desirable to have strands of rattan of a uniform diameter, and this could be achieved by means of a rattan grader, *pru ue* (BM108). This is a piece of metal with holes in it through which the rattan is passed; the metal shaves off excess pieces of rattan, producing an even piece of a certain diameter.

Working bamboo

Bamboo was used whole, in strips (**Pl. 90**), or, with large bore bamboo, as though it were a solid substance like wood (**Pls 93-94**). It was not wetted before working. Strips of bamboo might be used with or without the bark; if the bark is removed the bamboo becomes porous and *ubir* (BM143, SM102) will stick to it and have the effect of sealing the surface of the item being made (**Pl. 112**). Most items made of bamboo were lined with *ubir*. Using bamboo strips some of which have the bark on and some of which do not, a pattern can be created, and this was someimes done in making baskets. An example of this kind of pattern can be seen on BM66 (**Pl. 91**).

Pot-making

Kelabit earthenware pots – the bigger ones called *kudin* and the smaller ones *tuning* – were made in Pa' Dalih until the 1970s. They used to be the speciality of certain women in the community of Pa' Dalih, whose husbands assisted them in peripheral activities such as collecting wood for firing and assisting with glazing. The technology for making them remained, and in 1987, I commissioned a woman in Pa' Dalih, Na'an Tenan, to make a batch of *tuning* for me, and photographed and filmed the process as well as retaining most of the pots for the British Museum collection (BM117-121) and Sarawak Museum collection (SM41-44) (**Pls 112-118**) (see Janowski 1991b). Na'an Tenan kept five of the pots because she wanted to use them herself for making *kikid* (rice porridge). This illustrates the fact that *tuning* were still valued in Pa' Dalih for this purpose, and many women liked to have a couple of them. Another woman expressed an interest in learning how to make them from Na'an Tenan.

Na'an Tenan still had all of the necessary equipment for making pots: the *topah tana'* (BM132, SM50), a substantial stick made of heavy *belaban* wood for pounding the clay; the *okat* (BM133, SM49), a stick also made of *belaban* wood used to create the initial cavity in the pot; and the *pepe'* (BM134-135, SM47-48), paddles made of wood criss-crossed with parallel cuts and used together with the *batuh tuning* ('*tuning* stone') (BM136, SM46) to shape out the pot by the method described by Tom Harrisson as the 'paddle and anvil' method (Harrisson 1955).

Clay used for making earthenware is called *tana' kudin*, 'earth for *kudin*'. This occurs in pockets in the highlands. Na'an Tenan used clay from her own wet rice field (**Pl. 113**). She took it back to her field hut (*daan*) nearby, where she wrapped it in a mat and left it to rest for a number of days. It was in the field hut that she made the pots. When the clay was ready, she mixed in some pounded-up fragments of an old earthenware pot, described as *pra* (BM137, SM104); this is said to be necessary to stop the new pots from exploding when they are being fired. After mixing in the *pra*, she pounded the clay on an old mat with the *topah tana'* stick (**Pl. 114**). She then shaped it into cylinders by rolling the clay out on the mat with the *topah tana'*. The cavity of the pots was made using the pointed *okat* stick, around which the cylinders were rolled. They were then rolled with the larger *topah tana'* inside (**Pl. 115**). This was removed and one end of the cylinder was closed using the hands. The lid of the pot was formed roughly using the handle of a *pepe'* paddle. After this the crudely shaped pots were left to stand for a couple of hours to harden a little, sitting on circlets of rattan (**Pl. 116**). After this, the *tuning* were shaped more exactly using the *batuh tuning* and the *pepe'*. Na'an Tenan inserted one hand, holding the stone, into the pot, and held the stone against the side of the pot while the *pepe'* were gentled paddled against the corresponding outside part of the pot. She gradually moved her hand around the inside of the pot, paddling the whole of it. Thus she gradually enlarged and shaped the pot. The paddles have criss-cross lines of varying coarseness on them, and the coarsest were used first, with the incised side being used against the pot. The lines which they left on the pot were smoothed away at the end using the hand and some water. The lip of the pot was shaped using the handle of the paddle and a piece of bamboo which had been partially split in order to make it more flexible (**Pl. 117**). After shaping, the pots were placed over the fire in the

field hut, in the *raran* structure used for storing firewood (**Pl. 112** and **Fig. 4**). They remained there for two weeks until they were thoroughly dry. This, apparently, reduces the danger of their exploding in the firing.

The firing itself was done on a bonfire (described as a 'fence', *taa*) mainly constructed by Na'an Tenan's husband Bala Ukung, although she helped him. The 'fence' consisted of a square whose sides were made up of a number of layers of small logs that overlapped at the corners of the square at either end. The number of layers depends, they said, on the number of pots being fired. In this case eight layers were made and the total height was one and a half metres. The 'fence' covered an area of about three metres by two metres. The 17 *tuning* that Na'an Tenan had made were placed mouth down on the top layer of logs. A piece of resin, *natang*, (BM36) had been placed deep inside the heap and this was lit to start the fire, which burnt for two hours. The pots gradually descended as the heap burnt (**Pl. 118**). None exploded.

After firing, Na'an Tenan and Bala Ukung lifted the pots out of the fire using long sticks and immediately applied resin as a glaze, using sticks called *di'id* (BM131, SM51) which had been split and had had chunks of soft resin inserted into the splits. The glaze was applied inside and out.

Appendix 3

Botanical Names for Materials Used

My thanks are due to Hanne Christensen for the identifications below; she identified many of these before her recent book was published, and I have been able to make the rest of the identifications from that book (Christensen 2002). There is a small number of species which I recorded as being used but which Christensen did not record, and I have not been able to identify these.

I have put Christensen's transcription of the names of the species in brackets after my transcription. The transcriptions of some words are significantly different, although the identification of all of the plants is clear. She does not provide a discussion of the basis of her transcription, but some of the differences between her transcriptions and mine may be due to the fact that her assistant, Florence Lapu Apu, speaks the northern variety of Kelabit (see Appendix 1), which may have influenced the way in which some words were transcribed (e.g. the grass whose Kelabit name I have transcribed as *uduh kabir* is transcribed by Christensen as *uduh kabarr*; and this reflects the difference which I know to exist between the pronunciation of the word kabir/kabarr in southern and northern Kelabit respectively, with 'a' being used to transcribe the sound shwa in the second syllable of the word in northern Kelabit)

Rattans (*ue*)

Ue kusah (wae kusa)	*Calamus flabellatus* Bl.
Ue pa'it (wae pait)	*Calamus pogonacanthus* Becc. Ex. H. Winkl.
Ue lengan (wae lengan)	*Daemonorops sabut* Becc
Ue tuk (wae tok)	*Calamus caesius* Bl.
Ue rekun	Unidentified
Ue repit (wae rapit)	*Calamus marginatus* (Bl.) Mart.
Ue rabun (wae rabun)	*Calamus javensis* Bl.
Ue koran (wae koran)	*Plectocomia muelleri* Bl.

Bamboos (Kelabit: *bulu'*); botanical family: Poaceae

Bulu' telang (buluh talang)	*Schizostahyum brachycladum* Kurz.
Bulu' betong (buluh betong)	*Gigantoochloa levis* Merr.
Bulu' bayuh (buluh bayuh)	*Schizostahyum lima* (Blanco) Merr.
Bulu' poran (buluh poran)	*Schizostahyum blumei* Nees

Trees (Kelabit: *kayuh*); belonging to various botanical families

Kayuh mat (kayu mut)	Unidentified. Christensen collected a sample of this and lists it as indet. Sp. 3 (Christensen 2002: 179)
Kayuh takarau	Unidentified
Kayuh bua' meritem (maritam)	*Nephelium spp.; Sapindaceae*
Kayuh obong (obong)	no definite identification; Christensen believes that this may be a species of *Shorea* (Dipterocarpaceae)
Kayuh tomoh	probably *Agathis kinabaluensis* de Laub; Araucariaceae[57]
Kayuh ubir (ubarr atey)	*Syzygium rosulentum (*Ridl.) Merr. & Perry; Myrtaceae
Kayuh labakan (labakan)	*Syzygium sp* Mytraceae
Kayuh tara'	Unidentified
Kayuh menubun	Unidentified
Kayuh tai' la'al (tae la'al)	*Clausena excavata* Burm. F.; Rutaceae
Kayuh pul (kayu pul)	*Garcinia maingayi* Hook. f.; Clusaceae
Kayuh matah (mateh)	*Nephelium cuspidatum var.* Bl. Var. *robusta* Bl. vel aff.; Sapindaceae
Kayuh mata loang	Unidentified
Kayuh bua' bupu' (bubpu)	*Dimocarpus longan* Lour.*;* Sapindaceae
Kayuh ketong	Unidentified
Kayuh nato'	Unidentified
Kayuh kilid (kilid)	*Artocarpus elasticus* Reinw.*;* Moraceae
Kayuh rababar (rababar)	*Commersonia bartramia* (L.) Merr.; Sterculiaceae

Kayuh parir (kayu parir)	*Antiaris toxicaria* (Pers.) Lesch.; Moraceae
Kayuh belaban sia' (belaban siah)	*Tristaniopsis grandiflora (*Ridl.) P.G. Wilson & J.T. Waterhouse; Myrtaceae
Kayuh belaban buda' (belaban buda)	*Tristaniopsis whiteana* Griff.; Myrtaceae
Kayuh seboko (sebuko)	*Actinodaphne pruinosa* Nees*.;* Lauraceae
Kayuh ore	Unidentified
Kayuh payang (payang)	*Pangium edule* Reinw.; Flacourtiaceae

Leaves (Kelabit: *da'un*); belonging to various botanical families

Da'un ilad (ilad)	*Licuala valida* Becc.; Arecaceae
Da'un isip (daun isip)	*Phacelophrynium maximum* (Bl.) K. Schum.; Marantaceae

Grasses (Kelabit: *uduh*); belonging to various botanical families

Uduh berpah	unidentified; possibly a species of Pandanaceae
Uduh tamar (tamar)	*Curculigo villosa* (Kurz) Merr.: Hypoxidaceae
Uduh siar (siyar)	*Fimbristylis globulosa* Kunth.; Cyperaceae
Uduh kabir (kabarr)	*Pandanus kinabaluensis* St. John. vel aff.; Pandanaceae
Uduh kerubit(kerubat)	*Machaerina rubiginosa* (Spreng.) Koyana vel aff.; Cyperaceae
Uduh tepang	Unidentified

Creepers (Kelabit: *uar*); belonging to various botanical families

Uar reman	Unidentified[58]
Uar ubu	*Tetracera arborescens* Jack. vel aff.; Dilleniaceae
Uar bekar (war ubu)	Unidentified

Other

Reman belabo (reimand belabo)	*Caryota mitis* Lour. Reimand; Arecaceae
Bua' tabuh (tabu)	*Lagenaria siceraria* (Molina) Standl.; Cucurbitaceae
Kenangan (kanangan)	*Eugeissonia utilis Becc.; Arecaceae*
Basong	unidentified; possible species of Pandanaceae sp.
Derma (deramar)	*Arenga brevipes Becc.;* Arecaceae

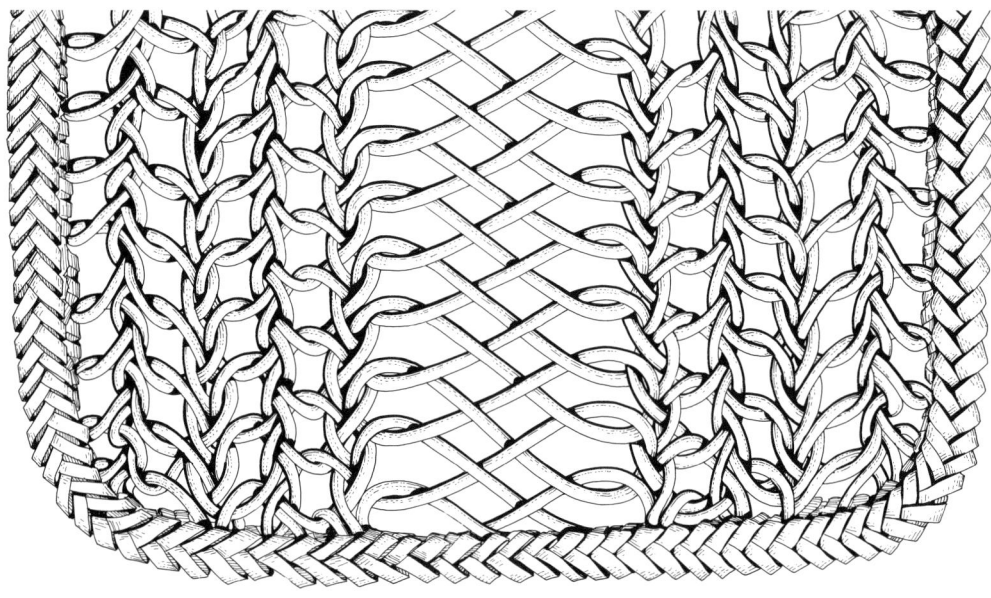

BM72 The flap of a *bekang dechur*, an expandable lady's basket. Item in the British Museum collection, drawing by Claire Thorne.

Catalogues

The British Museum and Sarawak Museum Collections

Catalogues are provided here for both the British Museum and Sarawak Museum collections. These are to a very large extent parallel collections, although the British Museum collection is somewhat fuller than that at the Sarawak Museum. The items in the British Museum collection are numbered BM followed by the numbers 1–161 for simplicity and in order to distinguish them from the items in the Sarawak Museum collection. The British Museum accession numbers are also given for each item. The numbers of the items in the Sarawak Museum collection are those which I gave them in the documentation deposited with the collection at the Sarawak Museum in 1988, with the distinguishing prefix 'SM'.

Except where otherwise stated, the makers of the items in the two collections lived in Pa' Dalih in 1986-88. Both used and new artefacts were bought for the two collections. Most of the new artefacts were commissioned. I have indicated in the catalogue where it was quite clear that items were either used or were new and had never been used.

Measurements are provided for most of the items in the British Museum collection but not for the items in the Sarawak Museum collection. This is because I was unfortunately not able to visit Sarawak to make measurements while writing this book. However, for most items in the Sarawak Museum collection there is a parallel item in the British Museum collection, and the size of an item can be estimated from this.

Editor's note

Measurements are given in feet (abbreviation ') and inches (abbreviation ")

    1 inch = 25.4mm
    1 foot = .3048m

Items in the British Museum collection

BM1

Belu'ing. Agricultural tool used for weeding. Iron part of tool made in the shape of an L, with the short arm bent over to form the blade and the other end fixed into a wooden handle, held in place with tree latex (*mat*) and rattan binding around the handle. Iron part forged in the Highlands. Used.

1' long; blade 5½" long.
Made by Bayah Ripuk (male), 1984.
Materials: blade iron (*belawan*), handle wood (*kayuh labakan*), binding rattan (*ue kusah*), tree latex (*mat*) used to fix iron in wood.
Bought from Bayah Ripuk 7/3/88 M$10
BM accession no. Ethno As1988,22.1

BM2

Uai tetad. 'Scooping out blade'; adze used for making boats and also for making *iong* (blocks with scooped out centres for pounding rice to husk and to make rice flour). Wooden handle with narrower wooden shaft set into it using tree latex (*mat*) and rattan binding. Blade, with wooden support, fixed to shaft using rattan binding and 'gunny' nylon. Used.

Handle and shaft 1' 8½" long; blade 8½" long.
Handle and binding made by Bayah Ripuk (male) 1978. Blade inherited by Bayah Ripuk from his ancestors.
Materials: blade iron (*belawan*), handle wood (*kayuh tara'*); shaft wood (*kayuh pul*); binding rattan (*ue pa'it*). Inside binding part of 'gunny' (nylon bag for rice etc.).
Bought from Bayah Ripuk 29/2/88 M$20.
BM accession no. Ethno As1988,22.2

BM3

Uai bara'. ('broad blade'). Axe used until approx 1966 for felling trees, still used for making boats. Wooden handle with narrower wooden shaft set into it using tree latex (*mat*) and rattan binding. Blade attached to shaft using rattan binding and deerskin (*kubir payo*). Used.

Handle made by Balang Pelaba (male) approx 1945. Blade made by Belong Elo (male) (Balang Pelaba's father) before 1920. Binding made by Balang Pelaba approx 1985.
Handle and shaft 1' 8" long; blade 7" long.
Materials: blade iron (*belawan*), shaft wood (*kayuh matah*); handle wood (*kayuh labakan*); binding rattan (*ue lengan*); additional binding deerskin (*kubir payo*); tree latex (*mat*) used for fixing shaft to handle.
Bought from Balang Pelaba 28/2/88 M$20.
BM accession no. Ethno As1988,22.3

BM4

Uai i'it ('small blade'). Axe (model). Same structure as BM3. Made for Esther, granddaughter of Lawe Padan, headman of Pa' Dalih, to exhibit at school (as required by the school) but said not to have been presented because it was felt to be inappropriate since she is a girl. She was supposed to have made it herself, but girls do not make axes. Never used; ornamental.

Handle and shaft 11½" long, blade 3½" long.
Blade and handle made by Lawe Padan. Binding by Makio' Ulun (male).
Materials: blade iron (*belawan*), shaft wood (*kayuh mata loang*), handle wood (*kayuh labakan*). Binding rattan (*ue lengan*).
Given to Monica and Kaz Janowski by Lawe Padan 2/3/88.
BM accession no. Ethno As1988,22.4

BM5 a,b

Tongol (bush knife) in *binan tongol* (sheath) with attached *labuh io* (sheath for small knife). Handle bought in Marudi in July 1987 for M$10. According to Bayah Ripuk, probably made by Penan. Blade, sheath and knife sheath made by Bayah Ripuk (male), February 1988. Used.

Materials: *binan tongol* (sheath for bush knife) made of wood (*kayuh labakan*), binding rattan (*ue pa'it*). *Labuh io* (sheath for small knife) made of bark of plant (*anit reman belabo*), bound with rattan (probably *ue pa'it*).
Tongol (bush knife) made of iron, wood (variety unknown), rattan binding (probably *ue tak* or *ue pa'it*); tree latex (*mat*) used for fixing blade in handle.
BM5a *Tongol* (bush knife). 1' 7" long.
BM accession no. Ethno As1988,22.5a
BM5b *Binan tongol* (sheath for bush knife) with attached *labuh io* (sheath for small knife).
BM accession no. Ethno As1988,22.5b
Whole of **BM5** bought from Bayah Ripuk February 1988 M$20.

BM6

Boso (labelled as "busu" on item). Spear for hunting wild pigs. Used.

Made by Bayah Ripuk (male), February 1988.
5' 6" long.
Materials: Handle wood (*kayuh bua' bupu'*); iron; binding rattan (*ue pa'it* and probably another variety, unknown; there are two types of binding, one finer than the other); probably also tree latex (*mat*) used for fixing blade in handle, although it is not evident.
Bought from Bayah Ripuk February 1988 M$20.
BM accession no. Ethno As1988,22.6

BM7

Put. Blowpipe for hunting. Used.

7' long.
Made by John Fred (male), Long Layu, Kerayan 1982.
Materials: wood (*kayuh ketong*), bound with rattan (*ue pa'it*), iron.
Bought from John Fred, Long Layu, Kerayan, February 1988 via Belaan Paran of Pa' Dalih, M$110.
BM accession no. Ethno As1988,22.7

BM8 a-e

Selongan. Quiver for blowpipe darts, and associated equipment. Quiver made of section of bamboo, bound with woven rattan to a large wooden, decoratively carved hook for attaching the quiver to belt (or loincloth in the past). Lid made of the end of another section of bamboo, also bound with woven rattan. Lid attached to quiver by a short metal chain. Attached to rattan binding by a nylon string decorated with beads is a gourd filled with spare blowpipe dart flights. Inside quiver are two squirrel skin pockets filled with blowpipe darts (*langan*), with flights (*ra'o*), tipped with poison (*parir*) (see **BM 11**). Used.

Made by Lajan (male), Long Layu, Kerayan date unknown.
Blowpipes were, in 1986-88, no longer made or used in the Kelabit Highlands because there are enough guns there, but were still made and used in the Kerayan.
BM8a *Selongan* (quiver).
11" long, 3" in diameter.
Materials: bamboo (*bulu' telang*), binding rattan (*ue kusah*), wood (*kayuh nato'*), string made of bark (*anit kayuh kilid*). Decorated with town-bought beads and tooth, monkey or dog.
BM accession no. Ethno As1988,22.8a
BM8b *Bua' tabuh kre'* (gourd) filled with *ra'o* (blowpipe dart flights).
Materials: gourd (*bua' tabuh*), beads (*ba'o*), nylon string, sago pith (*kenangan*).
BM accession no. Ethno As1988,22.8b
BM8c Awl (Kelabit term unknown) for making holes in blowpipe dart flights.
Materials: iron.
BM accession no. Ethno As1988,22.8c
BM8d Pocket made of squirrel skin (*anid belabo keter*) filled with blowpipe darts (*langan*) tipped with flights (*ra'o*) made of sago pith (*kenangan*). Some darts bamboo (*bulu'*), some palm (*derma*).
BM accession no. Ethno As1988,22.8d
BM8e as **BM8d**
BM accession no. Ethno As1988,22.8e
Set bought via Belaan Paran of Pa' Dalih, February 1988, M$40.

BM9 a-c

Tongol (bush knife) in *binan tongol* (sheath) and attached *labuh io* (sheath) containing *io* (small knife). Used.

Tongol and *binan tongol* made by Penan, date unknown. *Binan tongol* carved by Kalib Telutu Ayu (male), a Sa'aban from Long Banga' resident in Tang Ra'an in Kalimantan, at that time temporarily working at various jobs in Bario, presumably in 1987 or 1988. *Labuh io* and *io* made by Bayah Ripuk (male), February 1988.
BM9a *Tongol* (bush knife). 2' 1" long.
Materials: handle wood (variety unknown), iron, rattan binding (probably *ue pa'it*), tree latex (*mat*) used for fixing blade to handle.
BM accession no. Ethno As1988,22.9a
BM9b *Binan tongol* (sheath for bush knife) with attached *labuh io* (sheath for small knife). Materials: *binan tongol* – wood (probably *kayuh labakan*), rattan binding (probably *ue pa'it*); *labuh io* – bark of plant (*anit reman belabo*).
BM accession no. Ethno As1988,22.9b
BM9C *Io* (small knife). 1' 4" long.
Materials: iron, handle bamboo (*bulu' betong*), rattan binding (*ue pa'it*).
BM accession no. Ethno As1988,22.9c
Bush knife and its sheath bought from Sinah Pitan's shop in Bario May 1987 M$30. M$2.50 paid to Kalib Telutu Ayu for carving of sheath. Small knife and sheath bought from Bayah Ripuk February 1988 M$11 (sheath commissioned).

BM10

Batuh pian. Sharpening stone for sharpening iron blades. Used.

3" by 1".
Materials: stone (slate?).
No detailed documentation. Acquired in Pa' Dalih 1986-88. Donated by Monica and Kaz Janowski.
BM accession no. Ethno As1988,22.10

BM11

Parir. Poison for use on blowpipe darts, wrapped in leaf. Collected from the forest by Belaan Paran of Pa' Dalih at Pa' Bengar (abandoned Kelabit community a couple of hours' walk from Pa' Dalih, very close to the international border and to the Kerayan), 1986. Donated by Belaan Paran.

Materials: *parir* (sap of *parir* tree, mixed with water from unspecified creeper (*uar*) and boiled), leaves (*ilad*).
BM accession no. Ethno As1988,22.11

BM12

Io bulu' peraneh. Bamboo harvesting knife. New.

5½" long.
Made by Bayah Ripuk (male) 23/2/88.
Materials: bamboo (*bulu' bayuh*).
Bought from Bayah Ripuk 23/2/88 M$0.50.
Commissioned.
BM accession no. Ethno As1988,22.12

BM13

Bogo. Implement for stirring food while cooking. The handle has decorative parallel grooves. Used, darkened.

1' 6" long by 2" wide maximum
Made by Adun Rewat (male), 1968.
Materials: wood (*kayuh belaban*).
Bought from Siren Tauh (maker's widow), 30/9/87, M$2.50.
BM accession no. Ethno As1988,22.13

BM14

Bogo. Implement for stirring food while cooking. Handle decoratively carved. Hole for passing cord through for hanging. Used, darkened.

1' 8½" long, 2½" wide maximum.
Maker unknown.
Materials: wood (probably *kayuh belaban*).
No detailed documentation. Acquired Pa' Dalih 1986-88.
BM accession no. Ethno As1988,22.14

BM15

Bogo. Implement for stirring food while cooking. Used, darkened.

1' 3" long, 2½" wide maximum.
Made by Adun Rewat (male), 1968.
Materials: bamboo (*bulu' betong*).
Bought from Siren Tauh (maker's widow) 30/9/87 M$2.50.
BM accession no. Ethno As1988,22.15

BM16

Bogo. Implement for stirring food while cooking. Used, darkened.

1' 1" long, 2" wide maximum.
Made by Ngimat Ulun (male), 1978.
Materials: bamboo (*bulu' betong*).
Bought from Ngimat Ulun, 31/1/88 M$1.00.
BM accession no. Ethno As1988,22.16

BM17

Bogo. Implement for stirring food while cooking. Used.

1' 2½" long, 1" wide maximum.
Maker unknown.
Materials: wood (probably *kayuh belaban*).
No detailed documentation. Bought or donated to collection in Pa' Dalih 1986-88.
BM accession no. Ethno As1988,22.17

BM18 and 19

Bogo. Implement for stirring food while cooking. New, never used.

1' 2" long, 1¼" wide maximum.
Made by Bala Aran (male), 1988.
Commissioned.
Materials: bamboo (*bulu' betong*).
Bought from Bala Aran 1988 M$1.00.
BM accession no. Ethno As1988,22.18 and As1988,22.19

BM20

Pit karid. Tongs (*pit*) for cooking vegetables to be eaten at the rice meal (*krid*). Sometimes described as *pit naak* ('cooking tongs'). New.

1' 1¾" long, 1¾" wide.
Made by Belaan Paran (male), January 1987.
Commissioned.
Materials: bamboo (*bulu' betong*).
Bought from Belaan Paran 31/1/88 M$1.OO.
BM accession no. Ethno As1988,22.20

BM21

Bogo kikid. Implement for stirring rice porridge (*kikid*) and other thick soupy foods. Made of thick twig, branching at end. Used.

1' 4" long.
Made by Pun Ngelipo Ra'an Lewan (female) (originally from Kerayan) 1986.
Materials: wood (variety unknown).
Bought from Sinah Belaan Paran (Pun Ngelipo's daughter-in-law), 31/1/88 M$1.00.
BM accession no. Ethno As1988,22.21

BM22

Pit apui. Tongs (*pit*) used for moving wood in the fire (*apui*). Made of a strip of bamboo bent over. Held together by a strip of grass binding for storage. New.

1' 5½" long, 1" wide.
Made by Lawe Padan (male), 1/3/88.
Commissioned.
Materials: bamboo (*bulu' betong*).
Bought from Lawe Padan 2/3/88 M$1.00.
BM accession no. Ethno As1988,22.22

BM23

Pit apui. Tongs (*pit*) used for moving wood in the fire (*apui*). Made of a strip of bamboo bent over. New.

1' 5½" long, 1" wide.
Made by Lawe Padan (male), 1/3/88.
Commissioned.
Materials: bamboo (*bulu' betong*).
Bought from Lawe Padan 2/3/88 M$1.00.
BM accession no. Ethno As1988,22.23

BM24

Bogo. Implement for stirring food while cooking. Carved handle. New.

1' 4" long, 1½" wide maximum.
Made by Kalib Telutu Ayu (male), Sa'aban from Long Banga' living in Tang Ra'an, Kerayan during a visit to Pa' Dalih to make a boat for Lawe Padan, headman of Pa' Dalih, 15/2/88.
Materials: bamboo (*bulu' betong*).
Bought from Kalib Telutu Ayu 26/2/88 M$2.00.
BM accession no. Ethno As1988,22.24

BM25

Bogo. Implement for stirring food while cooking. Carved handle. New.

1' 2¾" long, 1½" wide maximum.
Made by Kalib Telutu Ayu (male), Sa'aban from Long Banga' living in Tang Ra'an, Kerayan during a visit to Pa' Dalih to make a boat for Lawe Padan, headman of Pa' Dalih. 15/2/88.
Materials: bamboo (*bulu' betong*).
Bought from Kalib Telutu Ayu 26/2/88 M$2.00.
BM accession no. Ethno As1988,22.25

BM26

Bogo. Implement for stirring food while cooking. Carved handle. New.

1' 3" long, 1½" wide maximum.
Made by Kalib Telutu Ayu (male), Sa'aban from Long Banga' resident
in Tang Ra'an, Kerayan, during a visit to Pa' Dalih to make a boat for
Lawe Padan, headman of Pa' Dalih.
15/2/88.
Materials: bamboo (bulu' betong).
Bought from Kalib Telutu Ayu in Pa' Dalih 16/2/88 M$2.00.
BM accession no. Ethno As1988,22.26

BM27

Bak bua' payang. Seed ladle for rice porridge, and previously
for rice beer (which the Kelabit no longer make). Made by
cutting top off seed pod and attaching it to a long stick
through a hole in the seed. Used.

Stick 1' 2" long, seed 2½" by 2½".
Made by Na'an Tepin (female) 14/11/87.
Materials: seed pod of *payang* tree (*ilong payang*), wood (variety
unknown).
Bought from Na'an Tepin 1988 M$1.00.
BM accession no. Ethno As1988,22.27

BM28

Kasib. Comb for removing lice eggs from hair and destroying
them by squashing the teeth of the comb together. Made of a
flat strip of bamboo with outside removed half way down;
below this the strip has been fringed, with the tips of the
fringe pointed, so as to create a comb. Used.

10½" long, 1" wide.
Made by Bayah Ripuk (male) 1987.
Materials: bamboo (*bulu' betong*).
Bought from Bayah Ripuk 16/1/88 M$2.50.
BM accession no. Ethno As1988,22.28

BM29 a,b

Longing (mortar) and *totok* (pestle). For pounding vegetables
before cooking. The mortar is carved out of a single block of
wood, with a wide lip around the hole and a handle for
hanging the mortar when not in use. Used.

1' 1" in diameter including lip; hole 4" in diameter; 5" in height, hole
4" in depth. Pestle 1' 5" long, 1½" in diameter.
Made by Maurice (male), Long Layu, Kerayan, father of Ribuh Paran
of Pa' Dalih, 1965 approx.
Bought via Belaan Paran of Pa' Dalih February 1988 M$30.
BM29a Longing. Materials: wood (*kayuh tara'*).
BM accession no. Ethno As1988,22.29a
BM29b Totok. Materials: wood (*kayuh nato'*).
BM accession no. Ethno As1988,22.29b

BM30

Bak bua' payang. Seed ladle (*bak*) for rice porridge and other
thick soupy foods, and previously for rice beer (which the
Kelabit no longer make). Made by cutting the end off a seed
pod (*bua'*) and attaching it to a stick through a hole in the
pod. Used.

Stick 10" long; seed 3½" by 3".
Seed found by Mada' Ulun (male) at Long Kelit already cut (i.e. an
old ladle with stick missing). He added a stick.
Materials: seed pod of *payang* tree (*ilong payang*), wood (variety
unknown).
Bought from Mada' Ulun, Pa' Dalih 29/2/88, M$1.00.
BM accession no. Ethno As1988,22.30

BM31

Tara bogo. Container for *bogo* – implements for stirring food
while cooking (see **BM13/14/15/16/17/18/19/24/25/26**).
Made of single segment of large-bore bamboo, with closed

end at the bottom. Extended tab of the bamboo, with a hole
bored in it to enable it to be hung by the hearth on a nail.
Blackened through use in the hearth area.

11" high, 5" in diameter.
Made by Riwed Bala (male), Batu Patong (40 minutes walk from Pa'
Dalih), 1984.
Materials: bamboo (*bulu' betong*).
Bought from Sinah Rang Bala, Batu Patong, 8/2/88, M$5.00.
BM accession no. Ethno As1988,22.31

BM32

Tara bogo. Container for *bogo* – implements for stirring food
while cooking (see **BM13/14/15/16/17/18/19/24/25/26**).
Made of single segment of large-bore bamboo, with closed
end at the bottom. Extended tab of bamboo above and
another below the body of the container. Hole drilled
through the container below this tab (not in it) by which it
was hung by the hearth on a nail. Names of members of
family (Pun Balang Tepun, Udau Lian, Lulau Pulu'. Selina
Bala, Laura Bala, Nora Bala, Samson Bala, Julia Bala,
Alexzander Bala, Supang Bala, Prescilla Bala) written in
black one under the other down the front, with the bark
removed from below alternate names. On the back the date of
making, 18.11.1987, has been carved around and left standing
out and coloured black. Used.

1' 5" high, 4" in diameter.
Made by Samson Bala Aran (male), November 1987.
Materials: Bamboo (*bulu' betong*).
Bought from Sinah Bala Aran (Samson Bala Aran's mother) 6/2/88,
M$10.
BM accession no. Ethno As1988,22.32

BM33

Tara bogo. Container for *bogo* – implements for stirring food
while cooking (see **BM13/14/15/16/17/18/19/24/25/26**).
Made of single segment of large-bore bamboo, with closed
end at the bottom. Extended tab, cut in a decorative hook
shape, above the body of the container has a hole drilled
through it by which it was hung by the hearth on a nail.
Decorated by leaving strips of bark on the bamboo, and
incising parallel and v-shaped lines into these. Used.

1' 5" high, 4" in diameter.
Made by Bala Aran (male), date unknown.
Materials: bamboo (*bulu' betong*).
Bought from Bala Aran, 1988, price unrecorded.
BM accession no. Ethno As1988,22.33

BM34

Obe. Drinking vessel. Used.

Made by Belalong Tepun (male) February 1987.
Materials: bamboo (*bulu' betong*).
Bought from Belalong Tepun 6/2/88 M$1.00.
BM accession no. Ethno As1988,22.34

BM35

Tik. Container for carrying fire-making equipment and
tobacco. Made of a section of large-bore bamboo, with
another piece of a section as a tightly-fitting lid. Rattan
binding on lid and on body of container. Lip of lid carved
decoratively. Cord made of creeper passes around bottom
and top, passing through the bamboo itself, holding lid in
place and enabling the container to be carried or hung. No
contents. Used, darkened. No longer used in Kelabit

Highlands but informants told me in 1988 that old people still use *tik* in the Kerayan.

Made by Pun Kemedan (unknown sex), Long Layu, Kerayan, Kalimantan Timur 1976.
Materials: bamboo (*bulu' telang*), creeper binding (*uar reman*).
Bought from Belalong Tepun, Pa' Dalih, 5/3/88 M$6.
BM accession no. Ethno As1988,22.35

BM36

Natang. Resin from damar tree (*kayuh tomoh*). Used for fire-making and, in past, for light (burnt on bamboo stands – *dawan natang* – see **BM102**).

Collected by Kaz Janowski in primary forest near Pa' Dalih, 1988.
BM accession no. Ethno As1988,22.36

BM37

Be'ong bua' tabuh. Container (*be'ong*) for storing seeds, made of a gourd. Round hole cut in pod through which to put in and take out seeds through. Small hole through pointed end of gourd with bark string passed through it, to make it possible to hang the gourd. Used.

5" by 2".
Made by Siren Tauh (female), approx 1970.
Materials: gourd (*bua' tabuh*), string made of bark (*anit kayuh kilid*).
Bought from Siren Tauh 11/11/87 M$0.50.
BM accession no. Ethno As1988,22.37

BM38 a,b

Pagang. Musical instrument with stick for playing. Consists of part of a section of bamboo with two strings cut out of the bamboo itself and held away from the body of the instrument with small pieces of bamboo. A hole between the two strings is covered with another piece of bamboo attached to the strings. Played by tapping the strings with a stick. New.

Made by Belalong Tepun (male), February 1988.
Commissioned.
Bought from him 29/2/88, M$10.
BM38a *Pagang*. 1' 7" long, 3½" in diameter.
Materials: bamboo (*bulu' telang*).
BM accession no. Ethno As1988,22.38a
BM38b Stick for playing *pagang*. 10" long, ¼" in diameter.
Materials: wood (variety unknown)
BM accession no. Ethno As1988,22.38b

BM39

Sape. Long narrow simple stringed musical instrument with two metal strings. Carved out of one piece of wood with a flat piece nailed on to bottom. Six holes burnt out of body along top to allow sound to come out. Strings held away from body of instrument with pieces of wood at each end. Pegs to adjust sound. Simple ornamental carving at end with pegs. New.

3' 6" long, 2" across and 2½" in depth.
Made by Belalong Tepun (male), February 1988.
Materials: wood (*kayuh menubun* plus *kayuh belaban* for pegs), beeswax (*ole bua tikan*) to stick stops, metal wire (bought in town).
Bought from Belalong Tepun 29/2/88 M$30.
BM accession no. Ethno As1988,22.39

BM40

Lotong. Musical instrument. Made of one section of large-bore bamboo, with end divisions between this section and other sections intact. Slit cut down one side, decoratively cut in the middle. On each side of the slit, two strings have been cut out of the bamboo itself and held away from the body of

the bamboo by small pieces of bamboo which act as tuning devices. Inside the body of the instrument there is a dried leaf which may be important in creating the type of sound desired. Bound by bark string at both ends to hold it together well. The instrument is played by plucking the strings. New.

1' 10" long, 5½" in diameter
Made by Balang Telian (male), March 1988.
Commissioned.
Materials: bamboo (*bulu' betong*), wood (variety unknown), string made of bark (*anit kayuh kilid*), leaves (probably *ilad*).
Bought from Balang Telian March 1988 M$20.
BM accession no. Ethno As1988,22.40

BM41

Lotong. Musical instrument. Made of one section of large-bore bamboo, with end divisions between this section and other sections intact. Slit cut down one side. On each side of the slit, two strings have been cut out of the bamboo itself and held away from the body of the bamboo by small pieces of bamboo which act as tuning devices. Used.

1' 8½" long, 5" in diameter.
Made by Belalong Tepun (male), December 1987.
Materials: bamboo (*bulu' betong*), wood (variety unknown).
Bought from Belalong Tepun 29/2/88 M$20.
BM accession no. Ethno As1988,22.41

BM42

Kelingut. Nose flute. Made of one section of bamboo with division with next section left intact except for a hole for blowing. Three triangular holes for stopping. New.

1' 9" long.
Made by Balang Pelaba (male), 9/2/88.
Materials: bamboo (*bulu' telang*).
Bought from Balang Pelaba 20/2/88 M$2.50.
BM accession no. Ethno As1988,22.42

BM43

Selingut. Flute. Detachable end piece (purpose not clear) fits over end; flute itself is one section of bamboo with division with next section intact at end with detachable end piece. Hole for blowing is on opposite side to three three triangular holes for stopping. New.

1' 11" long.
Made by Belalong Tepun (male), February 1988.
Commissioned.
Materials: bamboo (*bulu' telang*).
Bought from Belalong Tepun 29/2/88 M$10.
BM accession no. Ethno As1988,22.43

BM44

Selingut. Flute. Incised and blackened decoration at end with blowing hole. Six stopping holes on same side as blowing hole. New.

1' 9" long.
Made by Belalong Tepun (male), February 1988.
Materials: bamboo (*bulu' telang*).
Bought from Belalong Tepun 5/3/88 M$10.
Commissioned.
BM accession no. Ethno As1988,22.44

BM45 a,b

Tobong. Tubular gong made of one section of large bore bamboo. Wide slit cut in one side. Piece of rattan attached to top of slit for hanging. Stick for beating gong is a piece of wood with a natural twist in it. Used to summon people to meetings, *irau* feasts and to church. New.

Made by Balang Telian (male), February 1988.
Commissioned.
Bought from Balang Telian 7/3/88 M$10.
BM45a *Tobong*. 2' long, 6" in diameter.
Materials: bamboo (*bulu' betong*), wood (variety unknown), string made of bark (*anit kayuh kilid*), rattan.
BM accession no. Ethno As1988,22.45a
BM45b Stick for beating *tobong*. 10" long.
Materials: wood (*kayuh seboko*), nylon.
BM accession no. Ethno As1988,22.45b

BM46

Ra'ong. Sun hat made of palm leaf, with beaded centre and inner cap. Beaded centre carries message 'Selamat Pakai from Kelabit Girl 10.1.67' ('Happy wearing [Malay : *Selamat Pakai*] from a Kelabit girl, 10.1.67'). Hat has beaded hook to enable it to be hung up as a *bunga ruma'* (house decoration). Used.

1' 10" in diameter.
Hat possibly made by Sinah Rang Bala; her sister made the beaded centre of the hat at a later date. Said by some Pa' Dalih Kelabit to have been made for a British soldier during the Confrontation period. Unclear whether it was given to him and returned.
Materials: palm leaves (*ilad*), rattan for frame (*ue kusah*), beads, grass for cap (*da'un berpah*), cotton thread, cotton cloth (last two bought in town).
Bought from Sinah Rang Bala, Batu Patong, March 1988 M$30.
BM accession no. Ethno As1988,22.46

BM47

Ra'ong. Sun hat, with inner cap (*oloh*) made of palm leaf, with woollen thread decorations (concentric circles of different colours in centre, lines radiating out joined by other lines, some zigzag, pompoms attached to outer edge. Hook for hanging up as *bunga ruma'* (house decoration), probably in town. Cap has (*oloh*) with lining of blue cotton cloth. Used.

Made by Sinah Maran To'oh (female), Long Lellang approx 1982. Sold by her to Sinah Ben of Pa' Dalih for two 'medium-sized' cakes of Kelabit salt (*tusu'* – see **BM106-107**).
Materials: palm leaves (*ilad*), rattan frame (*ue kusah*), bamboo for cap (*bulu' poran*), wool, cotton thread, cotton cloth (latter three bought in town).
Bought from Sinah Ben, Pa' Dalih, 22/2/88 M$10.
BM accession no. Ethno As1988,22.47

BM48

Ra'ong Ba Rian. Sun hat made of grass, with inner cap (*oloh*). This type of sun hat is widely worn in the Kelabit Highlands. Embroidered decoration of woollen thread in centre in various colours and covered with strips of cloth in various colours around outside. Strips of rattan attached to centre with pieces of red cloth attached to them. Cap inside has cotton cloth around rim to make it more comfortable. Used.

Made in the Ba Rian area, Kalimantan Timur, Indonesia, one day's walk from Bario in the Kelabit Highlands, by unknown maker. Given to Pun Punang Kelapang of Pa' Dalih in 1987 by Simeon from the Ba Rian area, who adopted him (Pun Penang Kelapang) as his father. In January 1988 Ban (daughter of Sinah Rang Bala of Batu Patong), great grand niece of Pun Penang Kelapang, wrote on it 'Balang Punang' (previous parental name of Pun Punang Kelapang) and 'Pun Punang Kelapang' (his grandparental name).
Materials: grass (*da'un berpah*), rattan frame (*ue kusah*), rattan decorative strips (probably *ue pa'it*), wool, nylon thread, cotton cloth (last three bought in town).
Bought from Pun Punang Kelapang 12/2/88 M$5.
BM accession no. Ethno As1988,22.48

BM49

Ra'ong Lun Bawang. 'Lun Bawang' sun hat. Conical hat decorated with red and black paint. No inner cap. Almost certainly never worn, but used as *bunga' ruma'* (house decoration) by Meechang in Bario.

1' 2" in diameter
Made in Ba' Kelalan, Fifth Division of Sarawak (where the Lun Bawang, closely related culturally and linguistically to the Kelabit, live) by Bulan Pengiran (female), 1987 for Meechang, Lun Bawang headmaster at Bario secondary school in the Kelabit Highlands.
Materials: aerial root of palm tree (*basong*), leaves (*ilad*), rattan (variety unknown), string, paint (last two bought in town).
Given to Monica Janowski by Meechang January 1988.
BM accession no. Ethno As1988,22.49

BM50

Samit. Rain cape. Used.

Outer arc 4' 5", inner arc 1' 6", distance between them 1' 6".
Made by Mariam Ribuh Paran (female), Kerayan, 1987.
Materials: leaves (*ilad*), green and red wool (bought in town). Fan shaped, double thickness, opening out for use.
Bought from Mariam Ribuh Paran 1/10/87 M$4.
BM accession no. Ethno As1988,22.50

BM51

Uyut. Soft multipurpose basket, carried on back. Woven around the top is BALANG PUNANG (previous name of Pun Punang Kelapang) and around the bottom LOVE IN CHRIST, with an unnamed pattern in between. Used.

1' 3" in height, 11" in width.
Made by Sinah Aran Tuan (female), Long Peluan (Kelabit settlement outside the Kelabit Highlands, further downriver) approx 1974 for Pun Punang Kelapang of Pa' Dalih.
Materials: rattan (*ue tak*), nylon (bought in town), natural black dye made from *takarau* tree shoots and *bua' meritam* leaves
Bought from Pun Punang Kelapang, Pa' Dalih, 12/2/88 M$10.
BM accession no. Ethno As1988,22.51

BM52

Uyut. Soft multipurpose basket, carried on back. Woven around the top is ALOYSIUS T. GOH and around the bottom SING FOR JOY, with an unnamed pattern in between (the same as on 51). Used.

1' in height, 11" in width.
Made by Sinah Isaac (female), Long Peluan (Kelabit settlement outside the Kelabit Highlands, further downriver) in 1982 for the first husband of Sinamo' Selina Rip, daughter of Sinah Bala Aran of Pa' Dalih.
Materials: rattan (*ue tak*), natural black dye made from *takarau* tree shoots and *bua' meritam* leaves
Bought from Sinah Bala Aran, Pa' Dalih 7/2/88 M$26.
BM accession no. Ethno As1988,22.52

BM53

Uyut. Soft multipurpose basket, carried on back. 'GOD BLESS YOU ALL' is woven around the top and THE TRUTH OF GOD around the bottom, with an unnamed pattern in between. Used.

1' 6" in height, 1' 1½" in width.
Made by Sinah Rang Bala (female) of Batu Patong (40 minutes walk from Pa' Dalih) in Long Peluan (Kelabit settlement outside Kelabit Highlands, further downriver, her husband's settlement), approx 1970.
Materials: rattan (*ue tak*), natural black dye made from *takarau* tree shoots and *bua' meritam* leaves
Bought from Sinah Rang Bala, Batu Patong, 4/3/88.
BM accession no. Ethno As1988,22.53

BM54

Uyut. Soft multipurpose basket, carried on back.
Woven into pattern are words: *'Pesta Sukan SRK Long Banga'*
(Long Banga Lower Secondary School Sports Day). Long
Banga is a Sa'aban settlement further downriver from the
Kelabit Highlands, near the Kelabit settlement outside the
Highlands of Long Peluan. Given to Juliet, daughter of Balang
Darin of Pa' Dalih. Used.

Made by Sinah Aran Tuan (wife of brother of Balang Darin of Pa'
Dalih, originally of Long Peluan), in Long Peluan in 1980.
Materials: rattan (*ue tak*), nylon, natural black dye made from
takarau tree shoots and *bua' meritam* leaves
Bought from Juliet Balang Darin 7/2/88 M$25.
BM accession no. Ethno As1988,22.54

BM55

Uyut. Soft multipurpose basket, carried on back. With *kalang
monong* (nylon woven net around neck which can be
tightened to protect contents), with a thick nylon cord as
drawstring decorated with beads. There are also beads on the
nylon thread used to fix the shoulderstraps to the basket.
Woven into the basket are the words: *'Selamat P.A.K.'*, which
stand for *'Selamat Pakai Abang Ku'* (this is Malay; *Selamat
Pakai* means 'Happy Wearing' and *Abang Ku* means 'elder
brother') around the bottom of the basket and *'K. Telutu Ayu*
(*K.* stands for *Kalib*) around the top, with an unnamed
pattern in between. Used.

1' 1½" in height, 10" in width.
Made by Sinah Isaac (female) of Long Peluan (Kelabit settlement
outside Kelabit Highlands, further downriver) for her father's
second cousin, Kalib Telutu Ayu, who is from the Sa'aban settlement
of Long Banga' near Long Peluan but lives in Tang Ra'an in the
Kerayan.
Materials: rattan (*ue tak*), nylon, beads (last two bought in town),
natural black dye made from *takarau* tree shoots and *bua' meritam*
leaves.
Bought from Kalib Telutu Ayu on a visit to Pa' Dalih 9/2/88 M$50.
BM accession no. Ethno As1988,22.55

BM56

Uyut barit. Soft multipurpose basket, carried on back; *barit*
means 'coloured' and refers to the fact that this is a very finely
woven basket with a pattern which is considered beautiful.
However, the pattern has no name at least as far as the Kelabit
are concerned. Used.

10" in height, 7" in width.
Made by Penan from Long Beruang (Penan settlement in Kelabit
Highlands). Bought from them by Sinah Ngimat Ulun of Pa' Dalih, in
Bario, in 1987 for undisclosed price.
Materials: rattan (*ue tak*), string made of bark (*anit kayuh kilid*),
natural black dye made from *takarau* tree shoots and *bua' meritam*
leaves.
Bought from Sinah Ngimat Ulun in Pa' Dalih 20/2/88 M$40.
BM accession no. Ethno As1988,22.56

BM57

Gawang. Multipurpose soft basket, carried on back. Shoulder
straps fixed to body of basket at top, joined by rattan string at
bottom. Used.

Made by Penan from Long Beruang (Penan settlement in Kelabit
Highlands). Given by them to Sinah Paran Belaan, originally of Pa'
Dalih, now living in Remudu (Kelabit settlement three hours' walk
from Pa' Dalih).
1' 3" in height, 11" in width.
Materials: rattan (*ue tak*).

Given to Monica Janowski by Sinah Belaan, Remudu 14/2/88.
Donated to BM by Monica Janowski March 1988.
BM accession no. Ethno As1988,22.57

BM58

Uyut rawang. Open weave soft basket, carried on back. New.

1' 2" in height, 9" in width.
Made by Riwed Bala (male), Batu Patong (40 minutes walk from Pa'
Dalih), February 1988, using *ue tak* rattan brought from Long
Peluan. Beads added by his daughter Sinah Rang Bala.
Materials: rattan (*ue tak* for body of basket and *ue pa'it* for shoulder
straps), beads (bought in town).
Commissioned.
Bought from Riwed Bala February 1988 M$30.
BM accession no. Ethno As1988,22.58

BM59

Uyut ruma' tebupun. Church collection basket. Soft basket
(*uyut*), of a type usually made to be carried on back; but this
was made and was used for taking the collection in the
Remudu church (Remudu is a Kelabit settlement three hours'
walk from Pa' Dalih) until 1988, when it was purchased for
the collection. Woven on to the basket is SIDANG PA
REMUDU ('the parish of Pa' Remudu'). Used.

6½" in height, 5" in width.
Made by Penan from Long Beruang (Penan settlement in Kelabit
Highlands) at request of Remudu people in 1983 approx. Not clear
whether this was for payment.
Materials: rattan (*ue tak*), string made of bark (*anit kayuh kilid*),
natural black dye made from *takarau* tree shoots and *bua' meritam*
leaves
Bought from Sidang Pa Remudu (the parish of Remudu) 14/2/88 for
M$50 including donation to the parish.
BM accession no. Ethno As1988,22.59

BM60 a,b

Uyut ruma' tebupun. Pair of nearly identical church (*ruma'
tebupun*) collection baskets, of a type of soft basket (*uyut*)
usually made to be carried on back; but these were made and
were used until 1988 (when they were purchased for the
museum collection) for the collection of money in the Pa'
Dalih church. Decorated with beads at the tops and bottoms
of the shoulder straps. Woven into pattern are words:
Persembahan Kami ('Our Offering' in Malay, the language
used in church). Used.

Each is 8" in height, 7" in width.
Made by Sinah Ellie (female), 1980.
Materials: rattan (*ue tak*), beads (bought in town), string made of
bark (*anit kayuh kilid*), natural black dye made from *takarau* tree
shoots and *bua' meritam* leaves. Bought from Sidang Pa' Dalih (the
parish of Pa' Dalih) 1/3/88 M$100 including donation to the parish.
BM accession numbers As1988,22.60a and As1988,22.60b

BM61

Ra'ing with headstrap (*sengoloh*). Small rigid basket with flat
base used for harvesting rice and for collecting cultivated
vegetables and fruit in fields and wild vegetables and fruit in
secondary growth areas. Plain. Wide woven lip. Metal hooks
on basket for attaching headstrap. Base made of coiled *kusah*
rattan. Used.

10½" in height, 1' in diameter.
Said to have been made by Agil from Long Lungan (one day's walk
from Tangra'an, which is in Kerayan; however there must have been
two makers because men do rattan work, women bamboo work.
Bought by Laba Awa of Pa' Dalih (but originally from Kerayan
herself) in Long Lungan in about 1977.

Materials: bamboo (*bulu' poran*), rattan (probably including not only *ue kusah* for frame but also *ue rabun* and *ue pa'it*). Headstrap (*sengoloh*) made of grass (*da'un tamar*). Iron used for hooks.
Bought from Laba Awa 15/1/88 M$15.
BM accession no. Ethno As1988,22.61

BM62

Ra'ing with shoulder straps (*kela'e*). Rigid basket with flat base used for harvesting rice and for collecting vegetables and fruit in fields and wild vegetables and fruit in secondary growth areas. Woven using bamboo painted red, green, white and black to form a pattern. Name of pattern not known if there is one. Base formed by coiling split rattan. Rattan frame. Frame fixed and lip woven with rattan (lip quite wide). No *ubir* (BM143) has been applied inside. Used.

1' 5" high, 1' in diameter at top, 7" at bottom.
Made in Ba Rian area, one day's walk from Bario in Kalimantan Timur, Indonesia. Shoulder straps made by Nanad Bala (male), Remudu (Kelabit settlement three hours' walk from Pa' Dalih) in 1988.
Materials: bamboo (*bulu' poran*), string made of bark (*anit kayuh kilid*), paint (bought in town), rattan (probably including not only *ue kusah* for frame, but also *ue rabun* for lip and *ue pa'it* for binding frame). Shoulder straps rattan (*ue pa'it*).
Bought from Sinah Pitan at her shop in Bario, January 1988, M$20. Shoulder straps bought from Nanad Bala in Remudu, February 1988, M$3.00.
BM accession no. Ethno As1988,22.62

BM63

Boko'. Small storage container without lid. Square base, round top. Made of red, green and undyed bamboo strips. Used.

5" in height, 4½" in diameter.
Made by Sinah Matala Ulun (female), 1984.
Materials: bamboo (variety unknown), paint (bought in town).
Bought from Sinah Matala Ulun, 17/11/87 M$2.
BM accession no. Ethno As1988,22.63

BM64

Ra'ing uang bodok with headstrap (*sengoloh*). Small rigid basket with pointed (*bodok*) base, made in the old Kelabit style, used for harvesting rice and for collecting vegetables and fruit in fields and secondary growth areas. The term *uang*, literally 'inside', refers to the fact that the bamboo has been split so that the outside of the bamboo has been removed and the inner part faces both inside and outside the basket. *Ubir* (BM143) has been applied to inside of basket to make it proof against anything slipping through and to strengthen it. Bound with parallel strips of rattan, with woven base of rattan. Used.

1' 4" high, 11" in diameter.
Made by Pun Bupun (female), mother of Na'an Tenan (female) of Pa' Dalih, about 1958. Rattan work by Bala Ukung, Na'an Tenan's husband, 1958.
Base repaired by Bala Ukung 1/2/88. (**Pl. 112**).
Materials: bamboo (probably *bulu' poran*), rattan (probably *ue pa'it* for binding, *ue rabun* for lip of basket and *ue kusah* for frame), string made of bark to attach headstrap to basket, grass (*da'un tamar*) for headstrap, *ubir* (BM143).
Bought from Bala Ukung and Na'an Tenan 1/2/88 M$30.
BM accession no. Ethno As1988,22.64

BM65

Ra'ing with headstrap (*sengoloh*). Small rigid basket for harvesting rice and collecting vegetables and fruit in fields and wild, with headstrap (also used to fix basket around waist when harvesting). Body made of woven strips of bamboo. Bound with parallel and criss-cross strips of rattan. Frame rattan. Lip of basket rattan; simple pattern. Base made of coiled strips of rattan. Strip of rattan at base to allow the basket to be hung upside down. No *ubir* (BM143) has been applied inside. Used.

1' 5" in height, 1' 2" in diameter at top, 5" in diameter at bottom.
Made by Merua' Ulun (female), Remudu, 1987. Rattan work by her husband Unid Tala.
Materials: bamboo (*bulu' poran*), rattan (*ue kusah* for frame, *ue rabun* for lip of basket, *ue pa'it* for binding). Headstrap grass (*da'un tamar*).
Bought from Merua' Ulun, Remudu, 3/3/88 M$20.
BM accession no. Ethno As1988,22.65

BM66

Bu'an bodok barit. Large rigid basket made of bamboo bound to a rattan frame for use in carrying husked and unhusked rice. Pointed (*bodok*), then flattened, base, made in the old Kelabit style. This basket will not stand up by itself. *Ubir* (BM143) appears to have been applied both inside and outside of basket to make it proof against anything slipping through and to strengthen it, but it has adhered best to places where the inside of bamboo has been in contact with it. Much of the *ubir* on places where the slippery outside part of the bamboo has been in contact with it has come off. *Barit* refers to patterns woven into bamboo work by using inside or outside of bamboo, whose names are, from top to bottom: *barit lua'* (backbone pattern), *barit reko'* (crooked pattern), *barit bulan* (moon pattern), *barit peta'ud* (hooked pattern), *barit lua'* (*lua* is the pre-Christian ceremony of anointing those going through transitions with blood), *barit kukud ada'* (spirits' feet pattern). Used.

1' 11" in height, 1' 5" in diameter at top, 4" in diameter at bottom.
Made by Parai (female) (not known where resident) approximately 1976. Rattan work by Temagong (male), of Batu Patong, at same time. Bought by Malamud Ulun of Pa' Dalih from Temagong at unspecified date for three *bu'an*-full of unhusked rice.
Materials: bamboo (probably *bulu' poran*), rattan (probably *ue kusah* for frame, *ue rabun* for lip of basket, *ue pa'it* for binding), string made of bark (*anit kayuh kilid*), *ubir* (BM143). Bought from Malamud Ulun in Pa' Dalih 24/2/88 M$55.
BM accession no. Ethno As1988,22.66

BM67

Bu'an uang bodok. Large rigid basket with pointed (*bodok*), then flattened, base, made in the old Kelabit style, for use in harvesting rice. Will not stand up without support. Body made of strips of bamboo; *uang* refers to the fact that the slippery outside of the bamboo has been stripped off so that both the outside and the inside (*uang*) of the bamboo are visible. Frame made of rattan. Bound with parallel strips of rattan. Base made of closely woven rattan. *Ubir* (BM143) has been applied to inside of basket to make it proof against anything slipping through and to strengthen it and continues to adhere well. Plain; no pattern. Used.

1' 10" in height, 1' 5" at top, 3" at bottom.
Made by Pun Bupun (female), mother of Terawe Ulun of Pa' Dalih, approx 1960. Rattan work by Terawe Ulun (male), 1960. Bark string repaired by Sinah Terawe Ulun (female), Terawe Ulun's wife, Feb 1988. Repair commissioned.
Materials: bamboo (*bulu' poran*), rattan (probably *ue kusah* for frame, *ue rabun* for lip of basket and *ue pa'it* for binding), string made

of bark (*anit kayuh kilid*), *ubir* (BM143).
Bought from Sinah Terawe Ulun 7/2/88 M$40.
BM accession no. Ethno As1988,22.67

BM68

Bu'an. Large rigid basket for use in harvesting rice. Internal work bamboo, woven; outside this there is a tight parallel horizontal binding of rattan. Closely woven rattan strip around base, wide woven rattan lip. Frame rattan. Small woven rattan hooks on both sides, presumably for hanging when not in use. Headstrap and shoulder straps, attached using bark string. *Ubir* (BM143) has been applied to inside of basket to make it proof against anything slipping through and to strengthen it and continues to adhere well. Used.

1' 9" in height; 1' 3½" in diameter at top, 8½" in diameter at bottom. Probably made partly by Kapong Bawah, Long Layu, Kerayan; there must be another maker too, however, because rattan work is done by men, bamboo work by women.
Bought from Kapong Bawah about 1960 by Siren Tauh of Pa' Dalih.
Materials: bamboo (probably *bulu' poran*), rattan (*ue tak* – which is the best quality rattan for this purpose – for lip and strip around base; probably *ue kusah* for base and frame), string made of bark (*anit kayuh* kilid), *ubir* (BM143).
Bought from Siren Tauh 19/11/87 M$80.
BM accession no. Ethno As1988,22.68

BM69 a,b

Kalang basket for carrying fruit and vegetables or firewood, fitted with shoulder straps (*kela'e*) and lining mat (*liling*) inside for ease of packing and to prevent contents falling out through holes. Open-weave, made using criss-cross and parallel horizontal strips of split rattan. Used.

1' 6" in height, 10" in diameter.
Made by Balang Pelaba (male), 1987. Mat made by Sinah Matala Ulun, probably 1987/88.
Materials: rattan (*ue kusah*). Shoulder straps rattan (*ue pa'it*), attached by string made of bark (*anit kayuh kilid*). Mat grass (*da'un berpah*).
BM69a *Kalang* basket with shoulder straps (*kela'e*).
BM accession no. Ethno As1988,22.69a
BM69b *Liling* mat.
BM accession no. Ethno As1988,22.69b
Basket and mat bought from Balang Pelaba 4/3/88 $20

BM70

Kalang basket with headstrap (*sengoloh*). Open weave basket for carrying fruit and vegetables or firewood. This one was made using a complex technique involving looping whole rattan strips. Flat bottom. Used.

Height 1' 7", diameter 1' 3" at top, 5" at bottom.
Made by Sinah Pasan (female), Pa' Umor (Kelabit settlement near Bario) 1987.
Materials: rattan (frame *ue repit*, body *ue rabun*), headstrap grass (*da'un tamar*).
Bought from Cooperative shop in Bario, October 1987 M$20.
BM accession no. Ethno As1988,22.70

BM71 a,b

Bekang dechur. Expandable lady's basket (literally 'lady's *bekang*') with lining mat (*liling*) and headstrap (*sengoloh*) used for transporting things between settlements, constructed with flap at front attached only at bottom. Back of closely woven rattan, with wooden piece at bottom, attached with rattan, to provide strength. (Men's *bekang* used for hunting (see **BM73**)). Front and flap made of whole rattan

twisted and intertwined into a pattern, within a frame of larger rattan. Coiled and intertwined rattan at bottom to form flattish base. Bark string at front to close basket tightly. Used.

1' 5" in height, 7" in depth, 1' in width at top, 7" in width at bottom.
Made by Ribu Long (male), Pa' Lungan (Kelabit settlement near Bario) 1978, for Laba Awa of Pa' Dalih.
Materials: rattan (*ue rabun*, probably bound with *ue pa'it*), string made of bark (*anit kayuh kilid*). Headstrap grass (*da'un tamar*). Maker of headstrap unrecorded.
Liling mat of *berpah* grass made by Sina Niri, Remudu (Kelabit settlement three hours' walk from Pa' Dalih) February 1988.
BM71a *Bekang* basket with headstrap (*sengoloh*). Bought from Laba Awa 17/2/88 M$50.
BM accession no. Ethno As1988,22.71a
BM71b *Liling* lining mat. Maker unknown. Bought from Sinah Niri 17/2/88, $1.
BM accession no. Ethno As1988,22.71b

BM72 a,b

Bekang dechur. Expandable lady's basket (literally 'lady's *bekang*') with lining mat (*liling*) and headstrap (*sengoloh*) used for transporting things between settlements, constructed with flap at front attached at bottom. Bark string to bind at the front. This is a particularly ornate and beautifully made example of a ladies *bekang*. The wooden board at the back is carved and the rattan work is complex and well executed. The rattan binding on the frame is complex and well executed. Used.

1' 5" in height, 7" in depth, 1' in width at top, 7" in width at bottom.
Made by Milih Ulun (male), Ulung Palang Deta', Bario, 1967.
Acquired from him by Siren Tauh, Pa' Dalih, at an unspecified date and for an unspecified price.
Materials: rattan (*ue rabun* for body, probably bound with *ue pa'it*), string made of bark (*anit kayuh kilid*), wood (variety unknown). Headstrap grass (*da'un tamar*).
Bought from Siren Tauh 30/9/87 M$25.
BM72a *Bekang* basket with headstrap (*sengoloh*).
BM accession no. Ethno As1988,22.72a
BM72b *Liling* lining mat.
BM accession no. Ethno As1988,22.72b

BM73 a,b

Bekang dela'ih. Expandable man's basket (literally 'man's *bekang*') with lining mat (*liling*) and shoulder straps (*kela'e*) used for transporting things between settlements, for carrying meat and provisions when on hunting trips, and for bringing in firewood. Constructed with flap at front attached only at bottom. Used.

1' 11" in height, 1' 2" wide at top, 9" wide at bottom, 8" in depth.
Made by Balang Pelaba (male), July 1987 for Kaz Janowski (commissioned; price paid not available). Lining mat (*liling*) made by Pun Bian, Remudu (Kelabit settlement three hours' walk from Pa' Dalih), unknown date.
Materials: rattan (*ue lengan*, probably bound with *ue pa'it*), wood (*kayuh*; variety unknown). Shoulder straps rattan (*ue pa'it*). Lining mat (*liling*) grass (*da'un berpah*).
Bekang donated by Kaz Janowski March 1988. Lining mat bought from Pun Bian, Remudu, early 1988 M$1.00.
BM73a *Bekang* with shoulder straps.
BM accession no. Ethno As1988,22.73a
BM73b *Liling* lining mat.
BM accession no. Ethno As1988,22.73b

BM74 a,b

Bekang anak dela'ih. Expandable small boy's basket (literally 'small boys' *bekang*') with shoulder straps (*kela'e*) and lining mat (*liling*). Strip of split rattan to bind together at the front.

Such baskets are used by small boys to transport personal possessions between settlements, to carry firewood and to carry meat and provisions when on hunting trips. New.

1' 2" in height, 5" in width, 6" in depth.
Made by Nanad Bala (male), Remudu (Kelabit settlement three hours' walk from Pa' Dalih), February 1988.
Materials: rattan (*ue kusah* and probably *ue pa'it* for shoulder straps), wood (variety unknown). Lining mat (*liling*) grass (*da'un berpah*).
Bought from Nanad Bala 3/3/88 M$12.
BM74a *Bekang* basket with shoulder straps (*kela'e*).
BM accession no. Ethno As1988,22.74a
BM74b *Liling* lining mat.
BM accession no. Ethno As1988,22.74b

BM75 a,b

Bekang anak dechur. Expandable small girl's basket (literally 'small girls' *bekang*') with shoulder straps (*kela'e*) and lining mat (*liling*). Bark string to bind at front. Such baskets are used by small girls to transport personal possessions between settlements. New.

1' in height, 5" in depth, 5" in width at bottom, 7" in width at top.
Said to have been made by Doo Inan (female), Remudu (Kelabit settlement three hours' walk from Pa' Dalih), February 1988 (however, probably made by her husband since *bekang*, being made of rattan, are made by men).
Materials: rattan (variety unknown), wood (variety unknown), string made of bark (*anit kayuh kilid*). Lining mat grass (*da'un berpah*).
BM75a *Bekang* basket with shoulder straps (*kela'e*). BM accession no. Ethno As1988,22.75a
BM75b *Liling* lining mat. BM accession no. Ethno As1988,22.75b
Bought from Doo Inan, Remudu, February 1988, M$15.

BM76

Kalang anak Child's basket (literally 'child's *kalang*') with shoulder straps (*kela'e*) attached with bark string. Such open-weave baskets are used by children (usually girls) to carry fruit and vegetables gathered in the fields and in the wild. Normally used with lining mat (*liling*) such as **BM75b**. Wooden board fixed to bottom between shoulder straps to support base of back and contents. Used.

1' in height, 9" in diameter.
Made by Balang Pelaba (male) of Pa' Dalih in 1982 for Maureen, daughter of Raya Bala and Sinah Niri of Remudu (Kelabit settlement three hours' walk from Pa' Dalih).
Materials: rattan (*ue kusah*). Shoulder straps (*kela'e*) rattan (*ue pa'it*), string made of bark (*anit kayuh kilid*).
Bought from Raya Bala, Remudu, 3/3/88 M$10.
BM accession no. Ethno As1988,22.76

BM77

Liling. Mat for use inside basket, to facilitate packing and to keep contents in. Used.

Made by Sinah Paran Belaan (female), Remudu (Kelabit settlement 3 hours' walk from Pa' Dalih), 1987. Given by her to Sinah Paran To'oh, Pa' Dalih.
Materials: grass (*da'un berpah*).
Given to Monica Janowski by Laba Awa, Sinah Paran To'oh's mother, January 1988.
BM accession no. Ethno As1988,22.77

BM78

Gawang anak. Child's soft multipurpose basket (literally 'child's *gawang*') used for carrying personal possessions. Closely woven rattan, shoulder straps attached with bark string. Used.

10" in height, 7" across.
Materials: rattan (variety unknown), string made of bark (*anit kayuh kilid*).
No documentation.
Given to Molly Janowski during 1986-88. Donated by Monica and Kaz Janowski to BM March 1988.
BM accession no. Ethno As1988,22.78

BM79

Belalong la'al. Basket to keep hen with chicks in at night. Simple criss-cross rattan structure for body, looping pattern for lip of body and lid. New.

1' 3" in height, 10" maximum in diameter.
Made by Balang Pelaba (male) February 1988.
Commissioned.
Materials: rattan (*ue kusah*).
Bought from Balang Pelaba 29/2/88 M$15.
BM accession no. Ethno As1988,22.79

BM80

Belalong nuba'. Basket (literally '*belalong* for cooked rice') with lid to store rice packed in leaves between cooking and eating. Made of bamboo with outside stripped off, with frame and binding of rattan. Carrying handle of rattan which passes right round the basket. which also serves to hold on lid because it passes through rattan hooks on the lid.

1' in height, lid 6" in diameter, base 7" in diameter.
Made by Merua' Ulun (female), Long Dano (Kelabit settlement two hours' walk from Pa' Dalih). Rattan work by Unid Tala, her husband.
Materials: bamboo (*bulu' poran*), rattan (*ue kusah* for frame, *ue pa'it* for binding).
Bought from Merua' Ulun February 1987 M$10.
BM accession no. Ethno As1988,22.80

BM81

Sengoloh. Head strap for carrying baskets. New.

Made by Sinah Balang Lipang (female), Long Dano, niece of Na'an Tenan of Pa' Dalih, January 1988.
Materials: grass (*da'un tamar*).
Bought from Na'an Tenan, Pa' Dalih, 6/2/88, M$2.
BM accession no. Ethno As1988,22.81

BM82

A'ab. Basket for storage and serving of food. Square at bottom, rounded at top. Made of bamboo bound to rattan frame. *Ubir* (BM143) has been applied to inside of basket to make it proof against anything slipping through and to strengthen it. New.

9" in diameter (square at bottom), 3" deep.
Made by Sinah Matala Ulun (female), 23/11/87. Rattan work by Balang Pelaba (male).
Materials: bamboo (probably *bulu' poran*), rattan (*ue repit*), *ubir* (BM143)
Bought from Sinah Matala Ulun 23/11/87 M$4; M$1.50 paid to Balang Pelaba for rattan work.
BM accession no. Ethno As1988,22.82

BM83

A'ab. Basket for storage and serving of food. Square at bottom, rounded at top. Made of bamboo bound to rattan frame. *Ubir* (BM143) has been applied to inside of basket to make it proof against anything slipping through and to strengthen it. Used.

1' 2" in diameter (square at bottom), 5" deep.
Made by Pun Bupun (female), residence unknown, approximately 1955. Rattan work by unidentified man.
Materials: bamboo (probably *bulu' poran*), rattan (*ue*; variety unknown), *ubir* (BM143)
Bought from Na'an Tenan, Pa' Dalih 7/2/88 M$15.
BM accession no. Ethno As1988,22.83

BM84

A'ab. Basket for storage and serving of food. Square at bottom, rounded at top. Made of bamboo bound to rattan frame. *Ubir* (BM143) has been applied to inside of basket to make it proof against anything slipping through and to strengthen it. Some bamboo strips dyed pink and green, woven to make a pattern. Used.

1' 3½" in diameter (square at bottom), 4" deep.
Made by Sinah Rang Bala (female) of Batu Patong (40 minutes' walk from Pa' Dalih) 1985. Rattan work by Balang Pelaba (male) 29/2/88.
Materials: bamboo (*bulu' poran*), rattan (variety unknown), *ubir* (BM143).
Bought from Sinah Rang Bala 8/2/88 M$10. M$2 paid to Balang Pelaba for rattan work.
BM accession no. Ethno As1988,22.84

BM85

Agag bera. Rice sifter. Square, concave network of spaced out strips of bamboo bound to rattan frame. Used.

1' 2" square.
Made by Sekera Ayu (female), mother of Sinah Rang Bala of Batu Patong (40 minutes' walk from Pa' Dalih), 1982; rattan work by unidentified man.
Materials: bamboo (*bulu' poran*), rattan (variety unknown).
Bought from Sinah Allen, Pa' Dalih, 4/3/88 M$10.
BM accession no. Ethno As1988,22.85

BM86

Agag bera. Rice sifter. Square, concave network of spaced out strips of bamboo bound to rattan frame. Rattan hook for hanging. Darkened by storage in hearth area. Used.

1' 2" square.
Made by Sinah Ellie (female), 1985; rattan work by unidentified man.
Materials: bamboo (*bulu' poran*), rattan (variety unknown).
Bought from Na'an Tenan 6/2/88 M$10.
BM accession no. Ethno As1988,22.86

BM87

Agag ubi kayuh. Grated cassava sifter. Square, concave network of spaced out strips of bamboo bound to rattan frame. More closely spaced strips than BM85 and BM86. Blackened by storage in hearth area. Used.

10" square.
Made by Makatu Ulun (female) of Pa' Dalih (Balang Pelaba's first wife) approximately 1942. Rattan work presumably by Balang Pelaba (male).
Materials: bamboo (*bulu' poran*), rattan (variety unknown).
Bought from Balang Pelaba 23/2/88 M$5.
BM accession no. Ethno As1988,22.87

BM88

Reno. Rice winnowing tray, also used for cleaning vegetables, preparing food etc. Open at one end, closed at the other. *Ubir* (BM143) has been applied to inside of basket to make it proof against anything slipping through and to strengthen it.

1' 7" in length, 1' 3" maximum in width.

Made by Sinah Ellie (female), 1987. Rattan work by Balang Darin, her husband.
Materials: bamboo (probably *bulu' poran*), rattan (variety unknown), *ubir* (BM143).
Bought at auction in the church in Pa' Dalih intended to raise money for work on school electricity system 22/10/87 M$5. Donated for auction by Sinah Ellie.
BM accession no. Ethno As1988,22.88

BM89

Reno barit. Rice winnowing tray, also used for cleaning vegetables, preparing food etc. Open at one end, closed at the other. *Barit* ('patterned') refers to fact that the bamboo strips are painted white, black, red and yellow, and are woven in a pattern which shows on the underside (not in contact with rice or food). *Ubir* (BM143) has been applied to inside of basket to make it proof against anything slipping through and to strengthen it. Fitted with rattan hook for hanging.

1' 9" in length by 1' 6" maximum across.
Made by Merua' Ulun (female), Remudu, 1987. Rattan work probably by her husband, Unid Tala.
Materials: bamboo (probably *bulu' poran*), rattan (variety unknown), *ubir* (BM143), paint bought in town.
Bought from Merua' Ulun 14/2/88 M$15.
BM accession no. Ethno As1988,22.89

BM90

Reno. Rice winnowing tray, also used for cleaning vegetables, preparing food etc. Open at one end, closed at the other. Fitted with rattan hook for hanging. A pattern has been woven in by reversing the bamboo so that the shiny side shows in the inside and the inside of the bamboo on the outside in certain places. Used.

1' 9" in length, 1' 7" maximum across.
Made by Tepo Ben (female) 1986; rattan work (unusually, since she is a woman) also by Tepo Ben, using rattan collected by Ketuan Tepun (male).
Materials: bamboo (probably *bulu' poran*), rattan (variety unknown), *ubir* (BM143).
Bought from Tepo Ben 16/1/88 M$10.
BM accession no. Ethno As1988,22.90

BM91

Reno. Rice winnowing tray, also used for cleaning vegetables, preparing food etc. Unusual decorative rattan work 1" in from edge. Blackened from storage in a smokey kitchen. *Ubir* (BM143) has been applied to inside of basket to make it proof against anything slipping through and to strengthen it. Used.

1' 9" in length, 1' 8" maximum in width.
Made by Mariar Aran (female), 1985. Rattan work by Belalong Tepun (male).
Materials: bamboo (probably *bulu' poran*), rattan (variety unknown), *ubir* (BM143)
Bought from Mariar Aran 21/11/87 M$10.
BM accession no. Ethno As1988,22.91

BM92

Bakol tana'. Basket for transporting earth, open at one end. Handles at both sides for carrying. New.

1' 5" by 1' 2".
Made by Balang Pelaba (male) 3/3/88.
Commissioned.
Materials: rattan (*ue kusah*) for basket and handles, creeper for frame (*uar bekar*).
Bought from Balang Pelaba 3/3/88 M$10.
BM accession no. Ethno As1988,22.92

BM93

Be'ong bua' tabuh. Container made from a gourd with top cut off used for storing fish while fishing in small stream, or for storing snails while collecting in wet rice fields after harvest. Pierced for string used for hanging gourd at waist. Normally used by women. Used.

8" by 3½" maximum diameter.
Maker unknown.
Materials: gourd (*bua' tabuh*), string made of bark (*anit kayuh kilid*).
Bought from Sinah Bayah Ribuh, Pa' Dalih 4/2/88 M$2.
BM accession no. Ethno As1988,22.93

BM94

Iap. Fishing net used by women for fishing in small streams. Rounded rectangular rigid creeper frame with bucket net made of bark string bound to it. Used.

1' 7" by 1' 2".
Made by Na'an Padin (female), Long Dano (Kelabit settlement two hours' walk from Pa' Dalih) about 1980. Made for Siren Tauh, Pa' Dalih (female). Never used. Creeper frame made by Balang Pelaba (male), January 1988. Net made of bark string, bound on to frame 14/2/88 by Laba Awa (female), using bark string.
Materials: string made of bark (*anit kayuh kilid*), creeper (*uar bekar*).
Net bought from Siren Tauh 26/10/87 M$16. M$2.50 paid to Laba Awa for binding net to frame.
BM accession no. Ethno As1988,22.94

BM95

Iap. Fishing net used by women for fishing in small streams. Rounded rectangular rigid creeper frame with bucket net made of cotton string, nylon and bark string bound to frame with bark string. Appears new; not clear if used.

1' 7" by 1' 2".
Made by Pun Ribid Ayu (male), Long Dano (Kelabit settlement two hours' walk from Pa' Dalih), 1980's.
Materials: cotton string, string made of bark (*anit kayuh kilid*), nylon cord and creeper (*uar bekar*).
Bought from Pun Ribid Ayu 20/2/88 M$15.
BM accession no. Ethno As1988,22.95

BM96

Pukat. Fishing net, used by men in rivers. Stretched across the river and left to catch fish as they go by.

Made by Bayah Ripuk (male), 1987.
Materials: nylon string, rubber pieces, lead weights (all town-bought).
Bought from Bayah Ripuk 8/3/88 M$35.
BM accession no. Ethno As1988,22.96

BM97

Topi (orang) ulu. Decorative hat (literally 'hat of the people [of the interior]' – Malay) worn at festive occasions. Open at top. Made of fine woven strips of bamboo decorated with wool, sequins and other decorations bought in town. Brim on two sides made of bamboo bound with nylon. Used.

7" high by 6" maximum in diameter at brim.
Maker unknown.
Materials: bamboo (probably *bulu' poran*), wool, metal, cotton thread, velvet cloth, nylon (last five town-bought).
Given to Monica and Kaz Janowski by Lawe Padan, Pa' Dalih some time 1986-88. Donated by Monica and Kaz Janowski to BM March 1988
BM accession no. Ethno As1988,22.97

BM98

Apoh rongoh pade. Brush made of rice stalks for sweeping hearth area. Bound with grass. New.

2' 1" long by 2" in diameter.
Made by Bala Ukung (male), January 1988.
Materials: rice stalks (*rongoh pade*), bound with grass (*da'un tamar*).
Bought from Bala Ukung 6/2/88 M$1.50.
BM accession no. Ethno As1988,22.98

BM99

Apoh rongoh pade. Hearth broom made of rice stalks for sweeping hearth area. Bound with creeper. New.

2' 4" long by 2" in diameter.
Made by Bala Aran (male), February 1988.
Materials: rice stalks (*rongoh pade*), bound with creeper (*uar ubu*).
Bought from Bala Aran, 7/2/88 M$1
BM accession no. Ethno As1988,22.99

BM100

Apoh rongoh pade. Hearth broom made of rice stalks for sweeping hearth area. Bound with red nylon cord. New.

2' 5" long by 2" in diameter.
Made by Bala Aran (male), 12/2/88.
Materials: rice stalks (*rongoh pade*), red nylon cord (town-bought).
Bought from Bala Aran 12/2/88 M$1.
BM accession no. Ethno As1988,22.100

BM101

Iop apui. Tube for blowing on fire to make it grow. New.

1' 8" long, 1" in diameter.
Made by Balang Pelaba (male), 7/3/88.
Commissioned.
Materials: bamboo (*bulu' bayuh*).
Given by Balang Pelaba to Monica Janowski 7/3/88.
BM accession no. Ethno As1988,22.101

BM102

Dawan natang. Bamboo stand for burning damar resin (*natang*) from damar tree (*kayuh tomoh*) (see **BM36,139**). Rarely used nowadays; brass lamps filled with petrol with open flame at top, bought on coast, are now usual. Made by using one section of a large bore bamboo, split down its length and splayed out at one end so as to form legs, bound together with rattan. Top where damar is burnt is the joint at the other end of the section, which would be filled with earth before damar is burnt. New; no earth in top.

1' high by 10" wide at bottom, 3" wide at top.
Made by Lawe Padan (male), 1/3/88.
Materials: bamboo (*bulu' betong*), bound with rattan (variety unknown).
Bought from Lawe Padan 2/3/88 M$5.
Commissioned.
BM accession no. Ethno As1988,22.102

BM103

Laan. Low hearthside stool. Carved out of a single piece of wood. Used.

10" long, 4½" wide, 3½" high.
Made by Riwed Bala (male), Batu Patong (40 mins walk from Pa' Dalih) approx 1940.
Materials: wood (*kayuh belaban*).
Bought from Riwed Bala 8/2/88 M$10.
BM accession no. Ethno As1988,22.103

BM104

Laan oloh. Wooden 'stool' (literally 'head *laan*') used to support head when lying down, usually near the hearth. Carved out of a single piece of wood. Top carved in a slight curve and continuous with legs so that it is comfortable to lie on. New.

1' 1" in length, 6" in width, 3" in height.
Made by Riwed Bala (male), February 1988.
Commissioned.
Materials: wood (*kayuh belaban*).
Bought from Riwed Bala 2/3/88 M$15.
BM accession no. Ethno As1988,22.104

BM105

Laan. Low stool with legs for sitting on by hearth. Carved out of a single piece of wood. New.

1' 1" long, 7½" wide, 3" high.
Made by Riwed Bala (male), February 1988.
Commissioned.
Materials: wood (*kayuh belaban*).
Bought from Riwed Bala 2/3/88 M$15.
BM accession no. Ethno As1988,22.105

BM106

Tusuh. Kelabit/Kerayan salt, wrapped in leaves. Made from boiling down brine from springs in the forest. Tubular shape; this is the usual shape, made by packing salt in bamboo internodes while it is drying out.

9½" long by 1½" in diameter.
Made by people from the Kerayan and given or sold to Sinah Luun Ayu of Pa' Dalih. She gave it to the Pa' Dalih parish for sale at auction at the *Kuman Pade Bru* ('Eating New Rice', after harvest) on 18/2/88.
Materials: salt made from brine, leaves (*da'un ilad*), rattan for binding (*ue*; variety unknown).
Bought at auction held by Pa' Dalih parish (*sidang*) in short longhouse in Pa' Dalih, at *Kuman Pade Bru*, for M$6.
BM accession no. Ethno As1988,22.106

BM107

Tusuh. Kelabit salt, wrapped in leaves and bound with rattan. Hook for hanging made of rattan. Conical shape; this is an unusual shape, and it is not clear how it was made.

4" long by 2" in diameter at the base.
Made by Paran Belaan (male), Remudu (Kelabit settlement three hours' walk from Pa' Dalih), 1987.
Materials: salt made from brine, leaves (probably *da'un ilad*), rattan for binding (variety unknown).
Bought from Paran Belaan, February 1988, M$4.
BM accession no. Ethno As1988,22.107

BM108

Pru ue. Grader for passing rattan through to make it all the same diameter. Made of the lid of a tin, with holes of different sizes pierced in it and a rattan handle attached. Used and blackened by storage in the smokey hearth area.

Made by Belalong Tepun (male), 1984.
Materials: tin lid (from a town-bought tin), rattan (variety unknown).
Bought from Belalong Tepun M$1.
BM accession no. Ethno As1988,22.108

BM109

Gaing kedong. Spinning top (*gaing*). Single-ended. Played with after harvest by boys. New.

3½" long by 2" in diameter.

Made by Wel (male), 18/11/87.
Materials: wood (*kayuh ore*).
Bought from Wel 20/11/87 M$2.
BM accession no. Ethno As1988,22.109

BM110

Gaing kedong. Spinning top (*gaing*). Played with after harvest by boys. Double-ended. New.

3" long, 2" in diameter.
Made by Wel (male), 24/11/87.
Commissioned.
Materials: wood (variety unknown).
Bought from Wel 24/11/87 M$2.
BM accession no. Ethno As1988,22.110

BM111

Alud raut anak. Toy boat ('boat for play by a child'). Dugout carved out of a single piece of wood. Hook carved out at one end to which is attached a string made of bark string.

1' 3½" long, 3" wide, 1½" deep.
Made by Raan Kerayan (male), March 1988.
Materials: wood (*kayuh tara'*), string made of bark (*anit kayuh kilid*).
Bought from Raan Kerayan 7/3/88, M$10.
BM accession no. Ethno As1988,22.111

BM112

Bubuh raya. Big (*raya*) fish trap (*bubuh*) made of strips of bamboo bound with rattan. Tubular shape, with one pointed end and the other open for fish to enter. Inside, there are two rounds of bamboo prongs (*anga'*) to prevent the fish escaping. Opening with wooden door near pointed end to slide over it for access to fish once caught. Placed in rivers and streams overnight. New.

2' 5" long, 11" in diameter at wide end tapering to a point at the other.
Made by Bayah Ripuk (male), January 1988.
Commissioned.
Materials: bamboo (variety unknown), rattan (variety unknown), wood (variety unknown), creeper (variety unknown).
Bought from Bayah Ripuk 20/1/88 M$10.
BM accession no. Ethno As1988,22.112

BM113

Kelebong pakai ngarang. 'Clothing worn for dancing'. Skirt made of black cloth, in the style of a Malay *sarong*, decorated with machined-on lace and strips of cloth, with sequins and other metallic decorations, and with a sewn-on piece of cloth with a Kenyah/Kayan type of decoration in black and white; appears that the black part has been printed on to white cloth. Such skirts do not appear to be entirely Kelabit in style, being related more to Kenyah/Kayan styles and to some extent to Lun Bawang styles from the Fifth Division (a group closely related to the Kelabit). They are sometimes worn at festive occasions. When they are bought, they have usually been made on commission to Kelabit living in town, who buy them as *bunga ruma'* (house decorations, to display in a prominent place). They fetch prices much higher than the materials or even the workmanship would appear to warrant. It is likely that they have a symbolic value, displaying Kelabit cultural heritage to non-Kelabit; there are a number of other articles which enjoy a similar position (see BM116).

4' 4" by 3' 2".
Made by Gadong Ye, daughter of Tama Bulan, Long Peluan (Kelabit settlement outside the highlands, further downriver) and her

husband Keduis Apui, latter said to be a Kenyah from Long Banga' (although this is a Sa'aban longhouse); this couple now live in Marudi and the *kelebong* was made there. Tama Bulan brought the *kelebong* with him on a visit to Remudu (Kelabit settlement three hours' walk from Pa'Dalih), hoping to sell it (probably hoping to sell it to Monica and Kaz Janowski).
Materials: cotton cloth, sequins, beads, lace, dye (all town-bought).
Bought from Tama Bulan in Remudu 3/3/88 M$180.
BM accession no. Ethno As1988,22.113

BM114

Tabir puet. Rattan mat for one's bottom (for sitting on) with black cotton cloth string for tying around the waist. All Kelabit men used to have one of these when they wore loincloths (until about the 1960s). Now not worn. Rectangular shape, with point at one end. Illegible inscription. Made of plain rattan and rattan dyed black, woven together to create a pattern. Used.

1' 7" long maximum at point by 8½" wide.
Said by Riwed Bala to have been made by a Kalimantan Timur people whom the Kelabit call the Uang Paya a few days' walk from Pa'Dalih (probably a Kenyah group), approx 1968.
Materials: rattan (*ue tak*), cotton, dye (town-bought).
Bought from Riwed Bala, Batu Patong (40 mins from Pa'Dalih) 8/2/88 M$5.
BM accession no. Ethno As1988,22.114

BM115

Bane. Necklace made of town-bought small beads with tassel at end fitted round a piece of polystyrene with a button to hold it on. Beads pink, blue, red, yellow and orange. Label attached with 'Batang Kelapang' written on it.

Made by unidentified woman in Pa'Dalih to be given to one of *penaung* (sponsors) at a *Pesta memotong kek* ('Cake-cutting party', at which cakes are auctioned to raise money for the parish) in Pa'Dalih. It was eventually allocated to Batang Kelapang (Kaz Janowski's Kelabit name), who was one of the sponsors, and presented to him. Such necklaces are made to be presented on official occasions and to hang on walls in Kelabit houses in town as *bunga ruma'* ('house decorations') (see **BM113**). It is not clear whether they have much time depth in a Kelabit context; they may derive from a Kenyah/Kayan aesthetic tradition.
Materials: beads, polystyrene, button, nylon string (all town-bought).
Given to Kaz Janowski at *Pesta memotong kek* in Pa'Dalih, during 1986-88.
Donated by Kaz Janowski to the BM March 1988.
BM accession no. Ethno As1988,22.115

BM116

Bane. Necklace made of town-bought small beads with tassel at end fitted round a piece of polystyrene with a button to hold it on. Beads white, blue and red.

Made by unidentified Kelabit woman. Such necklaces are now made to be presented on official occasions or given to sponsors at 'cake cutting parties' (see **BM115**). They are often hung on walls in Kelabit houses in town as *bunga ruma'* ('house decorations') (see **BM113**). It is not clear whether they have much time depth in a Kelabit context; they may derive from a Kenyah/Kayan aesthetic tradition.
Materials: beads, polystyrene, button, nylon string (all town-bought).
No detailed documentation on acquisition. Given to Kaz, Monica or Molly Janowski some time 1986-88. Donated by Monica and Kaz Janowski to BM March 1988.
BM accession no. Ethno As1988,22.116

BM117

As **BM120 and 121**, broken in transport from Kuching to London.

BM accession no. Ethno As1988,22.117

BM118

As **BM120 and 121**, broken in transport from Kuching to London.

BM accession no. Ethno As1988,22.118

BM119

As **BM120 and 121**, broken in transport from Kuching to London.

BM accession no. Ethno As1988,22.119

BM120

Tuning. Glazed earthenware cooking pot with rounded bottom, for use in making rice porridge (*kikid*) and other side dishes (*penguman*) for the rice meal. Such pots were made and were in regular use until the 1970s. Those that remain are used by some women in Pa'Dalih but are no longer normally made. New.

6½" in height, 5" in diameter.
Made by Na'an Tenan (female), Jan/Feb 1988 as part of a batch made under commission from Monica Janowski.
Materials: clay, resin (*natang*) (see **BM36,139**).
Fee for making of complete batch M$150.
BM accession no. Ethno As1988,22.120

BM121

Tuning. Glazed earthenware cooking pot with rounded bottom, for use in making rice porridge (*kikid*) and other side dishes (*penguman*) for the rice meal. Such pots were made and were in regular use until the 1970s. Those that remain are used by some women in Pa'Dalih but are no longer normally made. New.

6½" in height, 5" in diameter.
Made by Na'an Tenan (female), Jan/Feb 1988 as part of a batch made under commission from Monica Janowski.
Materials: clay, resin (*natang*) (see **BM36,139**).
Fee for making of complete batch M$150.
BM accession no. Ethno As1988,22.121

BM122.

Tuning. Earthenware pot, rounded bottom. Unfired, unglazed example. 6½" in height, 5" in diameter.

Made by Na'an Tenan as part of same batch as **BM117-21**.
BM accession no. Ethno As1988,22.122

BM123

Tuning, broken in transport from Kuching to London. Glazed earthenware pot with rounded bottom used for making rice porridge (*kikid*) and other side dishes (*penguman*) for the rice meal. Blackened with use.

Made by Pun Ribuh (female), Long Dano (Kelabit settlement two hours' walk from Pa'Dalih) approx 1960.
Materials: clay, damar resin (*natang*) (see **BM36,139**).
Bought from Na'an Tepin, Pa'Dalih, 8/11/87 M$5.
BM accession no. Ethno As1988,22.123

BM124

Tuning. Glazed earthenware pot with rounded bottom used for making rice porridge (*kikid*) and other side dishes (*penguman*) for the rice meal, until 1970s. Decorated with v-shaped lines around rim. Rim broken in transport from Kuching to London. Used.

5½" in height, 5½" in diameter.
Made by Na'an Tenan (female), approx 1970.
Materials: clay, damar resin (*natang*) (see **BM36,139**).
BM accession no. Ethno As1988,22.124

BM125
Kudin. Large glazed earthenware pot with rounded botom, used for cooking rice until approx 1970's. Used.

8" in height, 7" in diameter.
Made by Pun Tengokan (female), mother of Sinah Luun Ayu, 1966.
Materials: clay, damar resin (*natang*) (see **BM36,139**).
Bought from Sinah Luun Ayu 1/10/87 M$6.
BM accession no. Ethno As1988,22.125

BM126
Tuning. Glazed earthenware pot with rounded bottom, used for cooking rice porridge (*kikid*) and other side dishes (*penguman*) for the rice meal until approx 1970's. Used.

4½" in height, 4" in diameter.
Made by Tepo Ben (female), 1973.
Given by Tepo Ben, 1987/88 as a gift; M$3 given to her as a return gift.
BM accession no. Ethno As1988,22.126

BM127
Tuning. Glazed earthenware pot with rounded bottom, used for cooking rice porridge (*kikid*) and other side dishes (*penguman*) for the rice meal until approx 1970's. Used.

3½" in height, 3½" in diameter.
Made by Sina Achin, grandmother of Jemry Pian of Pa' Dalih, unknown date.
Materials: clay, damar resin (*natang*) (see **BM36,139**).
Given by Siren Tauh, Pa' Dalih, 1987/8 as a gift; M$2 given to her as a return gift.
BM accession no. Ethno As1988,22.127

BM128
Kudin. Large used glazed earthenware pot with rounded bottom, used for cooking rice until approx 1970s. Decorated with parallel lines at three places around the lip. Blackened by use in cooking.

1' in height, 11" in diameter.
Made by Pun Ribuh (female), Long Dano (Kelabit settlement two hours' walk from Pa' Dalih), approx 1960.
Materials: clay, damar resin (*natang*) (see **BM36,139**).
Bought from Na'an Tepin, Pa' Dalih, 8/11/87 M$10.
BM accession no. Ethno As1988,22.128

BM129
Tuning. Unglazed, apparently unfired earthenware pot with rounded bottom, decorated with lines and squiggles. Such pots, when fired and glazed, were used until approx 1970's for cooking rice porridge (*kikid*) and other side dishes (*penguman*) for the rice meal. However this example was probably never used, and is unusual in having decorations; although Harrisson (1955: 303) says that the Kelabit used to decorate their earthenware pots, no others collected in Pa' Dalih or seen by the author in other communities in the southern part of the Kelabit Highlands in 1986-93 have any decoration of this complexity, although BM124 and BM125 have v-shaped lines around their rims and BM128 has parallel lines around its rim.

Maker unknown.
Materials: clay.
Bought from Malamud Ulun, Pa' Dalih 18/2/88 M$2.
BM accession no. Ethno As1988,22.129

BM130
Tuning, with flat base. Glazed earthenware pot, used. Blackened through use in cooking.

7" in height, 5½" in diameter.
Made by Merua', Pa' Potok, Kerayan, approx 1976. Brought to Pa' Dalih for reasons unknown; it is rare to find Kerayan style *tuning* in Kelabit settlements. Probably used for similar purposes to Kelabit *tuning* with rounded base – for cooking rice porridge (*kikid*) and other side dishes (*penguman*) for the rice meal.
Materials: clay, damar resin (*natang*) (see **BM36,139**).
BM accession no. Ethno As1988,22.130

BM131
Di'id. Stick with hardened 'soft damar resin' (*natang laya'*) on end, used for applying resin glaze to *tuning* earthenware pots made by Na'an Tenan 16/2/88, commissioned by Kaz and Monica Janowski (see **BM117-121, SM41-44**).

1' 5½" long.
Stick roughly peeled at one end, prepared by Bala Ukung for use in making commissioned pots.
Materials: wood (variety unknown), 'soft' damar resin (*natang*) (see **BM139**).
Given by Na'an Tenan together with batch of *tuning*; fee for making *tuning* M$150.
BM accession no. Ethno As1988,22.131

BM132
Topah tana'. Heavy stick bluntly pointed at one end used by Na'an Tenan (female) of Pa' Dalih to pound clay in making *tuning* earthenware pots commissioned by Kaz and Monica Janowski, Jan/Feb 1988 (see **BM117-121, SM41-44** and **Pl. 114**). Previously used by Na'an Tenan in making pots before early 1970s, when she stopped making pots.

2' 1" long, 1½" in diameter maximum.
Made by Bala Ukung, Na'an Tenan's husband, unknown date (pre-1970's).
Materials: wood (*kayuh belaban*). Covered with traces of clay.
Bought from Bala Ukung and Na'an Tenan 1/2/88 M$2.
BM accession no. Ethno As1988,22.132

BM133
Okat. Pointed stick used by Na'an Tenan (female) of Pa' Dalih to begin to shape *tuning* earthenware pots commissioned by Kaz and Monica Janowski, Jan/Feb 1988 (see **BM117-121, SM41-44**).

2' 1" long, ¾" in diameter maximum.
Made by Bala Ukung, Na'an Tenan's husband, unknown date (pre-1970's).
Materials: wood (*kayuh belaban*). Covered with traces of clay.
Bought from Bala Ukung and Na'an Tenan 1/2/88 M$2.
BM accession no. Ethno As1988,22.133

BM134
Pepe'. Paddle used by Na'an Tenan (female) to shape *tuning* earthenware pots commissioned by Kaz and Monica Janowski, Jan/Feb 1988 (see **BM117-121, SM41-44** and **Pl. 116**). Criss-crossed with incised lines to aid in working clay (further apart than lines on **BM135**). Previously used by Na'an Tenan to make pots before early 1970s, when she stopped making pots.

1' 3" long, 2½" wide maximum.
Made by Bala Ukung, Na'an Tenan's husband, unknown date (pre-1970's).
Materials: wood (*kayuh labakan*). Traces of clay.
Bought from Bala Ukung and Na'an Tenan 1/2/88 M$2.
BM accession no. Ethno As1988,22.134

BM135

Pepe'. Paddle used by Na'an Tenan (female) to shape *tuning* earthenware pots commissioned by Kaz and Monica Janowski, Jan/Feb 1988 (see **BM117-121, SM41-44** and **Pl. 116**). Criss-crossed with incised lines to aid in working clay (closer together than lines in **BM134**).

1' 2½" long, 2½" wide maximum.
Made by Bala Ukung, Na'an Tenan's husband, unknown date (pre-1970's).
Materials: wood (*kayuh belaban*). Traces of clay.
Bought from Bala Ukung and Na'an Tenan 1/2/88 M$2.
BM accession no. Ethno As1988,22.135

BM136

Batuh tuning. Stone used by Na'an Tenan (female) to shape *tuning* earthenware pots commissioned by Kaz and Monica Janowski, Jan/Feb 1988 (see **BM117-121, SM41-44**). Previously used by her to make pots before early 1970s, when she stopped making pots.

2½" in diameter.
Found by Na'an Tenan in Baram river at Lio Mato approx 1955.
Materials: stone
Bought from Na'an Tenan 1/2/88 M$3.
BM accession no. Ethno As1988,22.136

BM137

Sample of *prah*. Pounded up old *tuning*. *Prah* such as this was mixed with new clay in making *tuning* earthenware pots commissioned by Kaz and Monica Janowski, Jan/Feb (see **BM117-121, SM41-44**), and is said to stop new *tuning* from exploding during firing.

From old *tuning* belonging to Na'an Tenan, pounded up by her.
Bought from Na'an Tenan 1/2/88 M$1.
BM accession no. Ethno As1988,22.137

BM138

Gayut. Scraper for removing crust from pots used to cook 'soft rice' (*nuba laya'*). Iron bent over to form a hook at one end, and sharpened at other.

5" long, 1" wide at scraping edge.
Made by Bayah Ripuk (male), Feb 1988. In use in his hearth-group until purchase for the collection.
Materials: iron.
Bought from Bayah Ripuk 19/2/88 M$2.
BM accession no. Ethno As1988,22.138

BM139

Natang. Sample of resin from damar tree (*kayuh tomoh*). This is hard resin (*natang to'a*), and was, in the late 1980s, used for fire-making. Before the Second World War and probably for some time afterwards it was also used for light (burnt on bamboo stands, *dawan natang*) – see **BM102**. Soft damar resin (*natang laya'*) from the *obong* tree (SM103), also exists, which was until the 1970s used to glaze earthenware pots (**BM117-121, SM41-44**). In the late 1980s it was used to caulk the joins between plank sides and dugout bottoms of boats (*alud*).

Collected by Kaz Janowski in primary forest near Pa' Dalih, 1988.
Donated by him to BM March 1988.
BM accession no. Ethno As1988,22.139

BM140

Sample of *anit kayuh kilid*, the bark from the *kilid* tree. Bark used to make string (*nopar*) by twisting strands together (*ngopar*, literally 'to make string') on the thigh, for baskets of all kinds, musical instruments, containers (see **BM141**). Now often replaced by nylon string bought in town.

Collected by unidentified male.
Materials: bark from *kilid* tree (*anit kayuh kilid*).
Donated by Na'an Tepin of Pa' Dalih 26/10/87.
BM accession no. Ethno As1988,22.140

BM141

Sample of *nopar kayuh kilid*. Bark string used in making baskets of all kinds, musical instruments, containers. Now often replaced by nylon string bought in town. Made by twisting strands of bark around each other on the thigh and then letting them twist back, forming a tightly bound string.

Maker unrecorded.
Materials: bark from *kilid* tree (*anit kayuh kilid*).
Acquired in Pa' Dalih 1988, source unrecorded; price recorded as M$5.
BM accession no. Ethno As1988,22.141

BM142

Sample of *anit kayuh rababar*. Bark string used to bind fences (*taa*), rice stalks (*rongoh pade*) for brooms, for operating bird-scaring systems (*derur*). Wound up into a skein for storage.

Made by Bala Ukung (male), date unknown.
Materials: bark from *rababar* tree (*anit kayuh rababar*).
Bought from Bala Ukung, Pa' Dalih, 1/2/88, M$1.
BM accession no. Ethno As1988,22.142

BM143

Sample of *ubir*. Black paste used to strengthen and caulk inside of *ra'ing* and *bu'an* baskets, *a'ab* containers and *reno* winnowing trays. It is made from the inside of the bark of the *ubir* tree, which is scraped off, mixed with water and applied as a paste. This is then allowed to dry in the sun.

Collected by unidentified male.
Acquired from unrecorded source, Pa' Dalih 1987-88.
BM accession no. Ethno As1988,22.143

BM144

Batuh pade. 'Padi stone'. Also known as *batuh pera'it* ('thunder stone'). Such stones are believed to be or to derive from thunder and used to be (perhaps sometimes still are; the Kelabit, now Christian, would not admit this easily if it were still practised) kept in rice barns (*lepo pade*) because they are believed to make the rice last longer i.e. to increase in quantity. Cylindrical shape, pointed at one end, increasing in size at the other end, with a chunk missing at the thicker end. Almost certainly ancient manmade tool, possibly a sago-pounder or a candlenut-cracker (see Harrisson 1951; Sellato 1996).

6" long and 2" in diameter maximum.
Found by Na'an Tenan's (female, of Pa' Dalih) grandmother near Pa' Bengar (abandoned Kelabit settlement a few hours' walk from Pa' Dalih very near the border with the Kerayan).

Materials: stone (variety unknown).
Bought from Na'an Tenan and Bala Ukung (her husband) in Pa' Dalih 1/2/88 M$5.
BM accession no. Ethno As1988,22.144

BM145

Batuh pade. 'Padi stone'. Cylindrical shape. See **BM144**.

3" long and 1½" in diameter.
Found by Ngimat Ulun (male) of Pa' Dalih at Long Kelit (less than an hour's walk from Pa' Dalih), 1987.
Materials: stone (variety unknown.)
Bought from Sinah Ngimat Ulun, finder's wife, 31/1/88 in exchange for *tekip* worth M$30.
BM accession no. Ethno As1988,22.145

BM146 a,b

Abe ringgit. Big single loop white metal ear rings made of thick wire; ends meet but were separated slightly so that earring could be inserted into ear. Little girls gradually had their ears lengthened from shortly after birth by the insertion of ever heavier weights until their ears reached their shoulders; little boys also had their ears lengthened but only until they were an inch or two long (see **BM148**). These are one of many heavy varieties of earring worn by all Kelabit women until 1970's; now most have had their 'long ears' (*lalid kadang*) cut off.

These are said to have come originally from people described as 'Uang Paya', who are said by the Kelabit to live in Kalimantan Timur a few days' walk from Pa' Dalih. They are a Kenyah sub-group. They were bought by Doo Belaan (female) of Pa' Dalih from a group of Uang Paya who came to Pa' Dalih in about 1968 for a string of beads (*ba'o*) called *labang ote'*.
Materials: white metal (variety unknown).
1¾" in diameter.
Bought from Doo Belaan, Pa' Dalih, 12/2/88 M$50.
BM accession numbers As1988,22.146a and As1988,146b

BM147 a-f

Abe semera'. Bunch of six very heavy ear pendants made of lead (*semera'*). Four may have been cast in bamboo, but two have ridges indicating that they were made in some other way. See BM146.

2½" in diameter; lead itself ¼" in diameter.
Said by Sinah Ellie (female) of Pa' Dalih to have been made by her (but iron working is usually something men do, so it may have been her husband Tama Ellie who made them) approx 1965 for her eldest daughter Ellie (who in 1988 was an office worker in Miri, a town on the coast, and had cut off her long ears).
Materials: lead (*semera'*). Probably bought in town.
Bought from Sinah Ellie, 4/2/88 M$30.
BM accession numbers As1988,22.147a-f

BM148 a,b

Abe tawak. Men's brass ear pendants. Made of tubular piece of metal twisted round to form a round, overlapping ends not quite meeting so that the metal can be inserted into the ear. The ears of little boys, like those of little girls, were gradually lengthened by the insertion of ever heavier weights, but while men's ears were eventually an inch or so long, women's reached their shoulders (see **BM146,147**). These are one of number of varieties of heavy earring (apparently always brass, and thus bought in town) worn by all men until 1970's when the practice of lengthening boys' ears began to cease and men began to have their 'long ears' (*lalid kadang*) cut off. In 1986-88 there were still five older men in Pa' Dalih who

wore ear pendants.

1" in diameter.
Bought 'on the coast' (*la'ud*, literally 'downriver') by Tepo Ewan, the grandfather of Pun Punang Kelapang of Pa' Dalih (originally of Batu Patong, a settlement 40 minutes' walk from Pa' Dalih). After Tepo Ewan, Pun Punang Kelapang's father wore them, and then Pun Punang Kelapang himself, who wore them from when he was a small boy until 1983, when he ceased wearing ear pendants.
Materials: brass (*temaga*).
Bought from Pun Punang Kelapang, Pa' Dalih, 12/2/88 M$80.
BM accession numbers As1988,22.148a and b

BM149 a,b

Abe tawak. Men's brass ear pendants. See **BM149**. These ear pendants were Ngimat Ulun's, of Pa' Dalih. He inherited them from his *tetepo* (grandparents/ancestors); he doesn't know who bought them. He started to wear them at the age of seven. He had stopped wearing them some years before 1988 but the date he stopped was not noted.

Materials: brass (*temaga*).
Bought from Ngimat Ulun 19/2/88 M$80.
BM accession numbers As1988,22.149a and As1988,22.149b

BM150

Leko' olo. Bangle made of shell (*akap*). Appears to have been broken and mended at some point.

From outside the highland area. Not only Kelabit but many Borneo tribal peoples valued such bangles in the past. This bangle is from the Kerayan on an immediate basis, but may have travelled a good deal in its life. Both men and women wore such bracelets.
Materials: shell (*akap*).
Bought from Amos (male), resident in Pa' Dalih but originally from Kerayan; he got it from youngsters (*anak adi'*) in the Kerayan.
Purchase price: M$30.
BM accession no. Ethno As1988,22.150

BM151

Bua' payang. Seed of *payang* tree, used in making grass mats such as **BM155,157-59** to smooth out strips of grass as they are woven.

3" long, 3½" in diameter.
Materials: seed of *payang* tree.
Probably bought from Sinah Ngimat Ulun (details lost). Purchase price M$5.
BM accession no. Ethno As1988,22.151

BM152

Io tonan narit. Small long-handled knife with carved handle. Used both in the longhouse and in the forest. New.

1' 5" long.
Knife made by Bayah Ripuk (male) Feb 1988. Handle made by Danel Balang (male) from Long Layu, Kerayan. Danel also bound handle to knife.
Materials: wood (variety unknown), tree latex (*mat*) to fix blade in wood, bound with rattan (variety unknown) in pattern known as *kal belad* ('flat style').
M$5 paid to Bayah Ripuk for knife; M$8 paid to Danel for handle and binding.
BM accession no. Ethno As1988,22.152

BM153

Io. Small long-handled knife. Used both in the longhouse and in the forest. Used.

1' 2½" long.
Made by Doo Puun (male) of Pa' Dalih, 1982.
Materials: iron, bamboo (*bulu' betong*), brass (*sekiling*) for trimming.

Bought from Doo Puun July 1987 M$5.
BM accession no. Ethno As1988,22.153

BM154

Io kabing. Left-handed long-handled small knife. Used both in the longhouse and in the forest. 1' 3" long.

Knife made by Bayah Ripuk (male) for Belaan Paran, who is left-handed; handle made by Belaan Paran (male).
Materials: wood (*kayuh tai'la'al*).
Bought from Belaan Paran, 31/1/88 M$7.
BM accession no. Ethno As1988,22.154

BM155

Ugam berpah. Mat made of undyed *berpah* grass. Coarse grass; mats like these are made quickly. Used to sit on. May be covered by finer *tarub* mats.

5' 6" long, 4' 11" wide.
Made by Doo Inan, Remudu (Kelabit settlement three hours' walk from Pa' Dalih) Feb 88. Seed of *payang* tree used in making such mats (see **BM151**).
Materials: grass (*da'un berpah*).
Bought from Doo Inan, 3/3/88 M$2.
BM accession no. Ethno As1988,22.155

BM156

Pin ue. Mat made of undyed *tak* bamboo. Such mats could not be made in the Kelabit Highlands because this type of bamboo does not grow at that altitude. They could only be made in Kelabit settlements outside the highlands such as Long Peluan and Long Lellang. They are valued highly both in the Highlands and in town, where they are often to be seen in Kelabit houses.

Made by Guna Ulun (male), Long Lellang (a Kelabit settlement outside the Highlands), 1987. 11' long, 5' wide.
Materials: bamboo (*ue tak*), nylon string (town bought).
Bought from Guna Ulun in Miri (town on the coast where many Kelabit now live) January 1988 M$500.
BM accession no. Ethno As1988,22.156

BM157

Tarub siar barit. Mat made of *siar* grass. *Barit*, meaning striped/coloured/decorated, refers to the different colours used in the mat: green (dye from town), red (made using *bua'*

tepang fruit – see notes *re* this). Seed of *payang* tree is used in making such mats (see **BM151**). Used.

6' 2" long, 4' 9" wide.
Made by Dekan (female) from Long Kewang, Ba Rian (one day's walk from Bario in the northern part of the Kerayan). Sinah Bayah Ribuh of Pa' Dalih bought this mat from Dekan's husband in Bario in 1986.
Materials: *siar* grass, green dye from town, red dye from *bua' tepang*.
Bought from Sinah Bayahh Ribuh, Pa' Dalih, 26/2/88 M$40.
BM accession no. Ethno As1988,22.157

BM158

Tarub siar barit. Mat made of *siar* grass. See BM157.

6' 2" long, 4' 3" wide.
Maker unrecorded (details lost). Price unrecorded (details lost).
Donated by Monica and Kaz Janowski to BM March 1988.
BM accession no. Ethno As1988,22.158

BM159

Tarub siar barit. Mat made of *siar* grass. See BM157.

6' long, 4' 3" wide.
Maker unrecorded (details lost). Price unrecorded (details lost).
Donated by Monica and Kaz Janowski to BM March 1988.
BM accession no. Ethno As1988,22.159

BM160

Tabang pa'. Water carrier made of section of bamboo. Decoratively carved on lip. Cracked in one place on body. New.

4' 4" long, 4½" in diameter.
Made by Balang Pelaba (male) 29/2/88.
Commissioned.
Materials: bamboo (*bulu' betong*).
Bought from Balang Pelaba 1/3/88 M$10.
BM accession no. Ethno As1988,22.160

BM161

Apoh kenangan. Broom for sweeping inside house. New.

4' 7" long.
Made by Pian Ayu (female), Feb 1988.
Materials: sago palm (*kenangan*), rattan for binding (*ue pa'it*).
Bought from Pian Ayu 7/3/88 M$2.50.
BM accession no. Ethno As1988,22.161

Items in the Sarawak Museum Collection

SM1

Bogo. Implement for stirring rice while cooking. Used.

Made by Bala Ukung (male) 1975 approx.
Materials: wood (*kayuh rabulu*).
Bought from Na'an Tenan, Bala Ukung's wife, 7/2/88 M$2

SM2

Bogo. Implement for stirring rice while cooking. Used.

Made by Tama Puding, Long Layu, Kerayan 1986.
Materials: bamboo (*bulu' betong*).
Bought from Sinah Luun Ayu, Tama Puding's adopted daughter, Pa' Dalih, 17/11/87 M$1.50

SM3

Bogo. Implement for stirring food while cooking. Used.

Made by Balang Pelaba (male), 1986.
Materials: bamboo (*bulu' betong*).
Bought from Balang Pelaba 31/1/88 M$1

SM4

Bak payang. Ladle made of seed of *payang* fruit. Used for serving rice porridge (*kikid*). In the past, used to serve rice beer (*borak*). New.

Made by Doo Puun (male), 6/2/88.
Commissioned.
Materials: bamboo (*bulu' betong*), seed pod of payang tree (*ilong payang*).
Bought from Doo Puun 6/2/88 M$1

SM5

Bogo. Implement for stirring food while cooking. New.

Made by Bala Aran (male), Feb. 1988.
Commissioned.
Materials: bamboo (*bulu' betong*).
Bought from Bala Aran, Feb. 1988, M$1

SM6

Bogo. Implement for stirring food while cooking. New.

Made by Bala Aran (male), Feb. 1988.
Commissioned.
Materials: bamboo (*bulu' betong*).
Bought from Bala Aran Feb. 1988 M$1.50.

SM7, SM8, SM9, SM10

Bogo narit. Implements for stirring food while cooking with carved ends. New.

Made by Telutu Ayu (male), also known as Kalib, Sabaan from Long Banga' resident in Tang Ra'an, Kerayan on a visit to Pa' Dalih looking for temporary work.
Materials: bamboo (*bulu' betong*).
Bought from Telutu Ayu 15/2/88 and 26/2/88 M$2 each

SM11

Gayut. Iron scraper for removing traces of 'soft rice' (*nuba laya'*) from cooking pot. New.

Made by Bayah Ripuk (male), Feb. 1988.
Materials: iron.
Bought from Bayah Ripuk 19/2/88 M$2

SM12

Tusuh. Salt boiled down from brine from salt springs wrapped in leaves.

Made by group of people from Kerayan at a salt spring near Pa' Bengar, Kelabit Highlands. Bartered by them to Lawe Padan, Pa' Dalih, Dec. 1987, in return for cloth.
Materials: salt from salt spring, leaves (*ilad*), rattan (*ue pa'it*).
Bought from Lawe Padan 2/3/88 M$1

SM13, SM14

Pit. Tongs used to move pieces of wood on fire or for frying in wok. New.

Made by Lawe Padan (male), 1/3/88.
Commissioned.
Materials: bamboo (*bulu' betong*).
Bought from Lawe Padan 2/3/88 M$1 each.

SM15

Iop apui. Tube for blowing up fire. New.

Made by Balang Pelaba (male), 7/3/88.
Commissioned.
Materials: bamboo (*bulu' bayuh*).
Donated by Balang Pelaba 7/3/88.

SM16

Tara bogo. Holder for bamboo and wooden implements for cooking (*bogo*) (see **SM1,2,3,5,6**), hung on the frame of the hearth (*tetal*). New.

Made by Bala Aran (male), Feb. 1988.
Commissioned.
Materials: bamboo (*bulu' betong*).

SM17

Apoh rongoh pade. Small hearth broom. New.

Made by Bala Ukung (male), Jan. 1988.
Commissioned.
Materials: threshed paddy stalks (*rongoh pade*), grass for binding (*da'un tamar*).
Bought from Na'an Tenan, Bala Ukung's wife, Jan 1988 M$1.50.

SM18

Apoh rongoh pade. Hearth broom. New.

Made by Bala Aran (male), Feb. 1988.
Materials: threshed paddy stalks, woody creeper for binding (*uar ubu*).
Bought from Bala Aran, 7/2/88 M$2.

SM19

Io, tonan narit. Small long-handled knife with carved handle representing crocodile (*kabok*) head, used both in the longhouse and in the forest. New.

Made by Danel (male), Long Layu, Kerayan Sept. 1987.
Materials: iron, wood (*kayuh benibut*), rattan (*ue kusah*) for binding, tree latex (*mat*) used for fixing blade to handle.
Bought from Danel in Pa' Dalih 1/10/87 M$12.

SM20

Io, tonan narit. Small long-handled knife knife with carved handle, used both in the longhouse and in the forest. Used.

Made by Danel (male), Long Layu, Kerayan at date unknown.
Materials: wood (*kayuh belaban*), rattan (*ue kusah*) for binding, tree latex (*mat*) used for fixing blade to handle.
Bought from Miriam, Danel's wife, in Long Layu via Belaan Paran of Pa' Dalih, Feb. 1988 M$15.

SM21

Kasib. Lice comb for removing lice eggs from hair and

destroying them by squashing between teeth of comb (see **BM28**). New.

Made by Bayah Ripuk (male), Feb. 1988.
Commissioned.
Materials: bamboo (*bulu' betong*).
Bought from Bayah Ripuk 7/2/88 M$2.

SM22

Apoh kenangan. Broom for sweeping inside the house. New.

Made by Pian Ayu (female), Feb. 1988.
Materials: young unopened sago leaves (*belalok kenangan*), rattan (*ue pa'it*).
Bought from Pian Ayu 7/3/88 M$2.50.

SM23

Laan. Hearthside stool. New.

Made by Riwed Bala (male), Batu Patong, Feb. 1988.
Materials: wood (*kayuh belaban*).
Bought from Riwed Bala 22/2/88 M$10.

SM24

Laan oloh. Wooden 'stool' (literally 'head *laan*') used to support head when lying down, usually near the hearth. Used.

Made by Maran Balang (male), Long Dano, date unknown.
Materials: wood (*kayuh belaban*).
Donated by Maran Balang 26.2.88.

SM25

Dawan natang (not yet used). Bamboo stand for burning damar resin (*natang*) from damar tree (*kayuh tomoh*) (see **SM103**). Rarely used nowadays; brass lamps filled with petrol with open flame at top, bought on coast, are now usual. Made by using one section of a large bore bamboo, split down its length and splayed out at one end so as to form legs, bound together with rattan. Top where damar is burnt is the joint at the other end of the section, which would be filled with earth before damar is burnt. New; no earth in top.

Made by Lawe Padan (male), 1/3/88.
Commissioned.
Materials: bamboo (*bulu' betong*), rattan (*ue kusah*) for binding.
Bought from Lawe Padan 2/3/88 M$5.

SM26

Belalong nuba'. Basket with lid to store rice packed in leaves between cooking and eating. Made of bamboo with outside stripped off, with frame and binding of rattan. Carrying handle of rattan which passes right round the basket. which also serves to hold on lid because it passes through rattan hooks on the lid.

Made by Merua' Ulun (female), Remudu, Jan. 1987. Rattan binding by her husband, Unid Tala.
Materials: bamboo (*bulu' poran*) for basket, rattan (*ue kusah* and *ue pa'it*) for binding.
Bought from Merua' Ulun, July 1987, M$10.

SM27

Orong bua' tabuh. Container used to store husked rice (*bera*) until 1950s. Made of gourd (*bua' tabuh*), with a lid of bamboo. Used.

Made by Adin Tepun (female), 1945 approx.
Materials: gourd (*bua' tabuh*), bamboo (*bulu' telang*).
Bought from Doo Inan, Adin Tepun's daughter, 3/3/88 M$10.

SM28

Lotong. Musical instrument. Made of one section of large-bore bamboo, with end divisions between this section and other sections intact. Slit cut down one side, decoratively cut in the middle. On each side of the slit, two strings have been cut out of the bamboo itself and held away from the body of the bamboo by small pieces of bamboo which act as tuning devices. Inside the body of the instrument there is a dried leaf which may be important in creating the type of sound desired. Bound by bark string at both ends to hold it together well. The instrument is played by plucking the strings. Used.

Made by Balang Telian (male), date unknown.
Materials: bamboo (*bulu' betong*), leaf (*da'un isip*).
Bought from Balang Telian, March 1988 M$20.

SM29 and 29a

Pagang. Musical instrument with stick for playing. Consists of part of a section of bamboo with two strings cut out of the bamboo itself and held away from the body of the instrument with small pieces of bamboo. A hole between the two strings is covered with another piece of bamboo attached to the strings. Played by tapping the strings with a stick. New.

Made by Belalong Tepun (male), Feb. 1988.
Commissioned.
Materials: bamboo (*bulu' telang*).
Bought from Belalong Tepun, 29/2/88 M$10.

SM30

Selingut. Flute. Detachable end piece (purpose not clear) fits over end; flute itself is one section of bamboo with division with next section intact at end with detachable end piece. Hole for blowing is on opposite side to three three triangular holes for stopping. New.

Made by Belalong Tepun (male), Feb. 1988.
Commissioned.
Materials: bamboo (*bulu' telang*).
Bought from Belalong Tepun, 5/3/88 M$10.

SM31

Kelingut. Nose flute. Made of one section of bamboo with division with next section left intact except for a hole for blowing. Three triangular holes for stopping. New.

Made by Balang Pelaba (male), 19/2/88.
Commissioned.
Materials: bamboo (*bulu' telang*).
Bought from Balang Pelaba 20/2/88 M$2.50

SM32

Sape. Long narrow simple stringed musical instrument with two metal strings. Carved out of one piece of wood with a flat piece nailed on to bottom. Six holes burnt out of body along top to allow sound to come out. Strings held away from body of instrument with pieces of wood at each end. Pegs to adjust sound. Carved end represents cow's head. Used.

Made by Belalong Tepun (male), 1985.
Materials: wood (*kayuh menubuh* for instrument, *kayuh belaban* for pegs). Beeswax (*angat*) for sticking stops.
Bought from Belalong Tepun 29/2/88 M$30.

SM33

Tabang pa'. Water carrier made of one section of giant bamboo. New.

Made by Belaan Paran (male), Feb. 1988.
Ccommissioned.
Materials: bamboo (*bulu' betong*).
Bought from Belaan Paran Feb. 1988 M$10.

SM34 and SM34a

Tobong. Tubular gong, with stick (*tetik*) for hitting it, made of one section of large bore bamboo. Wide slit cut in one side. Piece of rattan attached to top of slit for hanging. Stick for beating gong is a piece of wood with a natural twist in it. Used to summon people to meetings, *irau* feasts and to church. New.

Made by Balang Telian (male), Feb. 1988.
Commissioned.
Materials: bamboo (*bulu' betong*), wood (*kayuh seboko*) for stick.
Bought from Balang Telian 7/3/88 M$10.

SM35

Kudin. Large earthenware cooking pot for use in cooking large quantities of rice for *irau* feasts and in making rice beer (*borak*) for *irau*. Blackened with use. No longer in use.

Made by Adin Tepun (female), Remudu, 1950 approx.
Materials: clay (*tana'*), resin (*natang*) for glazing.
Bought from Adin Tepun's daughter, Doo Inan, in Remudu 3/3/88 M$10.

SM36

Kudin. Large earthenware cooking pot for use in cooking rice, meat, vegetables. Blackened with use. No longer used.

Made by Na'an Tenan (female), 1960 approx.
Materials: clay (*tana'*), resin (*natang*) for glazing.
Bought fromLawe Padan, Pa' Dalih, Octo. 1987 M$7

SM37

Tuning. Small earthenware cooking pot. Such pots still used to some extent 1987 for cooking rice porridge (*kikid*).

Made by Na'an Tenan (female), 1979, for Rinai Adun (female), then a primary school child, to present at her craft class at school. Never used for cooking.
Materials: clay (*tana'*), resin (*natang*) for glazing.
Bought from Sinah Ellie, Pa' Dalih, 19/1/88 M$2.

SM38

Tuning. Small earthenware cooking pot. Such pots still used to some extent 1987 for cooking rice porridge (*kikid*). Used.

Made by Na'an Tenan (female), 1970 approx.
Materials: clay (*tana'*), resin (*natang*) for glazing.
Bought from Sinah Adun Rewat, Pa' Dalih, 24/11/87 M$5.

SM39

Tuning. Small earthenware cooking pot. Such pots still used to some extent 1987 for cooking rice porridge (*kikid*). Used.

Made by Tsung Balang (female), 1947 approx.
Materials: clay (*tana'*), resin (*natang*) for glazing.
Bought from Bayah Ripuk, her grandson, 1/10/87 M$5.

SM40

Tuning. Small earthenware cooking pot. Such pots still used to some extent 1987 for cooking rice porridge (*kikid*). Used.

Made by Na'an Tenan (female), 1973.
Materials: clay (*tana'*), resin (*natang*) for glazing.
Bought from Na'an Tenan, Oct. 1987 M$6.

SM41, SM42, SM43, SM44

Tuning. Glazed earthenware cooking pot with rounded bottom, for use in making rice porridge (*kikid*) and other side dishes (*penguman*) for the rice meal. Such pots were made and were in regular use until the 1970s. Those that remain are used by some women in Pa' Dalih but are no longer normally made. New.

Made by Na'an Tenan (female), Jan/Feb 1988 as part of a batch made under commission from Monica Janowski.
Materials: clay (*tana'*), resin (*natang*) for glazing.
Fee for making pots M$150.

SM45

Tuning. Small earthenware cooking pot. Part of batch made by Na'an Tenan Jan/Feb 1988 (see **SM41-44, BM117-121**). This example left unfired and unglazed.

SM46

Batuh tuning. Stone used until 1970s in making *tuning*, small earthenware pots. Used.

Found by Tepo Ben (female), Pa' Dalih, near her wet rice field (*baa'*) near Pa' Dalih, 1960s.
Materials: stone (variety unknown).
Donated by Tepo Ben 28/2/88.

SM47 and SM48

Pepe'. Paddles used by Na'an Tenan (female) to shape *tuning* earthenware pots commissioned by Kaz and Monica Janowski, Jan/Feb 1988 (see **BM117-121, SM41-44** and **Pl. 116**). Criss-crossed with incised lines to aid in working clay (further apart than lines on **BM135**). Previously used by Na'an Tenan to make pots before early 1970s, when she stopped making pots.

Made by Bala Ukung (male), Na'an Tenan's husband, 1960s.
Materials: wood (*kayuh labakan*).
Bought from Na'an Tenan 1/2/88 M$2.

SM49

Okat. Stick of the type used in shaping the inside of *tuning* and *kudin* earthenware pots until the 1970s.

Made by Bala Ukung (male), Feb. 1988.
Materials: wood (*kayuh belaban*).
Bought from Bala Ukung 6/2/88 M$1.

SM50

Topah tana'. Heavy stick of the type used in rolling and shaping the clay for *tuning* and *kudin* earthenware pots until the 1970s.

Made by Bala Ukung (male), Feb. 1988.
Materials: wood (*kayuh belaban*).
Bought from Bala Ukung March 1988 M$2.50.

SM51

Di'id. Stick with hardened 'soft' damar resin (*natang laya'*) on end, used for applying resin glaze to *tuning* earthenware pots made by Na'an Tenan 16/2/88, commissioned by Kaz and Monica Janowski (see **BM117-121, SM41-44**).

Materials: wood (variety unknown), 'soft' damar resin (*natang*). Stick roughly peeled at one end, prepared by Bala Ukung for use in making commissioned pots.
Given by Na'an Tenan together with batch of *tuning*; fee for making *tuning* M$150.

SM52 and SM52A

Longing (mortar) and *totok* (pestle). Used to pound vegetables or roasted wild boar meat (*belabo belatuh*) before cooking. This example is from the Kerayan but is the same as those used by the Kelabit and was, when bought, being used in a Pa' Dalih hearth-group.

Sold by Martin, originally of Long Layu, Kerayan, to Pian Tauh, Pa' Dalih, 1985.
Materials: wood (*kayuh tara'* for mortar, *kayuh belaban* for pestle).
Bought from Pian Tauh 5/3/88 M$25.

SM53

Alud raut anak. Toy dug-out boat. New.

Made by Ra'an Kerayan, March 1988.
Materials: wood (*kayuh tara'*).
Bought from Ra'an Kerayan 7/3/88 M$10.

SM54

Ra'ong. Sun hat made of leaves with rattan frame and inner cap. Decorated with wool.

Made by Sinah Telona Bala (female), 1986. Woolen decorations applied by Sinah Paran To'oh (her sister-in-law) 1986 and cap made by Laba Awa (her mother in law) Feb. 1988.
Materials: leaves (*da'un ilad*), rattan (*ue kusah*), grass (*da'un berpah*), wool bought in town.
Bought from Laba Awa, Pa' Dalih, 29/2/88 M$15.

SM55

Ra'ong. Sun hat made of leaves with rattan frame and bamboo cap. Decorated with wool and beads.

Made by Sinah Telona Bala (female) 1986; cap (*oloh*) made by Sinah Ellie (female). Presented without decorations by the children of Pa' Dalih primary school to Kaz Janowski, November 1986 (he had been teaching them English for some months). Decorations applied by Sinah Paran To'oh (Sinah Telona Bala's sister-in-law) using beads supplied by Monica Janowski in Feb. 1988.
Materials: grass for hat (*da'un berpah*), rattan for frame (*ue kusah*), bamboo for cap (*bulu' poran*), wool and beads from town.
Fee paid to Sinah Paran To'oh for applying beads M$7.

SM56

Ra'ong Ba Rian. Sun hat made of grass with a rattan frame and a grass cap. Decorated with bamboo strips, wool and cloth. Such hats are widely used in the Kelabit Highlands.

Made in the Ba Rian area, just over the border with Indonesia from the Bario area in the northern part of the Kelabit Highlands.
Materials: grass for hat (*da'un berpah*), rattan for frame (*ue kusah*), grass for cap (*da'un kabir*), bamboo for decoration (*bulu' poran*), wool and cloth from town.
Bought in Bario from the shop belonging to Sinah Pitan (female), M$10.

SM57

Bubuh. Fish trap made of strips of bamboo bound with rattan. Tubular shape, with one pointed end and the other open for fish to enter. Inside, there are two rounds of bamboo prongs (*anga'*) to prevent the fish escaping. Opening with wooden door near pointed end to slide over it for access to fish once caught. Placed in rivers and streams overnight. New.

Made by Belalong Tepun (male), Jan 1988.
Commissioned.
Materials: bamboo (*bulu' poran*), rattan (*ue pa'it*).
Bought from Belalong Tepun 19/1/88 M$10.

SM58

Be'ong bua' tabuh. Gourd with bark string (*nopar kilid*) used until about 1960s for storing *epa' kayuh* (flavouring substance made of pounded *epa'* leaves, now largely replaced by monosodium glutamate which is also described as *epa'*). Used.

Made by Adin Tepun (female), Remudu, approx 1945. Bark string made by Laba Awa (female) of Pa' Dalih, March 1988.
Materials: gourd (*bua' tabuh*), bark from *kilid* tree (*kilid*).
Bought from Doo Inan, daughter of Adin Tepun, 3/3/88 M$3

SM59

Io bulu' peraneh. Simple bamboo knife for harvesting rice. New.

Made by Bayah Ripuk (male), 23/2/88
Commissioned.
Materials: bamboo (*bulu' bayuh*).
Bought from Bayah Ripuk 23/2/88 M$0.50.

SM60

Belu'ing. Weeding tool made of iron with wooden handle bound close to blade with rattan. Used in dry rice fields, gardens and around the longhouse. Used.

Made by Bayah Ripuk (male), 1984.
Materials: wood (*kayuh labakan*), rattan (*ue kusah*), tree latex (*mat*) used for fixing blade to handle.
Bought from Bayah Ripuk 7/3/88 M$10.

SM61

Baru pian. Sharpening stone used to sharpen iron tools and knives.

Found by Balang Pelaba (male), Pa' Dalih, at the source of the Kelapang river (*Punang Kelapang*), which is in the southern part of the Kelabit Highlands, approximately 1945.
Materials: stone (unknown variety).
Donated by Balang Pelaba 8/3/88.

SM62

Tongol (bush knife) with wooden handle (*tonan*), *binan tongol* (sheath for bush knife) and *labuh io* (sheath for small *io* knife). The *labuh io* is attached to the *binan tongol*. The *binan tongol* is made of wood, while the *labuh io* is made of the bark of a plant. The *binan tongol* is bound with rattan, and the *labuh io* is attached to the *binan tongol* using rattan. The handle of the *tongol* is also bound with rattan. The *binan tongol* is carved. There is a cord made of rattan and bark attached to the *binan tongol* for hanging the whole ensemble from the waist. This is standard equipment for any man entering the forest.

Tongol and *binan tongol*, as well as the rattan part of the waist string near the *binan tongol*, made by Penan, who sold it to Sinah Pitan at her shop in Bario. Carving on *binan tongol* executed in Pa' Dalih Feb. 1988 by Kalib, Sabaan man from Long Banga' normally resident in the Kerayan but temporarily in Pa' Dalih working. *Labuh io* made by Bayah Ripuk (male), Feb. 1988. Bark string made by Sinah Matala Ulun (female), Feb. 1988.
Materials: wood for handle of *tongol* (unknown variety), wood for *binan tongol* (probably *kayuh labakan*), rattan for handle of *tongol* (probably *ue tak*), rattan for binding of *labuh io* (*ue kusah*), rattan for waist string (variety unknown), tree latex (*mat*) for setting blade

into knife), bark for *labuh io* (*anit reman belabo*), bark for string (*anit kayuh kilid*).

Tongol and *binan tongol* bought from Sinah Pitan at her shop in Bario, M$20. Fee paid to Telutu Ayu for executing carving M$2.50. Fee paid to Bayah Ripuk for making *labuh io* M$5. Fee paid to Sinah Matala Ulun for making bark string M$2.

SM63

Selongan. Quiver for blowpipe darts (*langan*) made of bamboo bound with rattan. Containing darts (*langan*) made of bamboo, one tipped with poison. Attached is a small gourd (*bua' tabuh kre'*) for storing flights (*ra'o*) made of wild sago pith, containing some flights, with wooden lid. Bark string and wooden hook to attach quiver to trousers or shorts (or in the past loincloth). Used.

Made by John Fred (male), Long Layu, Kerayan 1986.
Materials: bamboo for quiver (*bulu' telang*), rattan for binding quiver (*ue pa'it*), bamboo for darts (probably *bulu' betong*), poison from the sap of *parir* tree (made from sap boiled with water from creepers – *uar* – to make paste), wild sago pith (*kenangan)* for flights, bark for string (*anit kayuh kilid*), wood for hook (*kayuh belaban*), wood for lid of gourd (variety unknown).
Bought from John Fred in Long Layu via Belaan Paran, Pa' Dalih Feb 1988 M$30.

SM64

Put. Blowpipe made of wood, with spear bound on with rattan. Used.

Made by Lajan (male), Long Layu, Kerayan 1982.
Materials: wood (*kayuh ketong*), rattan (*ue pa'it*), iron (*belawan*).
Bought from Lajan in Long Layu via Belaan Paran, Pa' Dalih, Feb. 1988 M$110.

SM65

Boso. Spear for hunting pigs made of wood with spear bound on to end of shaft with rattan. New.

Made by Bayah Ripuk (male), Feb. 1988.
Commissioned.
Materials: wood (*kayuh bua' bupu*), rattan (*ue pa'it*), iron (*belawan*).
Bought from Bayah Ripuk, Feb. 1988 M$20.

SM66

Samit. Rain cape made of leaves stitched together with wool and nylon. New.

Made by Mariam Ribuh Paran (female), Long Layu, Kerayan 1987.
Materials: leaves (*da'un ilad*), wool and nylon from town.
Bought from Mariam Ribuh Paran in Pa' Dalih where she was visiting, 1/10/87 M$4.

SM67

Reno. Winnowing tray also used for cleaning vegetables and preparing food, made of bamboo bound with rattan to rattan frame. Open at one end, closed at the other. *Ubir* (**SM102**) has been applied to inside of basket to make it proof against anything slipping through and to strengthen it.

Made by Merua' Ulun (female), Remudu, 1987; rattan work by her husband, Unid Tala.
Materials: bamboo (*bulu' poran*), rattan for frame (*ue kusah*), rattan for binding (*ue pa'it*), *ubir* (**SM102**), enamel paint from town.
Bought from Merua' Ulun, Remudu, 3/3/88 M$10.

SM68

Reno barit. Winnowing tray also used for cleaning vegetables and preparing food, made of bamboo bound with rattan to rattan frame. Open at one end, closed at the other. *Ubir* (**SM102**) has been applied to inside of basket make it proof against anything slipping through and to strengthen it. Bamboo strips used to make it have been coloured using paint from town before weaving so that a coloured pattern has been created – this is why it is called *barit*, which means 'decorated, coloured, patterned'.

Made by Sinah Kakim (female), Remudu, 1986; rattan work done by unidentified man. *Ubir* applied by Sinah Matala Ulun (female), Feb. 1988.
Materials: bamboo (*bulu' poran*), rattan for frame (*ue kusah*), rattan for binding (*ue pa'it*), *ubir* (**SM102**), enamel paint from town.
Bought from Sinah Kakim, Remudu, Feb. 1988 M$15.

SM69

Reno barit. Winnowing tray also used for cleaning vegetables and preparing food, made of bamboo bound with rattan to rattan frame. Open at one end, closed at the other. *Ubir* (**SM102**) has been applied to inside of basket make it proof against anything slipping through and to strengthen it. Bamboo strips used to make it have been coloured using paint from town before weaving so that a coloured pattern has been created – this is why it is called *barit*, which means 'decorated, coloured, patterned'. Used.

Made by Sinah Kakim, (female), Remudu, 1986; rattan work by unidentified man. *Ubir* applied by unidentified woman, probably Sinah Kakim.
Materials: bamboo (*bulu' poran*), rattan for frame (*ue kusah*), rattan for binding (*ue pa'it*), *ubir* (**SM102**), enamel paint from town.
Bought from Sinah Kakim April 1987 M$10.

SM70

Agag ubi kayuh. Sieve made of bamboo bound to rattan frame for sieving grated cassava root (*ubi kayuh*). Used.

Made by Pun Bupun (female), Pa' Bengar, 1955 approx.
Materials: bamboo (*bulu' poran*), rattan for frame (*ue kusah*), rattan for binding (*ue pa'it*)
Bought from Pun Bupun's daughter, Na'an Tenan, Pa' Dalih, 6/2/88 M$6.

SM71

Agag bera. Sieve made of bamboo bound to rattan frame for sieving husked rice (*bera*).

Made by Merua' Ulun (female) Remudu, 1986.
Materials: bamboo (*bulu' poran*), rattan for frame (*ue kusah*), rattan for binding (*ue pa'it*).
Bought from Merua' Ulun, Remudu, 3/3/88 M$8.

SM72

Iap. Fishing net used by women in streams and wet rice fields. Rounded rigid rectangular creeper frame with bucket net made of bark string bound to it with bark string. Net used; frame new.

Net made by Na'an (female), Long Dano, 1984. Creeper frame applied by Balang Pelaba (male), Feb. 1988.
Materials: string made of bark (*anit kayuh kilid*) for net and binding, creeper for frame (*uar bekar*).
Obtained from Sinah Matala Ulun, Pa' Dalih 6/3/88 in exchange for a new *iap* made of shop-bought cotton string, bought from Pun Ribid Ayu, Long Dano 20/2/88 for M$15.

SM73

Pukat. Fishing net, used by men in rivers. Stretched across the river and left to catch fish as they go by.

Made by Bayah Ripuk (male), 1987.

Materials: nylon string, rubber pieces, lead weights (all town-bought).
Bought from Bayah Ripuk 8/3/88 M$20.

SM74

A'ab. Basket for storage and serving of food. Square at bottom, rounded at top. Made of bamboo bound to rattan frame. *Ubir* (**SM102**) has been applied to inside of basket make it proof against anything slipping through and to strengthen it.

Made by Sinah Matala Ulun (female), 1985. Rattan work by Balang Pelaba (male), Feb 1988. *Ubir* applied by Sinah Matala Ulun.
Materials: bamboo (*bulu' poran*), rattan for frame (*ue kusah*), rattan for binding (*ue pa'it*), *ubir* (**SM102**).
Bought from Sinah Matala Ulun 5/3/88 M$7.50.

SM75

A'ab. Basket for storage and serving of food. Square at bottom, rounded at top. Made of bamboo bound to rattan frame. *Ubir* (**SM102**) has been applied to inside of basket make it proof against anything slipping through and to strengthen it. New.

Made by Sinah Matala Ulun (female), Feb 1988. Rattan work by Balang Pelaba (male), Feb 1988. *Ubir* applied by Sinah Matala Ulun. Commissioned.
Materials: bamboo (*bulu' poran*), rattan for frame (*ue kusah*), rattan for binding (*ue pa'it*), *ubir* (**SM102**).
Bought from Sinah Matala Ulun 5/3/88 M$7.50.

SM76

Bakol tana'. Basket for transporting earth, open at one end. Handles at both sides for carrying. New.

Made by Balang Pelaba 3/3/88.
Commissioned.
Materials: rattan (*ue kusah*) for basket and handles, frame made of creeper (*uar bekar*).
Bought from Balang Pelaba 3/3/88 M$10.
Commissioned.

SM77

A'ab. Basket for storage and serving of food. Square at bottom, rounded at top. Made of bamboo bound to rattan frame. *Ubir* (**SM102**) has been applied to inside of basket make it proof against anything slipping through and to strengthen it. Some of the bamboo strips painted with enamel paint before weaving to create a pattern. Used.

Made by relative of Sinah Doo Puun, date unknown.
Materials: bamboo (*bulu' poran*), rattan for frame (*ue kusah*), rattan for binding (*ue pa'it*), *ubir* (**SM102**) enamel paint from town.
Donated by Sinah Doo Puun 7/3/88.

SM78 and SM79

Bekang dela'ih. Expandable man's basket (literally 'man's *bekang*") with lining mat (*liling*) and shoulder straps (*kela'e*) used for transporting things between settlements, for carrying meat and provisions when on hunting trips, and for bringing in firewood. Constructed with flap at front attached only at bottom.

Made by Balang Pelaba (male), July 1987.
Materials: rattan (*ue lengan*, bound with *ue pa'it*), wood (*kayuh*; variety unknown). Shoulder straps rattan (*ue pa'it*). Lining mat (*liling*) grass (*da'un berpah*).
Bought from Balang Pelaba 31/1/88 M£25.

SM80 and SM81

Bekang dechur. Expandable lady's basket (literally 'lady's *bekang*') with lining mat (*liling*), headstrap (*sengoloh*) and shoulder straps (*kela'e*), used for transporting things between settlements. Constructed with flap at front attached at bottom. Back of closely woven rattan, with wooden piece at bottom, attached with rattan, to provide strength. Front and flap made of whole rattan twisted and intertwined into a pattern, within a frame of larger rattan. Coiled and intertwined rattan at bottom to form flattish base. Bark string at front to close basket tightly. Used.

Made by Ra'an Kerayan (male), 1970. Headstrap made by his wife, Malamud Ulun, Feb. 1988.
Materials: rattan (*ue rabun*, probably bound with *ue pa'it*), string made of bark (*anit kayuh kilid*), (variety unknown). Headstrap grass (*da'un tamar*). Lining mat grass (*da'un kabir*).
Bought from Malamud Ulun 29/2/88 M$50.

SM82 and SM83

Bekang anak dela'ih. Expandable small boy's basket (literally 'small boy's *bekang*') made of rattan with grass lining mat (*liling*) and shoulder straps (*kela'e*). Strip of split rattan to bind together at the front. Such baskets are used by small boys to transport personal possessions between settlements, to carry firewood and to carry meat and provisions when on hunting trips. New.

Made by Ketuan Aran (male), Remudu, Feb. 1988.
Materials: rattan (*ue kusah* and probably *ue pa'it* for shoulder straps), wood (variety unknown). Lining mat (*liling*) grass (*da'un berpah*).
Bought from Ketuan Aran 3/3/88 M$12.

SM84

Uyut. Soft carrying basket made of rattan for personal possessions, with shoulder straps made of rattan. Used.

Made by Penan. Given by Pastor Remat (who is Penan), pastor of Pa' Dalih until 1987, to Balang Pelaba, Pa' Dalih.
Materials: rattan (*ue tak*).
Bought from Balang Pelaba 30/9/98 M$7.

SM85

Uyut rawang. Soft loosely woven carrying basket made of basket for personal possessions, with shoulder straps made of rattan. Used.

Materials: rattan (*ue tak*). Cord for shoulder straps made of rattan (*ue pa'it*).
Made by Ketuan Bala (male), Batu Patong, 1984. String replaced by Riwed Bala, Feb. 1988.
Bought from Sinah Luun Ayu, Pa' Dalih, 11/2/88 M$12.

SM86

Gawang barit. Soft carrying basket made of rattan with patterns (*barit*) woven in, fitted with shoulder straps.

Made by Penan of Long Beruang, Baram. Given by them to Raya Bala, Remudu, Feb. 1988.
Materials: rattan (*ue tak*). Natural black dye used to dye some strips of rattan (see section on materials).
Bought from Raya Bala 27/2/88 M$20.

SM87

Bu'an. Rigid basket made of bamboo bound to rattan frame for carrying rice, both husked and unhusked. Fitted with headstrap (*sengoloh*) and shoulder straps (*kela'e*). Used.

Made by Pun Ngelipo Ra'an Lewan (female), 1984. Headstrap made by her. Rattan work by her husband, Belalong Tepun (male). Materials: bamboo for basket (probably *bulu' poran*), rattan for frame (probably *ue kusah* and *ue pa'it*), rattan for binding (*ue pa'it*), rattan for cord (*ue koran*), grass for headstrap (*da'un tamar*). Bought from Sinah Rang Bala, Batu Patong, 7/3/88 M$30.

SM88

Kalang. Rigid open-weave basket made of bamboo for carrying fruit, roots, vegetables. Fitted with shoulder straps (*kelu'e*) made of rattan attached with bark string. Used with *liling* mat inside for ease of packing and to prevent contents falling out through holes. Made using criss-cross and parallel horizontal strips of split rattan. Used.

Made by Medang Aran (female), Long Peluan, 1985. Rattan binding by her husband, Tso Tepun.
Materials: rattan (*ue kusah*), bark for string (*anit kayuh kilid*), rattan for shoulder straps (*ue pa'it*).
Bought from Sinah Ellie, Pa' Dalih, Medang Aran's daughter in law, 6/3/88 M$30

SM89

Ra'ing barit. Small rigid carrying basket made of bamboo bound to a rattan frame for harvesting and for gathering vegetables.. The strips of bamboo have been dyed using paint from town before weaving so that a pattern (*barit*) is created. *Ubir* (**SM102**) has been applied to inside of basket make it proof against anything slipping through and to strengthen it. Fitted with shoulder straps (*kela'e*) made of rattan, attached with string made of bark.

Made by Mada (female), Binuang, Ba Rian, Kalimantan, Nov. 1987. Rattan work by her husband, Yus. Shoulder straps made by Nanad Bala (male), Remudu, Feb. 1988. Bark string made by Sinah Matala Ulun (female), Pa' Dalih, Feb. 1988.
Materials: bamboo probably (*bulu' poran*), rattan for frame (probably *ue kusah*), rattan for binding (probably *ue pa'it*), rattan for shoulder straps (*ue pa'it*).
Basket bought from Mada, Pa' Dalih, 29/2/88 M$20. Shoulder straps bought from Nanad Bala, Feb. 1988 M$2.50. Bark string donated by Sinah Matala Ulun.

SM90

Ra'ing. Small rigid carrying basket made of bamboo bound to a rattan frame for harvesting, gathering vegetables. Fitted with headstrap (*sengoloh*) made of grass. Used.

Made by Pun Ngelipo Ra'an Lewan 1982. Rattan work by her husband, Belalong Tepun. Headstrap made by Pun Ngelipo Ra'an Lewan.
Materials: bamboo (probably *bulu' poran*), rattan for frame (probably *ue kusah*), rattan for binding (probably *ue pa'it*), leaves for headstrap (*da'un tamar*).
Bought from Pun Ngelipo Ra'an Lewan 16/1/88 M$15.

SM91

Bu'an barit kulit bodok. Large rigid basket made of bamboo bound to a rattan frame for use in carrying husked and unhusked rice. Fitted with headstrap (*sengoloh*) made of grass and shoulders straps (*kela'e*) made of rattan. Pointed (*bodok*), then flattened, base, made in the old Kelabit style. This basket will not stand up by itself. It is made of both stripped and unstripped bamboo (*kulit*, meaning 'bark', refers to the fact that on some of the bamboo this visible), in order to be able to create patterns (*barit*). *Ubir* (**SM102**) has been applied to inside of basket make it proof against anything slipping through and to strengthen it, but has

adhered best to places where stripped bamboo has been in contact with it. Much of the *ubir* on places where the slippery outside part of the bamboo has been in contact with it has come off. *Barit* refers to patterns woven into bamboo work by using inside or outside of bamboo, whose names are, from top to bottom: *barit reko'* (crooked pattern), *barit bulan* (moon pattern), *barit peta'ud* (hooked pattern), *barit lua'* (*lua'* is the pre-Christian ceremony of anointing those going through transitions with blood), barit *kukud ada'* (spirits' feet pattern). Used.

Made by Parai (female), Batu Patong, 1972. Rattan work by Bala Ukung (male), 1972. Shoulder straps made by Balan Ukung (male), at unknown date, headstrap made by Na'an Tenan (female) at unknown date.
Materials: bamboo for basket (*bulu' poran*), rattan for frame (*ue kusah*), rattan for binding and base (*ue pa'it*), rattan for shoulder straps (*ue pa'it*), leaves for headstrap (*da'un tamar*), *ubir* (SM102).

SM92

Bu'an uang bodok. Large rigid basket with pointed (*bodok*), then flattened, base, made in the old Kelabit style, for use in harvesting rice. Will not stand up without support. Body made of strips of bamboo; *uang* refers to the fact that the slippery outside of the bamboo has been stripped off so that both the outside and the inside (*uang*) of the bamboo are visible. Fitted with headstrap (*sengoloh*) made of grass. No shoulder straps – to be carried from head only. *Ubir* (**SM102**) has been applied to both the inside and outside of basket make it proof against anything slipping through and to strengthen it. Used.

Made by Laba Awa (female), Long Dano, 1970s. Rattan work by Ngemong Raja (male), Long Dano 1986. *Ubir* (SM102) applied by Mengeh Aran (female) 1986.
Materials: bamboo for basket (*bulu' poran*), rattan for frame (*ue kusah*), rattan for binding (*ue pa'it*), grass for headstrap (*da'un tamar*).
Bought from Mengeh Aran, Pa' Dalih 19/2/88 M$30.

SM93

Ra'ing. Small rigid carrying basket made of stripped bamboo bound to a rattan frame for harvesting and gathering vegetables. Fitted with headstrap (*sengoloh*) made of grass. Coated inside and out with *ubir* (**SM102**) to make it proof against anything slipping through and to strengthen it. Used.

Made by Merua' Ulun (female), Remudu, 1986. Rattan work by her husband, Unid Tala (male). Headstrap made by Merua' Ulun.
Materials: bamboo (*bulu' poran*), rattan for frame (probably *ue kusah*), rattan for binding (probably *ue pa'it*), leaves for headstrap (*da'un tamar*).
Bought from Merua' Ulun, 3/3/88 M$20.

SM94

Be'ong. Gourd on nylon string used to collect small fish, crabs and smails by women in wet rice fields and streams. Worn around waist or on head. Used.

Made by Sinah Adun Rewat (female) 1970 approx.
Materials: gourd (*bua' tabuh*), nylon string.
Bought from Sinah Adun Rewat, 11/11/87 M$1

SM95

Ugam berpah. Mat made of undyed *berpah* grass. Coarse grass; mats like these are made quickly. Used to sit on. May be covered by finer *tarub* mats. Seed of *payang* tree (**BM151**) used in making such mats.New.

Made by Doo Inan, Remudu (Kelabit settlement three hours' walk from Pa' Dalih) Feb 88.
Commissioned.
Materials: grass (*da'un berpah*).
Bought from Doo Inan, 3/3/88 M$2.

SM96

Tarub kerubit barit. Grass mat with red and purple pattern (*barit*) woven in. Seed of *payang* tree used in making such mats. New.

Made by Sarah, Ba Rian, Indonesia, Sep. 1987.
Materials: grass (*da'un kerubit*), *tepang* fruit (*bua' tepang*) for red dye, black and purple dyes from town.
Bought from Sarah in Pa' Dalih 29/2/88 M$14

SM97

Tarub kerubit barit. Grass mat with red pattern (*barit*) woven in.

Made by Mariam Ribuh Paran (female), Long Layu, Kerayan, 1987.
Materials: grass (*da 'un kerubit*), *tepang* fruit (*bua' tepang*) for red dye, dyes from town.
Bought from Mariam Ribuh Paran in Pa' Dalih, 1/10/87 M$12.

SM98

Tarub siar barit. Grass mat with pink, yellow and green pattern (*barit*) woven in.

Made by Sinah Ellie (female), 1987.
Materials: grass (*da'un siar*), dyes from town.
Bought at auction at 'cake party' (*pesta kek*) held to raise money for work on Pa' Dalih school electricity system (Sinah Ellie donated the mat to be auctioned), 22/10/87 M$22.

SM99

Liling. Small grass mat for use inside *bekang* carrying basket.

Made by Pun Bian, Remudu, Feb. 1988.
Materials: grass (*da'un berpah*).
Bought from Pun Bian 3/3/88 M$2.

SM100

Sample of bark from the *rababar* tree. Used for binding fences, tying back paddy stalks, making bird-scaring devices (*derur*), etc.

Collected by Bala Ukung (male), Pa' Dalih, 1988.
Materials: bark from *rababar* tree (*anit kayuh rababar*).
Bought from Bala Ukung 1/2/88 M$0.50

SM101

Sample of *anit kayuh kilid*, the bark from the *kilid* tree. Bark used to make string (*nopar*) by twisting strands together (*ngopar*, literally 'to make string') on the thigh, for baskets of all kinds, musical instruments, containers (see **BM141**). Now often replaced by nylon string bought in town.

Collected by unidentified male.
Materials: bark from *kilid* tree (*anit kayuh kilid*).
Donated by Sinah Matala Ulun (female), Pa' Dalih, Feb. 1988.

SM102

Sample of *ubir*. Black paste used to strengthen and caulk inside of *ra'ing* and *bu'an* baskets, *a'ab* containers and *reno* winnowing trays. It is made from the inside of the bark of the *ubir* tree, which is scraped off, mixed with water and applied as a paste. This is then allowed to dry in the sun.

Collected by Batang Ribuh (male), Remudu.
Fee paid to him for collecting M$20.

SM103

Natang. Sample of resin from the *obong* tree. The resin from this tree is soft and was used until the 1970s to glaze earthenware pots. It was used in the late 1980s to caulk the joins between plank sides and dugout bottoms of boats (*alud*).

Collected by Kaz Janowski in the headwaters of the Di'it river (a source of the Baram in the Kelabit Highlands) January 1988.
Donated by Kaz Janowski to the BM March 1988.

SM104

Sample of *prah*, pounded up old earthenware pot (*tuning* – SM37-45). Used mixed with fresh clay to make new *tuning*.

Donated by Na'an Tenan (female), Pa' Dalih, Feb. 1988.

Kelabit Artefacts held in UK Museums

Outside Malaysia, the largest number of Kelabit artefacts is deposited in museums in the UK; this is related to the fact that the Brooke Rajahs were British and they were succeeded by a British colonial administration until Sarawak became part of Malaysia in 1963.

The British Museum

The British Museum holds 29 items listed as Kelabit in addition to the Janowski collection. Most of these have multiple ethnic group listings (being listed as Kenyah, Kayan, Murut, Madang or Sea Dayak – i.e. Iban – as well as Kelabit or Kalabit) and cannot therefore be definitely identified as Kelabit. Most were collected by Charles Hose, who was Divisional Resident in the Baram Division of Sarawak (under which the Kelabit Highlands fell) from 1891 to 1904, and the majority of these were bought using money from the Christy fund in 1900. The rest were acquired between 1896 and 1908, except for one item donated by Mrs. E. Pollard in 1967 (probably the widow of F.H. Pollard, a Brooke-era administrator who spent part of his working life stationed in the Baram district). The Ranee Margaret Brooke donated one item and four items come from unidentified sources at unrecorded times. Included are a sword with sheath, bead necklaces, a tobacco pipe, tobacco boxes and a tobacco pouch, sharpening stones (hones), a bark loin cloth, some rattan/bamboo basketry items, a bone (man's) hair pin, two stone hammers, a skin (man's) jacket, a (blowpipe) quiver and a woman's hat decorated with shells and beads.

The Cambridge University Museum of Archaeology and Anthropology

The Cambridge University Museum of Archaeology and Anthropology holds five items listed as `Kalabit'. Three were collected by Charles Hose and donated by him to the Museum at an unrecorded date. These are a skull in a `wicker' (rattan) casing; an old Chinese jar; and a boy's necklace. The other two items, two head hunter's swords with sheaths, come from the Woolley collection and were acquired in 1929. However, these are listed as `Kalabit?'.

The Pitt Rivers Museum in Oxford

At the Pitt Rivers Museum in Oxford there are 11 items listed as Kelabit. Three were donated by the widow of Robert Shelford, who was Curator of the Sarawak Museum from 1897 to 1905, and include a spear and two tobacco boxes. One, a box made out of an internode of bamboo with phyllomorphic engraved design, was donated either by Prof. C.G. Seligman or by his widow Mrs. B.Z. Seligman after his death in 1940. Four items were donated by G. Arnold, and were collected on the Oxford University Expedition to Borneo in 1956. These include two tobacco boxes, a lidded basket used by women to keep beads, and a leopard-skin sitting mat. One Kelabit item held at the Museum, a white-metal ear pendant (its Kelabit name is listed, *abih*, the same as that I recorded for ear pendants) was donated by Rajah Charles Vyner Brooke in 1923, and may have been collected by Charles Hose. Finally, one item was donated in 1997 by Dorothy Wright, a basketry expert and is a women's plaited rattan headband. However, this is listed as being either Kayan, Kenyah or Kelabit.

The Liverpool Museum

The Liverpool Museum holds two items listed as Kelabit: a sword and sheath with sharpening stone, and a tobacco box. Both are listed as donated by Charles Hose.

The National Museums of Scotland in Edinburgh

The National Museums of Scotland in Edinburgh holds six items listed as Kelabit. One, a mouse trap made of bamboo or rattan, comes from the Charles Hose collection and was acquired in 1908. The rest are boxes made of bamboo internodes, carved and decorated, with lids. All but one, from the John Hewitt Collection (acquired in 1909), are from unnamed sources. These were acquired in 1902.

BM46 Beaded centre of sunhat, *ra'ong*, made for a British soldier in 1967 but never given to him. Item in the British Museum collection, drawing by Claire Thorne.

Notes

1. See below for a discussion of the term 'Kelabit'.
2. I have also heard the Ba Rian area referred to as the Berian area and the people of the area as the Lun Berian (also see Bala 2000, where this term is used).
3. See King (1993) for an overview of the major groups in Borneo. Divisions between what are described as 'tribal groups' are hard to define, since some ways of dividing people up are meaningful in one context, others more meaningful in another. Not only on the part of outsiders but even on the part of members of tribal groups themselves, distinctions tend to vary contextually.
4. Literally Labid stream/river; Kelabit settlements are often named after the stream/river on which they are situated.
5. Although Talla states that the people of the Kelabit Highlands had been referred to by the Kayan and Kenyah of the area as 'Kelabit', deriving from the longhouse of Pa' Labid (a longhouse outside the Kelabit Highlands on the Labid river, a tributary of the Tutoh, itself a tributary of the Baram), for some time before this, since it was through this longhouse that all contact with the highlands took place (Talla, 1979: 5-6).
6. It has been estimated that there were 1800 Kelabit in 1946 (Harrisson 1949) and there appear to have been a similar number in the Kelabit Highlands in 1990 (Rousseau 1990). Another source gives a figure of 5,059 Kelabit in 1987 and suggests that there was a growth rate among them of 4% between 1970 and 1980 (Ko 1987). This would indicate that there are now (2002) about 7,500 Kelabit. Bala, Lien *et al* however estimate a lower figure of 5,000 in 2000 (Bala, Lien, *et al*. 2000). Many Kelabit now live in town, mostly in Miri at the mouth of the Baram. The migration that has led to this is fairly recent, starting in the 1970s, which means that most Kelabit living outside the highlands were born in highland communities. Many of those living in town move back and forth between town and highlands depending on the availability of work and other factors. For this reason it is difficult to generate an accurate figure for the proportion of the Kelabit population living in the highlands or in town. However, since there were calculated to be 993 people registered formally as resident in the Highlands in 1998 (ibid), it is clear that the majority of the Kelabit now live in town. This is confirmed by the survey carried out by Amster, which found that for those people originating from the Highlands community of Pa' Ukat, 73.7% were now resident in town (Amster 1998: 57).
7. See Appendix 1 for a discussion of the different varieties of Kelabit.
8. By 1997, a number of Kelabit had converted to Catholicism (Kit Pearce, pers. comm.).
9. It has been suggested (Sellato, 1997) that the present people of the highland area are fairly recent immigrants, having moved into the area from an area much further downriver in what is now Indonesia – the area around the town of Malinau – in the 17th century. On the other hand other authors have suggested that the highland area is the homeland of the Apo Duat peoples of the highlands, and that they expanded out of this area into the coastal area (Schneeberger 1945) and that peoples of the Apo Duat language group may have inhabited much more extensive areas outside the highlands than they now occupy, being pushed into the highland area by marauding Kayan and Kenyah invaders in the 19th century (Harrisson, 1958: 187-191).
10. Cultivated vegetables, eaten at the daily rice meal together with wild vegetables and wild meat, were treated very differently from rice. They were freely shared with neighbours and kin, unlike rice. Although they were planted, they were not weeded as rice is. They were, in fact, treated in much the same way as are wild vegetables.
11. I am tempted to hypothesise that this may have been because of the killing involved in both hunting and soldiering.
12. See Rousseau (1990) for a discussion of the stratified groups of Central Borneo, the part of Borneo where such groups are mainly concentrated.
13. In the early 1990s Batu Patong increased in size through the immigration of relatives of Batu Patong residents from nearby communities across the border in the Kerayan area of East Kalimantan.
14. Yahya Talla, writing of Pa' Ramapoh longhouse in the Bario area in the 1970s (Talla 1979), says that these rooms are there described as *takap* and were built as additions to the *dalim*; in the southern part of the Highlands, however, where Pa' Dalih is situated, it is clear that these rooms, here called *télong*, were built in part of the *tawa'*.
15. Amster (Amster 1998: footnote page 233) suggests that this analysis, which I first presented in my thesis (Janowski 1991), is incorrect. He appears to assume that my data derives from Kelabit statements about 'going to play in the forest' on the part of informants, statements which were really intended to downplay their own activities there. In fact my data does not derive from informants making such statements about what they are themselves doing, or have done, in the forest. I am well aware that the Kelabit tend to downplay their success and their commitment to work by referring to 'work' activities as 'play'. My analysis derives rather from conversations with many informants about their views on hunting, and to comments by some individuals on other individuals' habits which implied a view of hunting and gathering as an enjoyable activity, to be described as 'play'. A good illustration of this view of hunting was expressed privately by one informant in relation to a young man who, although married with a child, persisted in spending most of his time hunting, and who was criticised as wanting to spend all of his time 'playing' (*raut*) in the forest.
16. Schooling in the Kelabit Highlands was in Malay in the late 1980s, but until the mid-1970s was in English.
17. There was also considerable interest in the beads which my mother brought to Pa' Dalih in 1987, bought in the Bead Shop in Covent Garden in London. I donated these to the Pa' Dalih parish of the SIB church and they were auctioned to raise money for the church, bringing in quite high sums of money.
18. Saging and Bulan use the term *lauk* to describe side dishes (Lian-Saging and Bulan 1989: 110), but this term was not in common use in Pa' Dalih, and I use the term which was usual during my time there, *nok penguman*.
19. The Kelabit have radically changed a number of their living habits since being made aware, largely through the Christian missionaries, of the importance of hygiene and how certain diseases are transmitted. In the late 1980s they always boiled drinking water, penned pigs and used mosquito nets at night.
20. This is contrary to what Christensen was told in Pa' Dalih, which is that irrigated rice has always been their most important crop, only supplemented by minor amounts of dry rice, and that it is only in the 50-year period just before the Second World War that they cultivated only dry rice fields (Christensen 2002: 39). However, this is not what I was told by informants.
21. Christensen is mistaken in saying that dry rice fields are 'only occasionally found' (Christensen 2002: 39); my data show that all hearth-groups made both types of field during the two years that I lived in the community.
22. Yahya Talla says that transplanting was practised in the old-style wet rice cultivation in Bario (Talla 1979: 314), although it would seem that transplanting may not always have been part of the system, since it was only introduced around 1956 in the Kerayan area (Padoch 1981: 35).
23. Talla however says that when the Kelabit followed the bird calendar (which would have been up to the 1950s or 1960s) rice

24 This is a cylindrical stone with rounded ends, which appears to have been a tool used in the past throughout the interior Kerayan-Kelabit tableland. The implication of the term 'thunder stone' is that these stones fell from the sky with thunder, or that they 'were' in some sense the thunder. Harrisson has described these tools as sago-pounders (Harrisson 1951); it has been suggested recently by Sellato that they may have been used to crack candlenuts (Sellato 1996). The dating of these tools has not so far been possible since they have not been unearthed in association with dateable organic remains but rather collected from inhabitants of the area. The belief that stone tools originate in thunderbolts is to be found throughout the Indonesian archipelago (ibid).

25 This appears to derive from the now obsolete system of organizing labour before the Second World War called *ngerupan*, where the host provided not only side dishes for the rice meal but also *borak* (rice beer) to drink for the participants.

26 There was a third way of organizing labour, for projects which were not related to rice-growing such as path maintenance. In Pa' Dalih while I was there, this was used for work on lengthening the Mission airstrip, undertaken in the hope of being able to receive at least charter planes so as to be able to export rice. This was called *gotong royong* (Malay) (see Lian-Saging and Bulan: 113).

27 It has been estimated that it would cost at least M$63,200 to purchase replacement vegetables and meat in the market for those gathered and hunted in the forest by and for a longhouse community of 25-30 households over a year (Christensen 2000). It is much more difficult to estimate how much it would cost to replace the materials taken from the forest used for handicrafts – indeed many of the materials simply could not be replaced with anything as good – but it is clear that the cost would be very considerable.

28 For the Kelabit the distinction between primary and secondary forest is not a dichotomous one as in English. In Pa' Dalih, 'big forest' (*polong raya*) and 'little forest' (*polong i'it*) were distinguished on a continuum with any particular piece of forest being 'smaller' or 'bigger' according to how recently it was utilised by humans. They do not find it useful, as does Euro-American culture, to emphasise whether forest has never been used by humans or not. Forest that has not been used by humans for a very long time is described as being, simply, 'big'. It is not distinguished conceptually from forest which has never been used by humans. Therefore it was not possible, from information gathered from informants, for me to establish whether forest was 'truly' primary (in the English sense), and I do not have the expert background to make this assessment myself.

29 There were two types of natang – 'soft resin', *natang laya'* (from the *obong* tree), for caulking boats (and for glazing earthenware pots until the 1970s) and what was simply called 'resin', *natang*. This is from the *tomoh* tree and is a hard resin. It was used for lighting fires and was, in the past, burnt to make light on props made of bamboo, *dawan natang* (BM102, SM25).

30 This list is the same as that provided in my Ph.D. thesis (Janowski 1991). Since then, I have been able to identify many of the plants in the list from the information provided by Hanne Christensen, who carried out ethnobotanical research in Pa' Dalih for short periods between October 1992 and November 1993 and between February 1995 and June 1995 (Christensen 2000 and Christensen 2002). However, some of the plants which I recorded as being eaten are not recorded by Christensen and some of those Christensen lists are not ones I recorded.

31 Although *beruk* or *berak* is the name for the pig-tailed macaque in most Central Bornean languages, it is the term for the domestic pig in Kelabit.

32 Talla says that in the 1970s men in Pa' Ramapoh in Bario were already hunting only rarely, and states that there was little game left in the Kelabit Highlands since guns had decimated the animal population (Talla 1979: 394). This was certainly not the case in the area around Pa' Dalih in the late 1980s, although it is possible that there may have been even more game before guns were introduced after the Second World War.

33 Christensen has a list of the animals, insects and fish eaten by the Kelabit, with the frequency with which they were consumed by

was normally stored in alternate layers of *rongo'* and loose grain (which he terms *urah*) (Talla 1979: 326).

the household in Pa' Dalih which kept a food diary for her for 77 days in 1992-3 (Christensen 2000). This confirms that wild boar was by far the most frequently eaten meat (eaten 137 times), closely followed by deer (24 times) – and snails (*akap*) (23 times), taken from wet rice fields. The household in question also ate monkey (19 times) and porcupine (14 times) regularly. Although there were many other living things eaten, these were eaten extremely infrequently.

34 BM5 has a handle bought in Marudi, said to have been made by Penan.

35 In Bario, where, in the late 1980s, access to the forest was limited and there was more cash due to the possibility of selling rice to town by air, the situation was quite different and meat was regularly sold. Men from settlements which had easier access to the forest and less cash sometimes brought meat to Bario for sale.

36 Talla also refers to belief in longhouses which had been turned to stone for laughing at animals (Talla 1979: 284-5).

37 Both Talla and Lian-Saging, however, say that Guma is the Kelabit Creator Deity. Talla and Lian-Saging say that Baru is a god living in the sky, but not the Creator Deity (Talla 1979: 265-267; Lian-Saging 1976/77: 236-237).

38 Talla says that the Kelabit believed that the *lun rabada'* were a heterogenous group of proto-humans, the ancestors of all humans, while the *lun seluyah* were a group of *lun rabada'* who were the ancestors of the Kelabit (Talla 1979: 266). The greater *lalud* of the *lun rabada'* and *lun seluyah* is believed by some present-day Kelabit to be demonstrated through their erection of certain of the megalithic monuments in the Kelabit Highlands, which are beyond the technological competence of the Kelabit themselves (ibid: 242).

39 In each generation, only one child, together with his or her spouse, remained within his or her natal hearth-group. It was this child's first child who was the first co-resident grandchild. Where a couple was resident in town, they counted as being resident in a hearth-group in the Highlands, and the parents of one of the couple would hold an *irau* to name their first child (sometimes their first two or three children, since it was sometimes only after a few years that an *irau* was held for a young couple living in town).

40 Talla points out that although in theory anyone could become *la'ih raya*, in practice it would be very difficult for anyone who does not come of a family which is of high status (Talla, 1979: 87-88).

41 The last fully megalithic act was performed, according to Harrisson, who witnessed it, in 1951 (Harrisson 1958b: 699, pl. XVII [a] and pl. XVIII [a]).

42 Jars within living memory have been ceramic, Chinese or Chinese-style. However, in the past they were also made of stone, although informants in Pa' Dalih told me that they and their immediate ancestors no longer knew how to work stone to make such stone jars.

43 Although Lian-Saging does not mention that ordinary people were only kept for ten days, saying that all the dead were kept in the *dalim* for a year (Lian-Saing 1976/77: 146).

44 In Bario there was limited land and not everyone had enough to grow rice. Also, those belonging to communities outside the Bario area – Pa' Dalih, Remudu and Long Dano – had limited possibilities of selling rice to town, and were therefore excluded from the main source of income in Bario.

45 *Ngelua'*, smearing of blood, was apparently believed to generate a symbolic transition between a pre-human and a human status on the part of the child, judging from material provided by Robert Lian-Saging (Lian-Saging 1976/77: 138-145). It was no longer practiced once the Kelabit became Christian.

46 In Pa' Dalih in the late 1980s, and presumably before that as well, one became *lun merar* (literally 'big people'; here, adults) gradually, not suddenly: the beginning of the process was at the birth of a couple's first child, and its culmination was when one was fully accepted as a grandparent.

47 Matthew Amster's informants told him that names were not changed at *borak ngelua' anak* (which he terms *burak lua'*), but five days after the birth of a child (Amster 1998: 251). Amster argues therefore that the holding of name-changing *irau* is a recent cultural practice for the Kelabit. Although it is true that name-changing *irau* as they are held nowadays are new, and

appear to originate in the 1960s, it seems clear that, assuming that Talla is correct – his data were gathered in the mid-1970s when memories of pre-Christian times were fresh, and are probably more accurate than Amster's, gathered in the late 1990s – the older *borak ngelua' anak* can also be seen as an earlier type of name-changing *irau*. The changing of names is fundamental to the change in status from 'child' (*anak*) to adult or 'big person' (*lun merar*), and this, as well as the initiation of the child into the social universe, was marked at *borak ngelua' anak*.

48 According to Yahya Talla, Deraya was the supreme pre-Christian Kelabit deity, who gave life to man, was omnipotent and was consulted in relation to almost every activity in which people engaged (Talla 1979: 261). However, in Pa' Dalih informants associated this deity specifically with rice and with women.

49 The distribution of meat by men and rice by women at feasts is referred to in the song-story of Balang Lipang as recorded by Rubenstein (Rubenstein 1973: 831).

50 The association of borak with high status is emphasised through the reference later to the old and valuable jars in which it is made and to the valuable beads which decorate them, as well as to the big, hard, old planks on which they stand (only high-status hearth-groups would have had such planks as floor for their longhouse apartments; other hearth-groups would have used split bamboo or smaller planks made from softer wood).

51 Mention of the centre of the longhouse underlines the high status of Aruring Salud Bulan, since the centre of the longhouse is where the leading hearth-group of the longhouse, the *lun merar* of the longhouse, has its apartment.

52 In 1987, Kaz Janowski, my husband, accompanied Pa' Dalih inhabitants on one of these pilgrimages, to Batu Lawi (**Pl. 101**).

53 The SIB church seemed to have an ambivalent attitude to praying on mountains. When an outdoor 'church' on a hill at some distance from the community was established in 1987 by the people of Pa' Dalih, circulars were sent by the church authorities stating that it was not appropriate to pray in such places and that the right place to pray was in the church building within the community. However, the SIB church was in the 1990s formally involved in the annual pilgrimage to Mt. Murud, and built the church on its summit (Amster 1998: 305).

54 Although Blust lists *batuh* in the vocabulary, he spells it as *batu* in Batu Patung, probably because this is the way it is normally spelt in the place name. He uses the spelling patung for the second part of the place name. Both the spellings *patung* and *patong* may be used in this place name. However, since in the southern Kelabit area, which includes the place concerned, the word is pronounced *patong*, I have chosen to use this spelling.

55 Christensen noted two ways of making black dye in Pa' Dalih, which are different from this: one involved pounding and boiling the bark of trees of species of *Nephelium* (one of which is the tree which the Kelabit call *bua' meritem*); the other involved boiling the leaves of a plant which she records as having the Kelabit name *kararuh and* which she identified as *Archidendron clypearia* (Leg.) with those of another plant with the Kelabit name *mirirr*, which she identified as *Macaranga costulata* Euph. (Christensen 2002: 122).

56 Christensen noted a different method of making red dye in Pa' Dalih, which involved the use of the resin covering the scales on the fruits of Calamus marginatus (Kelabit: *ue repit*) and *Daemonorops didymophylla* (according to Christensen, known by the Kelabit as *ue kurad*), two types of rattan, mixed with water and heated before use, with the optional addition of the sap from the shoot tips of *Fragraea ridleyi* to make a brighter, pinkish colour (Christensen 2002: 122)

57 Christensen notes that the resin of this species is used to seal pottery (Christensen 2002: 178) but does not give its Kelabit name. Since the species known in Kelabit as *kayuh tomoh*, together with that known as *kayuh obong*, are used for this purpose according to my informants, and Christensen has identified *kayuh obong* as a species of *Shorea* (see above) I think it likely that *kayuh tomoh* is *Agathis kinabaluensis*

58 Christensen has suggested (pers. comm.) that this may be *Calamus blumeii* Becc (Arec.), a rattan, the Kelabit name for which she noted as *wae mara raimand*.

Bibliography

Amster, M. 1998. Community, Ethnicity and Modes of Association among the Kelabit of Sarawak, East Malaysia. Ph.D. thesis, Department of Anthropology, Brandeis University.

Amster, M. 1999. '"Tradition", Ethnicity and Change: Kelabit Practices of Name Changing'. *Sarawak Museum Journal* LIV(75)n.s.: 183-200.

Amster, M. 2000. 'It takes a Village to Dismantle a Longhouse'. *Thresholds* 20: 54-71.

Anderson, B. 1972. 'Power'. *Culture and Politics in Indonesia*. C. Holt (ed). Ithaca: Cornell University Press.

Appell, G N. 1964. 'The Long House Apartment of the Rungus Dusun'. *Sarawak Museum Journal* XI(23-24)n.s.: 570-573.

Appell, G.N. 1969a. 'Social Anthropological Research in Borneo'. *Anthropologica* 11: 45-57.

Appell, G.N. 1969b. 'The Status of Research among the Northern and Southern Murut.' *Borneo Research Bulletin* 1: 18-21.

Appell, G.N. 1978. 'The Rungus Dusun'. *Essays on Borneo Societies*. V.T. King (ed). Hull: Oxford University Press for the University of Hull.

Appell, G.N. 1976. *Studies in Borneo Societies: Social Process and Anthropological Explanation*. Center for Southeast Asian Studies, Northern Illinois University.

Atkinson, J.M. and S. Errington 1990. *Power and Difference. Gender in Island Southeast Asia*. Stanford: Stanford University Press.

Ave, J. and V.T. King 1986. *The People of the Weeping Forest. Tradition and Change in Borneo*. Leiden: Rijksmuseum voor Volkenkunde.

Bala, P. 2001. 'Interethnic Ties along the Kalimantan-Sarawak Border in Highlands Borneo: the Kelabit and Lun Berian Case in the Kelabit-Kerayan Highlands'. *Borneo Research Bulletin* 32: 103-111.

Bala, P., K.G. Lien, *et al.* 2000. 'Potential Users Profile and Existing Communication Pattern among the Rural Community of Bario: A Need Analysis for the Development of a Telecentre'. Paper presented at the Borneo 2000 Conference in Kuching, Sarawak, organised by the Borneo Research Council.

Banks, E. 1937a. 'Native Drink in Sarawak'. *Sarawak Museum Journal* 4: 439-447.

Banks, E. 1937b. 'Some Megalithic Remains from the Kelabit Country in Sarawak with some notes on the Kelabits themselves'. *Sarawak Museum Journal* 4: 411-438.

Beccardi, O. 1904. *Wanderings in the Great Forests of Borneo*. London: Archibald Constable and Co.

Bloch, M. and J. Parry, 1982. 'Introduction: Death and the Regeneration of Life'. *Death and the Regeneration of Life*. M. Bloch and J. Parry (eds). Cambridge: Cambridge University Press.

Blust, R. 1993. 'Kelabit-English Vocabulary'. *Sarawak Museum Journal* XLIV(65)n.s.: 141-226.

Bulan, L., n.d. *A Kelabit Discourse*. Unpublished manuscript.

Bulan, L. and D. Labang, 1979. 'The Kelabit Harvest'. *Sarawak Museum Journal* XXVII(48)n.s.: 43-52.

Carsten, J. 1997. *The Heat of the Hearth: The Process of Kinship in a Malay Fishing Community*. Oxford: Clarendon Press.

Carsten, J. 2000. 'Introduction: cultures of relatedness'. *Cultures of Relatedness. New Approaches to the Study of Kinship*. J. Carsten (ed). Cambridge: Cambridge University Press.

Chin, L. a. M. V., Ed. 1991. *Sarawak Cultural Legacy: A Living Tradition*. Kuching, Sarawak: Society Atelier Sarawak.

Chong, A.O. 1954. 'Some Kelabit Customs and Practices'. *Sarawak Gazette* 80: 187-188.

Christensen, H. 2000. 'Economic Importance of Wild Food in a Kelabit Longhouse Community in Sarawak, Malaysia'. Paper presented at the Borneo 2000 Conference in Kuching, Sarawak, organized by the Borneo Research Council.

Christensen, H. 2002. *Ethnobotany of the Iban and the Kelabit*.

Aarhus, Denmark and Kuching, Sarawak: Forest Dept., Sarawak; NEPCon; and the University of Aarhus.

Christie, J.W. and V.T. King 1988. *Metal Working in Borneo. Essays on Iron and Silver Working in Sarawak*. Hull: The University of Hull, Centre for South-East Asian Studies.

Crain, J.B. 1970a. *The Lun Dayeh of Sabah, East Malaysia: Aspects of Marriage and Social Exchange*. Cornell University; published by University Microfilms.

Crain, J.B. 1970b. 'The Domestic Family and Longhouse among the Mengalong Lun Dayeh'. *Sarawak Museum Journal* XVIII(36-37)n.s.: 186-192.

Crain, J.B. 1970c. 'The Mengalong Lun Dayeh Longhouse'. *Sarawak Museum Journal* XVIII(36-37)n.s.: 169-185.

Crain, J.B. 1976. 'Ngerufan: Ritual Process in a Bornean Rice Harvest'. *Studies in Borneo Societies: Social Process and Anthropological Explanation*. G.N. Appell (ed). Centre for Southeast Asian Studies, Northern Illinois University.

Crain, J.B. and V. Pearson-Rounds 2000. 'Constructing the Lun Dayeh: Contradictions Past and Present'. Paper presented at the Borneo 2000 Conference in Kuching Sarawak, organized by the Borneo Research Council.

Deegan, J.L. 1973. *Change among the Lun Bawang, a Borneo People*. Washington University; published by University Microfilms.

Deegan, J.L. 1974. 'Community Fragmentation among the Lun Bawang'. *Sarawak Museum Journal* XXII(43)n.s.: 229-247.

Douglas, R.S. 1907. 'A Journey into the Interior of Borneo to visit the Kelabit Tribe'. *Journal of the Royal Asiatic Society*, Straits Branch 49: 53-62.

Douglas, R.S. 1909a. 'The "Pun mein" or Salt Springs of the upper Baram'. *Sarawak Gazette* 39: 52-53.

Douglas, R.S. 1909b. 'Visit to the Kelabits of Ulu Baram'. *Sarawak Gazette* 39: 29-30.

Douglas, R.S. 1912. 'An expedition to the Bah country of Central Borneo'. *Sarawak Museum Journal* 1(2): 17-29.

Dove, M.R. 1980. 'The Swamp Rice Swiddens of the Kantu' of West Kalimantan'. *Tropical Ecology and Development*. J.I. Furtado (ed). Kuala Lumpur: The International Society of Tropical Ecology.

Eilers, R.G. and K.S. Loi, 1982. *The Soils of Northern Interior Sarawak (East Malaysia)*. Kuching: Soils Survey Division Research Branch, Sarawak Department of Agriculture.

Errington, S. 1989. *Meaning and Power in a Southeast Asian Realm*. Princeton: Princeton University Press.

Errington, S. 1990. 'Recasting Sex, Gender and Power. A Theoretical and Regional Overview'. *Power and Difference. Gender in Island Southeast Asia*. S. Errington and J.M. Atkinson (eds). Stanford: Stanford University Press.

Freeman, J.D. 1955. *Report on the Iban of Sarawak*. Kuching.

Geddes, W.R. 1954. *The Land Dayaks of Sarawak*. London.

Geertz, C. 1980. *Negara*. Princeton: Princeton University Press.

Harrisson, T. 1949a. 'Explorations in Central Borneo'. *The Geographical Journal* CXIV (4-6): 129-150.

Harrisson, T. 1949b. 'The Upland Plateau'. *Sarawak Gazette* 79 (August 6): 190-192.

Harrisson, T. 1951a. 'Notes on some Neolithic Implements from Borneo'. *Man* 51: 21-24.

Harrisson, T. 1951b. 'The Kelabits of Borneo'. *The Geographical Magazine* 24: 32-39.

Harrisson, T. 1958a. 'Megaliths of Central and West Borneo'. *Sarawak Museum Journal* VIII(11): 394-401.

Harrisson, T. 1958b. 'A Living Megalithic in Upland Borneo'. *Sarawak Museum Journal* VIII(12): 694-703.

Harrisson, T. 1958c. 'The Peoples of Sarawak VII and VIII. The Kelabits and Muruts'. *Sarawak Gazette* 84 (October 31): 187-191.

Harrisson, T. 1959. *World Within,* The Cresset Press. Republished by Oxford in Asia paperbacks 1984; reissued as an Oxford University Press paperback 1986.

Harrisson, T. 1960a. 'Birds and Men in Borneo'. *Birds of Borneo.* B.E. Smythies (ed). London: Oliver and Boyd.

Harrisson, T. 1960b. 'A Kelabit Diary Part IV. Upland Irrigation and Irritation'. *Sarawak Gazette* 86 (March 31).

Harrisson, T. 1962a. 'Megaliths of Central Borneo and Western Malaya, compared'. *Sarawak Museum Journal* XI(19-20): 376-382.

Harrisson, T. 1962b. 'Borneo Death'. *Bijdragen tot de Taal-, Land- en Volkenkunde* 118: 1-41.

Harrisson, T. 1964. 'Inside Borneo'. *Geographical Journal* 125: 299-311.

Heimann, J.M. *The most offending soul alive. Tom Harrisson and his Remarkable Life.* Honolulu: University of Hawai'i Press.

Helliwell, C. 1992. 'Evolution and Ethnicity: A Note on Rice Cultivation Practices in Borneo'. *The Heritage of Traditional Agriculture among the Western Austronesians.* J.J. Fox (ed). Canberra: Department of Anthropology in association with the Comparative Austronesian Project, Research School of Pacific Studies, Australian National University.

Helliwell, C. 1993. 'Good walls make bad neighbours: the Dayak Longhouse as a Community of Voices'. *Inside Austronesian Houses - Perspectives on Domestic Designs for Living.* J.J. Fox (ed). Canberra: Department of Anthropology, Research School of Pacific Studies, Australian National University.

Highland Development Technical Committee, 1985. *Highland Development Study.* Kuching: Department of Agriculture, Sarawak, Malaysia.

Hose, C. and W. McDougall 1912. *The Pagan Tribes of Borneo,* Macmillan. Reissued by Oxford University Press 1993.

Hoskins, J. 1996. 'Introduction: Headhunting as Practice and as Trope'. *Headhunting and the Social Imagination in Southeast Asia.* J. Hoskins (ed). Stanford: Stanford University Press.

Howell, S. 1995. 'Many Contexts, Many Meanings? Gendered Values among the Northern Lio of Flores, Indonesia'. *Journal of the Royal Anthropological Institute* 2, no. 2: 253-269.

Hudson, A.B. 1977. 'Linguistic relations among Borneo peoples with special reference to Sarawak: an interim report'. *Studies in Third World Societies* 3: 1-44 Special Issue: Linguistics and Development Problems. M.D. Zamora, V. Sutlive and N. Altshuler (eds).

Izikowitz, K.G. and P. Sorensen 1982. *The House in East and South East Asia.* London: Curzon Press.

Janowski, M. 1988. 'The motivating forces behind changes in the wet rice agricultural system in the Kelabit Highlands'. *Sarawak Gazette* CXIV (1504): 9-20.

Janowski, M. 1991a. *Rice, Work and Community among the Kelabit of Sarawak.* Ph.D. thesis, Department of Anthropology, London School of Economics, University of London.

Janowski, M. 1991b. 'The Making of Earthenware Cooking Pots in the Kelabit Highlands'. *Sarawak Cultural Legacy: A Living Tradition.* L. Chin and V. Mashman (eds). Kuching, Sarawak: Society Atelier Sarawak.

Janowski, M. 1992. 'Southeast Asian "Centres" and the Generation of Human Life: An Attempt to Understand how the Kelabit of Sarawak see themselves'. Paper presented at the Department of Social Anthropology, University of Cambridge, 23 October 1992.

Janowski, M. 1995. 'The Hearth-group, the Conjugal Couple and the Symbolism of the Rice Meal among the Kelabit of Sarawak'. *About the House: Lévi-Strauss and Beyond.* J. Carsten and S. Hugh-Jones (eds). Cambridge: Cambridge University Press.

Janowski, M. 1996. 'Gender, Power and Christianity among the Kelabit of Sarawak'. Paper presented at ASEASUK annual meeting, SOAS, 25-27 April.

Janowski, M. 1997a. 'Heirlooms, Status and Identity in Town among the Kelabit of Sarawak'. Paper presented at the Association of South East Asian Studies in the United Kingdom (ASEASUK) conference, Hull.

Janowski, M. 1997b. 'The Kelabit Attitude to the Penan: Forever Children'. *La ricerca folklorica* 34: 55-58.

Janowski, M. 1998a. 'Kelabit Beads'. *Beads and Bead Makers. Gender, Material Culture and Meaning.* L.D. Sciama and J.B. Eicher (eds). Oxford: Berg.

Janowski, M. 1998b. '"To have strong life": "big people" and the generation of rice-based kinship and status among the Kelabit of Sarawak'. Paper presented at European Association of South East Asian Studies conference, Hamburg, September 1998.

Janowski, M. 2000. 'Kelabit Names and Kelabit Titles: Grandparenthood, Prestige and Kinship'. Paper presented at the University of Hull.

Janowski, M. 2001a. 'The Wet or the Dry: the Development of Rice Growing in the Kelabit Highlands, Sarawak'. Paper presented at the European Association of South East Asian Studies (EUROSEAS) Conference, London.

Janowski, M. 2001b. 'Rice, Women, Men and the Natural Environment among the Kelabit of Sarawak'. *Sacred Custodians of the Earth? Women, Spirituality and the Environment.* S. Tremayne and A. Low (eds). Oxford and New York: Berghahn.

Janowski, M. 2003. 'Who's in charge around here? Rank, Kinship and the House among the Kelabit of Sarawak'. *The House in South East Asia - a Changing Social, Economic and Political Domain.* S. Sparkes and S. Howell (eds). London: Curzon.

Janowski, M. forthcoming a. 'Of Meat and Men: the Kelabit of Sarawak'. *Meat* (provisional title). A. Hubert (ed). Oxford and New York: Berghahn.

Janowski, M. forthcoming b. 'Rice Beer and Social Cohesion in the Kelabit Highlands, Sarawak'. *Fluid Bread* (provisional title). W. Schiefenhovel (ed). Oxford and New York: Berghahn.

Janowski, M. forthcoming c. 'Rice as a Bridge between two Symbolic Economies: Migration within and out of the Kelabit Highlands, Sarawak'. *Environmental Change in Native and Colonial Histories of Borneo: Lessons from the Past, Prospects for the Future.* R. Wadley (ed), KITLV press.

King, V.T. 1978. 'The Maloh'. *Essays on Borneo Societies.* V.T. King (ed). Oxford: Oxford University Press for the University of Hull.

King, V.T. 1991. 'Cognation and Rank in Borneo'. *Cognation and Social Organization in South East Asia.* F. Husken and J. Kemp (eds). Leiden: KITLV Press.

King, V.T. 1993. *The Peoples of Borneo.* Oxford and Cambridge: Blackwell.

Ko, 1987. 'Minor Indigenous Groups in Sarawak'. *Sarawak Gazette* CXIII (1501): 31-35.

Labang, L. 1962. ' "Married Megaliths" in Upland Kalimantan'. *Sarawak Museum Journal* XI (19-20): 383-385.

Leach, E.R. 1950. *Social Science Research in Sarawak.* London.

LeBar, F.M. 1972. 'Kelabitic Murut'. *Ethnic Groups of Southeast Asia. Vol 1. Indonesia, Andaman Islands and Madagascar.* New Haven: Human Relations Area Files Press.

Lees, S. 1979. *Drunk before Dawn.* Sevenoaks, Kent: Overseas Missionary Fellowship.

Lian-Saging, R. 1976/77. *An Ethno-History of the Kelabit Tribe of Sarawak. A Brief Look at the Kelabit Tribe before World War II and after.* Graduation Exercise submitted in partial fulfilment of the requirements for the Degree of Bachelor of Arts, Hons. Jabatan Sejarah, University of Malaya, Kuala Lumpur.

Lian-Saging, R. and L. Bulan, 1989. 'Kelabit ethnography: a brief report'. *Sarawak Museum Journal* Special Issue no. 4, part III (XL(61)n.s.): 89-119.

Mjoberg, E. 1925. 'An Expedition to the Kalabit Country and Mt. Murud, Sarawak'. *Geographical Review* 15: 411-427.

Moore, H. 1994. *A Passion for Difference: Essays on Anthropology and Gender.* Cambridge: Polity Press.

Padoch, C. 1981. *A Study of a Bornean System of Intensive Agriculture as a Model for Development.* Final report presented to the Consortium for the Study of Man and his Global Environment.

Padoch, C. 1983. 'Agricultural Practices of the Kerayan Lun Dayeh'. *Borneo Research Bulletin* 15 (1): 33-38.

Padoch, C. 1985. 'Labor Efficiency and Intensity of Land Use in Rice Production: an example from Kalimantan'. *Human Ecology* 13 (3): 271-289.

Prentice, D.J. 1970. *The Linguistic Situation in Northern Borneo.* Canberra: Pacific Linguistic Studies.

Rousseau, J. 1978. 'The Kayan'. *Essays on Borneo Societies.* V.T. King. Oxford: Oxford University Press.

Rousseau, J. 1979. 'Kayan Stratification'. *Man* 14 (2): 215-236.

Rousseau, J. 1980. 'Iban Inequality'. *Bijdragen tot de -taal, -land en volkenkunde* 136: 52-63.

Rousseau, J. 1990. *Central Borneo. Ethnic Identity and Social Life in a Stratified Society.* Oxford: Clarendon Press.

Rousseau, J. 1998. 'Hereditary Stratification in Middle-Range

Societies'. Paper presented at 14th International Congress of Anthropological and Ethnological Sciences, Williamsburg, VA, July 1998.

Rubenstein, C. 1973. 'Poems of Indigenous Peoples of Sarawak - Some of the Songs and Chants. Part II'. *Sarawak Museum Journal* XXI(12)n.s.: 723-1127.

Rubenstein, C. 1985. *The Honey Tree Song: Poems and Chants of Sarawak Dayaks*. Athens, Ohio: Ohio University Press.

Rubenstein, C. 1990. *The Nightbird Sings: Chants and Songs of Sarawak Dayaks*. Dumfriesshire, Scotland, and Singapore: Tynron Press and Graham Brash Publishers.

Schneeberger, W.F. 1945. 'The Kerayan-Kalabit Highland of Central Northeast Borneo'. *Geographical Review* 35: 544-562.

Schneeberger, W.F. 1979. *Contributions to the Ethnology of Central Northeast Borneo*. Berne: Institute of Ethnology, University of Berne.

Sellato, B. 1983. 'Le Mythe du Tigre au Centre de Borneo'. *ASEMI* 14 (1-2): 25-49.

Sellato, B. 1989. *Hornbill and Dragon*. Jakarta: Elf Aquataine. Republished by Sun Tree Publishing Pte. Ltd., Singapore, 1992.

Sellato, B. 1994. *Nomads of the Borneo Rainforest*. Honolulu: University of Hawaii Press.

Sellato, B. 1996. 'Stone Nutcrackers and other Recent Finds of Lithic Industry in Interior Northeastern Kalimantan'. *Sarawak Museum Journal* L(71)n.s.: 39-67.

Sellato, B. 1997. 'Agricultural Practices, Social Organization, Settlement Patterns and Ethnogenetic Processes in East Kalimantan'. *People and Plants of Kayan Mentarang*. K.W. Sorensen and B. Morris (eds). London: World Wide Fund for Nature.

Strathern, M. 1988. *The gender of the gift*. Berkeley: University of California Press.

Talla, Y. 1979. 'The Development of Education among the Kelabit'. *Sarawak Gazette* 10 (1455): 55-60.l.

Talla, Y. 1979. *The Kelabit of the Kelabit Highlands, Sarawak*. Penang: Universiti Sains. Report No. 9, Social Anthropology Section, School of Comparative Social Sciences. Edited by Clifford Sather.

Watson Andaya, B. 2003. 'History, Headhunting and Gender in Monsoon Asia: Comparative and Longitudinal Views'. Paper presented to an International Workshop on Indigenous Warfare in Precolonial Monsoon Asia', SOAS, University of London, January 2003.

Whittier, H.L. 1973. *Social organization and symbols of social differentiation; an ethnographic study of the Kenyah Dayak of East Kalimantan (Borneo)*. Michigan State University.

Whittier, H.L. 1978. 'The Kenyah'. *Essays on Borneo Societies*. V.T. King. Oxford: Oxford University Press for the University of Hull.